SCHOLASTIC

ALPHA Mathematics

Develops mathematical thinking and problem-solving skills

Coursebook

5

Scholastic ALPHA™ Mathematics is adapted from the Primary Mathematics Project series (3rd Edition), originally developed by the Ministry of Education, Singapore. This edition contains new content developed by Scholastic Education International (Singapore) Private Limited, which is not attributable to the Ministry of Education, Singapore.

First edition: 2014
Reprinted: 2014 (twice), 2015 (twice), 2016, 2017, 2018, 2020, 2021, 2022 (twice), 2023, 2024, 2025 (twice), 2026

ISBN 978-93-5103-033-1

About ALPHA™ Mathematics

Welcome to **Scholastic ALPHA™ Mathematics.**

The programme covers four strands of mathematics across five grades: **Numbers and Operations**, **Measurement**, **Geometry** and **Data Analysis**.

Numbers and Operations

Geometry

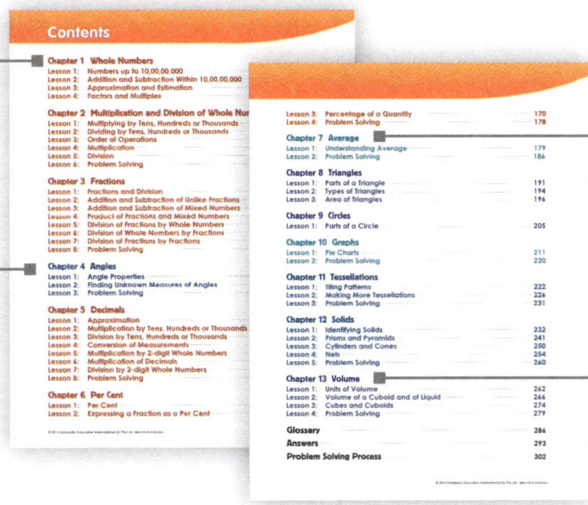

Data Analysis

Measurement

Each chapter of the Coursebook comprises two parts, **Lessons** and **Practice**.

1 Each chapter contains **lessons**, each focusing on a concept or an aspect of it. Concepts and skills are introduced in **Let's Learn**, and **Let's Do** provides opportunities for immediate formative assessment.

In **Let's Learn**, concepts and skills are introduced and developed to mastery using the *concrete-pictorial-abstract* approach. This proven, research-based approach develops deep conceptual understanding.

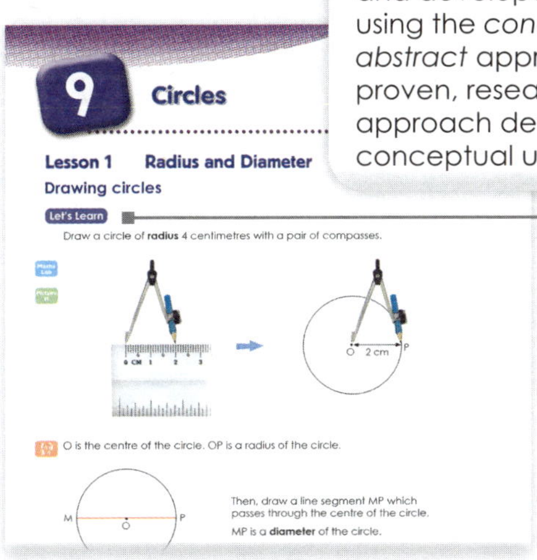

Let's Do provides opportunities for formative assessment. Systematic variation of tasks reinforces students' understanding and enables teachers to check learning and identify remediation needs.

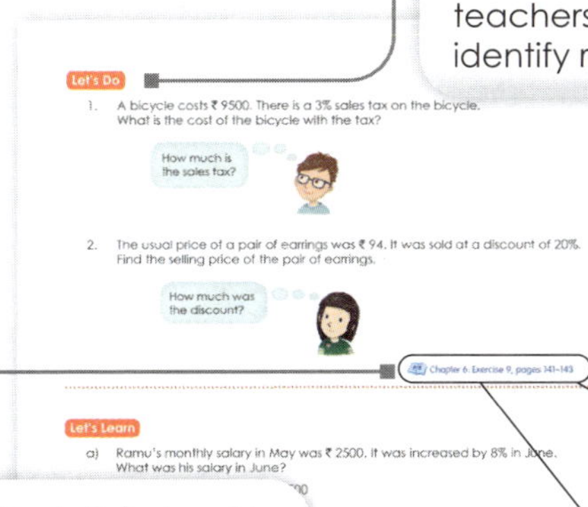

Practice Book links lead to exercises in the Practice Book to further reinforce understanding of the concepts and skills learnt.

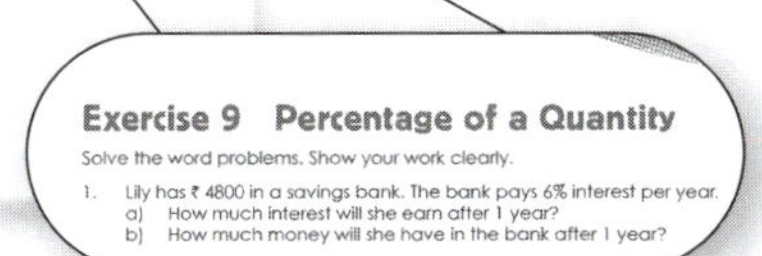

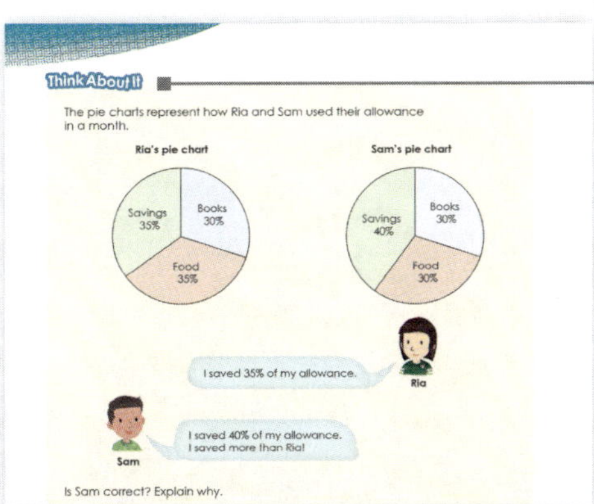

Think About It develops metacognitive skills by providing opportunities for mathematical communication, reasoning and justification.

 ISBN 978-93-5103-033-1

2 **Practice** provides opportunities for summative assessment and independent practice.

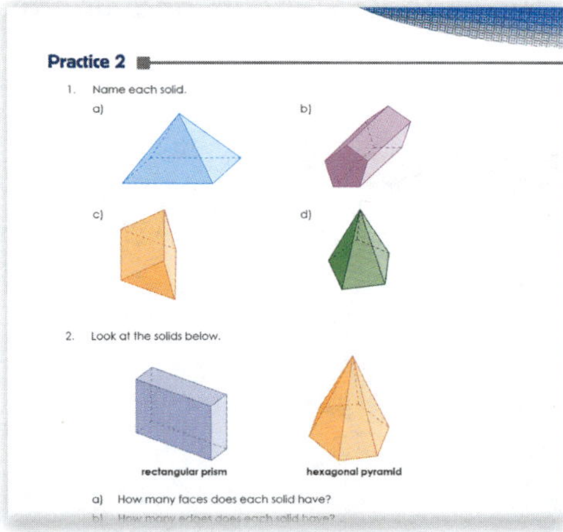
Practice 2

1. Name each solid.
a)
b)
c)
d)

2. Look at the solids below.

rectangular prism
hexagonal pyramid

a) How many faces does each solid have?

The questions are graded and allow for consolidation of concepts and skills learnt within the lesson.

Chapters end with a **Problem Solving** lesson.
Word problems provide a meaningful context for students to apply mathematical knowledge.
The focus is on both the strategies and the process of problem solving.

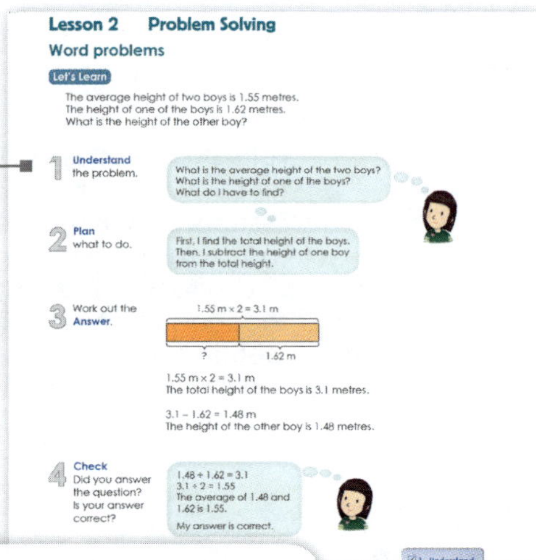
Lesson 2 Problem Solving
Word problems
Let's Learn
The average height of two boys is 1.55 metres.
The height of one of the boys is 1.62 metres.
What is the height of the other boy?

1 Understand the problem.
What is the average height of the two boys?
What is the height of one of the boys?
What do I have to find?

2 Plan what to do.
First, I find the total height of the boys.
Then, I subtract the height of one boy from the total height.

3 Work out the Answer.
1.55 m × 2 = 3.1 m
1.55 m × 2 = 3.1 m
The total height of the boys is 3.1 metres.
3.1 − 1.62 = 1.48 m
The height of the other boy is 1.48 metres.

4 Check
Did you answer the question?
Is your answer correct?
1.48 + 1.62 = 3.1
3.1 ÷ 2 = 1.55
The average of 1.48 and 1.62 is 1.55.
My answer is correct.

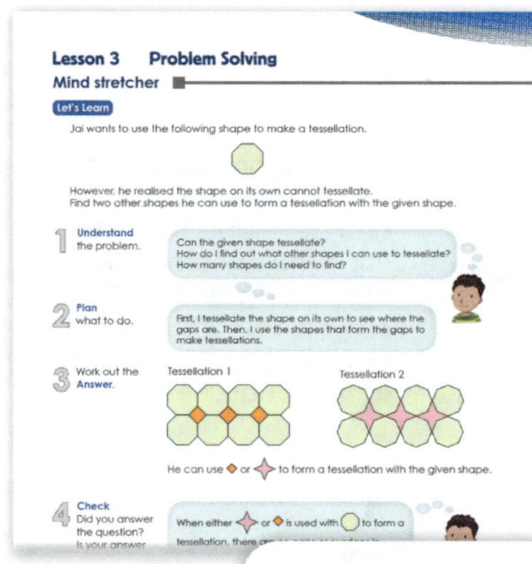
Lesson 3 Problem Solving
Mind stretcher
Let's Learn
Jai wants to use the following shape to make a tessellation.
However, he realised the shape on its own cannot tessellate.
Find two other shapes he can use to form a tessellation with the given shape.

1 Understand the problem.
Can the given shape tessellate?
How do I find out what other shapes I can use to tessellate?
How many shapes do I need to find?

2 Plan what to do.
First, I tessellate the shape on its own to see where the gaps are. Then, I use the shapes that form the gaps to make tessellations.

3 Work out the Answer.
Tessellation 1
Tessellation 2
He can use or to form a tessellation with the given shape.

4 Check
Did you answer the question?

A 4-step process guides students to systematically solve problems and to apply appropriate problem-solving strategies.

Mind Stretcher allows students to apply knowledge gained to non-routine problem situations to develop higher-order thinking skills.

The **Glossary** combines pictorial representation and simple explanations for easy reference by students.

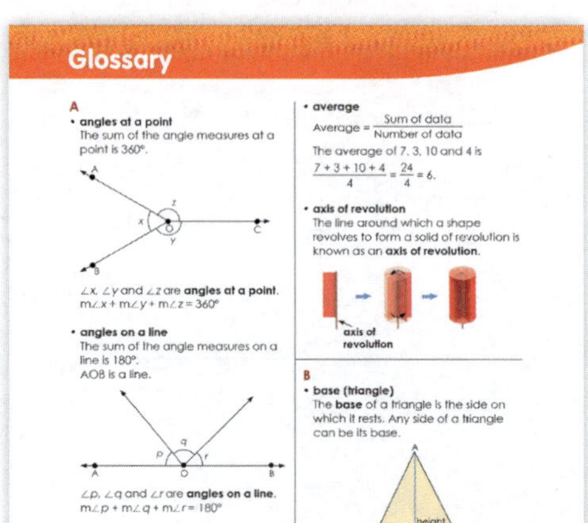
Glossary

A
• angles at a point
The sum of the angle measures at a point is 360°.
∠x, ∠y and ∠z are angles at a point.
m∠x + m∠y + m∠z = 360°

• angles on a line
The sum of the angle measures on a line is 180°.
AOB is a line.
∠p, ∠q and ∠r are angles on a line.
m∠p + m∠q + m∠r = 180°

• average
Average = Sum of data / Number of data
The average of 7, 3, 10 and 4 is
(7 + 3 + 10 + 4)/4 = 24/4 = 6.

• axis of revolution
The line around which a shape revolves to form a solid of revolution is known as an axis of revolution.
axis of revolution

B
• base (triangle)
The base of a triangle is the side on which it rests. Any side of a triangle can be its base.
height

 ISBN 978-93-5103-033-1

Contents

 ISBN 978-93-5103-033-1

 ISBN 978-93-5103-033-1

1 Whole Numbers

Lesson 1 Numbers up to 10,00,00,000

Reading and writing numbers within 10,00,000

Let's Learn

a) This block is made up of unit cubes. How many unit cubes are there?

Maths Lab

Picture It

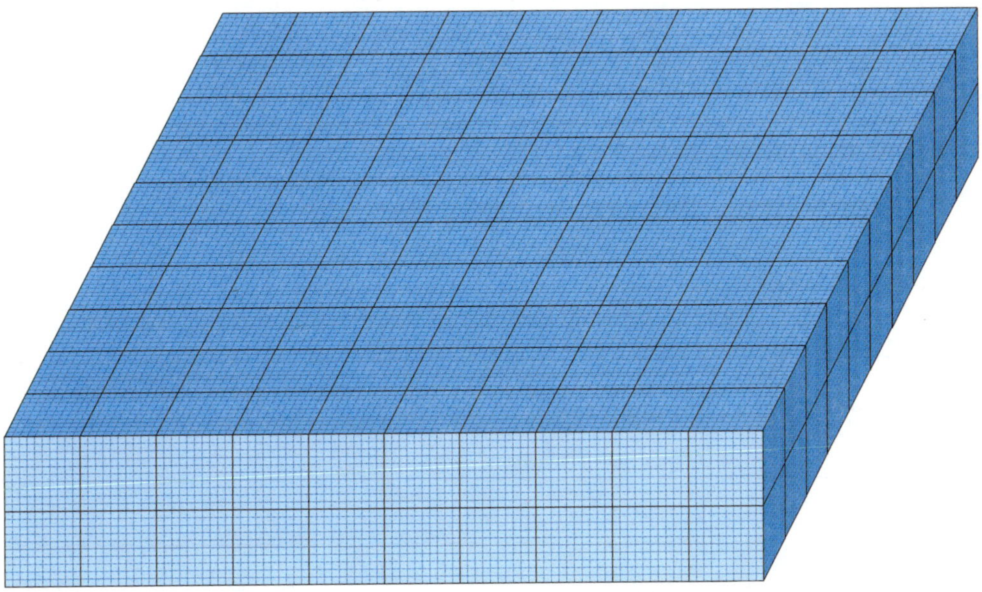

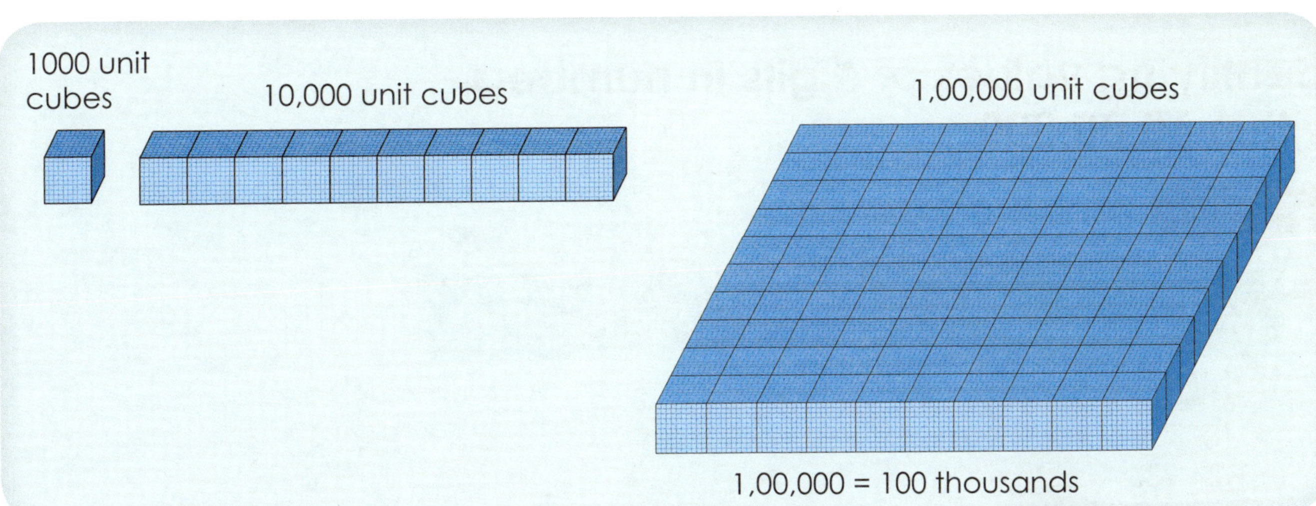

There are 2,00,000 unit cubes.
Read 2,00,000 as **two lakh**.

 ISBN 978-93-5103-033-1

b) A library has a collection of 1,24,936 books.

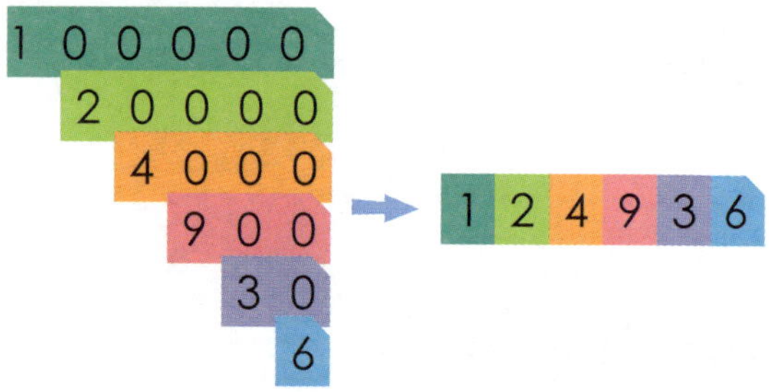

1,00,000 + 20,000 + 4000 + 900 + 30 + 6 = 1,24,936
1,24,000 + 936 = 1,24,936

Read 1,24,936 as **one lakh twenty-four thousand nine hundred thirty-six**.

Let's Do

1. Write the numbers.
   a) four lakh one thousand sixty-two ________
   b) nine lakh seventy thousand five hundred five ________

2. Write the numbers in words.
   a) 4,35,672 ____
   ____
   b) 3,11,012 ____
   ____

Identifying values of digits in numbers within 10,00,000

Let's Learn

Lakhs	Ten thousands	Thousands	Hundreds	Tens	Ones
1	2	4	9	3	6

In 1,24,936,
the digit 2 is in the ten thousands place and its value is 20,000.
the digit 1 is in the lakhs place and its value is ____.
the digit ____ is in the thousands place and its value is ____.

 ISBN 978-93-5103-033-1

Let's Do

1. Fill in the blanks.

   a) In 3,45,713, the digit _______ is in the lakhs place.

   Its value is _______.

   b) In 8,40,382, the digit 4 is in the _________________ place.

   Its value is _______.

   c) 2,70,846 = 2,00,000 + _______ + 800 + 40 + 6

Comparing numbers within 10,00,000

Let's Learn

Compare 6,52,470, 6,25,470 and 67,470.

	Lakhs	Ten thousands	Thousands	Hundreds	Tens	Ones
6,52,470	6	5	2	4	7	0
6,25,470	6	2	5	4	7	0
67,470		6	7	4	7	0

First, compare the lakhs. There are no lakhs in 67,470. 67,470 is the smallest number.

Then, compare the ten thousands in 6,52,470 and 6,25,470.
2 ten thousands is smaller than 5 ten thousands.
6,25,470 is smaller than 6,52,470.
6,52,470 is the greatest number.

Arranging the numbers in order from the smallest, we have:

67,470, 6,25,470, 6,52,470
(smallest)

 ISBN 978-93-5103-033-1

Let's Do

1. Compare 2,31,358, 2,13,538 and 2,31,375.

   a) _______ is the greatest number.

   b) _______ is the smallest number.

   c) Arranging the numbers in order from the greatest, we have:

   _______, _______, _______
   (greatest)

P/B Chapter 1: Exercise 1, pages 7–8

Reading and writing numbers within 1,00,00,000

Let's Learn

a)

The selling price of the house is ₹ 70 lakh.
How many one-thousand-rupee notes do you need to buy the house?

10 lakh = 10,00,000 (1000 thousands)

70 lakh = 70,00,000 (☐ thousands)

The selling price of the house is ₹ 70,00,000.
Read 70,00,000 as **70 lakh**.

 ISBN 978-93-5103-033-1

b) The land area of India is about 32,87,263 square kilometres.

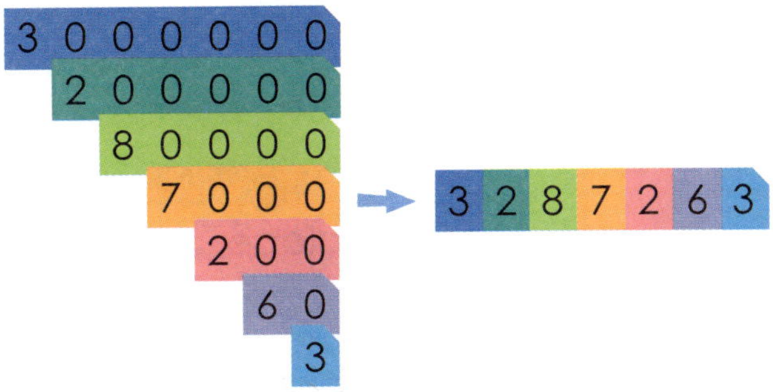

30,00,000 + 2,00,000 + 80,000 + 7000 + 200 + 60 + 3 = 32,87,263
32,00,000 + 87,000 + 263 = 32,87,263

Read 32,87,263 as thirty-two lakh eighty-seven thousand two hundred sixty-three.

Let's Do

1. Write the numbers.
   a) seventy lakh three thousand ____________
   b) ninety lakh twenty-three thousand ____________
   c) twenty-four lakh five thousand forty-nine ____________

2. Write the numbers in words.
   a) 41,26,000 ______________________________
   ____
   b) 36,90,580 ______________________________
   ____

Identifying values of digits in numbers within 1,00,00,000

Let's Learn

Ten Lakhs	Lakhs	Ten thousands	Thousands	Hundreds	Tens	Ones
3	2	8	7	2	6	3

In 32,87,263,
the digit in the ten lakhs place is 3 and its value is 30,00,000.
the digit in the lakhs place is ____ and its value is ____.
the digit 8 stands for ____.

 ISBN 978-93-5103-033-1

Let's Do

1. Fill in the blanks.

   a) In 35,74,621, the digit ________ is in the lakhs place.
   Its value is ________.

   b) In 48,36,152, the digit 4 is in the ________ place.
   Its value is ________.

   c) 24,03,510 = ________ + 4,00,000 + 3000 + 500 + 10

P/B Chapter 1: Exercise 2, pages 9–10

Reading and writing numbers within 10,00,00,000

Let's Learn

a) There are about 1 **crore** vehicles in Delhi.

1 crore = 100 lakh
1 crore = 1,00,00,000

The number of vehicles is about 1,00,00,000.
Read 1,00,00,000 as one **crore**.

b) According to the 2011 Census, the population of the National Capital Region of Delhi is about 2,17,53,486.

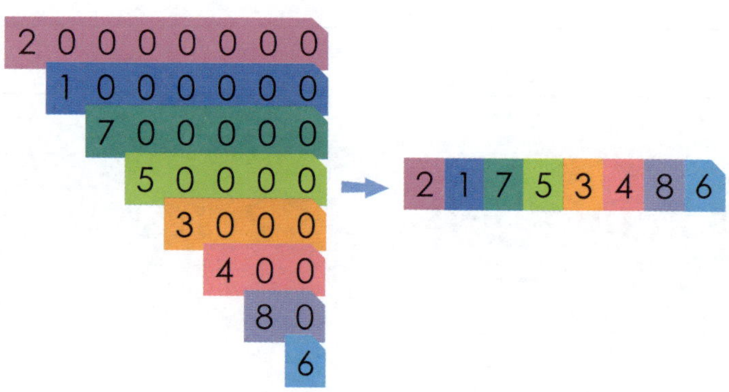

Read 2,17,53,486 as **two crore seventeen lakh fifty-three thousand four hundred eighty-six**.

 ISBN 978-93-5103-033-1

Let's Do

1. Write the numbers.

   a) four crore thirty lakh twenty thousand three hundred ______________

   b) eight crore nineteen lakh twelve thousand two hundred one ______________

2. Write the numbers in words.

   a) 9,16,80,300 ______________________________

   b) 2,02,75,834 ______________________________

Identifying values of digits in numbers within 10,00,00,000

Let's Learn

Crores	Ten lakhs	Lakhs	Ten thousands	Thousands	Hundreds	Tens	Ones
1	3	8	4	7	4	6	5

In 1,38,47,465,
the digit in the crores place is 1 and its value is 1,00,00,000.
the digit 3 is in the ten lakhs place and its value is ____.
the digit 7 stands for ____.

Let's Do

1. Fill in the blanks.

   a) In 3,14,65,790, the digit ______________ is in the ten lakhs place.
   Its value is ______________.

   b) In 5,34,21,709, the digit 3 is in the ______________ place.
   Its value is ______________.

Chapter 1: Exercise 3, page 11

 ISBN 978-93-5103-033-1

Comparing Indian and international systems of numbers

Let's Learn

Picture It

Indian System	International System
10,000 ten thousand	10,000 ten thousand
1,00,000 one lakh	100,000 one hundred thousand
10,00,000 ten lakh	1,000,000 one million
1,00,00,000 one crore	10,000,000 ten million
10,00,00,000 ten crore	100,000,000 one hundred million

For five-digit numbers and above,

- in the international system, the commas are put at regular intervals of three place values from the right.
- in the Indian system, the first comma is put between the thousands and hundreds place. Thereafter, the commas are put after every two place values to the left.

Let's Do

1. a) There are 7 lakh cars produced in a factory in a year. Express this in the international system in words and numbers.

   b) Mr. Bal bought a house for ₹ 20 million. Express the amount in the Indian system.

   c) A toy factory made two crore fourteen lakh seventy thousand three hundred toys in a year. Write the amount in numbers and express it in words in the international system.

 ISBN 978-93-5103-033-1

Practice 1

1. Write the numbers.

   a) one lakh fifteen thousand six hundred

   b) eight lakh eighty thousand five

   c) three crore fifty-two lakh forty-one thousand seventy

2. Write the numbers in words.

   a) 2,07,306 b) 5,60,003 c) 34,50,000 d) 1,65,08,070

3. What is the value of the digit **8** in each of the following numbers?

   a) 9,01,9**8**2 b) 96,4**8**,000 c) 1,**8**1,40,050

4. What are the missing numbers?

   a) 2,25,430 = _____ + 20,000 + 5000 + 400 + 30

   b) 85,32,000 = 80,00,000 + 5,00,000 + _____ + 2000

   c) 8,14,10,060 = _____ + 10,00,000 + 4,00,000 + 10,000 + 60

5. a) Which number is greater, 4,21,668 or 4,61,668?

   b) Which number is smaller, 56,32,000 or 56,23,000?

6. Complete the number patterns.

   a) 70,500, 71,500, 72,500, _____, _____

   b) 83,002, 93,002, _____, _____, 1,23,002

   c) 9,74,20,000, 8,74,20,000, _____, 6,74,20,000, _____

7. Arrange the numbers in order. Begin with the greatest.

   5,32,760, 5,32,670, 5,62,370, 5,32,607

8. Arrange the numbers in order. Begin with the smallest.

   7,25,37,000, 7,23,57,000, 7,32,57,000, 74,25,700

9. Write the place value of the underlined digit in the Indian and international systems.

	Number	Indian System	Place Value	International System	Place Value
a)	5934<u>8</u>192	5,93,48,192		59,348,192	
b)	6<u>2</u>18379	62,18,379		6,218,379	
c)	7<u>5</u>436821	7,54,36,821		75,436,821	

 ISBN 978-93-5103-033-1

Lesson 2 Addition and Subtraction Within 10,00,00,000

Adding within 10,00,00,000

Let's Learn

Find the sum of 3,71,940 and 45,328.

3,71,940 + 45,328 = ☐

	L	T Th	Th	H	T	O
	1		1			
	3	7	1	9	4	0
+		4	5	3	2	8
	4	1	7	2	6	8

3,71,940 + 45,328 = 4,17,268

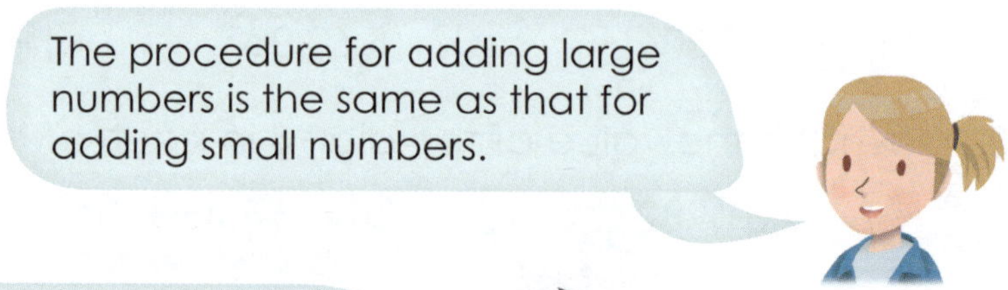

Let's Do

1. Add.

a)
```
    1 4 2 4 6 1 0
+     6 5 7 3 6 1
```

b)
```
    3 2 6 1 4 7 2
+     1 2 9 5 2 4
```

c)
```
    1 7 9 3 5 2 8
+   4 1 7 3 9 4 1
```

2. 1,97,32,546 + 11,79,410 = ________

Chapter 1: Exercise 4, page 12

 ISBN 978-93-5103-033-1

Subtracting within 10,00,00,000

Let's Learn

Find the difference between 2,45,36,543 and 12,78,521.

2,45,36,543 – 12,78,521 = ▢

Cr	TL	L	T Th	Th	H	T	O
		4	12	1			
2	4	~~5~~	~~3~~	6	5	4	3
–	1	2	7	8	5	2	1
2	3	2	5	8	0	2	2

The procedure for subtracting large numbers is the same as that for subtracting small numbers.

I need to regroup twice here.

2,45,36,543 – 12,78,521 = 2,32,58,022

Let's Do

1. Subtract.

a)
```
   9 9 9 8 9 8
 –   9 6 9 8 7
 _____________

 _____________
```

b)
```
   2 3 8 6 9 4 1
 –   1 9 4 7 1 2
 _______________

 _______________
```

c)
```
   4 6 5 2 7 1 3
 – 2 8 3 0 7 9 2
 _______________

 _______________
```

2. 1,62,27,056 – 1,03,23,564 = ________

P/B Chapter 1: Exercise 5, page 13

 ISBN 978-93-5103-033-1

Solving word problems

Let's Learn

An industrialist owned a plot of land worth ₹ 3,12,70,000. He then bought the plot of land next to it for ₹ 1,98,67,500. What was the total value of the two plots of land he owned?

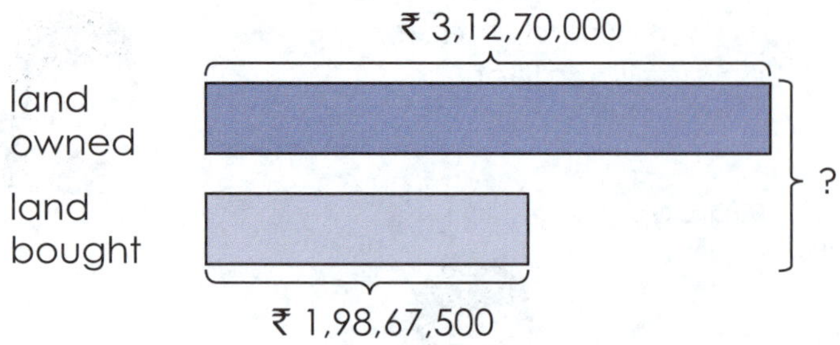

$$\begin{array}{r} {}^{1\ 1\ 1} \\ 3\,1\,2\,7\,0\,0\,0\,0 \\ +\ 1\,9\,8\,6\,7\,5\,0\,0 \\ \hline 5\,1\,1\,3\,7\,5\,0\,0 \\ \hline \end{array}$$

If 3,12,70,000 + 1,98,67,500 = 5,11,37,500,
then, 5,11,37,500 – 1,98,67,500 = 3,12,70,000.

$$\begin{array}{r} 5\,1\,1\,3\,7\,5\,0\,0 \\ -\,1\,9\,8\,6\,7\,5\,0\,0 \\ \hline 3\,1\,2\,7\,0\,0\,0\,0 \\ \hline \end{array}$$

My answer is correct.

The total value of the two plots of land he owned was ₹ 5,11,37,500.

Let's Do

1. The total number of female voters at a state election was 59,19,989. The number of male voters was 73,89,000. What was the total number of voters?

2. Mars has a diameter of 67,92,000 metres. The Earth's diameter is 1,27,56,000 metres. What is the difference between their diameters?

3. The population of Country A in 2005 was 2,05,44,060. By 2015, it was 4,38,25,200. By how much did the population of Country A increase in ten years?

PB Chapter 1: Exercise 6, page 14

 ISBN 978-93-5103-033-1

Practice 2

1. Add.

   a) 4,86,789 + 2,10,001   b) 1,11,888 + 12,37,160

   c) 58,23,609 + 73,82,154   d) 1,16,90,009 + 75,79,238

2. Subtract.

   a) 5,24,610 – 84,375   b) 64,50,010 – 2,40,009

   c) 28,02,984 – 17,93,420   d) 6,98,53,208 – 1,95,45,304

   Solve the word problems. You may draw bar models to help you.
   Show your work clearly.

3. Company A collected 5,53,078 clothes at a charity drive. Company B collected 78,021 more clothes than Company A. How many clothes did Company B collect?

4. A property developer needs 3,76,39,523 bricks to build a township. It has 2,83,26,416 bricks now. How many more bricks must it buy?

5. Mr. Rao had ₹ 14,39,444 in savings. Mr. Mathur saved ₹ 68,732 more than Mr. Rao. Mr. Lee saved ₹ 16,076 less than Mr. Mathur. How much did Mr. Lee save?

Lesson 3 Approximation and Estimation

Rounding numbers to the nearest thousand

Let's Learn

a) 4865 people watched a tennis match.

Picture It

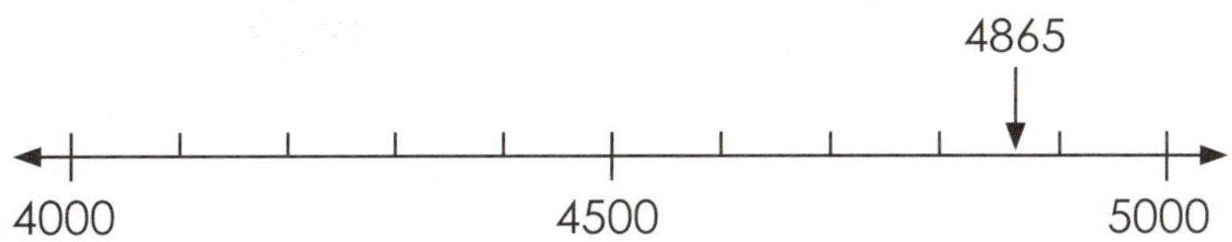

4865 is between 4000 and 5000.
It is nearer to 5000 than to 4000.

4865 is 5000 when rounded to the nearest thousand.
4865 ≈ 5000
4865 is approximately 5000.
There were about 5000 people.

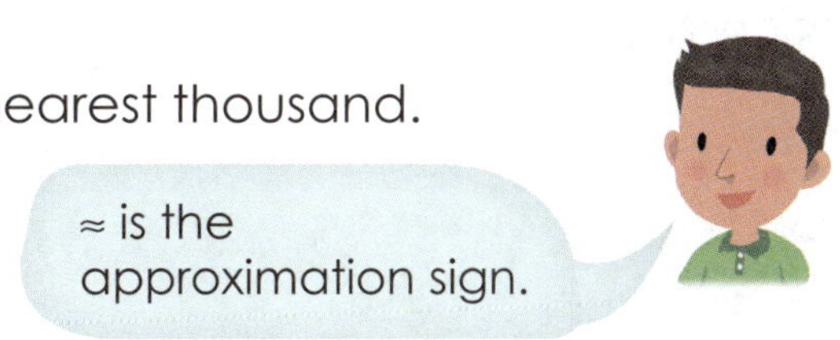

 ISBN 978-93-5103-033-1

b) Round 18,300 to the nearest thousand.

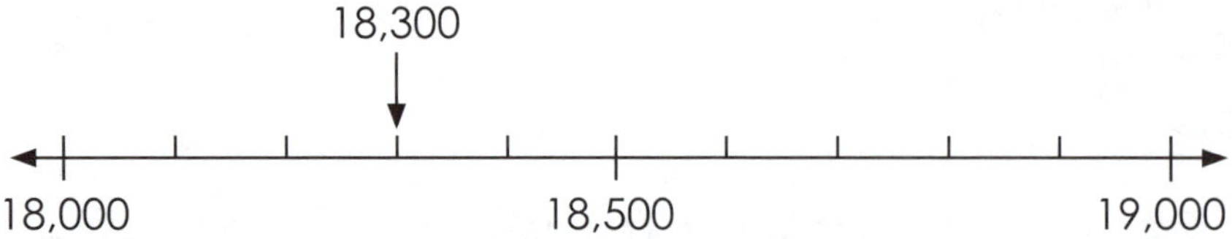

18,300 is less than halfway between 18,000 and 19,000.
18,300 is nearer to 18,000 than to 19,000.

18,300 is 18,000 when rounded to the nearest thousand.
$18,300 \approx 18,000$

c) Round 16,500 to the nearest thousand.

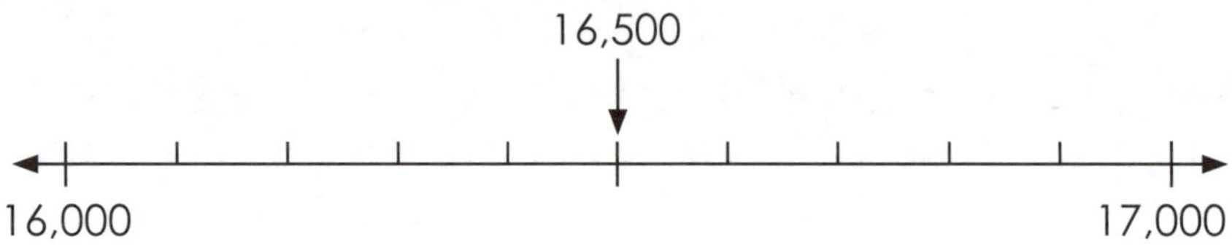

16,500 is halfway between 16,000 and 17,000.
Take 17,000 to be the nearest thousand.
$16,500 \approx 17,000$

To round a number to the nearest thousand, look at the digit in the hundreds place. If it is 5 or greater than 5, we round up. If it is smaller than 5, we round down.

Let's Do

1. Round each number to the nearest thousand.

a)

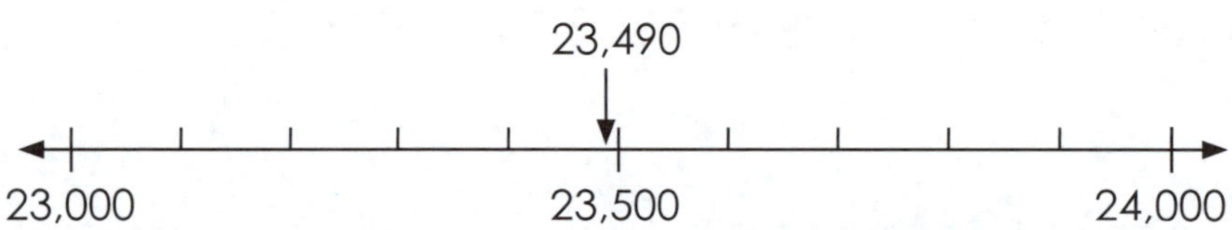

$23,490 \approx$ ______

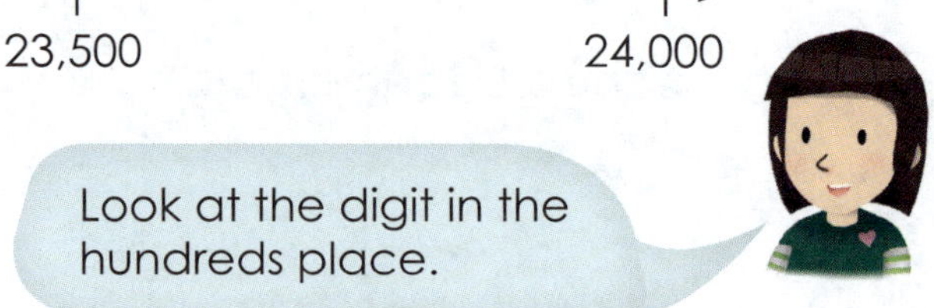

b)

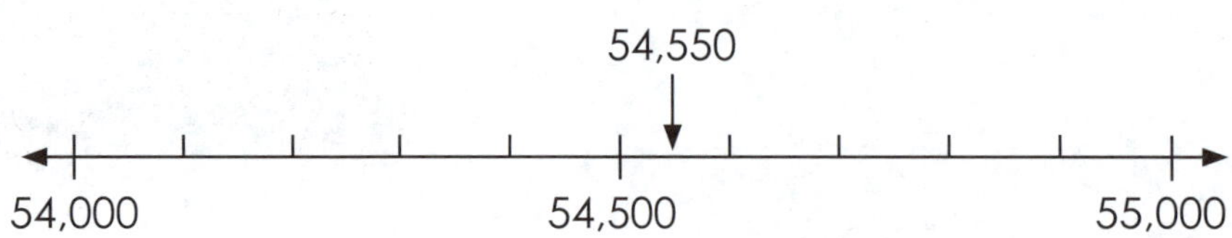

$54,550 \approx$ ______

 ISBN 978-93-5103-033-1

c)

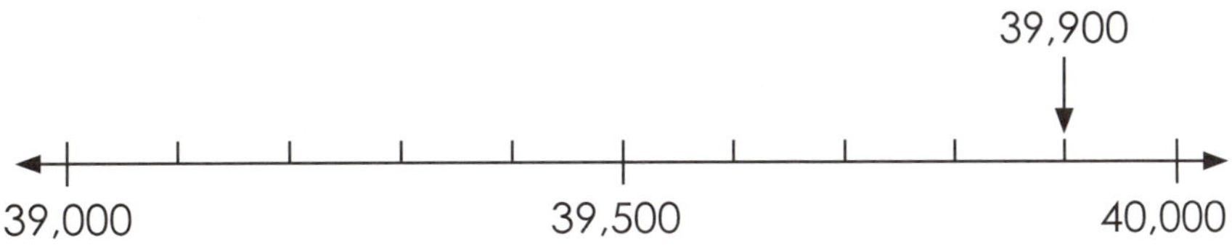

39,900 ≈ ________

Chapter 1: Exercise 7, page 15

Rounding numbers to the nearest ten thousand, lakh, ten lakh or crore

Let's Learn

a) Round 2,48,360 to the nearest ten thousand.

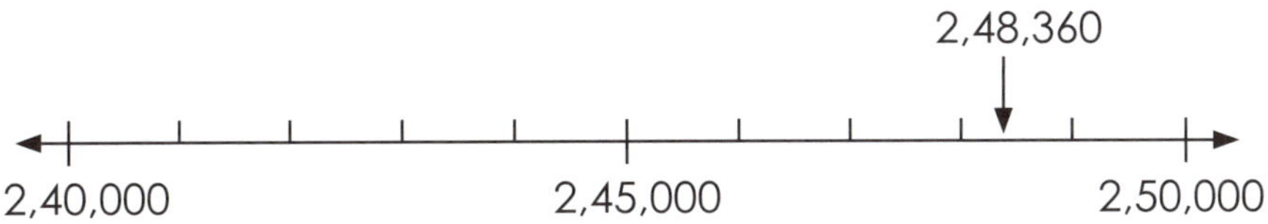

In 2,48,360, the digit 8 is in the thousands place.
So, we round up.
2,48,360 ≈ 2,50,000

b) Round 13,26,450 to the nearest lakh.

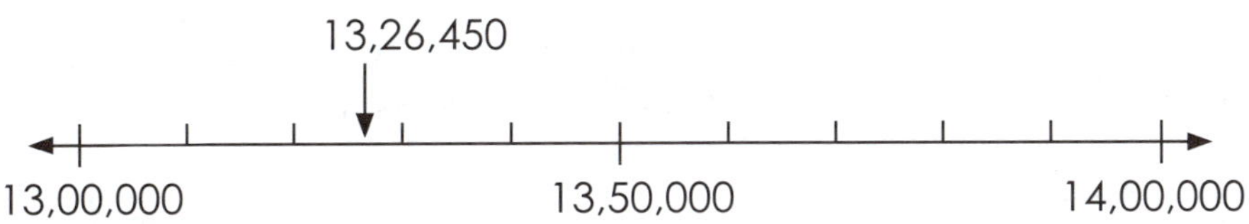

In 13,26,450, the digit 2 is in the ten thousands place.
So, we round down.
13,26,450 ≈ ☐

c) Round 1,52,89,000 to the nearest ten lakh.

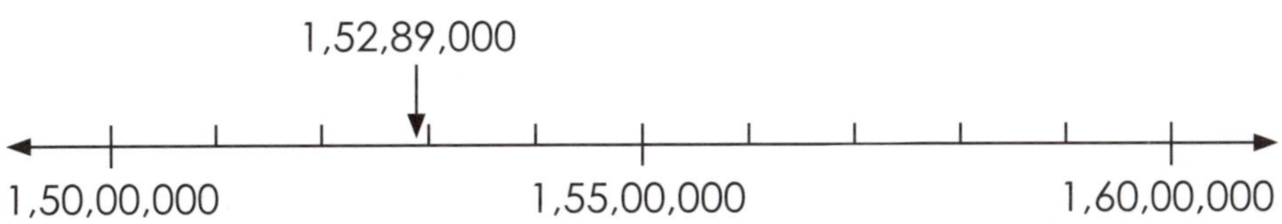

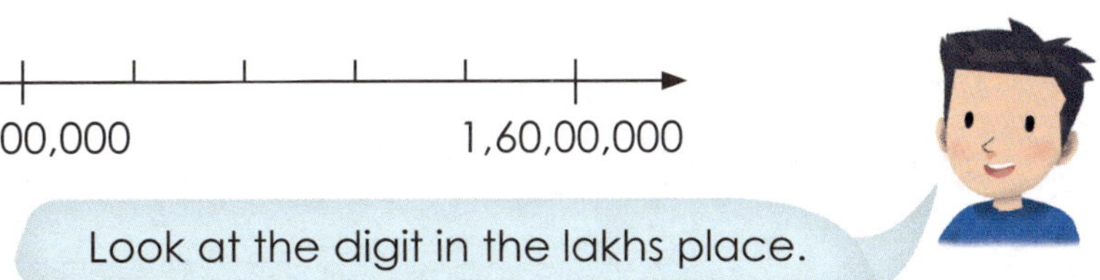

In 1,52,89,000, the digit 2 is in the lakhs place.
So, we round down.
1,52,89,000 ≈ ☐

 ISBN 978-93-5103-033-1

d) Round 1,52,89,000 to the nearest crore.

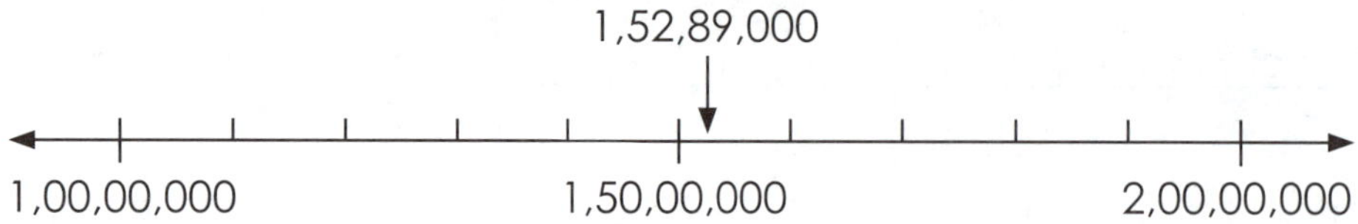

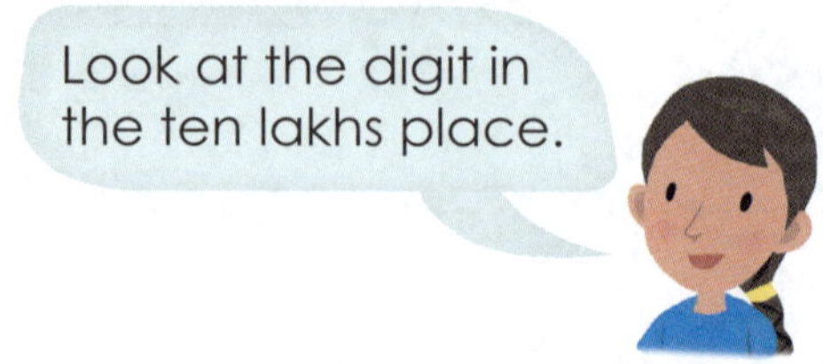

In 1,52,89,000, the digit 5 is in the ten lakhs place.
So, we round up.
1,52,89,000 ≈ ______

Let's Do

1. Round 2,34,56,780 to the nearest
   a) ten thousand. ______ b) lakh. ______
   c) ten lakh. ______ d) crore. ______

P/B Chapter 1: Exercise 8, page 16

Estimating sums and differences

Let's Learn

a) Estimate the value of 63,900 + 59,920.

63,900 + 59,920 ≈ 64,000 + 60,000
= 1,24,000

b) Estimate the value of 4,59,970 – 32,400.

4,59,970 – 32,400 ≈ 4,60,000 – 30,000
= 4,30,000

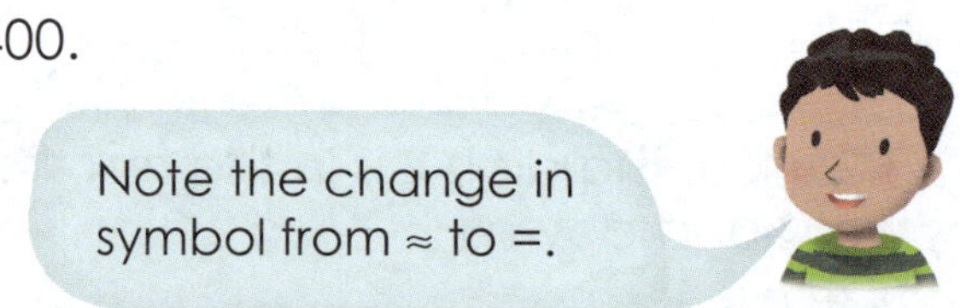

Let's Do

1. Estimate the value of each of the following.
   a) 7,80,230 + 9985 ≈ ______ + ______
   = ______
   b) 5,89,12,000 – 2,90,11,888 ≈ ______ – ______
   = ______

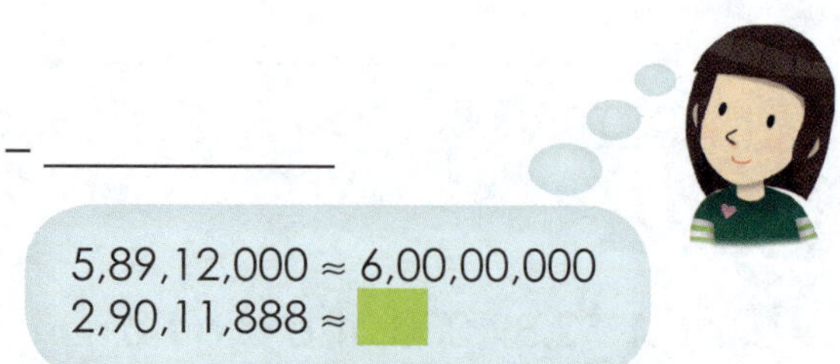

P/B Chapter 1: Exercise 9, page 17

 ISBN 978-93-5103-033-1

Estimating products and quotients

Let's Learn

a) Estimate the value of 29,840 × 6.

Round 29,840 to the nearest thousand.

$29{,}840 \times 6 \approx 30{,}000 \times 6$
$= 1{,}80{,}000$

30 thousands × 6 = 180 thousands
= 1 lakh 80 thousands

b) Estimate the value of 5,42,300 ÷ 8.

Multiples of 8:
... 40, 48, 56
... 4,00,000, 4,80,000, 5,60,000

5,42,300 is nearer to 5,60,000 than to 4,80,000.

5,42,300 ≈ 5,60,000

$5{,}42{,}300 \div 8 \approx 5{,}60{,}000 \div 8$
$= \square$

5 lakh 60 thousands ÷ 8
560 thousands ÷ 8 = $\square$ thousands

Let's Do

1. Estimate the value of each of the following.

a) 4,87,204 × 5 ≈ ______ × 5
= ______

4,87,204 ≈ ______

b) 3,78,200 ÷ 4 ≈ ______ ÷ 4
= ______

3,78,200 ÷ 4 → 3,60,000 ÷ 4
3,78,200 ÷ 4 → 4,00,000 ÷ 4

PB Chapter 1: Exercise 10, page 18

Practice 3

1. Round each number to the nearest thousand.

   a) 6850 b) 10,500 c) 1,25,498

2. A spaceship travelled 9,99,540 kilometres.
   Round this distance to the nearest ten thousand kilometres.

3. David bought a car for ₹ 10,56,200.
   Round this amount to the nearest lakh rupees.

4. Mr. Raju bought a plot of land for ₹ 1,80,93,000.
   Round this amount to the nearest crore rupees.

5. Estimate the value of each of the following.

   a) 32,370 + 44,959 b) 24,890 + 50,016

   c) 4,80,207 – 98,640 d) 5,40,500 – 68,920

6. The number of people living in three cities is shown below.
   Estimate the total number of people living in the three cities.

   Number of people

   City A : 17,99,200
   City B : 17,63,920
   City C : 17,05,000

7. Estimate the value of each of the following.

   a) 38,659 × 4 b) 60,230 × 9

   c) 7,08,000 ÷ 8 d) 4,37,800 ÷ 7

 ISBN 978-93-5103-033-1

Lesson 4 Factors and Multiples

Prime factorisation

Let's Learn

a) $12 = 1 \times 12$ $\quad 12 = 2 \times 6$ $\quad 12 = 3 \times 4$

The factors of 12 are 1, 2, 3, 4, 6 and 12.
12 has more than two factors. So, it is a composite number.

Two of the factors, 2 and 3, are prime numbers.
We can write 12 as a product of its prime factors, 2 and 3.
$12 = 2 \times 2 \times 3$

When we write a number as a product of its prime factors, it is called **prime factorisation**.

$12 = 2 \times 6 = 2 \times 2 \times 3$ | $12 = 3 \times 4 = 3 \times 2 \times 2$

b) Write the prime factorisation of 36.

Method 1: Factor tree method

36
2×18 ← Express 36 as a product of its smallest prime factor and another number.
$2 \times 2 \times 9$ ← Express 18 as a product of its smallest prime factor and another number.
$2 \times 2 \times 3 \times 3$ ← Express 9 as a product of its smallest prime factor and another number. Stop when the last row has only prime numbers.

The prime factors of 36 are 2 and 3.
$36 = 2 \times 2 \times 3 \times 3$

Method 2: Division method

$$\begin{array}{r|l} 2 & 36 \\ \hline & 18 \end{array} \rightarrow \begin{array}{r|l} 2 & 36 \\ \hline 2 & 18 \\ \hline & 9 \end{array} \rightarrow \begin{array}{r|l} 2 & 36 \\ \hline 2 & 18 \\ \hline 3 & 9 \\ \hline & 3 \end{array}$$

Divide 36 by its smallest prime factor.

Divide 18 by its smallest prime factor.

Divide 9 by its smallest prime factor. Stop dividing when the quotient is a prime number.

The prime factors of 36 are 2 and 3.
$36 = 2 \times 2 \times 3 \times 3$

$$\begin{array}{r|l} (2) & 36 \\ \hline (2) & 18 \\ \hline (3) & 9 \\ \hline & (3) \end{array}$$

 ISBN 978-93-5103-033-1

Let's Do

1. Write the prime factorisation of each of the following numbers. Use the factor tree method to find the answer and the division method to check your answer.

   a) 60 ______   b) 210 ______

Finding out if a number is a common factor of given numbers

Let's Learn

a) Is 5 a common factor of 75 and 80?

```
   15            16
5 ) 75        5 ) 80
    5             5
   ---           ---
    25            30
    25            30
   ---           ---
     0             0
```

75 can be divided by 5 exactly.
5 is a factor of 75.

80 can be divided by 5 exactly.
5 is a factor of 80.

5 is a factor of both 75 and 80.
So, 5 is a **common factor** of 75 and 80.

b) Is 4 a common factor of 96, 84 and 78?

```
   24            21            19
4 ) 96        4 ) 84        4 ) 78
    8             8             4
   ---           ---           ---
    16             4            38
    16             4            36
   ---           ---           ---
     0             0             2
```

96 can be divided by 4 exactly.
4 is a factor of 96.

84 can be divided by 4 exactly.
4 is a factor of 84.

78 cannot be divided by 4 exactly.
4 is not a factor of 78.

So, 4 is not a common factor of 96, 84 and 78.

 ISBN 978-93-5103-033-1

Let's Do

1. Is 8 a common factor of 56, 72 and 96?

$8\overline{)56}$	$8\overline{)72}$	$8\overline{)96}$
56 ________ be divided by 8 exactly.	72 ________ be divided by 8 exactly.	96 ________ be divided by 8 exactly.

So, 8 ________ a common factor of 56, 72 and 96.

Finding common factors and greatest common factor

Let's Learn

a) $1 \times 30 = 30$
$2 \times 15 = 30$
$3 \times 10 = 30$
$5 \times 6 = 30$

(1), (2), (3), 5, (6), 10, 15 and 30 are factors of 30.

$1 \times 42 = 42$
$2 \times 21 = 42$
$3 \times 14 = 42$
$6 \times 7 = 42$

(1), (2), (3), (6), 7, 14, 21 and 42 are factors of 42.

1, 2, 3 and 6 are common factors of 30 and 42.
The **greatest common factor (G.C.F.)**, also known as the highest common factor (H.C.F.), of 30 and 42 is 6.

We can also find the G.C.F. using the division method.

b) Find the greatest common factor of 40, 60, 200.

(2)	40, 60, 200 ← Divide the numbers by their common prime factor.
(2)	20, 30, 100
(5)	10, 15, 50
	2, 3, 10 ← Stop here as there is no common prime factor for these numbers.

→ $2 \times 2 \times 5 = 20$

Multiply the common prime factors to get the G.C.F.

The greatest common factor of 40, 60 and 200 is 20.

 ISBN 978-93-5103-033-1

Let's Do

1. Find the common factors and greatest common factor of 50 and 40.

1 × 50 = 50	1 × 40 = 40
2 × _____ = 50	2 × _____ = 40
_____ × _____ = 50	4 × _____ = 40
	_____ × _____ = 40

   a) The common factors of 50 and 40 are _____, _____, _____ and _____.

   b) The greatest common factor of 50 and 40 is _____.

2. Find the greatest common factor of 24, 48 and 60 using the division method.

P/B Chapter 1: Exercise 11, pages 19–20

Finding out if a number is a common multiple of given numbers

Let's Learn

a) Is 96 a common multiple of 2 and 3?

$$\begin{array}{r} 48 \\ 2\overline{)96} \\ \underline{8} \\ 16 \\ \underline{16} \\ 0 \end{array} \qquad \begin{array}{r} 32 \\ 3\overline{)96} \\ \underline{9} \\ 6 \\ \underline{6} \\ 0 \end{array}$$

96 can be divided by 2 exactly.
96 is a multiple of 2.

96 can be divided by 3 exactly.
96 is a multiple of 3.

So, 96 is a **common multiple** of 2 and 3.

b) Is 124 a common multiple of 4, 6 and 8?

$$\begin{array}{r} 31 \\ 4\overline{)124} \\ \underline{12} \\ 4 \\ \underline{4} \\ 0 \end{array} \qquad \begin{array}{r} 20 \\ 6\overline{)124} \\ \underline{12} \\ 4 \\ \underline{0} \\ 4 \end{array} \qquad \begin{array}{r} 15 \\ 8\overline{)124} \\ \underline{8} \\ 44 \\ \underline{40} \\ 4 \end{array}$$

124 can be divided by 4 exactly.
124 is a multiple of 4.

124 cannot be divided by 6 exactly.
124 is not a multiple of 6.

124 cannot be divided by 8 exactly.
124 is not a multiple of 8.

So, 124 is not a common multiple of 4, 6 and 8.

 ISBN 978-93-5103-033-1

Let's Do

1. Is 126 a common multiple of 5, 7 and 9?

$5\overline{)126}$	$7\overline{)126}$	$9\overline{)126}$
126 ____ be divided by 5 exactly.	126 ____ be divided by 7 exactly	126 ____ be divided by 9 exactly.

So, 126 ____ a common multiple of 5, 7 and 9.

Finding common multiples and least common multiple

Let's Learn

a)

$1 \times 4 = 4$	$2 \times 4 = 8$	$3 \times 4 = 12$
$4 \times 4 = 16$	$5 \times 4 = 20$	$6 \times 4 = 24$
$7 \times 4 = 28$	$8 \times 4 = 32$	$9 \times 4 = 36$

The multiples of 4 are 4, 8, (12), 16, 20, (24), 28, 32, (36)...

$1 \times 6 = 6$	$2 \times 6 = 12$	$3 \times 6 = 18$
$4 \times 6 = 24$	$5 \times 6 = 30$	$6 \times 6 = 36$

The multiples of 6 are 6, (12), 18, (24), 30, (36)...

12 is a common multiple of 4 and 6.

The next two common multiples of 4 and 6 are ____ and ____.

The **least common multiple (L.C.M.)** of 4 and 6 is 12.

We can also find the L.C.M. using the division method.

 ISBN 978-93-5103-033-1

b) Find the least common multiple of 20, 30 and 50.

②	20, 30, 50
⑤	10, 15, 25
	②, ③, ⑤

← Divide the numbers by their common prime factor.

← Stop here as there is no common prime factor for these numbers.

$2 \times 5 \times 2 \times 3 \times 5 = 300$

Multiply the common prime factors and the quotients to get the L.C.M.

The least common multiple of 20, 30 and 50 is 300.

Let's Do

1. Find the first two common multiples and the least common multiple of 3 and 5.

   a) The first ten multiples of 3 are _____, _____, _____, _____, _____, _____, _____, _____, _____ and _____.

   b) The first ten multiples of 5 are _____, _____, _____, _____, _____, _____, _____, _____, _____ and _____.

   c) The first two common multiples of 3 and 5 are _____ and _____.

   d) The least common multiple of 3 and 5 is _____.

2. Find the least common multiple of 36, 54 and 81 using the division method.

P/B Chapter 1: Exercise 12, pages 21–22

Think About It

John has some sweets. He can pack them equally into bags of 3 or bags of 5.

Ria

Can you find the greatest possible number of sweets John has?

Yes, I can.

Sam

Is Sam correct? Explain why.

 ISBN 978-93-5103-033-1

Divisibility rules of 3, 4, 6, 7, 8 and 9

Let's Learn

Divisibility by 3 and 9

A number is divisible by	If the sum of its digits is divisible by	Example
3	3	Is 75 divisible by 3? Check: 7 + 5 = 12 12 is divisible by 3. So, 75 is divisible by 3.
9	9	Is 765 divisible by 9? Check: 7 + 6 + 5 = 18 18 is divisible by 9. So, 765 is divisible by 9.

Divisibility by 4

A number is divisible by	If the number formed by its last two digits is divisible by	Example
4	4	Is 324 divisible by 4? Check: 3**24** ↓ 24 is divisible by 4. So, 324 is divisible by 4.

Divisibility by 6

A number is divisible by	If it is divisible by both	Example
6	2 and 3	Is 84 divisible by 6? Check: Divisible by 2? ⟶ 84 has a digit 4 in the ones place. So, 84 is divisible by 2. Divisible by 3? ⟶ 8 + 4 = 12 The sum of its digits, 12, is divisible by 3. So, 84 is divisible by 3. So, 84 is divisible by 6.

ISBN 978-93-5103-033-1

Divisibility by 7		
A number is divisible by	**If the difference between twice its ones digit and the number formed by the other digits is**	**Example**
7	0 or a multiple of 7	a) Is 126 divisible by 7? Check: **12 6** 12 – (6 × 2) = 12 – 12 = 0 So, 126 is divisible by 7. b) Is 329 divisible by 7? Check: **32 9** 32 – (9 × 2) = 32 – 18 = 14 14 is divisible by 7. So, 329 is divisible by 7.

Divisibility by 8		
A number is divisible by	**If the number formed by its last three digits is divisible by**	**Example**
8	8	Is 3112 divisible by 8? Check: 3**112** ↓ 112 is divisible by 8. So, 3112 is divisible by 8.

Let's Do

1. Which of the following numbers is divisible by 3?
   a) 108 b) 574 c) 2079
2. Which of the following numbers is divisible by 4?
   a) 2152 b) 3274 c) 4140
3. Which of the following numbers is divisible by 6?
   a) 162 b) 409 c) 1458
4. Which of the following numbers is divisible by 7?
   a) 175 b) 236 c) 1668

ISBN 978-93-5103-033-1

5. Which of the following numbers is divisible by 8?
   a) 439 b) 2584 c) 4280
6. Which of the following numbers is divisible by 9?
   a) 535 b) 9125 c) 6579

P/B Chapter 1: Exercise 13, page 23

Practice 4

1. Find the common factors of each group of numbers.
   a) 6 and 15 b) 12 and 16 c) 15, 45 and 60 d) 24, 40 and 56
2. a) Is 4 a factor of 60? Why?
   b) Is 4 a factor of 84? Why?
   c) Is 4 a common factor of 60 and 84? Why?
3. Find the greatest common factor of each group of numbers in Question 1.
4. Is 4158 a common multiple of 2, 3 and 9?
5. a) List the first ten multiples of 2.
   b) List the first ten multiples of 7.
   c) Name the least common multiple of 2 and 7.
6. Find the least common multiple of each group of numbers.
   a) 33 and 110 b) 18 and 144 c) 28, 42 and 56 d) 90, 135 and 180
7. Complete the table with **Yes** or **No**.

Number	**Is the number divisible by...?**					
	3	**4**	**6**	**7**	**8**	**9**
513						
319						
3642						
4050						
6566						
1920						

 ISBN 978-93-5103-033-1

2 Multiplication and Division of Whole Numbers

Lesson 1 Multiplying by Tens, Hundreds or Thousands

Multiplying by 10, 100 or 1000

Let's Learn

a)

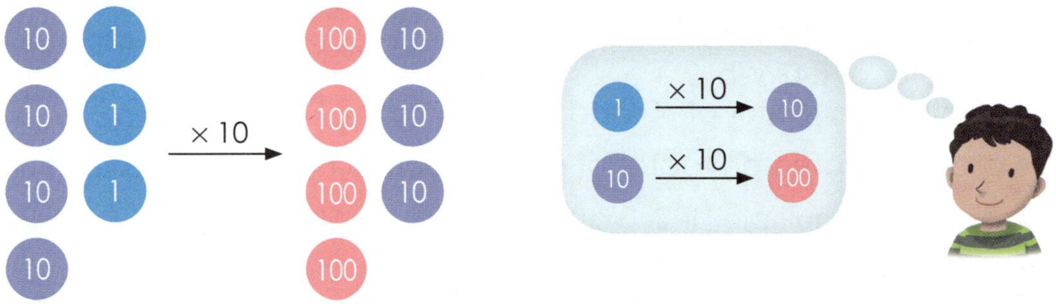

$43 \times 10 = 430$

b)

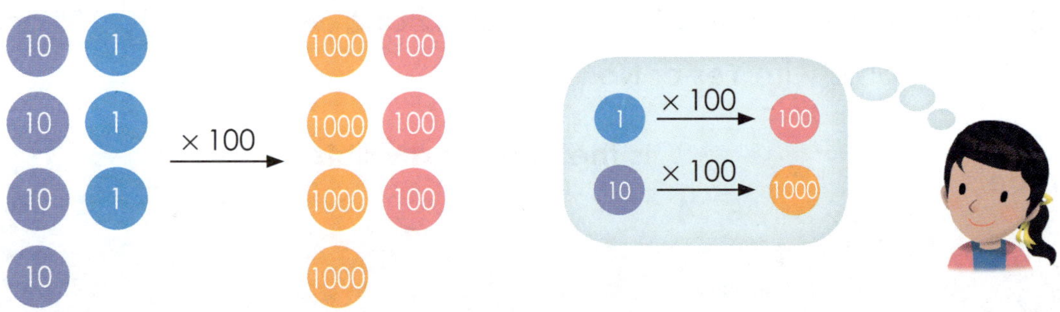

$43 \times 100 = 4300$

c)

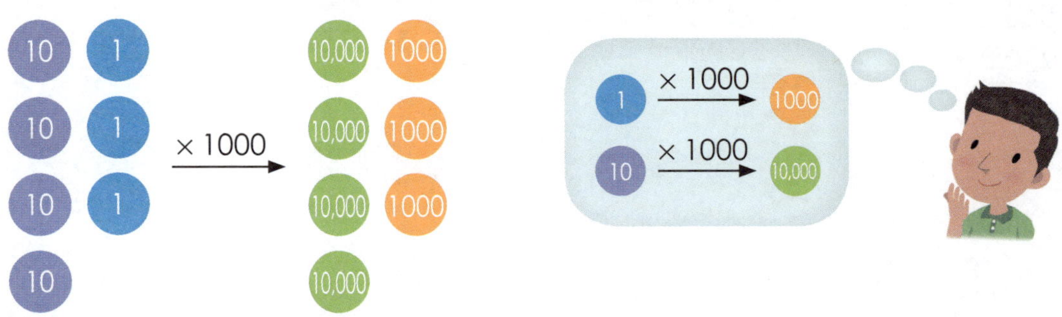

$43 \times 1000 = 43,000$

 ISBN 978-93-5103-033-1

Let's Do

1. Multiply.

   a) $328 \times 10 =$ ______ b) $536 \times 100 =$ ______ c) $1000 \times 630 =$ ______

P/B Chapter 2: Exercise 1, page 24

Multiplying by tens, hundreds or thousands

Let's Learn

a) Multiply 16 by 70.

$$16 \times 70 = 16 \times 7 \times 10$$
$$= 112 \times 10$$
$$= 1120$$

b) Multiply 16 by 700.

$$16 \times 700 = 16 \times 7 \times 100$$
$$= 112 \times 100$$
$$= 11,200$$

c) Multiply 16 by 7000.

$$16 \times 7000 = 16 \times 7 \times 1000$$
$$= 112 \times 1000$$
$$= 1,12,000$$

Let's Do

1. Multiply.

   a) $48 \times 30 = 48 \times 3 \times 10$

   $=$ ______ $\times 10$

   $=$ ______

   b) $48 \times 300 = 48 \times 3 \times$ ______

   $=$ ______ $\times$ ______

   $=$ ______

   c) $48 \times 3000 = 48 \times 3 \times$ ______

   $=$ ______ $\times$ ______

   $=$ ______

P/B Chapter 2: Exercise 2, page 25

 ISBN 978-93-5103-033-1

Estimating products

Let's Learn

a) Estimate the value of 702×19.

Round 702 to the nearest hundred.
$702 \approx 700$
Round 19 to the nearest ten.
$19 \approx 20$

$702 \times 19 \approx 700 \times 20$
$= 14{,}000$

$7 \times 2 = 14$

b) Mrs. Chandra needs 543 caps for students to take part in a parade. Each cap costs ₹ 35. Estimate the total cost of the caps.

$543 \times$ ₹ $35 \approx 500 \times$ ₹ 40
$=$ ₹ $20{,}000$

$5 \times 4 = 20$

The total cost of the caps is about ₹ 20,000.

Let's Do

1. Estimate the value of each of the following.

a) $529 \times 34 \approx$ ______ $\times$ ______
$=$ ______

$529 \approx 500$
$34 \approx 30$

b) $75 \times 386 \approx$ ______ $\times$ ______
$=$ ______

$75 \approx$ ______
$386 \approx$ ______

c) $7804 \times 59 \approx$ ______ $\times$ ______
$=$ ______

$7804 \approx$ ______
$59 \approx$ ______

P/B Chapter 2: Exercise 3, page 26

 ISBN 978-93-5103-033-1

Practice 1

1. Multiply.

a)	238×10	b)	700×100	c)	37×1000
d)	10×400	e)	100×280	f)	1000×520

2. Multiply 56 by 7.
Then, find the value of each of the following.

a)	56×70	b)	56×700	c)	56×7000

3. Multiply 450 by 6.
Then, find the value of each of the following.

a)	450×60	b)	450×600	c)	450×6000

4. Estimate the value of each of the following.

a)	689×42	b)	553×49	c)	549×67
d)	64×734	e)	54×762	f)	8903×38

Lesson 2 Dividing by Tens, Hundreds or Thousands

Dividing by 10, 100 or 1000

Let's Learn

a)

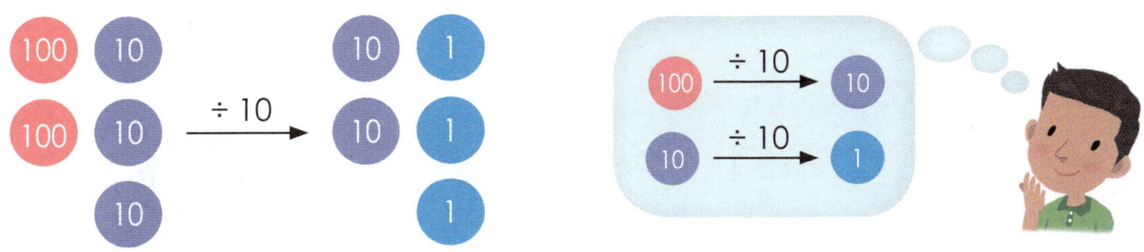

$230 \div 10 = 23$

b)

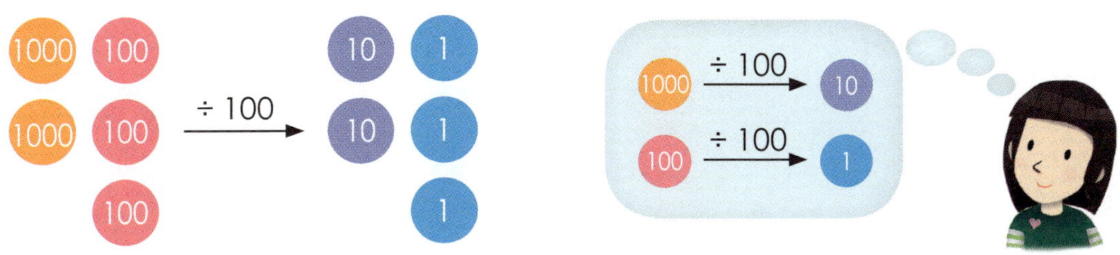

$2300 \div 100 = 23$

c) 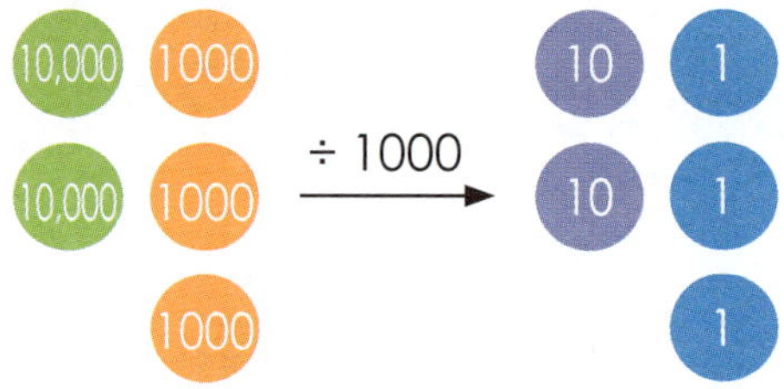

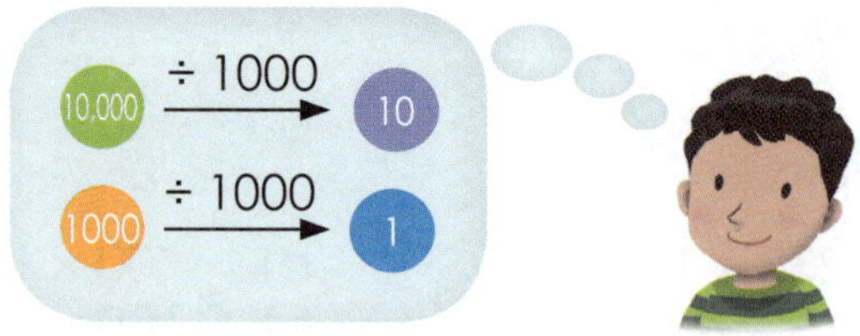

23,000 ÷ 1000 = 23

Let's Do

1. Divide.
   a) 520 ÷ 10 = ______
   b) 7400 ÷ 100 = ______
   c) 40,000 ÷ 1000 = ______

P/B Chapter 2: Exercise 4, page 27

Dividing by tens, hundreds or thousands

Let's Learn

a) Divide 15,000 by 30.

15,000 ÷ 30 = 15,000 ÷ 10 ÷ 3
= 1500 ÷ 3
= 500

b) Divide 15,000 by 300.

15,000 ÷ 300 = 15,000 ÷ 100 ÷ 3
= 150 ÷ 3
= 50

c) Divide 15,000 by 3000.

15,000 ÷ 3000 = 15,000 ÷ 1000 ÷ 3
= 15 ÷ 3
= 5

  ISBN 978-93-5103-033-1

Let's Do

1. Divide.

   a) $280 \div 40 = 280 \div 10 \div 4$

   $= \_\_\_\_\_\_ \div 4$

   $= \_\_\_\_\_\_$

$28\not{0} \div 4\not{0}$

   b) $64{,}000 \div 800 = 64{,}000 \div 100 \div \_\_\_\_\_\_$

   $= \_\_\_\_\_\_ \div \_\_\_\_\_\_$

   $= \_\_\_\_\_\_$

$64{,}0\not{0}\not{0} \div 8\not{0}\not{0}$

   c) $2{,}00{,}000 \div 5000 = 2{,}00{,}000 \div 1000 \div \_\_\_\_\_\_$

   $= \_\_\_\_\_\_ \div \_\_\_\_\_\_$

   $= \_\_\_\_\_\_$

PB Chapter 2: Exercise 5, page 28

Estimating quotients

Let's Learn

a) Estimate the value of 2992 ÷ 38.

Round 38 to the nearest ten.
$38 \approx 40$

Think of multiples of 40.
... 240, 280, 320, ...
... **240**0, **280**0, **320**0, ...

2992 is nearer to 2800 than to 3200.
$2992 \approx 2800$

$2992 \div 38 \approx 2800 \div 40$

$= \square$

b) Mr. Lal paid ₹ 959 for 33 copies of a brochure. Estimate the cost per copy.

₹ $959 \div 33 \approx$ ₹ $\square \div 30$

$=$ ₹ $\square$

$33 \approx 30$

959 → 1200
959 → 900

The cost per copy was about ₹ $\square$.

 ISBN 978-93-5103-033-1

Let's Do

1. Estimate the value of each of the following.

a) $6398 \div 81 \approx$ ______ $\div 80$

$=$ ______

b) $2205 \div 34 \approx$ ______ $\div$ ______

$=$ ______

c) $6380 \div 67 \approx$ ______ $\div$ ______

$=$ ______

P/B Chapter 2: Exercise 6, page 29

Practice 2

1. Divide.

a)	$470 \div 10$	b)	$4700 \div 100$	c)	$47,000 \div 1000$
d)	$720 \div 10$	e)	$7200 \div 100$	f)	$72,000 \div 1000$

2. Divide 72 by 8.
Then, find the value of each of the following.

a)	$7,20,000 \div 80$	b)	$7,20,000 \div 800$	c)	$7,20,000 \div 8000$

3. Divide 900 by 6.
Then, find the value of each of the following.

a)	$90,000 \div 60$	b)	$90,000 \div 600$	c)	$90,000 \div 6000$

4. Estimate the value of each of the following.

a)	$3287 \div 38$	b)	$6204 \div 82$	c)	$5460 \div 65$
d)	$43,920 \div 63$	e)	$18,500 \div 48$	f)	$70,900 \div 94$

 ISBN 978-93-5103-033-1

Lesson 3 Order of Operations

Adding and subtracting whole numbers

Let's Learn

a) Find the value of 12 + 8 – 10.

Work from left to right when there is only addition and subtraction.

12 + 8 – 10
= 20 – 10
= 10

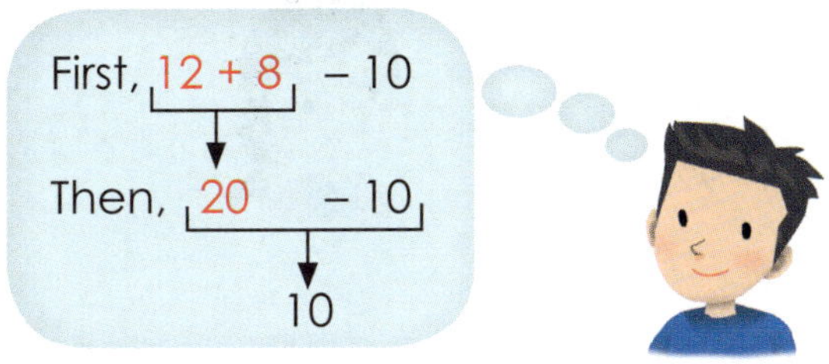

b) Find the value of 31 – 19 + 11.

31 – 19 + 11
= 12 + 11
= ☐

Let's Do

1. Find the value of each of the following.

a) 43 + 16 – 27
= ______ – ______
= ______

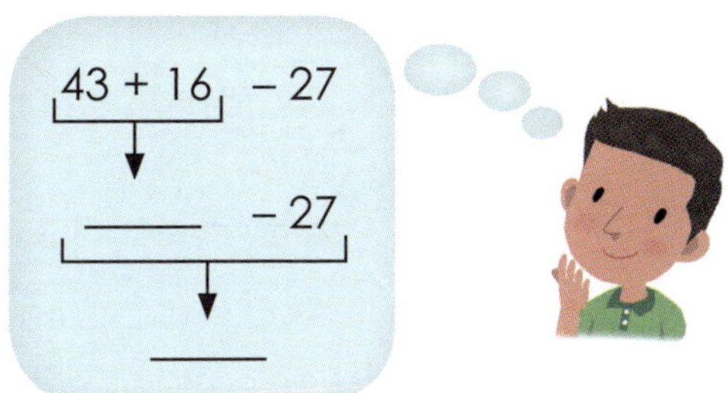

b) 38 – 23 + 29 = ______ + ______
= ______

Chapter 2: Exercise 7, page 30

 ISBN 978-93-5103-033-1

Multiplying and dividing whole numbers

Let's Learn

a) Find the value of 54 ÷ 6 × 3.

Work from left to right when there is only multiplication and division.

54 ÷ 6 × 3
= 9 × 3
= 27

First, 54 ÷ 6 × 3
Then, 9 × 3
27

b) Find the value of 4 × 24 ÷ 8.

4 × 24 ÷ 8
= 96 ÷ 8
= $\square$

First, 4 × 24 ÷ 8
Then, 96 ÷ 8
$\square$

Let's Do

1. Find the value of each of the following.

a) 60 ÷ 4 × 3 = ______ × 3
= ______

b) 9 × 81 ÷ 9 = ______ ÷ ______
= ______

60 ÷ 4 × 3
______ × 3
______

P/B Chapter 2: Exercise 8, page 31

 ISBN 978-93-5103-033-1

Carrying out mixed operations

Let's Learn

a) Find the value of $10 + 4 \times 3$.

Working from left to right, carry out multiplication and division before addition and subtraction.

$10 + 4 \times 3$
$= 10 + 12$
$= 22$

First, $10 + 4 \times 3$

Then, $10 + 12$

22

b) Find the value of $27 - 12 \div 3$.

$27 - 12 \div 3$
$= 27 - 4$
$= \square$

First, $27 - 12 \div 3$

Then, $27 - 4$

$\square$

c) Find the value of $56 - 8 \times 5 + 4$.

$56 - 8 \times 5 + 4$
$= 56 - 40 + 4$
$= \square + 4$
$= \square$

First, $56 - 8 \times 5 + 4$

Then, $56 - 40 + 4$

Lastly, $16 + 4$

$\square$

d) Find the value of $70 + 80 \div 5 \times 4$.

$70 + 80 \div 5 \times 4$
$= 70 + 16 \times 4$
$= 70 + \square$
$= \square$

First, $70 + 80 \div 5 \times 4$

Then, $70 + 16 \times 4$

Lastly, $70 + 64$

$\square$

 ISBN 978-93-5103-033-1

Let's Do

1. Find the value of each of the following.

   a) $9 + 3 \times 6$

   $= 9 +$ ________

   $=$ ________

   b) $96 \div 8 - 6 \times 2$

   $=$ ________ $- 6 \times 2$

   $=$ ________ $-$ ________

   $=$ ________

Chapter 2: Exercise 9, pages 32–33

Carrying out mixed operations with parentheses

Let's Learn

a) Find the value of $60 \div (12 - 7)$.

When there are **parentheses**, first carry out the operations in the parentheses. Then, carry out multiplication and division before addition and subtraction.

$60 \div (12 - 7)$
$= 60 \div 5$
$= 12$

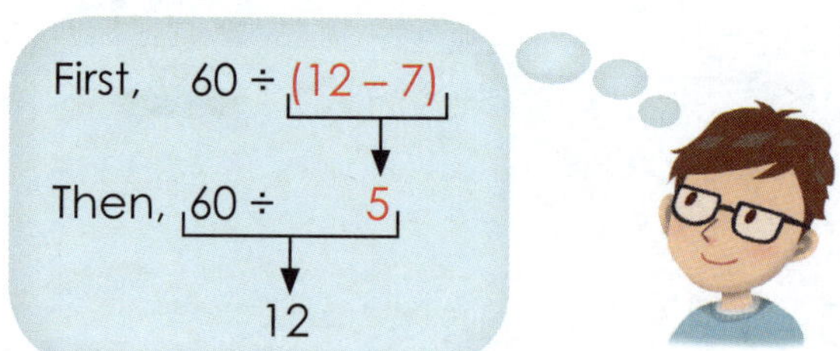

b) Find the value of $27 - 2 \times (3 + 5)$.

$27 - 2 \times (3 + 5)$
$= 27 - 2 \times 8$
$= 27 -$ ____
$=$ ____

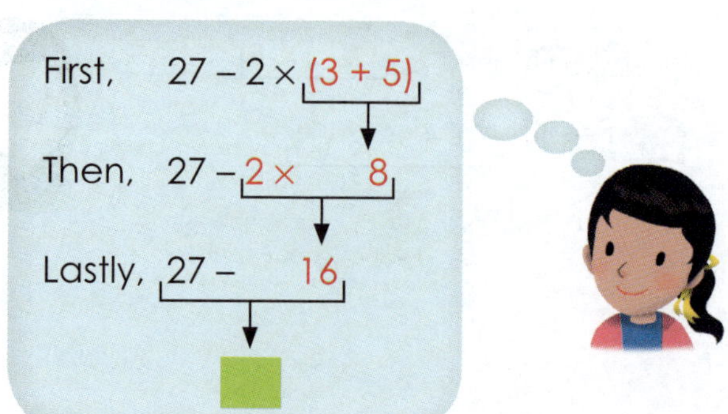

 ISBN 978-93-5103-033-1

c) Find the value of $(22 + 10) \div 8 \times 5$.

$(22 + 10) \div 8 \times 5$
$= 32 \div 8 \times 5$
$= \square \times 5$
$= \square$

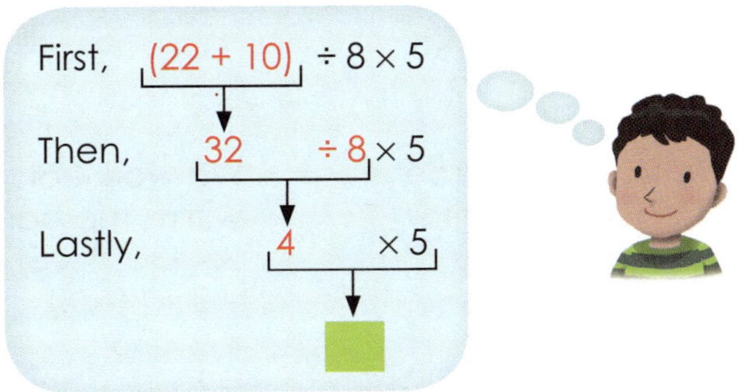

Let's Do

1. Find the value of each of the following.

a) $76 + (36 + 164) = 76 +$ ________
$=$ ________

b) $60 \div (4 + 8) = 60 \div$ ________
$=$ ________

c) $20 - 2 \times (18 \div 6) =$ ________ $-$ ________ $\times$ ________
$=$ ________ $-$ ________
$=$ ________

P/B Chapter 2: Exercise 10, pages 34–36

Think About It

What is the value of $2 \times (3 + 4 \times 5)$?

Ria

We follow the order of operations within the parentheses.
$2 \times (3 + 4 \times 5)$
$= 2 \times (3 + 20)$
$= 2 \times 23$
$= 46$

We work from left to right within the parentheses.
$2 \times (3 + 4 \times 5)$
$= 2 \times (7 \times 5)$
$= 2 \times 35$
$= 70$

Sam

Who is correct? Explain why.

Practice 3

1. Find the value of each of the following.

   a) $372 - (45 - 29)$
   b) $372 - 45 + 29$
   c) $372 - 45 - 29$
   d) $372 - (45 + 29)$

2. Find the value of each of the following.

   a) $128 \div 4 \div 2$
   b) $128 \div (4 \div 2)$
   c) $128 \div 4 \times 2$
   d) $128 \div (4 \times 2)$

3. Find the value of each of the following.

   a) $48 - 17 + 25$
   b) $6 \times 5 \times 10$
   c) $81 \div 9 \div 3$
   d) $50 \div 5 + 5$
   e) $64 - 3 \times 9$
   f) $72 - 36 \div 9$
   g) $27 + 15 \div 3 \times 2$
   h) $40 \div 2 - 2 \times 5$
   i) $10 + 24 \div 8 + 8$
   j) $(38 - 17) \div 3 \times 10$
   k) $35 \div (10 - 3) \times 10$
   l) $(13 + 7) \div (9 - 4)$

 ISBN 978-93-5103-033-1

Lesson 4 Multiplication

Multiplying 4-digit whole numbers by 2-digit whole numbers

Let's Learn

Multiply 4635 by 26.

1 Multiply 4635 by 6.

$$\begin{array}{r} {}^{3}4\,{}^{2}6\,{}^{3}3\,5 \\ \times\quad 2\,6 \\ \hline 2\,7\,8\,1\,0 \end{array}$$

2 Multiply 4635 by 20.

$$\begin{array}{r} {}^{1}_{3}4\,{}^{2}6\,{}^{1}_{3}3\,5 \\ \times\quad 2\,6 \\ \hline 2\,7\,8\,1\,0 \\ 9\,2\,7\,0\,0 \end{array}$$

3 Add.

$$\begin{array}{rl} 4\,6\,3\,5 & \\ \times\quad 2\,6 & \\ \hline 2\,7\,8\,1\,0 & \leftarrow 4635 \times 6 \\ 9\,2\,7\,0\,0 & \leftarrow 4635 \times 20 \\ \hline 1\,2\,0\,5\,1\,0 & \leftarrow 4635 \times 26 \\ \hline \end{array}$$

Let's Do

1. Multiply.

a)
$$\begin{array}{r} 3\,0\,5\,9 \\ \times\quad 5\,3 \\ \hline \\ \hline \\ \hline \end{array}$$

b)
$$\begin{array}{r} 7\,1\,0\,5 \\ \times\quad 6\,2 \\ \hline \\ \hline \\ \hline \end{array}$$

 ISBN 978-93-5103-033-1

Multiplying 3-digit or 4-digit whole numbers by 3-digit whole numbers

Let's Learn

a) Multiply 532 by 427.

$$
\begin{array}{r l}
{\scriptstyle 1} & \\
{\scriptstyle 2\ 1} & \\
5\ 3\ 2 & \\
\times \quad 4\ 2\ 7 & \\
\hline
3\ 7\ 2\ 4 & \leftarrow 532 \times 7 \\
1\ 0\ 6\ 4\ 0 & \leftarrow 532 \times 20 \\
2\ 1\ 2\ 8\ 0\ 0 & \leftarrow 532 \times 400 \\
\hline
2\ 2\ 7\ 1\ 6\ 4 & \leftarrow 532 \times 427 \\
\hline
\end{array}
$$

b) Multiply 3518 by 294.

$$
\begin{array}{r l}
{\scriptstyle 1\ \ 1} & \\
{\scriptstyle 4\ 1\ 7} & \\
{\scriptstyle 2\ \ 3} & \\
3\ 5\ 1\ 8 & \\
\times \quad 2\ 9\ 4 & \\
\hline
1\ 4\ 0\ 7\ 2 & \leftarrow 3518 \times 4 \\
3\ 1\ 6\ 6\ 2\ 0 & \leftarrow 3518 \times 90 \\
7\ 0\ 3\ 6\ 0\ 0 & \leftarrow 3518 \times 200 \\
\hline
1\ 0\ 3\ 4\ 2\ 9\ 2 & \leftarrow 3518 \times 294 \\
\hline
\end{array}
$$

Let's Do

1. Multiply.

a)
$$
\begin{array}{r}
5\ 6\ 8 \\
\times \quad 3\ 0\ 5 \\
\hline
\\
\hline
\\
\hline
\end{array}
$$

b)
$$
\begin{array}{r}
6\ 2\ 2\ 7 \\
\times \quad 4\ 8\ 3 \\
\hline
\\
\hline
\\
\hline
\end{array}
$$

PB Chapter 2: Exercise 11, page 37

 ISBN 978-93-5103-033-1

Solving word problems

Let's Learn

There are 3860 building blocks in a box. How many building blocks are there in 69 such boxes?

$3860 \times 69 = \square$

There are $\square$ building blocks in 69 such boxes.

$3860 \times 69 \approx 4000 \times 70$
$= 2,80,000$

My answer is close to 2,80,000.
It is reasonable.

Let's Do

1. A company sold 5482 ferry tickets at ₹ 124 for each ticket. How much money did the company collect altogether?

   _______ × ₹ _______ = ₹ _______

   The company collected ₹ _______ altogether.

Chapter 2: Exercise 12, page 38

Practice 4

1. Multiply.

   a) 4070×84 b) 6980×49 c) 941×736
   d) 539×512 e) 7404×852 f) 3092×633

Solve the word problems. Show your work clearly.

2. A worker uses 1077 bricks to build a wall. Each brick costs ₹ 13. How much does it cost to build the wall with the bricks?

3. A Republic Day float is decorated with 526 balloons. How many balloons are needed to decorate 150 such floats?

4. There are 2314 almonds in a bag. How many almonds are there in 128 such bags?

 ISBN 978-93-5103-033-1

Lesson 5 Division

Dividing by tens

Let's Learn

a) Divide 140 by 20.

Method 1

$140 \div 20 = 7$

$14\not{0} \div 2\not{0}$

Method 2

$$\begin{array}{r}7\\20\overline{)\,1\;4\;0}\\1\;4\;0\\\hline 0\end{array}$$

$7 \times 20 = 140$

b) Divide 150 by 20.

$$\begin{array}{r}7\\20\overline{)\,1\;5\;0}\\1\;4\;0\\\hline 1\;0\end{array}$$

$150 \div 20$
I cannot divide 15 by 2 exactly.
So, I use Method 2.

Let's Do

1. Divide.

a) $30\overline{)\,7\;0}$

b) $20\overline{)\,8\;9}$

c) $70\overline{)\,6\;2\;5}$

 ISBN 978-93-5103-033-1

Estimating the quotient when dividing by a 2-digit whole number

Let's Learn

a) Divide 74 by 21.

$21 \approx 20$

$$\begin{array}{r} 3 \\ 20\overline{)\,7\;4} \\ 6\;0 \\ \hline \end{array}$$

The estimated quotient is 3.

$$\begin{array}{rl} 3 & \\ 21\overline{)\,7\;4} & \\ 6\;3 & \leftarrow 21 \times 3 \text{ ones} = 63 \text{ ones} \\ \hline 1\;1 & \leftarrow \text{remainder } 11 \text{ ones} \end{array}$$

b) Divide 256 by 47.

$47 \approx 50$

$$\begin{array}{r} 5 \\ 50\overline{)\,2\;5\;6} \\ 2\;5\;0 \\ \hline \end{array}$$

The estimated quotient is 5.

$$\begin{array}{rl} \square & \\ 47\overline{)\,2\;5\;6} & \\ 2\;3\;5 & \leftarrow 47 \times 5 \text{ ones} = 235 \text{ ones} \\ \hline \square\;\square & \leftarrow \text{remainder } \square \text{ ones} \end{array}$$

Let's Do

1. Divide.

a) $17\overline{)\,6\;3}$

b) $67\overline{)\,1\;4\;9}$

c) $84\overline{)\,5\;0\;9}$

PB Chapter 2: Exercise 13, page 39

 ISBN 978-93-5103-033-1

Estimating and adjusting the quotient when dividing a 2-digit whole number by another 2-digit whole number

Let's Learn

a) Divide 89 by 24.

$24 \approx 20$

$$\begin{array}{r} 4 \\ 20\overline{)\,8\ 9} \\ 8\ 0 \\ \hline \end{array}$$

The estimated quotient is 4.

$$\begin{array}{rl} 4 & \\ 24\overline{)\,8\ 9} & \\ 9\ 6 & \leftarrow 24 \times 4 \text{ ones} = 96 \text{ ones} \\ \hline \end{array}$$

The estimated quotient is too big.
Try 3.

$$\begin{array}{rl} 3 & \\ 24\overline{)\,8\ 9} & \\ 7\ 2 & \leftarrow 24 \times 3 \text{ ones} = 72 \text{ ones} \\ \hline 1\ 7 & \leftarrow \text{remainder 17 ones} \end{array}$$

b) Divide 78 by 26.

$26 \approx 30$

$$\begin{array}{r} 2 \\ 30\overline{)\,7\ 8} \\ 6\ 0 \\ \hline \end{array}$$

The estimated quotient is 2.

$$\begin{array}{rl} 2 & \\ 26\overline{)\,7\ 8} & \\ 5\ 2 & \leftarrow 26 \times 2 \text{ ones} = 52 \text{ ones} \\ \hline 2\ 6 & \leftarrow \text{remainder 26 ones} \end{array}$$

The estimated quotient is too small.
Try 3.

$$\begin{array}{rl} \square & \\ 26\overline{)\,7\ \ 8} & \\ 7\ \ 8 & \leftarrow 26 \times 3 \text{ ones} = 78 \text{ ones} \\ \hline \square & \leftarrow \text{remainder } \square \text{ ones} \end{array}$$

 ISBN 978-93-5103-033-1

Let's Do

1. Divide.

a) $17\overline{)68}$

b) $33\overline{)94}$

c) $21\overline{)83}$

Estimating and adjusting the quotient when dividing a 3-digit whole number by a 2-digit whole number

Let's Learn

a) Divide 285 by 33.

33 ≈ 30

```
      9
30 ) 2 8 5
     2 7 0
```

The estimated quotient is 9.

```
      9
33 ) 2 8 5
     2 9 7 ← 33 × 9 ones = 297 ones
```

The estimated quotient is too big.
Try 8.

```
      8
33 ) 2 8 5
     2 6 4 ← 33 × 8 ones = 264 ones
       2 1 ← remainder 21 ones
```

b) Divide 473 by 78.

78 ≈ 80

```
      5
80 ) 4 7 3
     4 0 0
```

The estimated quotient is 5.

```
      5
78 ) 4 7 3
     3 9 0 ← 78 × 5 ones = 390 ones
       8 3 ← remainder 83 ones
```

The estimated quotient is too small.
Try 6.

```
      ▢
78 ) 4 7 3
     4 6 8 ← 78 × 6 ones = 468 ones
         ▢ ← remainder ▢ ones
```

 ISBN 978-93-5103-033-1

Let's Do

1. Divide.

   a) $23\overline{)2\ 0\ 7}$

$23 \approx 20$

$$\begin{array}{r} 1\ 0 \\ 20\overline{)2\ 0\ 7} \\ 2\ 0\ 0 \\ \hline \end{array}$$

The estimated quotient is 10.

   b) $79\overline{)4\ 7\ 4}$

   c) $64\overline{)5\ 7\ 2}$

PB Chapter 2: Exercise 14, page 40

Dividing a 3-digit whole number by a 2-digit whole number to get a 2-digit quotient

Let's Learn

a) Divide 870 by 34.

Step 1 Divide the tens by 34.

$34 \approx 30$

$$\begin{array}{r} 2 \\ 30\overline{)8\ 7\ 0} \\ 6\ 0 \\ \hline \end{array}$$

The estimated quotient is 2 tens.

$$\begin{array}{r} 2 \\ 34\overline{)8\ 7\ 0} \\ 6\ 8 \\ \hline 1\ 9 \end{array}$$

$\leftarrow 34 \times 2$ tens $= 68$ tens

 ISBN 978-93-5103-033-1

Step 2 Divide the ones by 34.

```
      2
34 ) 8 7 0
     6 8
     1 9 0
```

34 ≈ 30

```
       6
30 ) 1 9 0
     1 8 0
```

The estimated quotient is 6.

```
      2 6
34 ) 8 7 0
     6 8
     1 9 0
     2 0 4  ← 34 × 6 ones
               = 204 ones
```

```
      2 ___
34 ) 8 7 0
     6 8
     1 9 0
     1 7 0  ← 34 × 5 ones = 170 ones
     ___ ___  ← remainder ___ ones
```

The estimated quotient is too big.
Try 5.

b) Divide 570 by 16.

Step 1 Divide the tens by 16.

16 ≈ 20

```
      2
20 ) 5 7 0
     4 0
```

The estimated quotient is 2 tens.

```
      2
16 ) 5 7 0
     3 2    ← 16 × 2 tens
     2 5       = 32 tens
```

```
      3
16 ) 5 7 0
     4 8    ← 16 × 3 tens = 48 tens
       9
```

The estimated quotient is too small.
Try 3 tens.

 ISBN 978-93-5103-033-1

Step 2 Divide the ones by 16.

```
      3
16 ) 5 7 0
     4 8
     ----
       9 0
```

16 ≈ 20

```
      4
20 ) 9 0
     8 0
     ---
```

The estimated quotient is 4.

```
      3 4
16 ) 5 7 0
     4 8
     -----
       9 0
       6 4  ← 16 × 4 ones = 64 ones
       ---
       2 6  ← remainder 26 ones
```

```
      3 ▢
16 ) 5 7 0
     4 8
     -----
       9 0
       8 0  ← 16 × 5 ones = 80 ones
       ---
       ▢ ▢  ← remainder ▢ ones
```

The estimated quotient is too small.
Try 5.

Let's Do

1. Divide.

a) $28\overline{)862}$

b) $47\overline{)703}$

c) $15\overline{)612}$

P/B Chapter 2: Exercise 15, pages 41–42

 ISBN 978-93-5103-033-1

Dividing a 4-digit whole number by a 2-digit whole number to get a 2-digit or 3-digit quotient

Let's Learn

a) Divide 6552 by 28.

Step 1 Divide the hundreds by 28.

$28 \approx 30$

$$\begin{array}{r|l} & 2 \\ \hline 30 & 6\;5\;5\;2 \\ & 6\;0 \\ \hline \end{array}$$

The estimated quotient is 2 hundreds.

$$\begin{array}{r|l} & 2 \\ \hline 28 & 6\;5\;5\;2 \\ & 5\;6 \\ \hline & 9 \end{array}$$

$\leftarrow 28 \times 2$ hundreds = 56 hundreds

Step 2 Divide the tens by 28.

$$\begin{array}{r|l} & 2 \\ \hline 28 & 6\;5\;5\;2 \\ & 5\;6 \\ \hline & 9\;5 \end{array}$$

$28 \approx 30$

$$\begin{array}{r|l} & 3 \\ \hline 30 & 9\;5 \\ & 9\;0 \\ \hline \end{array}$$

The estimated quotient is 3 tens.

$$\begin{array}{r|l} & 2\;3 \\ \hline 28 & 6\;5\;5\;2 \\ & 5\;6 \\ \hline & 9\;5 \\ & 8\;4 \\ \hline & 1\;1 \end{array}$$

$\leftarrow 28 \times 3$ tens = 84 tens

 ISBN 978-93-5103-033-1

Step 3 Divide the ones by 28.

```
       2 3
28 ) 6 5 5 2
     5 6
     ----
       9 5
       8 4
       -----
       1 1 2
```

28 ≈ 30

```
        3
30 ) 1 1 2
       9 0
     -----
```

The estimated quotient is 3.

```
       2 3 3
28 ) 6 5 5 2
     5 6
     ----
       9 5
       8 4
       -----
       1 1 2
         8 4 ← 28 × 3 ones = 84 ones
       -----
         2 8
```

→

```
       2 3 4
28 ) 6 5 5 2
     5 6
     ----
       9 5
       8 4
       -----
       1 1 2
       1 1 2 ← 28 × 4 ones = 112 ones
       -----
           0 ← remainder 0 ones
```

The estimated quotient is too small.
Try 4.

b) Divide 4328 by 52.

Step 1 Divide the tens by 52.

52 ≈ 50

```
         8
50 ) 4 3 2 8
     4 0 0
     -------
       3 2
```

The estimated quotient is 8 tens.

```
         8
52 ) 4 3 2 8
     4 1 6    ← 52 × 8 tens = 416 tens
     -----
       1 6
```


 ISBN 978-93-5103-033-1

Step 2 Divide the ones by 52.

```
        8
52 ) 4 3 2 8
     4 1 6
     -------
       1 6 8
```

52 ≈ 50

```
          3
50 ) 1 6 8
     1 5 0
     -----
       1 8
```

The estimated quotient is 3.

```
        8 3
52 ) 4 3 2 8
     4 1 6
     -------
       1 6 8
       1 5 6 ← 52 × 3 ones = 156 ones
       -----
         1 2 ← remainder 12 ones
```

Let's Do

1. Divide.

a) 45) 3 1 8 5

b) 45) 1 4 9 5

c) 64) 6 8 2 0

 ISBN 978-93-5103-033-1

Dividing 5-digit or 6-digit whole numbers by 2-digit whole numbers

Let's Learn

a) Divide 76,548 by 34.

```
         2 2 5 1
     ___________
  34 ) 7 6 5 4 8
       6 8
     -------
         8 5
         6 8
       -------
       1 7 4
       1 7 0
       -------
           4 8
           3 4 ← 34 × 1 = 34 ones
          -----
           1 4 ← remainder 14 ones
```

b) Divide 2,81,252 by 45.

```
          6 2 5 0
     _____________
  45 ) 2 8 1 2 5 2
       2 7 0
     ---------
         1 1 2
           9 0
         -------
           2 2 5
           2 2 5
         ---------
                 2
                 0 ← 45 × 0 = 0 ones
             -------
                 2 ← remainder
                     2 ones
```

Let's Do

1. Divide.

a)

```
     __________
  33 ) 4 3 8 6 9
```

b)

```
     ____________
  58 ) 6 1 2 6 7 8
```

Chapter 2: Exercise 16, pages 43–44

 ISBN 978-93-5103-033-1

Think About It

```
      1 4
40 ) 4 1 6 0
     4 0
     -------
       1 6 0
       1 6 0
       -----
           0
```

Ria

Is Ria's answer correct? Explain why.

Solving word problems

Let's Learn

486 stickers are shared equally among 23 children. How many stickers does each child receive? How many stickers are left?

486 ÷ 23 = 21 R3

Each child receives 21 stickers.
3 stickers are left.

Each child receives 21 stickers.
21 × 23 = 483
483 stickers are given.
486 – 483 = 3
3 stickers are left.

My answer is correct.

Let's Do

1. Ravi collected ₹ 3672 from the sale of 54 circus tickets. The price of each ticket was the same. What was the price of each ticket?

   ₹ ______ ÷ ______ = ₹ ______

   The price of each ticket was ₹ ______.

2. A company has to pack 10,962 bottles of water into boxes for shipment. Each box can only hold 85 bottles. How many boxes are needed to hold all the bottles of water?

   ______ ÷ ______ = ______

   ______ boxes are needed.

PB Chapter 2: Exercise 17, page 45

ISBN 978-93-5103-033-1

Practice 5

1. Divide.

   a) 94 ÷ 43   b) 57 ÷ 29   c) 69 ÷ 31
   d) 668 ÷ 72   e) 279 ÷ 56   f) 183 ÷ 44

2. Divide.

   a) 890 ÷ 24   b) 924 ÷ 33   c) 569 ÷ 18
   d) 8485 ÷ 16   e) 4031 ÷ 67   f) 5052 ÷ 53
   g) 72,258 ÷ 38   h) 88,965 ÷ 23   i) 99,910 ÷ 42
   j) 7,68,412 ÷ 78   k) 1,34,050 ÷ 23   l) 9,67,078 ÷ 54

Solve the word problems. Show your work clearly.

3. Mrs. Mehta divided ₹ 6048 equally into 16 envelopes. How much money did each envelope hold?

4. Mr. Gupta has ₹ 2145. What is the maximum number of fountain pens he can buy if each fountain pen costs ₹ 64?

5. 10,650 special edition balloons were distributed equally among 38 schools. How many balloons did each school receive? How many balloons were left?

Lesson 6 Problem Solving

Word problems

Let's Learn

Mrs. Lee had 8400 paper flowers. She sold them in packets of 24 paper flowers each. How much money did she receive if she sold each packet at ₹ 13?

1 Understand the problem.

How many paper flowers were there altogether?
How many paper flowers were there in each packet?
What do I have to find?

2 Plan what to do.

First, I find the number of packets of paper flowers.
Then, I multiply the number of packets by the selling price of each packet.

 ISBN 978-93-5103-033-1

3 Work out the **Answer.**

Number of packets of paper flowers = 8400 ÷ 24
= 350

Amount of money she received = 350 × ₹ 13
= ₹ 4550

She received ₹ 4550 altogether.

4 **Check**
Did you answer the question?
Is your answer reasonable?

8400 ÷ 24 ≈ 8000 ÷ 20
= 400
400 × ₹ 13 ≈ 400 × ₹ 10
= ₹ 4000

My answer is close to ₹ 4000.
It is reasonable.

- ☑ **1. Understand**
- ☑ **2. Plan**
- ☑ **3. Answer**
- ☑ **4. Check**

Let's Do

1. Mita sold 11,904 metres of fabric. The fabric was sold in bales of 96 metres each. How much money did she receive if she sold each bale of fabric at ₹ 56?

How many bales of fabric did she sell?

- ☐ **1. Understand**
- ☐ **2. Plan**
- ☐ **3. Answer**
- ☐ **4. Check**

 ISBN 978-93-5103-033-1

Let's Learn

Miss Lata sold 2034 Diwali lamps at ₹ 16 per lamp. She also sold 840 small candles at ₹ 3 each. How much money did she collect altogether?

Amount of money collected from selling Diwali lamps = 2034 × ₹ 16
= ₹ 32,544

Amount of money collected from selling small candles = 840 × ₹ 3
= ₹ 2520

Total amount of money collected = ₹ 32,544 + ₹ 2520
= ₹ ____

She collected ₹ ____ altogether.

2034 × ₹ 16 ≈ 2000 × ₹ 20
= ₹ 40,000
840 × ₹ 3 ≈ 800 × ₹ 3
= ₹ 2400
₹ 40,000 + ₹ 2400 = ₹ 42,400

My answer is close to ₹ 42,400.
It is reasonable.

☑ 1. Understand
☑ 2. Plan
☑ 3. Answer
☑ 4. Check

Let's Do

1. Arun buys a cell phone and pays for it in instalments. Each instalment is ₹ 830. Arun still has to pay ₹ 310 after paying 15 instalments. How much does he have to pay for each instalment if he pays for the cell phone in 44 instalments?

How much does the cell phone cost?

☐ 1. Understand
☐ 2. Plan
☐ 3. Answer
☐ 4. Check

P/B Chapter 2: Exercise 18, pages 46–47

Practice 6

Solve the word problems. Show your work clearly.

1. A company manufactured 1,55,640 erasers. The erasers were packed in packs of 24 each. If the erasers were sold at ₹ 70 per pack, how much money did the company make after the sale of all the erasers?

  ISBN 978-93-5103-033-1

2. A tailor bought 368 bags of buttons. Each bag contains 144 buttons. How many buttons did he buy altogether?

3. 7840 students were divided into 14 schools. In each school, there were 240 girls. How many boys were there altogether?

4. There are 1104 red chairs and yellow chairs in a school auditorium. The yellow chairs are arranged in 42 rows with 16 chairs in each row. The red chairs are arranged in rows of 18. How many rows of red chairs are there?

Mind stretcher

Let's Learn

560 ÷ 14 – 12 × 10 + 16 = 7280

Place two pairs of parentheses in the number sentence so that it is correct.

1 **Understand** the problem.

How many pairs of parentheses are missing? Where should the parentheses be placed?

2 **Plan** what to do.

I can **guess and check** to decide where to place the two pairs of parentheses.

3 Work out the **Answer**.

Number sentence	Equal to 7280?
(560 ÷ 14) – 12 × (10 + 16) = 40 – 12 × 26 = 40 – 312	✗
560 ÷ (14 – 12) × (10 + 16) = 560 ÷ 2 × 26 = 280 × 26 = 7280	✓

4 **Check**
Did you answer the question?
Is your answer correct?

I carried out the operations in the parentheses first and then worked from left to right. My answer is correct.

☑ 1. Understand
☑ 2. Plan
☑ 3. Answer
☑ 4. Check

ISBN 978-93-5103-033-1

3 Fractions

Lesson 1 Fractions and Division

Associating fractions with division

Let's Learn

a) 3 waffles are shared equally among 4 children.
Each child receives 3 quarters of a waffle.

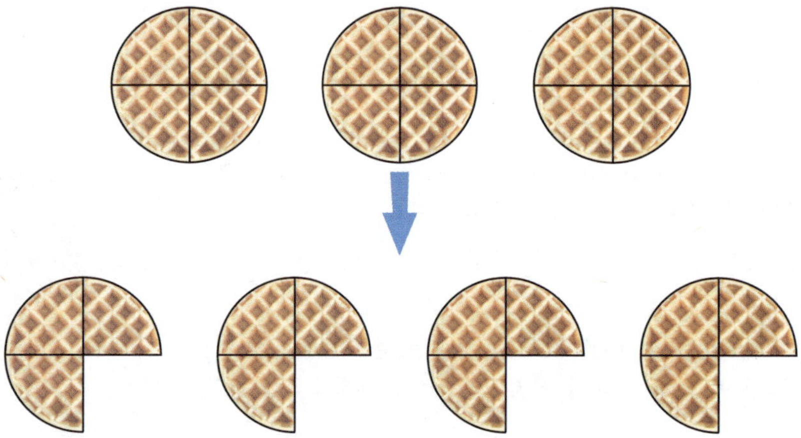

$3 \div 4 = \frac{3}{4}$

b) 5 waffles are shared equally among 4 children.
Each child receives 5 quarters of a waffle.

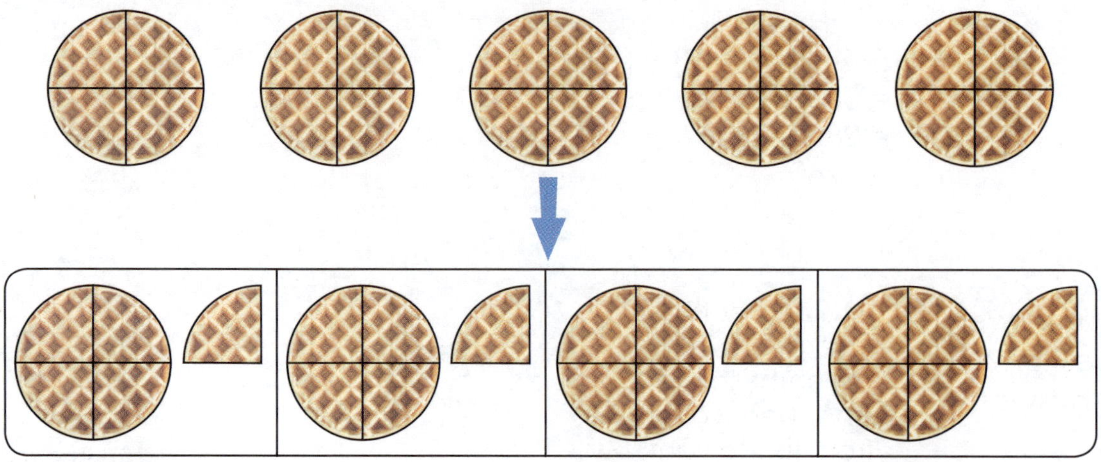

$5 \div 4 = \frac{\square}{\square}$

 ISBN 978-93-5103-033-1

Here is another way to show that $5 \div 4 = \frac{5}{4}$.

$$5 \div 4 = 1\frac{1}{4}$$
$$= 1 + \frac{1}{4}$$
$$= \frac{4}{4} + \frac{1}{4}$$
$$= \frac{5}{4}$$

$$\begin{array}{r} 1 \\ 4 \overline{)\,5} \\ \underline{4} \\ 1 \end{array} \leftarrow \text{remainder}$$

$$1 \div 4 = \frac{1}{4}$$

Expressing improper fractions as whole numbers or mixed numbers

Let's Learn

Express $\frac{11}{4}$ as a mixed number.

Method 1

$$\frac{11}{4} = \frac{8}{4} + \frac{3}{4}$$
$$= 2 + \frac{3}{4}$$
$$= 2\frac{3}{4}$$

Method 2

$$\frac{11}{4} = 11 \div 4$$
$$= 2\frac{3}{4}$$

$$\begin{array}{r} 2 \\ 4 \overline{)\,1\;1} \\ \underline{8} \\ 3 \end{array}$$

Let's Do

1. Express each improper fraction as a whole number or a mixed number in its simplest form.

a) $\frac{15}{5}$ = ______

$$\begin{array}{r} \square \\ 5 \overline{)\,1\;\;5} \\ \underline{1\;\;5} \\ \square \end{array}$$

b) **Method 1**

$$\frac{13}{5} = \frac{\square}{5} + \frac{\square}{5}$$
$$= \text{\_\_\_\_\_\_} + \frac{\square}{5}$$
$$= \text{\_\_\_\_\_\_}$$

Method 2

$\frac{13}{5}$ = ______

$$\begin{array}{r} \square \\ 5 \overline{)\,1\;\;3} \\ \underline{\square\square} \\ \square \end{array}$$

 ISBN 978-93-5103-033-1

Dividing whole numbers to get mixed numbers

Let's Learn

Express the value of 22 ÷ 8 as a mixed number.

Method 1

$22 \div 8 = 2\frac{6}{8}$

$= 2\frac{\square}{4}$

$$\begin{array}{r} 2 \\ 8\overline{)\,2\ 2} \\ 1\ 6 \\ \hline 6 \end{array}$$

Express the answer in its simplest form.

Method 2

$22 \div 8 = \frac{22}{8}$

$= \frac{\square}{4}$

$= \square$

2 is a common factor of 22 and 8. Divide 22 and 8 by 2.

Let's Do

1. Divide. Express each answer as a mixed number in its simplest form.

a) **Method 1**

$7 \div 3 =$ ______

$$\begin{array}{r} 2 \\ 3\overline{)\,7} \\ 6 \\ \hline 1 \end{array}$$

Method 2

$7 \div 3 = \frac{7}{3}$

= ______

b) **Method 1**

$14 \div 8 =$ ______

= ______

$$\begin{array}{r} \square \\ 8\overline{)\,1\ \ 4} \\ \square \\ \hline \square \end{array}$$

Method 2

$14 \div 8 = \frac{14}{8}$

$= \frac{\square}{4}$

= ______

P/B Chapter 3: Exercise 1, pages 48–49

 ISBN 978-93-5103-033-1

Expressing improper fractions as decimals

Let's Learn

Express $\frac{11}{6}$ as a decimal rounded to 1 decimal place.

$\frac{11}{6} = 11 \div 6$

≈ 1.8

$$\begin{array}{r} 1.83 \\ 6\overline{)11.00} \\ \underline{6} \\ 50 \\ \underline{48} \\ 20 \\ \underline{18} \\ 2 \end{array}$$

Divide to 2 decimal places. Then, round the answer to 1 decimal place.

$1.83 \approx 1.8$

Note the change in symbol from = to ≈.

Let's Do

1. Express each improper fraction as a decimal.
   Round the answer to 1 decimal place.

   a) $\frac{16}{3} \approx$ ______ $3\overline{)1\ 6}$

   b) $\frac{41}{8} \approx$ ______ $8\overline{)4\ 1}$

Chapter 3: Exercise 2, page 50

Solving word problems

Let's Learn

A bucket contains 8 litres of water. If the water is poured equally into 3 jugs, how much water is there in each jug? Express the answer as a mixed number.

$8 \div 3 =$ ☐

There are ☐ litres of water in each jug.

 ISBN 978-93-5103-033-1

Let's Do

1. A tin of tea with a weight of 4 kilograms was divided into 3 bags of equal weight. What was the weight of each bag of tea? Express the answer as a decimal rounded to 1 decimal place.

   $4 \div 3 \approx$ ______

   The weight of each bag of tea was ______ kilograms.

P/B Chapter 3: Exercise 3, page 51

Practice 1

1. Express each improper fraction as a whole number or a mixed number in its simplest form.

   a) $\frac{21}{3}$ b) $\frac{24}{9}$ c) $\frac{50}{6}$ d) $\frac{72}{9}$

2. Divide. Express each answer as a mixed number in its simplest form.

   a) $30 \div 8$ b) $21 \div 4$ c) $35 \div 10$ d) $78 \div 7$

3. Express each improper fraction as a decimal. Round the answer to 1 decimal place.

   a) $\frac{5}{3}$ b) $\frac{7}{6}$ c) $\frac{25}{4}$ d) $\frac{50}{9}$

Solve the word problems. Show your work clearly.

4. Varun cut a ribbon into 8 equal pieces. If the ribbon was 26 metres long, what was the length of each piece?

5. Mrs. Amrit bought 3 metres of fabric. She used the fabric to make 9 pillow covers of the same size. How many metres of fabric did she use for each pillow cover?

6. A baker made 10 cakes. She divided the cakes into 4 equal shares. How many cakes were there in each share?

7. Nancy poured 2 litres of milk equally into 5 jugs. How much milk was there in each jug?

8. A red ribbon 11 metres long is 5 times as long as a blue ribbon. How long is the blue ribbon?

 ISBN 978-93-5103-033-1

Lesson 2 Addition and Subtraction of Unlike Fractions

Adding unlike fractions

Let's Learn

a) Hannah painted $\frac{1}{3}$ of a paper plate red.
She painted $\frac{1}{2}$ of the same plate green.
What fraction of the plate was painted red and green?

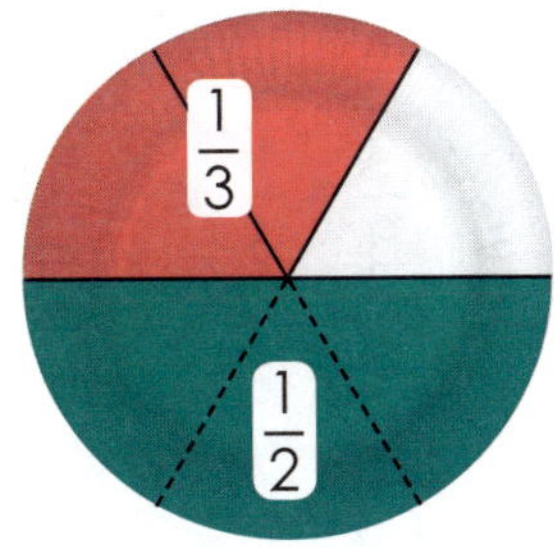

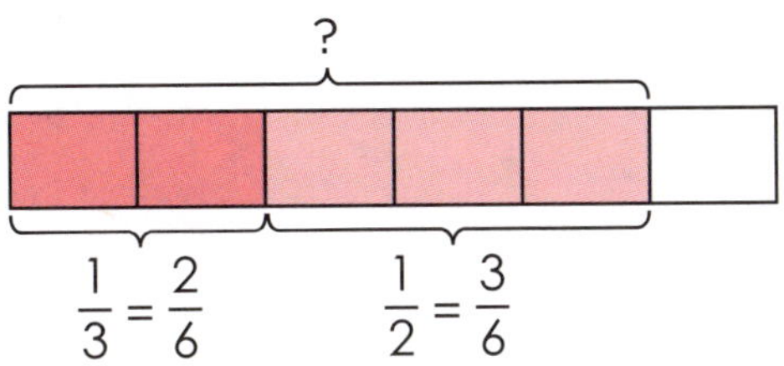

The plate is divided into 6 equal parts.
2 parts are red and 3 parts are green.

$$\frac{1}{3} + \frac{1}{2} = \frac{2}{6} + \frac{3}{6}$$
$$= \frac{5}{6}$$

Change $\frac{1}{3}$ and $\frac{1}{2}$ to fractions with the same denominator.
$\frac{1}{3}, \frac{2}{\mathbf{6}}, \ldots$
$\frac{1}{2}, \frac{2}{4}, \frac{3}{\mathbf{6}}, \ldots$

$\frac{5}{6}$ of the plate was painted red and green.

$\frac{1}{3}$ and $\frac{1}{2}$ do not have the same denominator.
They are called **unlike fractions**.

$\frac{2}{6}$ and $\frac{3}{6}$ have the same denominator.
They are called **like fractions**.

To add unlike fractions, change them to like fractions.

 ISBN 978-93-5103-033-1

b) Add $\frac{3}{8}$ and $\frac{1}{6}$.

Picture It

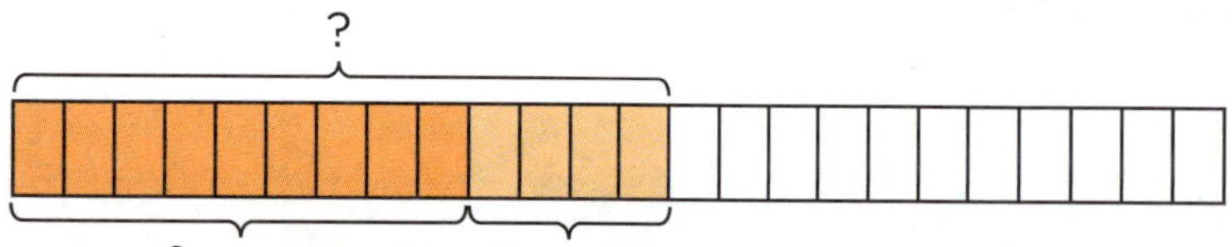

$\frac{3}{8} = \square$ $\frac{1}{6} = \square$

$\frac{3}{8} + \frac{1}{6} = \frac{\square}{24} + \frac{\square}{24}$

$= \frac{\square}{24}$

$\frac{3}{8}, \frac{6}{16}, \frac{9}{\mathbf{24}}, \ldots$

$\frac{1}{6}, \frac{2}{12}, \frac{3}{18}, \frac{4}{\mathbf{24}}, \ldots$

24 is the least common multiple of 8 and 6.

Let's Do

1. Add. Express each answer in its simplest form.

a) $\frac{2}{3} + \frac{2}{5} = \frac{\square}{15} + \frac{\square}{15}$

$= \frac{\square}{15}$

= ________

$\frac{2}{3}, \frac{\square}{6}, \frac{\square}{9}, \frac{\square}{12}, \frac{\square}{15}, \ldots$

$\frac{2}{5}, \frac{\square}{10}, \frac{\square}{15}, \ldots$

15 is the least common multiple of 3 and 5.

b) $\frac{7}{10} + \frac{5}{6} = \frac{\square}{30} + \frac{\square}{30}$

$= \frac{\square}{30}$

= ________

= ________

$\frac{7}{10}, \frac{\square}{20}, \frac{\square}{30}, \ldots$

$\frac{5}{6}, \frac{\square}{12}, \frac{\square}{18}, \frac{\square}{24}, \frac{\square}{30}, \ldots$

30 is the lowest common multiple of 10 and 6.

P/B Chapter 3: Exercise 4, pages 52–53

 ISBN 978-93-5103-033-1

Subtracting unlike fractions

Let's Learn

a) Amy had $\frac{3}{4}$ of a pizza. She gave $\frac{1}{3}$ of the pizza away.
What fraction of the pizza did she have left?

Maths Lab

Picture It

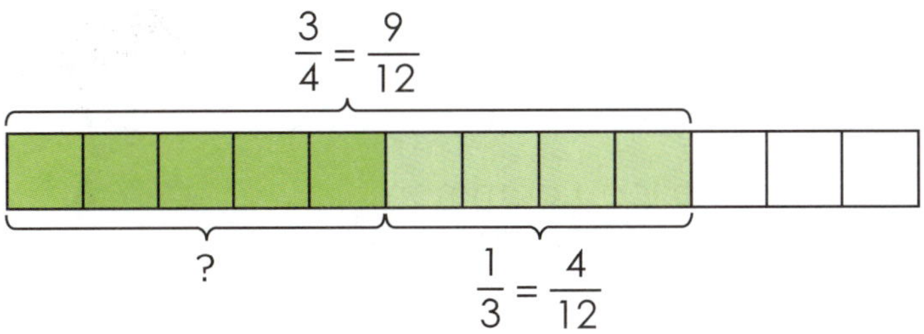

The pizza is divided into 12 equal slices. Amy had 9 slices of pizza and she gave away 4 slices.

$$\frac{3}{4} - \frac{1}{3} = \frac{9}{12} - \frac{4}{12}$$
$$= \frac{5}{12}$$

She had $\frac{5}{12}$ of the pizza left.

Change $\frac{3}{4}$ and $\frac{1}{3}$ to fractions with the same denominator.

$\frac{3}{4}, \frac{6}{8}, \frac{9}{\mathbf{12}}, \ldots$

$\frac{1}{3}, \frac{2}{6}, \frac{3}{9}, \frac{4}{\mathbf{12}}$

12 is the least common multiple of 4 and 3.

b) Subtract $\frac{5}{6}$ from $1\frac{7}{10}$.

$$1\frac{7}{10} - \frac{5}{6} = 1\frac{21}{30} - \frac{25}{30}$$
$$= \frac{51}{30} - \frac{25}{30}$$
$$= \frac{26}{30}$$
$$= \frac{\square}{15}$$

$\frac{7}{10}, \frac{14}{20}, \frac{21}{\mathbf{30}}, \ldots$

$\frac{5}{6}, \frac{10}{12}, \frac{15}{18}, \frac{20}{24}, \frac{25}{\mathbf{30}}$

30 is the least common multiple of 10 and 6.

Express the answer in its simplest form.

ISBN 978-93-5103-033-1

Let's Do

1. Subtract. Express each answer in its simplest form.

a) $\frac{7}{8} - \frac{1}{6} = \frac{\square}{24} - \frac{\square}{24}$

$= \underline{\qquad}$

$\frac{7}{8}, \frac{\square}{16}, \frac{\square}{24}, \ldots$

$\frac{1}{6}, \frac{\square}{12}, \frac{\square}{18}, \frac{\square}{24}, \ldots$

24 is the least common multiple of 8 and 6.

b) $1\frac{1}{4} - \frac{5}{6} = 1\frac{\square}{12} - \frac{\square}{12}$

$= \frac{\square}{12} - \frac{\square}{12}$

$= \underline{\qquad}$

$\frac{1}{4}, \frac{\square}{8}, \frac{\square}{12}, \ldots$

$\frac{5}{6}, \frac{\square}{12}, \ldots$

12 is the least common multiple of 4 and 6.

PB Chapter 3: Exercise 5, pages 54–55

Solving word problems

Let's Learn

Peter bought $\frac{4}{5}$ kilogram of grapes. John bought $\frac{2}{3}$ kilogram of grapes. What was the total weight of grapes bought?

$\frac{4}{5} + \frac{2}{3} = \frac{12}{15} + \frac{10}{15}$

$= \frac{22}{15}$

$= \square$

$\frac{4}{5}, \frac{8}{10}, \frac{12}{\mathbf{15}}, \ldots$

$\frac{2}{3}, \frac{4}{6}, \frac{6}{9}, \frac{8}{12}, \frac{10}{\mathbf{15}}, \ldots$

15 is the least common multiple of 5 and 3.

The total weight of grapes bought was $\square$ kilograms.

 ISBN 978-93-5103-033-1

Let's Do

1. Veda and Suraj each made a banner to publicise a charity sale. Veda's banner was $1\frac{1}{9}$ metres long and Suraj's banner was $\frac{7}{12}$ metre long. How much longer was Veda's banner than Suraj's banner?

$$1\frac{1}{9} - \frac{7}{12} = 1\frac{\square}{36} - \frac{\square}{36}$$

$$= \frac{\square}{36} - \frac{\square}{36}$$

$$= \_\_\_\_\_$$

$\frac{1}{9}, \frac{\square}{18}, \frac{\square}{27}, \frac{\square}{36}, \ldots$

$\frac{7}{12}, \frac{\square}{24}, \frac{\square}{36}, \ldots$

36 is the least common multiple of 9 and 12.

Veda's banner was _____ metre longer than Suraj's banner.

P/B Chapter 3: Exercise 6, pages 56–57

Practice 2

1. Add. Express each answer in its simplest form.

a) $\frac{7}{12} + \frac{5}{6}$ b) $\frac{2}{3} + \frac{1}{12}$ c) $\frac{5}{12} + \frac{1}{8}$

d) $\frac{1}{6} + \frac{3}{10}$ e) $\frac{5}{6} + \frac{7}{8}$ f) $\frac{9}{10} + \frac{1}{6}$

2. Subtract. Express each answer in its simplest form.

a) $\frac{2}{3} - \frac{5}{12}$ b) $\frac{3}{4} - \frac{1}{6}$ c) $\frac{5}{6} - \frac{7}{10}$

d) $1\frac{3}{8} - \frac{7}{12}$ e) $1\frac{1}{3} - \frac{7}{10}$ f) $1\frac{3}{10} - \frac{5}{6}$

Solve the word problems. Show your work clearly.

3. Mary spent $\frac{2}{5}$ of her money on clothes and $\frac{1}{4}$ of it on shoes. What fraction of her money did she spend altogether?

4. Karan took $\frac{3}{4}$ hour to travel from his house to the beach. He took $1\frac{1}{3}$ hours to return home. How much longer did he take to return home than to go to the beach?

 ISBN 978-93-5103-033-1

Lesson 3 Addition and Subtraction of Mixed Numbers

Adding mixed numbers

Let's Learn

a) Hari bought $2\frac{1}{2}$ kilograms of apples. He also bought $1\frac{1}{4}$ kilograms of oranges. What was the total weight of fruits he bought?

Maths Lab

Picture It

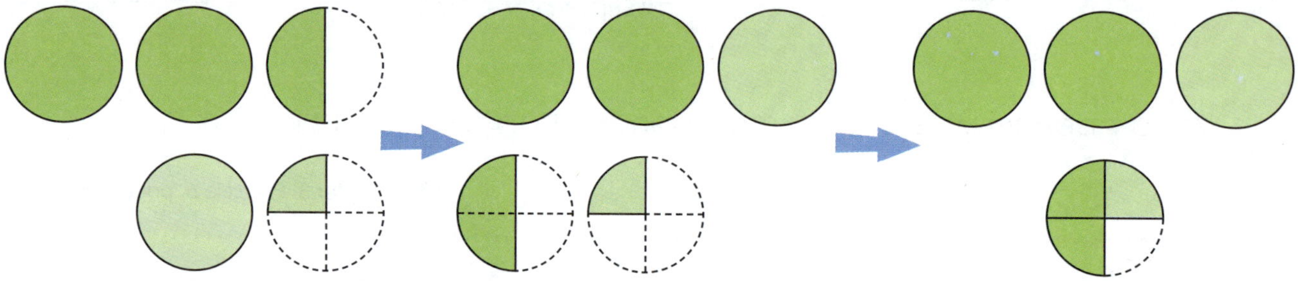

$$2\frac{1}{2} + 1\frac{1}{4} = 3\frac{1}{2} + \frac{1}{4}$$
$$= 3\frac{2}{4} + \frac{1}{4}$$
$$= 3\frac{3}{4}$$

$$2\frac{1}{2} \xrightarrow{+1} 3\frac{1}{2} \xrightarrow{+\frac{1}{4}} 3\frac{3}{4}$$

The total weight of fruits he bought was $3\frac{3}{4}$ kilograms.

 ISBN 978-93-5103-033-1

b) Add $2\frac{5}{6}$ and $1\frac{3}{4}$.

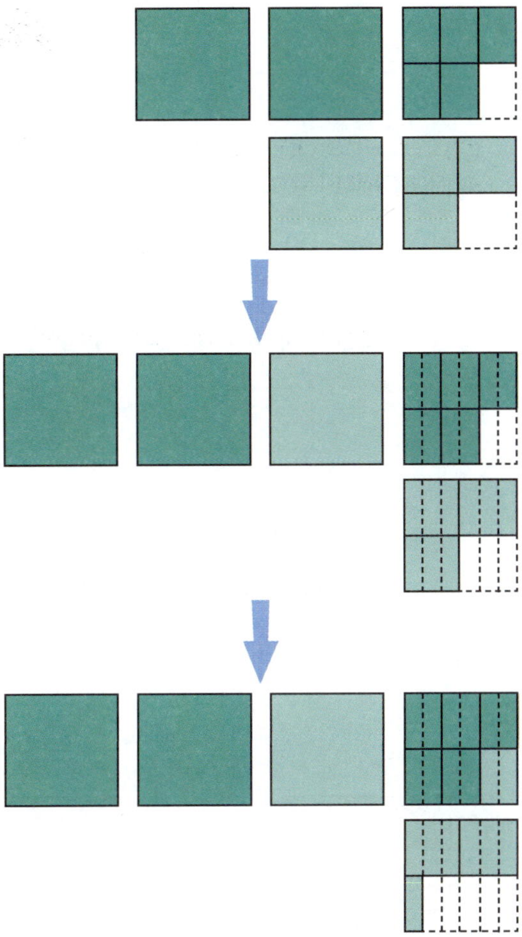

$2\frac{5}{6} + 1\frac{3}{4}$

$= 3\frac{5}{6} + \frac{3}{4}$

$= 3\frac{\square}{12} + \frac{\square}{12}$

$= 3\frac{\square}{12}$

$= 3 + 1 + \frac{\square}{12}$

$= \square$

Let's Do

1. Add. Express each answer in its simplest form.

a) $3\frac{5}{6} + 1\frac{7}{12} = 4\frac{5}{6} + \frac{7}{12}$

$= 4\frac{\square}{12} + \frac{\square}{12}$

= ______

= ______

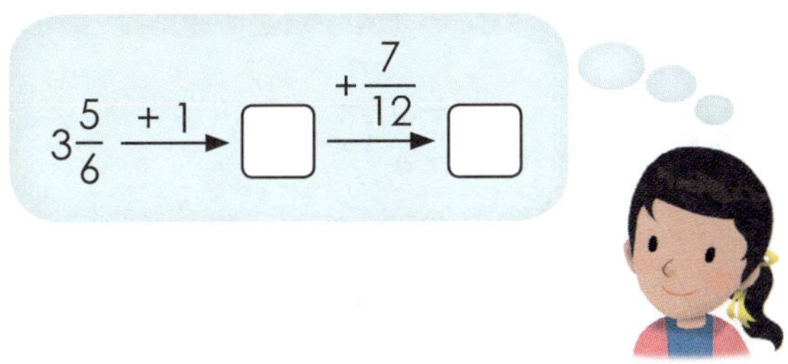

 ISBN 978-93-5103-033-1

b) $3\frac{1}{6} + 1\frac{9}{10} = 4\frac{1}{6} + \frac{9}{10}$

$= 4\frac{\square}{30} + \frac{\square}{30}$

= ______

= ______

= ______

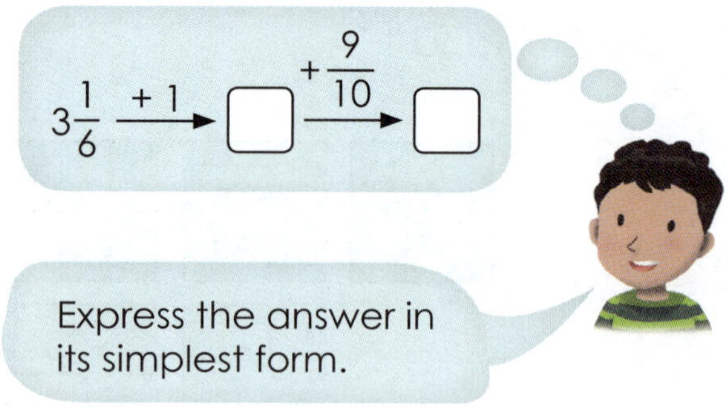

P/B Chapter 3: Exercise 7, pages 58–59

Subtracting mixed numbers

Let's Learn

a) Ram has $4\frac{3}{4}$ litres of juice. He uses $3\frac{7}{12}$ litres of juice to make a fruit punch. How much juice is left?

Maths Lab

Picture It

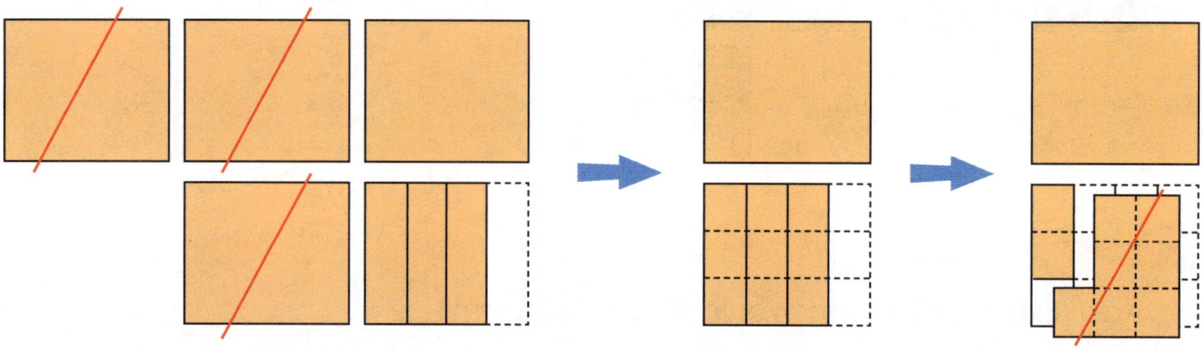

$4\frac{3}{4} - 3\frac{7}{12} = 1\frac{3}{4} - \frac{7}{12}$

$= 1\frac{9}{12} - \frac{7}{12}$

$= 1\frac{2}{12}$

$= 1\frac{1}{6}$

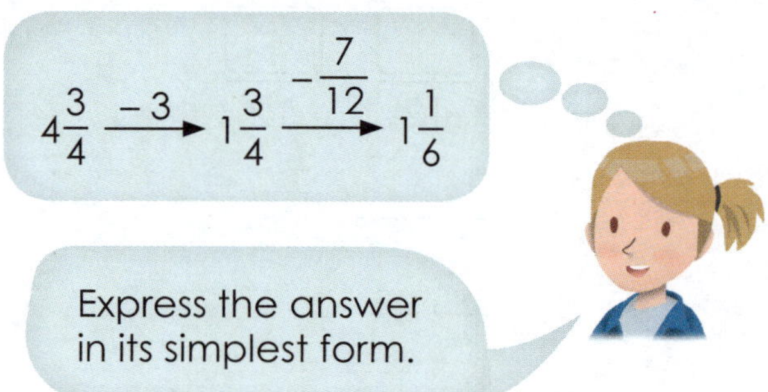

$1\frac{1}{6}$ litres of juice are left.

 ISBN 978-93-5103-033-1

b) Subtract $1\frac{4}{5}$ from $2\frac{1}{2}$.

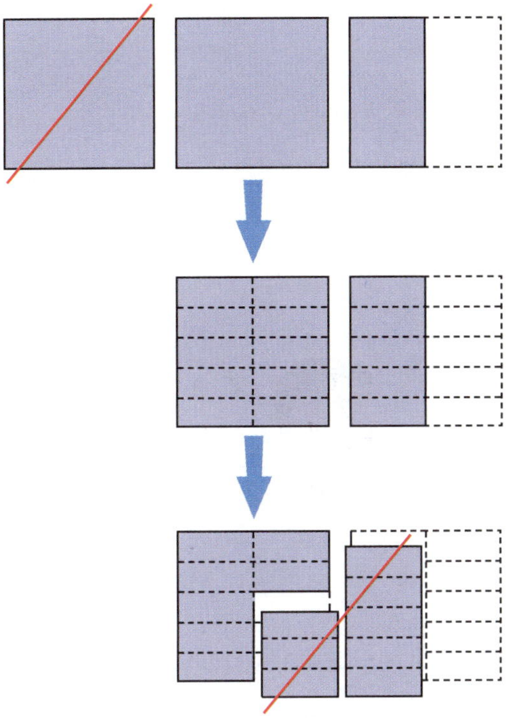

$$2\frac{1}{2} - 1\frac{4}{5}$$

$$= 1\frac{1}{2} - \frac{4}{5}$$

$$= 1\frac{5}{10} - \frac{8}{10}$$

$$= \frac{15}{10} - \frac{8}{10}$$

$$= \frac{\square}{10}$$

10 is a common multiple of 2 and 5.

Let's Do

1. Subtract. Express the answer in its simplest form.

a) $2\frac{3}{4} - 1\frac{1}{8} = 1\frac{3}{4} - \frac{1}{8}$

$= 1\frac{\square}{8} - \frac{1}{8}$

$=$ ______

$2\frac{3}{4} \xrightarrow{-1} \square \xrightarrow{-\frac{1}{8}} \square$

b) $4\frac{1}{6} - 1\frac{3}{10} = 3\frac{1}{6} - \frac{3}{10}$

$= 3\frac{\square}{30} - \frac{9}{30}$

$= 2\frac{\square}{30} - \frac{9}{30}$

$=$ ______

$=$ ______

$4\frac{1}{6} \xrightarrow{-1} \square \xrightarrow{-\frac{3}{10}} \square$

30 is a common multiple of 6 and 10.

Chapter 3: Exercise 8, pages 60–61

 ISBN 978-93-5103-033-1

Solving word problems

Let's Learn

A container has a capacity of $3\frac{1}{3}$ litres. It contains $1\frac{3}{4}$ litres of water. How much more water is needed to fill the container completely?

$$3\frac{1}{3} - 1\frac{3}{4} = 2\frac{1}{3} - \frac{3}{4}$$
$$= 2\frac{4}{12} - \frac{9}{12}$$
$$= 1\frac{16}{12} - \frac{9}{12}$$
$$= 1\frac{\square}{12}$$

$3\frac{1}{3} \xrightarrow{-1} 2\frac{1}{3} \xrightarrow{-\frac{3}{4}} \square$

12 is a common multiple of 3 and 4.

□ more litres of water are needed to fill the container completely.

Let's Do

1. Miss Dutta painted a table and some chairs. She used $2\frac{5}{6}$ litres of paint for the table and $1\frac{1}{4}$ litres of paint for the chairs. How much paint did she use altogether?

$$2\frac{5}{6} + 1\frac{1}{4} = 3\frac{5}{6} + \frac{1}{4}$$
$$= 3\frac{\square}{12} + \frac{\square}{12}$$
$$= 3\frac{\square}{12}$$
$$= \_\_\_\_\_$$

$2\frac{5}{6} \xrightarrow{+1} \square \xrightarrow{+\frac{1}{4}} \square$

12 is a common multiple of 6 and 4.

She used _______ litres of paint altogether.

P/B Chapter 3: Exercise 9, pages 62–63

 ISBN 978-93-5103-033-1

Practice 3

1. Add. Express each answer in its simplest form.

a) $2\frac{2}{3} + 1\frac{5}{9}$

b) $2\frac{5}{6} + 5\frac{1}{2}$

c) $4\frac{7}{12} + 1\frac{3}{4}$

d) $2\frac{1}{8} + 1\frac{5}{6}$

e) $3\frac{2}{9} + 1\frac{1}{6}$

f) $1\frac{1}{4} + 2\frac{5}{6}$

2. Subtract. Express each answer in its simplest form.

a) $3\frac{5}{6} - 1\frac{1}{3}$

b) $3\frac{4}{5} - 1\frac{3}{10}$

c) $4\frac{1}{6} - 1\frac{2}{3}$

d) $4\frac{5}{6} - 1\frac{1}{4}$

e) $3\frac{1}{6} - 2\frac{1}{10}$

f) $3\frac{3}{10} - 1\frac{1}{6}$

Solve the word problems. Show your work clearly.

3. Tasha spent $1\frac{1}{2}$ hours cooking lunch. She spent $1\frac{1}{12}$ hours cooking dinner. How much time did she spend cooking altogether?

4. Nisha jogged $2\frac{1}{2}$ kilometres. Her brother jogged $1\frac{2}{5}$ kilometres. How much further did Nisha jog than her brother?

5. The total length of two ribbons is $2\frac{3}{4}$ metres. If one ribbon is $1\frac{1}{3}$ metres long, what is the length of the other ribbon?

6. Mrs. Paulson bought $3\frac{1}{6}$ kilograms of potatoes and $1\frac{2}{3}$ kilograms of carrots. How much more potatoes than carrots did she buy?

 ISBN 978-93-5103-033-1

Lesson 4 Product of Fractions and Mixed Numbers

Finding the product of fractions through an activity

Let's Learn

a) Colour $\frac{3}{4}$ of a rectangle. Cut out $\frac{1}{2}$ of the coloured parts.
What fraction of the rectangle is cut out?

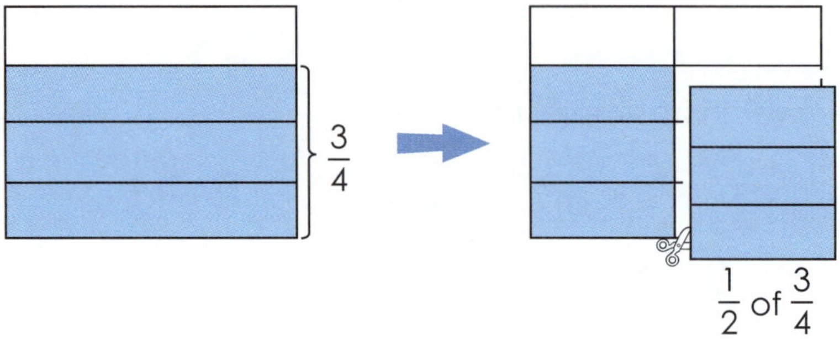

$$\frac{1}{2} \text{ of } \frac{3}{4} = \frac{1}{2} \times \frac{3}{4}$$
$$= \frac{3}{8}$$

$\frac{3}{8}$ of the rectangle is cut out.

b) Colour $\frac{1}{2}$ of a rectangle. Cut out $\frac{3}{4}$ of the coloured parts.
What fraction of the rectangle is cut out?

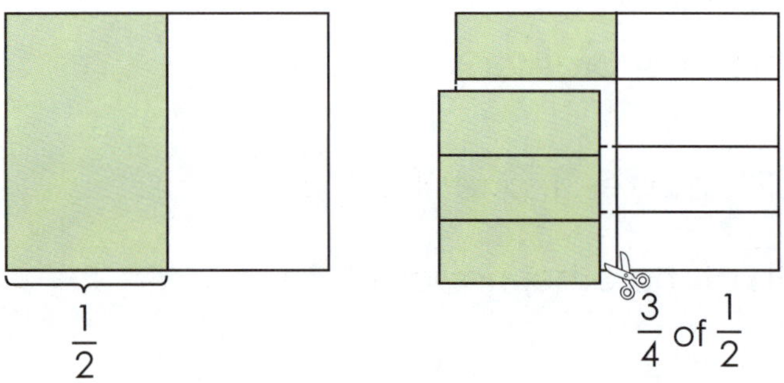

$$\frac{3}{4} \text{ of } \frac{1}{2} = \frac{3}{4} \times \frac{1}{2}$$
$$= \frac{3}{8}$$

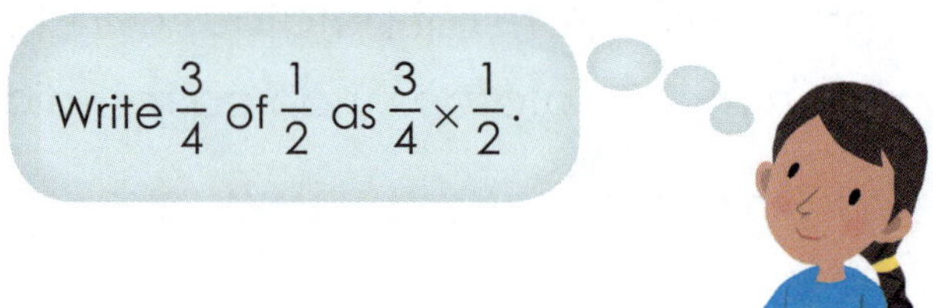

$\frac{3}{8}$ of the rectangle is cut out.

$\frac{1}{2}$ of $\frac{3}{4}$ and $\frac{3}{4}$ of $\frac{1}{2}$ have the same result of $\frac{3}{8}$.

So, $\frac{1}{2} \times \frac{3}{4} = \frac{3}{4} \times \frac{1}{2}$.

 ISBN 978-93-5103-033-1

Let's Do

1. A vegetable garden occupies $\frac{1}{2}$ of a piece of land. $\frac{3}{5}$ of the garden is used for growing radishes. What fraction of the land is used for growing radishes?

$\frac{3}{5}$ of $\frac{1}{2} = \frac{3}{5} \times \frac{1}{2}$

$= $ ______

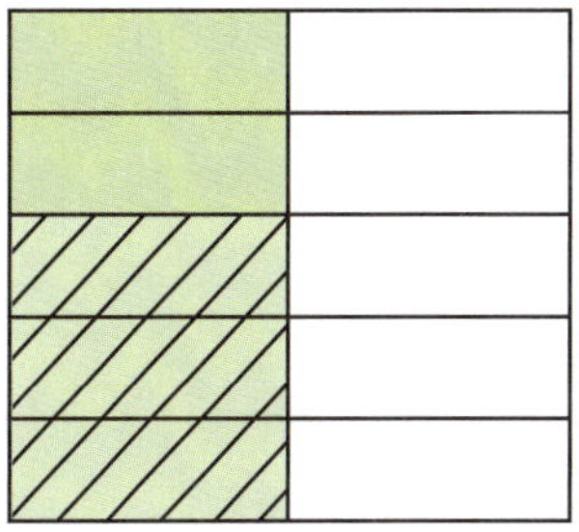

______ of the land is used for growing radishes.

2. Find the area of a rectangle measuring $\frac{1}{3}$ metre by $\frac{5}{6}$ metre.

$\frac{1}{3}\ \text{m} \times \frac{5}{6}\ \text{m}$

$= $ ______ m^2

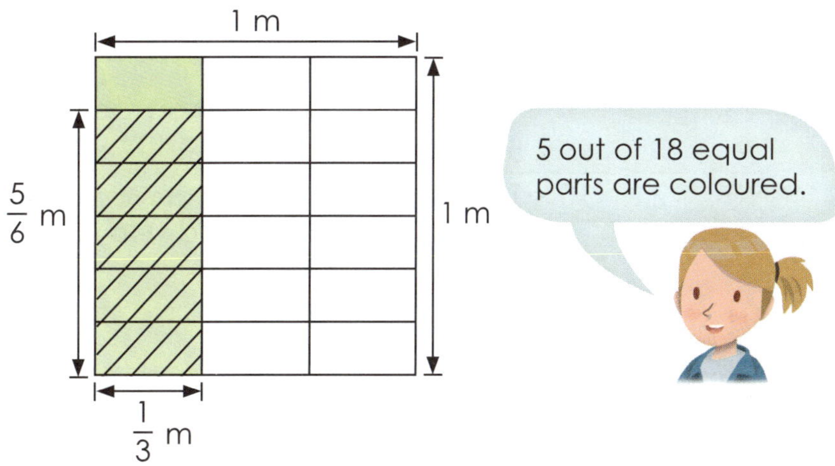

The area of the rectangle is ______ square metres.

Finding the product of fractions by calculation

Let's Learn

Picture It

a) Multiply $\frac{4}{5}$ by $\frac{2}{3}$.

$$\frac{4}{5} \times \frac{2}{3} = \frac{4 \times 2}{5 \times 3}$$
$$= \frac{8}{15}$$

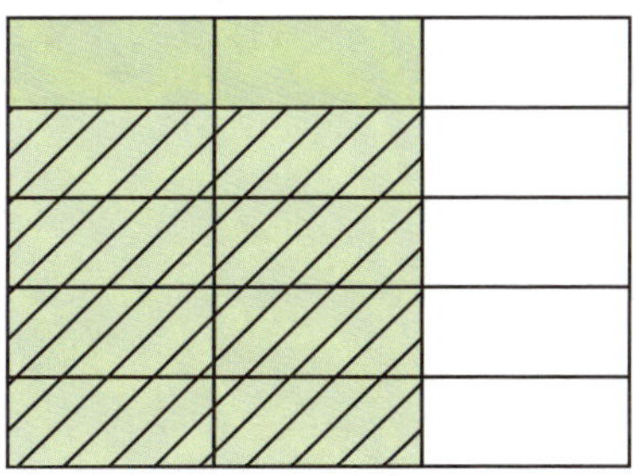

 ISBN 978-93-5103-033-1

b) Multiply $\frac{3}{4}$ by $\frac{7}{12}$.

Method 1

$$\frac{3}{4} \times \frac{7}{12} = \frac{{}^{1}\cancel{3} \times 7}{4 \times \cancel{12}_{4}}$$
$$= \square$$

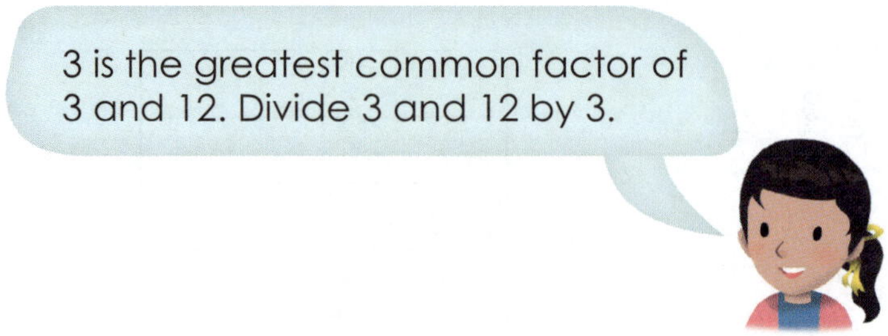

Method 2

$$\frac{{}^{1}\cancel{3}}{4} \times \frac{7}{\cancel{12}_{4}} = \frac{1 \times 7}{4 \times 4}$$
$$= \square$$

c) Find the product of $\frac{9}{10}$ and $\frac{5}{12}$.

Method 1

$$\frac{9}{10} \times \frac{5}{12} = \frac{{}^{3}\cancel{9} \times \cancel{5}^{1}}{{}_{2}\cancel{10} \times \cancel{12}_{4}}$$
$$= \square$$

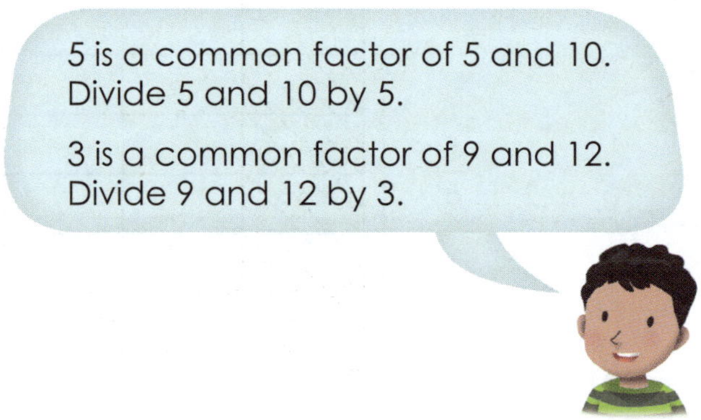

Method 2

$$\frac{{}^{3}\cancel{9}}{{}_{2}\cancel{10}} \times \frac{\cancel{5}^{1}}{\cancel{12}_{4}} = \frac{3 \times 1}{2 \times 4}$$
$$= \square$$

Let's Do

1. Multiply. Express each answer in its simplest form.

a) $\frac{1}{3} \times \frac{3}{4} = \frac{1 \times \cancel{3}^{1}}{{}_{1}\cancel{3} \times 4}$

= ______

b) $\frac{15}{4} \times \frac{8}{3} = \frac{\square \times \cancel{8}^{2}}{{}_{1}\cancel{4} \times \square}$

= ______

PB Chapter 3: Exercises 10–11, pages 64–66

 ISBN 978-93-5103-033-1

Multiplying whole numbers by mixed numbers

Let's Learn

a) There are 3 students in a group. Each student spends $2\frac{1}{2}$ hours on a group project. How many hours do they spend on the project altogether?

Picture It

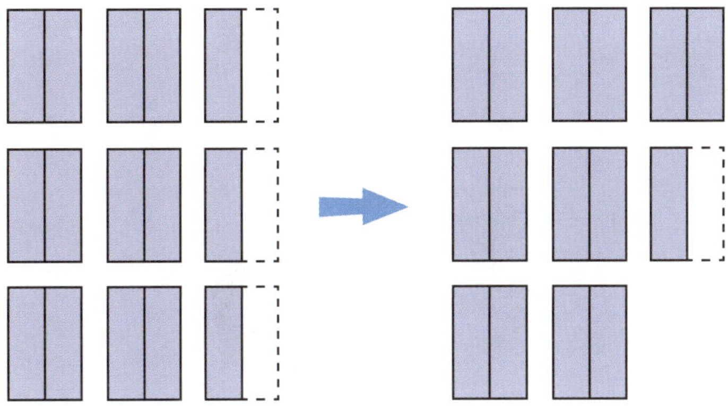

$$3 \times 2\frac{1}{2} = 3 \times \frac{5}{2}$$
$$= \frac{3 \times 5}{2}$$
$$= \frac{15}{2}$$
$$= 7\frac{1}{2}$$

They spend $7\frac{1}{2}$ hours on the project altogether.

b) Multiply $1\frac{5}{8}$ by 6.

$$1\frac{5}{8} \times 6 = \frac{13}{\cancel{8}_{4}} \times \cancel{6}^{3}$$
$$= \frac{39}{4}$$
$$= \square$$

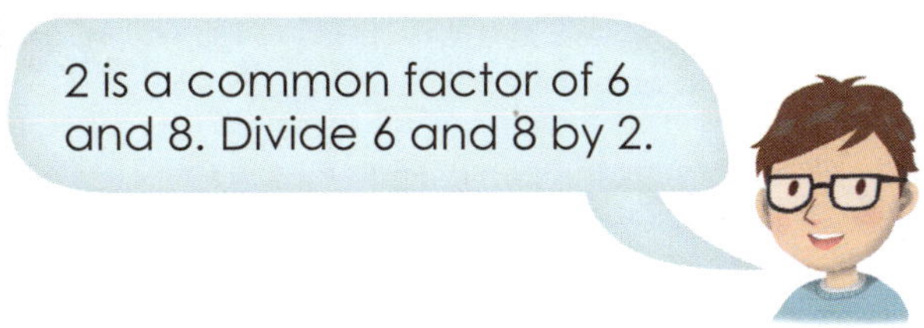

 ISBN 978-93-5103-033-1

Let's Do

1. Multiply. Express the answer as a mixed number in its simplest form.

a) $2\frac{3}{5} \times 4 = \frac{\square}{\square} \times 4$

$= \_\_\_\_\_\_$

$= \_\_\_\_\_\_$

$2\frac{3}{5} = \frac{\square}{5}$

b) $1\frac{5}{6} \times 4 = \frac{\square}{\square} \times 4$

$= \_\_\_\_\_\_$

$= \_\_\_\_\_\_$

$1\frac{5}{6} = \frac{\square}{6}$

Multiplying fractions or mixed numbers by mixed numbers

Let's Learn

a) Multiply $\frac{3}{4}$ by $2\frac{1}{5}$.

$$\frac{3}{4} \times 2\frac{1}{5} = \frac{3}{4} \times \frac{11}{5}$$
$$= \frac{33}{20}$$
$$= 1\frac{13}{20}$$

$2\frac{1}{5} = \frac{11}{5}$

b) Multiply $1\frac{1}{2}$ by $2\frac{2}{3}$.

$$1\frac{1}{2} \times 2\frac{2}{3} = \frac{3}{2} \times \frac{8}{3}$$
$$= \frac{{}^{1}\cancel{3} \times \cancel{8}^{4}}{{}_{1}\cancel{2} \times \cancel{3}_{1}}$$
$$= 4$$

$1\frac{1}{2} = \frac{3}{2}$

$2\frac{2}{3} = \frac{8}{3}$

 ISBN 978-93-5103-033-1

Let's Do

1. Multiply. Express each answer in its simplest form.

a) $1\frac{2}{9} \times \frac{2}{3} = \frac{\square}{9} \times \frac{2}{3}$

$= $ ______

$1\frac{2}{9} = \frac{\square}{9}$

b) $2\frac{1}{3} \times 3\frac{3}{7} = \frac{\square}{3} \times \frac{\square}{7}$

$= $ ______

$2\frac{1}{3} = \frac{\square}{3}$

$3\frac{3}{7} = \frac{\square}{7}$

PB Chapter 3: Exercise 12, page 67

Solving word problems

Let's Learn

Nitin had a piece of string $\frac{1}{2}$ metre long. He used $\frac{1}{3}$ of it to tie up a box.
Find the length of the string used to tie up the box.

$$\frac{1}{3} \times \frac{1}{2}\text{ m} = \frac{1 \times 1}{3 \times 2}\text{ m}$$

$$= \frac{1}{6}\text{ m}$$

▢ metre of the string was used to tie up the box.

Let's Do

1. A part of a wall was painted red. The painted part was a rectangle measuring $2\frac{1}{4}$ metres by $1\frac{2}{3}$ metres. What was the area of the wall that was painted red?

$2\frac{1}{4}\text{ m} \times 1\frac{2}{3}\text{ m} = \frac{9}{4}\text{ m} \times \frac{5}{3}\text{ m}$

$= $ ______ m^2

$= $ ______ m^2

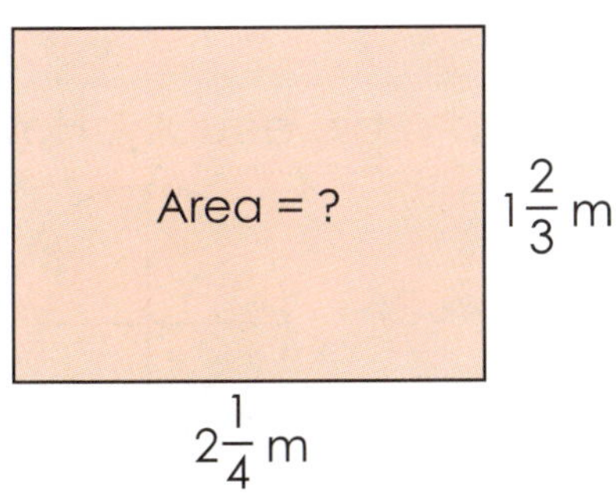

The area of the wall that was painted red was ______ square metres.

PB Chapter 3: Exercise 13, pages 68–69

 ISBN 978-93-5103-033-1

Practice 4

1. Multiply. Express each answer in its simplest form.

a) $\frac{1}{2} \times \frac{1}{2}$ b) $\frac{1}{4} \times \frac{8}{9}$ c) $\frac{5}{6} \times \frac{1}{5}$

d) $\frac{3}{4} \times \frac{5}{6}$ e) $\frac{4}{5} \times \frac{5}{8}$ f) $\frac{5}{12} \times \frac{9}{10}$

2. Multiply. Express each answer in its simplest form.

a) $\frac{9}{4} \times \frac{16}{3}$ b) $\frac{14}{9} \times \frac{12}{7}$ c) $\frac{10}{7} \times \frac{14}{5}$

d) $\frac{20}{7} \times \frac{7}{4}$ e) $\frac{11}{5} \times \frac{20}{11}$ f) $\frac{15}{8} \times \frac{8}{3}$

3. Multiply. Express each answer in its simplest form.

a) $1\frac{3}{5} \times \frac{3}{8}$ b) $\frac{3}{4} \times 2\frac{5}{6}$ c) $1\frac{5}{9} \times 1\frac{5}{7}$

d) $1\frac{3}{7} \times 2\frac{4}{5}$ e) $2\frac{6}{7} \times 1\frac{3}{4}$ f) $2\frac{1}{5} \times 1\frac{9}{11}$

Solve the word problems. Show your work clearly.

4. Arif has $2\frac{3}{4}$ kilograms of flour. He uses $\frac{2}{3}$ of the flour to bake a pie. How much flour does he use?

5. Mr. Bakshi has a large piece of land measuring $2\frac{1}{2}$ kilometres by $3\frac{3}{4}$ kilometres. What is the area of the land?

Lesson 5 Division of Fractions by Whole Numbers

Dividing fractions by whole numbers

Let's Learn

a) 4 friends shared a pie equally. How much pie did each friend receive?

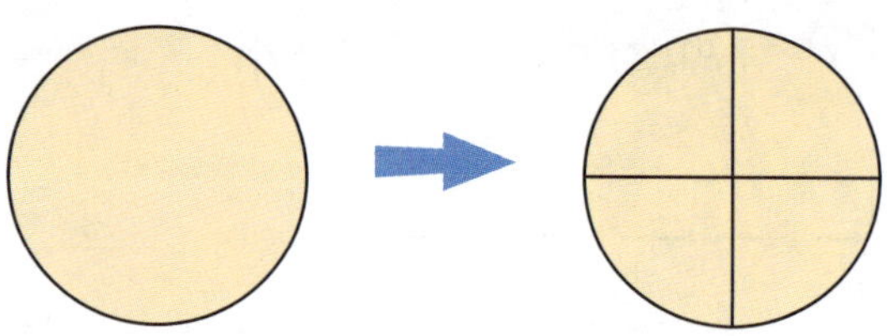

$1 \div 4 = \frac{1}{4}$

Each friend received $\frac{1}{4}$ of the pie.

 ISBN 978-93-5103-033-1

b) 4 friends shared 3 pies equally.
How much pie did each friend receive?

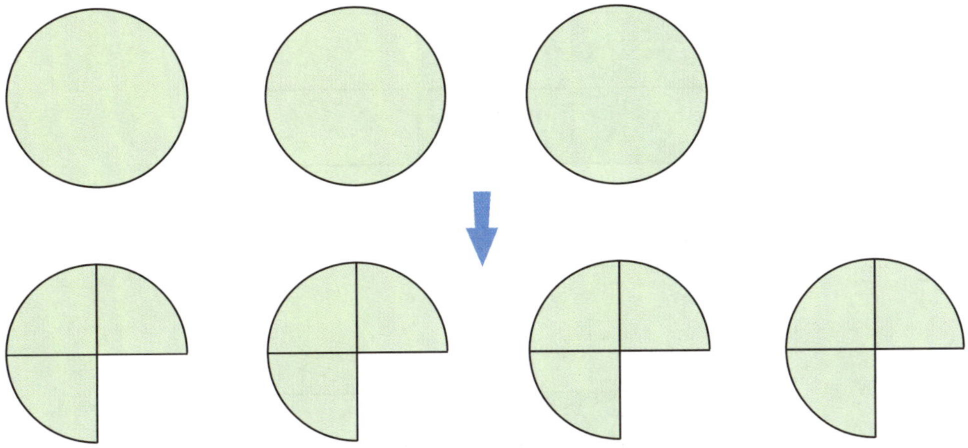

Each friend received $\frac{1}{4}$ of 3 pies.

$$3 \div 4 = \frac{1}{4} \text{ of } 3$$
$$= \frac{1}{4} \times 3$$
$$= \frac{3}{4}$$

Each friend received $\frac{3}{4}$ of a pie.

c) 4 friends shared $\frac{2}{3}$ of a pie equally.
How much pie did each friend receive?

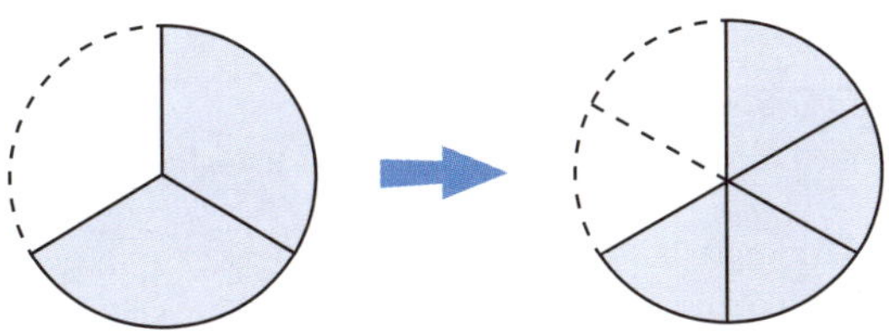

Each friend received $\frac{1}{4}$ of $\frac{2}{3}$ of a pie.

$$\frac{2}{3} \div 4 = \frac{1}{4} \text{ of } \frac{2}{3}$$
$$= \frac{1}{{}_{2}\cancel{4}} \times \frac{\cancel{2}^{1}}{3}$$
$$= \frac{1}{6}$$

We can also divide $\frac{2}{3}$ by 4 in another way.

$$\frac{2}{3} \div 4 = \frac{{}^{1}\cancel{2}}{3} \times \frac{1}{\cancel{4}_{2}}$$
$$= \frac{1}{6}$$

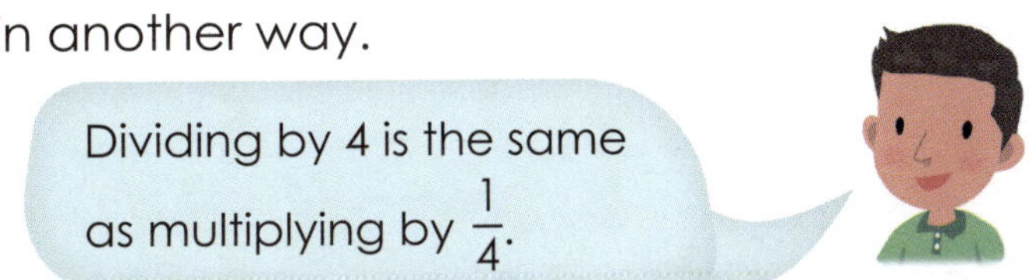

 ISBN 978-93-5103-033-1

Let's Do

1. Divide $\frac{2}{3}$ by 3.

$$\frac{2}{3} \div 3 = \frac{\square}{\square} \times \frac{\square}{\square}$$

$$= \underline{\hspace{2cm}}$$

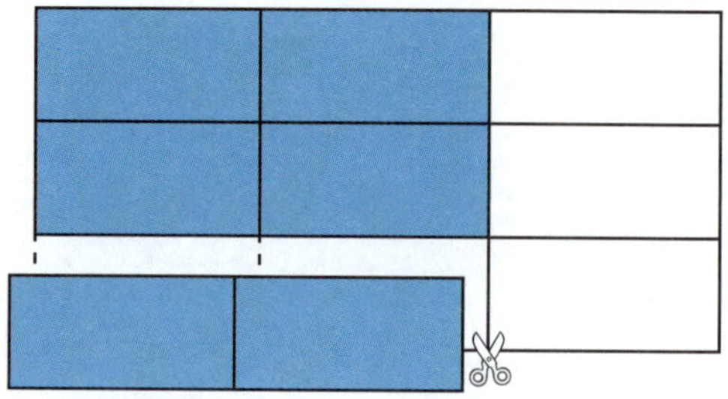

2. Divide $\frac{3}{4}$ by 6.

$$\frac{3}{4} \div 6 = \frac{\square}{\square} \times \frac{\square}{\square}$$

$$= \underline{\hspace{2cm}}$$

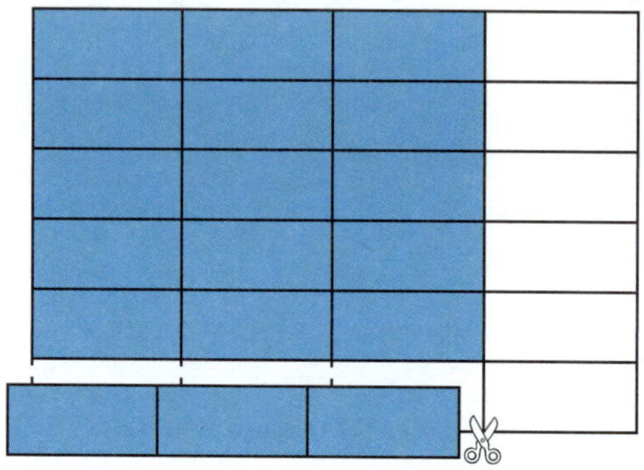

Chapter 3: Exercises 14–15, pages 70–72

Solving word problems

Let's Learn

A string of length $\frac{4}{5}$ metre is cut into 2 equal pieces.
What is the length of each piece?

Picture It

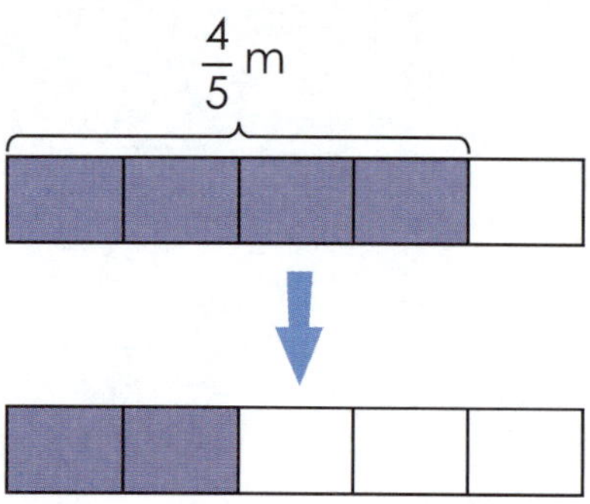

$$\frac{4}{5} \div 2 = \frac{\cancel{4}^{2}}{5} \times \frac{1}{\cancel{2}_{1}}$$

$$= \frac{2}{5}$$

The length of each piece is $\frac{2}{5}$ metre.

 ISBN 978-93-5103-033-1

Let's Do

1. 6 similar packets of raisins have a weight of $\frac{3}{10}$ kilogram.
Find the weight of 1 packet of raisins.

$$\frac{3}{10} \div 6 = \frac{3}{10} \times \frac{\square}{\square}$$

$$= \_\_\_\_\_$$

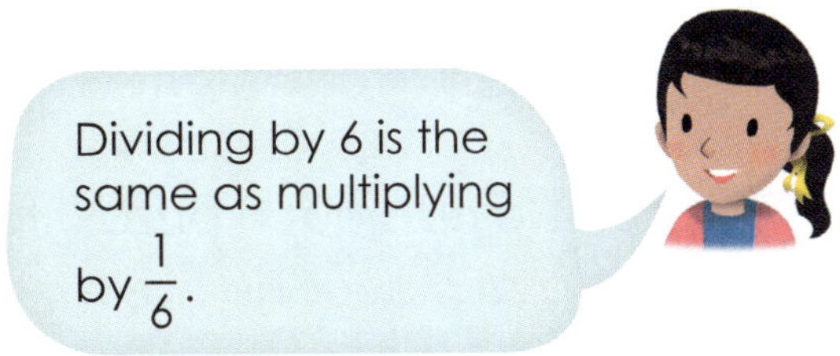

The weight of 1 packet of raisins is _____ kilogram.

P/B Chapter 3: Exercise 16, pages 73–74

Practice 5

1. Divide. Express each answer in its simplest form.

a) $\frac{4}{5} \div 3$ b) $\frac{5}{7} \div 4$ c) $\frac{4}{5} \div 4$

d) $\frac{6}{7} \div 2$ e) $\frac{2}{3} \div 8$ f) $\frac{9}{10} \div 6$

Solve the word problems. Show your work clearly.

2. $\frac{7}{8}$ of the money collected at a bake sale was divided equally among 4 clubs in a school. What fraction of the money did each club receive?

3. Samuel poured $\frac{2}{5}$ litre of fruit juice equally into 3 cups.
How much fruit juice was there in each cup?

4. The perimeter of a square flower bed is $\frac{3}{4}$ metre.
Find the length of each side in metres.

5. Mrs. Patil divided $\frac{3}{4}$ kilogram of walnuts equally among 6 children. How many kilograms of walnuts did each child receive?

 ISBN 978-93-5103-033-1

Lesson 6 Division of Whole Numbers by Fractions

Dividing whole numbers by fractions

Let's Learn

a) Atul has 3 pizzas. He cuts each pizza into halves.
How many half-pizzas does he have?

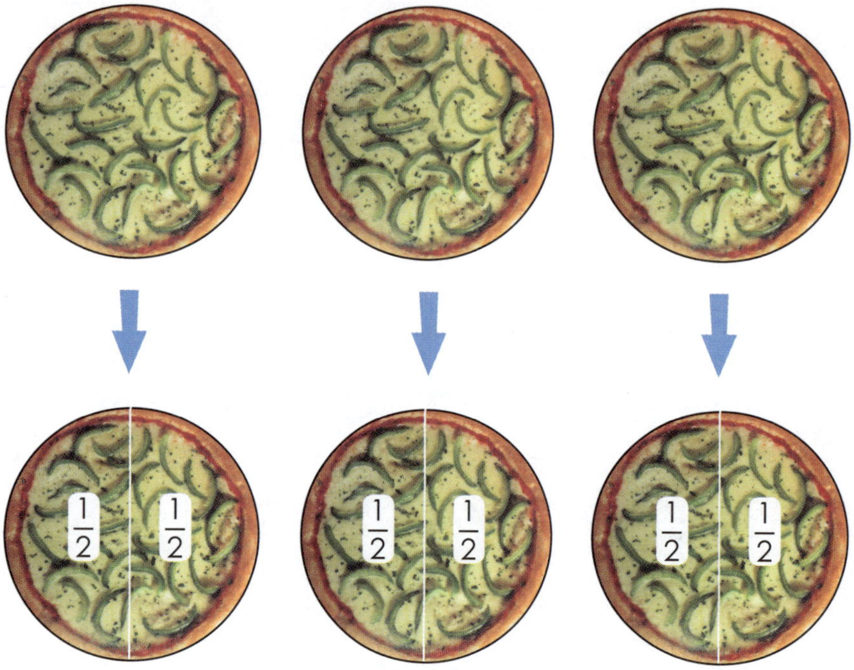

There are 3 whole pizzas. How many halves are there in 3 wholes?

In 1 pizza, there are 2 halves.
In 3 pizzas, there are (3 × 2) halves.

$$3 \div \frac{1}{2} = 6$$

He has 6 half-pizzas.

$$\begin{aligned} 3 \div \frac{1}{2} &= 3 \times \frac{2}{1} \\ &= \frac{3 \times 2}{1} \\ &= 6 \end{aligned}$$

He has 6 half-pizzas.

Dividing by $\frac{1}{2}$ is the same as multiplying by $\frac{2}{1}$.

 ISBN 978-93-5103-033-1

b) To bake a cake, Aisha uses $\frac{3}{5}$ of a bag of flour. If she has 2 bags of flour, how many cakes can Aisha bake?

Picture It

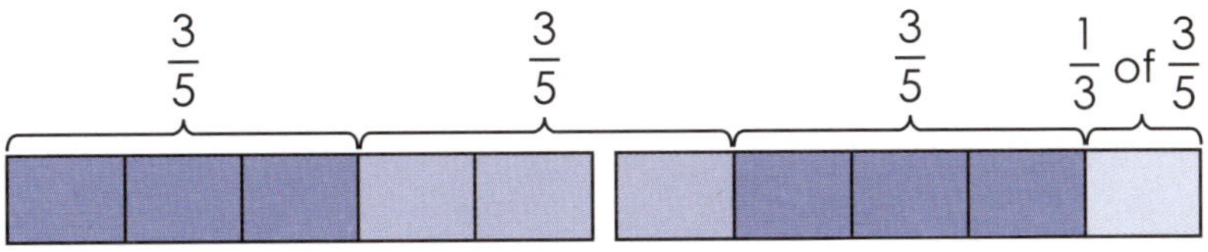

There are 2 whole bags of flour.
How many $\frac{3}{5}$s are there in 2 wholes?

In 1 whole, there are $1\frac{2}{3}$ or $\frac{5}{3}$ three-fifths.
In 2 wholes, there are $\left(2 \times \frac{5}{3}\right)$ three-fifths.

$$
\begin{aligned}
2 \div \frac{3}{5} &= 2 \times \frac{5}{3} \\
&= \frac{2 \times 5}{3} \\
&= \frac{10}{3} \\
&= 3\frac{1}{3}
\end{aligned}
$$

Aisha can bake 3 cakes.

Dividing by $\frac{3}{5}$ is the same as multiplying by $\frac{5}{3}$.

Aisha cannot bake $\frac{1}{3}$ of a cake.

Think About It

Look at the above example. How much flour is left after Aisha baked 3 cakes?

$2 \div \frac{3}{5} = 3\frac{1}{3}$

$\frac{1}{3}$ bag of flour is left.

Ria

Is Ria correct? Explain why.

 ISBN 978-93-5103-033-1

Let's Do

1. Divide. Express each answer in its simplest form.

a) $5 \div \frac{1}{4} = 5 \times \frac{\square}{1}$
$= \frac{\square}{1}$
$=$ ______

b) $7 \div \frac{7}{8} = 7 \times \frac{\square}{7}$
$= \frac{\square}{7}$
$=$ ______

c) $2 \div \frac{3}{10} = 2 \times \frac{\square}{3}$
$= \frac{\square}{3}$
$=$ ______

PB Chapter 3: Exercise 17, pages 75–76

Think About It

$12 \div \frac{2}{3} = \square$

Ria

Dividing by $\frac{2}{3}$ is the same as multiplying by $\frac{3}{2}$.

$12 \div \frac{2}{3} = 12 \times \frac{3}{2}$
$= \frac{36}{2}$
$= 18$

Divide 12 by the numerator.

$12 \div \frac{2}{3} = \frac{6}{3}$
$= 2$

Sam

Who is correct? Explain why.

Solving word problems

Let's Learn

A water pump can drain $\frac{3}{4}$ of the water in a swimming pool in an hour. How long does it take the water pump to drain 3 such swimming pools?

Picture It

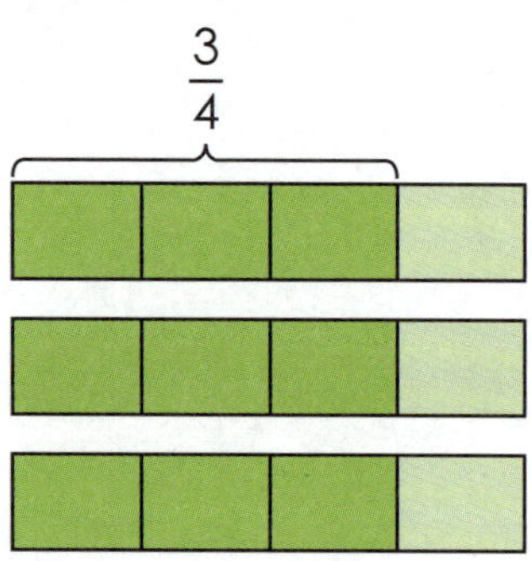

$3 \div \frac{3}{4} = {}^{1}\cancel{3} \times \frac{4}{\cancel{3}_{1}}$
$= 4$

It takes the water pump 4 hours to drain 3 such swimming pools.

 ISBN 978-93-5103-033-1

Let's Do

1. Wendy uses up $\frac{5}{6}$ of a bottle of glue in a month.
   How many months will 4 such bottles of glue last?

   $4 \div \frac{5}{6} = 4 \times \frac{\square}{\square}$

   $= \_\_\_\_\_\_$

   $= \_\_\_\_\_\_$

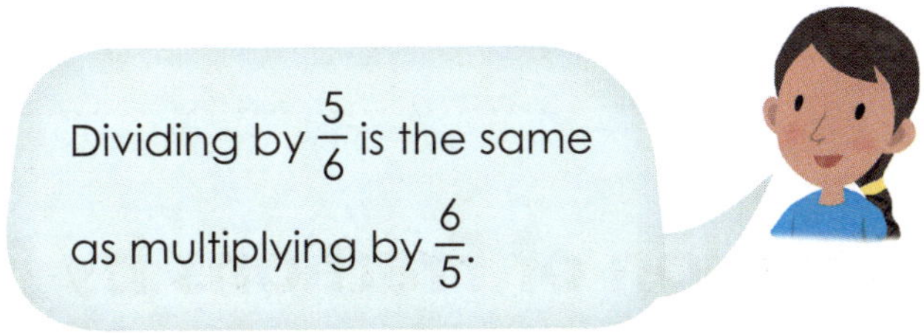

   4 such bottles of glue will last ______ months.

P/B Chapter 3: Exercise 18, pages 77–78

Practice 6

1. Divide. Express each answer in its simplest form.

   a) $5 \div \frac{1}{2}$ b) $7 \div \frac{1}{3}$ c) $4 \div \frac{1}{4}$

   d) $3 \div \frac{1}{8}$ e) $9 \div \frac{1}{5}$ f) $8 \div \frac{1}{7}$

   g) $12 \div \frac{1}{6}$ h) $6 \div \frac{1}{11}$ i) $10 \div \frac{1}{12}$

2. Divide. Express each answer in its simplest form.

   a) $4 \div \frac{2}{3}$ b) $5 \div \frac{5}{6}$ c) $6 \div \frac{4}{5}$

   d) $12 \div \frac{8}{9}$ e) $6 \div \frac{5}{6}$ f) $9 \div \frac{7}{8}$

Solve the word problems. Show your work clearly.

3. In a week, Henry uses $\frac{1}{5}$ of a bottle of detergent to wash dishes.
   How many weeks will 5 such bottles of detergent last?

4. Mr. Gupta has 10 kilograms of milk powder. If he packs all the milk powder into tins of $\frac{1}{4}$ kilogram each, how many tins does he need?

5. $\frac{3}{4}$ litre of water can be used to make a pot of soup. How many pots of soup can be made with 6 litres of water?

 ISBN 978-93-5103-033-1

6. Lily pours 3 litres of lemonade into mugs. Each mug can hold $\frac{2}{9}$ litre of lemonade. How many mugs will Lily be able to fill completely?

7. What is the greatest number of $\frac{4}{7}$-metre pieces that you can cut from a 3-metre length of wire?

Lesson 7 Division of Fractions by Fractions

Dividing fractions by fractions

Let's Learn

a) A baker sold $\frac{1}{2}$ of a large cake to a group of customers. Each customer bought $\frac{1}{6}$ of the cake. How many customers were there in the group?

Maths Lab

Picture It

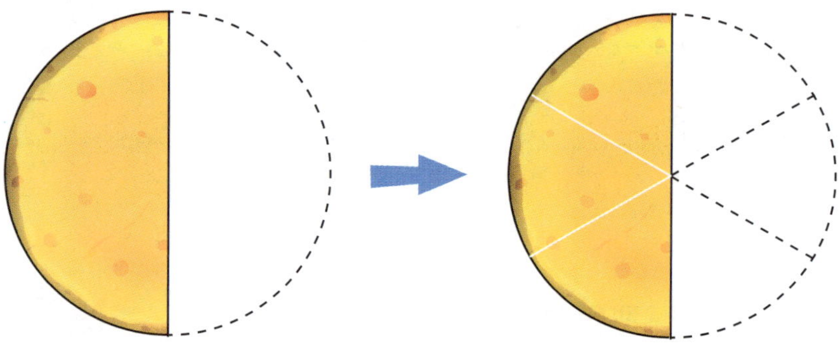

$\frac{1}{2} \div \frac{1}{6} = 3$

There were 3 customers in the group.

In 1 cake, there are 6 sixths.

In $\frac{1}{2}$ of a cake, there are $(6 \div 2)$ sixths.

$$\frac{1}{2} \div \frac{1}{6} = \frac{1}{2} \times \frac{6}{1}$$
$$= \frac{6}{2}$$
$$= 3$$

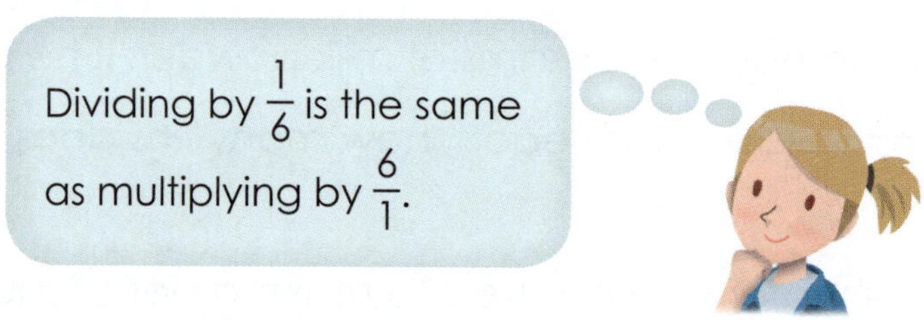

There were 3 customers in the group.

 ISBN 978-93-5103-033-1

b) Divide $\frac{2}{3}$ by $\frac{2}{9}$.

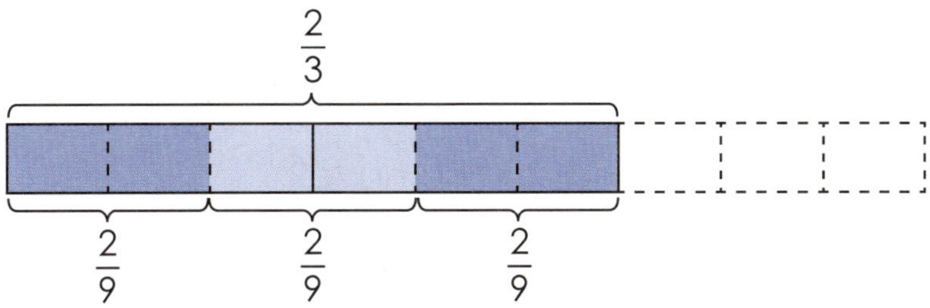

In 1 whole, there are 9 ninths.
In $\frac{2}{3}$ of a whole, there are $\left(\frac{2}{3} \times 9\right)$ ninths.

$$\frac{2}{3} \div \frac{2}{9} = \frac{\cancel{2}^{1}}{\cancel{3}_{1}} \times \frac{\cancel{9}^{3}}{\cancel{2}_{1}}$$
$$= 3$$

Dividing by $\frac{2}{9}$ is the same as multiplying by $\frac{9}{2}$.

Let's Do

1. Divide. Express each answer in its simplest form.

a) $\frac{3}{4} \div \frac{1}{8} = \frac{3}{4} \times \frac{\square}{1}$
$= \frac{\square}{\square}$
$=$ ______

b) $\frac{4}{5} \div \frac{3}{10} = \frac{4}{5} \times \frac{\square}{3}$
$= \frac{\square}{\square}$
$=$ ______

P/B Chapter 3: Exercise 19, pages 79–80

 ISBN 978-93-5103-033-1

Solving word problems

Let's Learn

Tom bought $\frac{11}{12}$ kilogram of almonds. He packed them into bags of $\frac{1}{4}$ kilogram each. How many full bags of almonds did he have?

Picture It

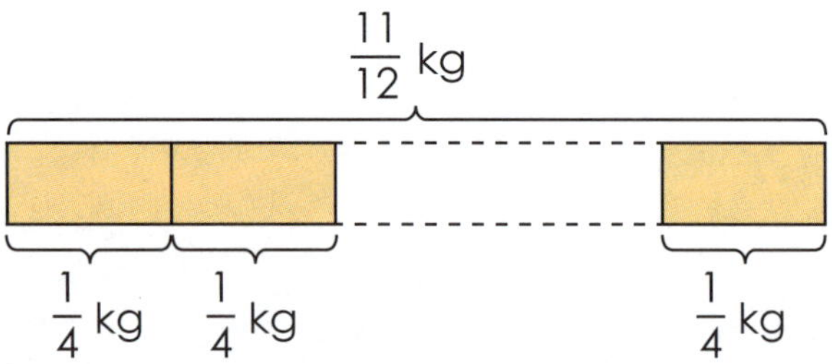

$$\frac{11}{12} \div \frac{1}{4} = \frac{11}{\cancel{12}_{3}} \times \frac{\cancel{4}^{1}}{1}$$
$$= \frac{11}{3}$$
$$= 3\frac{2}{3}$$

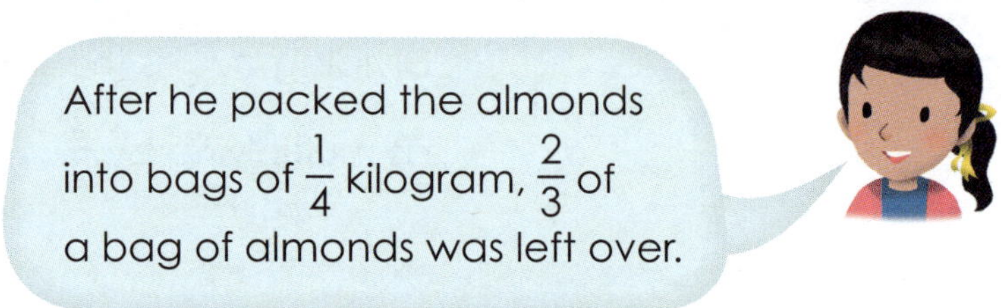

He had 3 full bags of almonds.

Let's Do

1. Shobha has $\frac{7}{8}$ litre of ketchup. She divides the ketchup into containers of $\frac{3}{16}$ litre each. How many containers can she fill with ketchup completely?

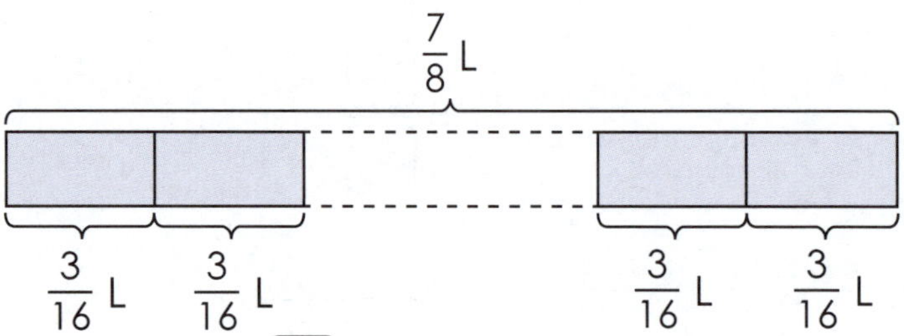

$$\frac{7}{8} \div \frac{3}{16} = \frac{7}{8} \times \frac{\square}{\square}$$
$$= \_\_\_\_\_$$
$$= \_\_\_\_\_$$

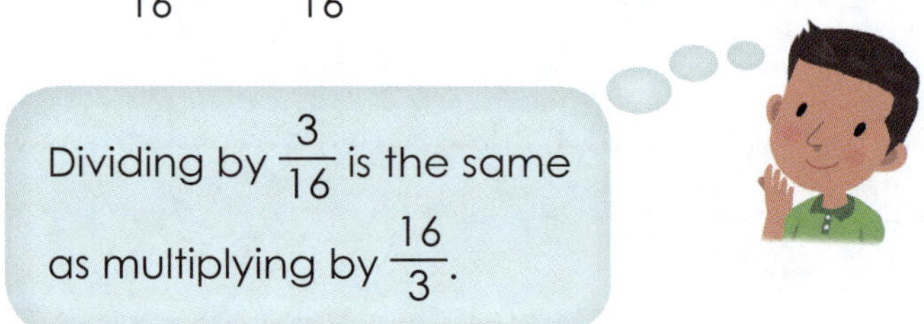

She can fill _____ containers with ketchup completely.

P/B Chapter 3: Exercise 20, page 81

 ISBN 978-93-5103-033-1

Think About It

A machine makes $\frac{1}{2}$ kilogram of cement in one minute. How long does it take for the machine to make $\frac{3}{4}$ kilogram of cement?

Ria

$\frac{3}{4} \div \frac{1}{2} = \frac{3}{\not{4}_{2}} \times \frac{\not{2}^{1}}{1}$

$= \frac{3}{2}$

$= 1\frac{1}{2}$

It takes the machine $1\frac{1}{2}$ minutes.

$\frac{3}{4} \div \frac{1}{2} = \frac{{}^{2}\not{4}}{3} \times \frac{1}{\not{2}_{1}}$

$= \frac{2}{3}$

It takes the machine $\frac{2}{3}$ minute.

Sam

Who is correct? Explain why.

Practice 7

1. Divide.

a) $\frac{1}{2} \div \frac{1}{4}$　　b) $\frac{2}{3} \div \frac{1}{12}$　　c) $\frac{5}{6} \div \frac{5}{12}$

d) $\frac{1}{3} \div \frac{5}{9}$　　e) $\frac{4}{5} \div \frac{7}{9}$　　f) $\frac{7}{12} \div \frac{3}{8}$

Solve the word problems. Show your work clearly.

2. Shelly colours $\frac{3}{4}$ of a paper plate blue. She cuts the blue part into a number of pieces such that each piece is $\frac{1}{12}$ of the whole plate. Find the number of blue pieces Shelly has.

3. A rectangular piece of wrapping paper has an area of $\frac{7}{12}$ square metre. If the width of the paper is $\frac{3}{8}$ metre, what is the length of the paper?

4. $\frac{1}{4}$ metre of a ribbon is needed to make a decorative bow. What is the greatest number of bows that can be made from $\frac{7}{8}$ metre of ribbon?

5. What is the smallest number of $\frac{2}{5}$-litre containers that are needed to hold $\frac{11}{12}$ litre of orange juice?

 ISBN 978-93-5103-033-1

Lesson 8 Problem Solving

Word problems

Let's Learn

Nicole had ₹ 125. She spent $\frac{2}{5}$ of the money and saved the rest.
How much money did she save?

1 Understand the problem.

How much money did she have?
How much money did she spend?
What do I have to find?

Method 1

2 Plan what to do.

First, I find the fraction of money saved.
Then, I find the amount of money saved.

3 Work out the **Answer**.

$1 - \frac{2}{5} = \frac{3}{5}$

She saved $\frac{3}{5}$ of the money.

$\frac{3}{\cancel{5}_1} \times ₹\,\cancel{125}^{25} = 3 \times ₹\,25$
$= ₹\,75$

She saved ₹ 75.

4 Check
Did you answer the question?
Is your answer reasonable?

$\frac{3}{5} > \frac{1}{2}$

She saved more than $\frac{1}{2}$ of the amount of money.

$\frac{1}{2}$ of ₹ 125 is ₹ 62.50.

₹ 75 > ₹ 62.50

My answer is reasonable.

 ISBN 978-93-5103-033-1

Method 2

2 Plan what to do.

First, I find the amount spent.
Then, I find the amount of money saved.

3 Work out the **Answer**.

$$\frac{2}{\cancel{5}_1} \times \text{₹}\,\cancel{125}^{25} = 2 \times \text{₹}\,25$$
$$= \text{₹}\,50$$

She spent ₹ 50.

₹ 125 – ₹ 50 = ₹ 75

She saved ₹ 75.

4 Check
Did you answer the question?
Is your answer reasonable?

I compare the fraction of money saved with the fraction of money spent.

$$\frac{3}{5} > \frac{2}{5}$$

₹ 75 > ₹ 50

My answer is reasonable.

Method 3

2 Plan what to do.

I **draw a bar model** to help me solve the problem.

3 Work out the **Answer**.

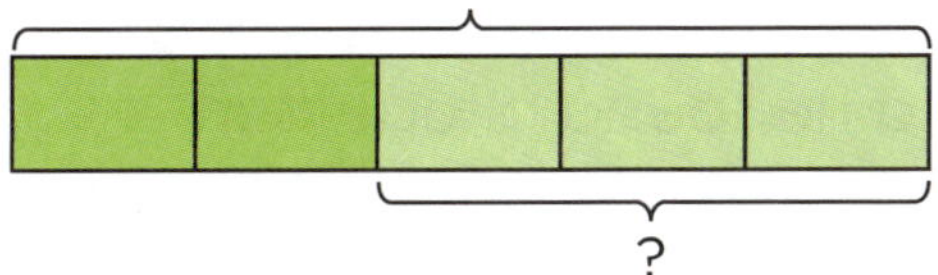

5 units → ₹ 125
1 unit → ₹ 125 ÷ 5 = ₹ 25
3 units → 3 × ₹ 25 = ₹ 75

She saved ₹ 75.

4 Check
Did you answer the question?
Is your answer correct?

2 units → 2 × ₹ 25 = ₹ 50
₹ 75 + ₹ 50 = ₹ 125

My answer is correct.

☑ **1. Understand**
☑ **2. Plan**
☑ **3. Answer**
☑ **4. Check**

 ISBN 978-93-5103-033-1

Let's Do

1. There are 96 children in a park. $\frac{5}{8}$ of them are girls. How many boys are there?

- ☐ 1. Understand
- ☐ 2. Plan
- ☐ 3. Answer
- ☐ 4. Check

2. A bakery had some rolls. $\frac{5}{8}$ of the rolls were sold. If 300 rolls were sold, how many rolls were there at first?

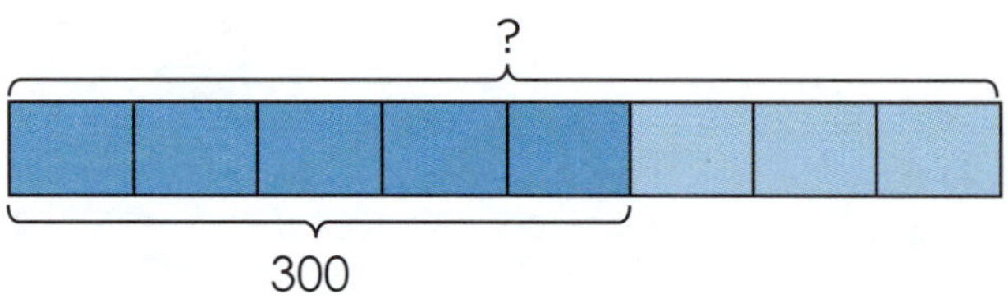

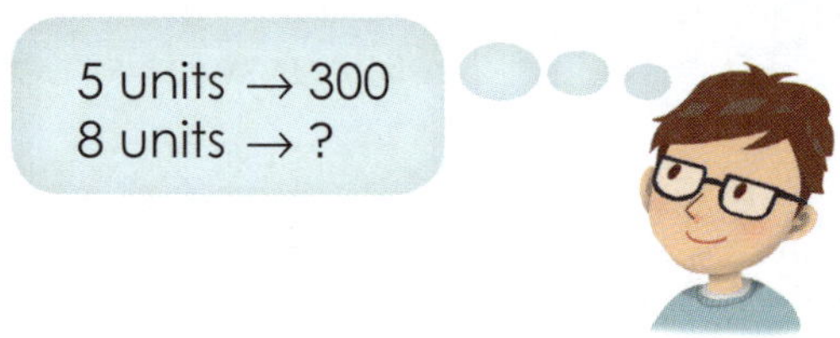

- ☐ 1. Understand
- ☐ 2. Plan
- ☐ 3. Answer
- ☐ 4. Check

Let's Learn

Alex had ₹ 80. He spent $\frac{1}{5}$ of the money on a notepad and $\frac{3}{10}$ on a pen. How much money did he spend altogether?

Picture It

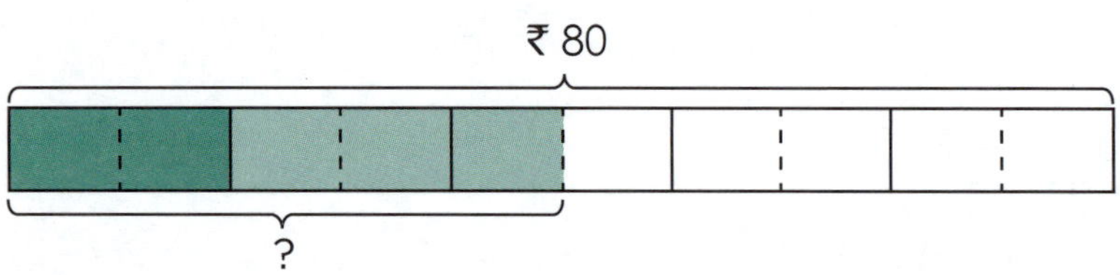

10 units → ₹ 80

1 unit → ₹ 80 ÷ 10

= ₹ 8

5 units → 5 × ₹ 8

= ₹ ☐

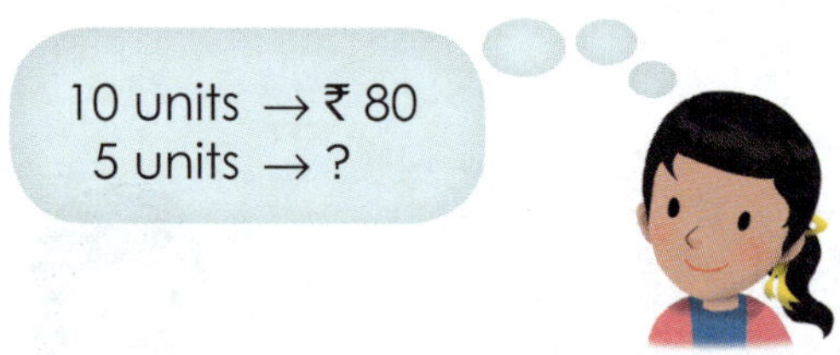

He spent ₹ ☐ altogether.

- ☑ 1. Understand
- ☑ 2. Plan
- ☑ 3. Answer
- ☑ 4. Check

 ISBN 978-93-5103-033-1

Let's Do

1. Ira had 192 marbles. $\frac{1}{4}$ of the marbles were blue and $\frac{3}{8}$ of the marbles were green. How many marbles were not blue or green?

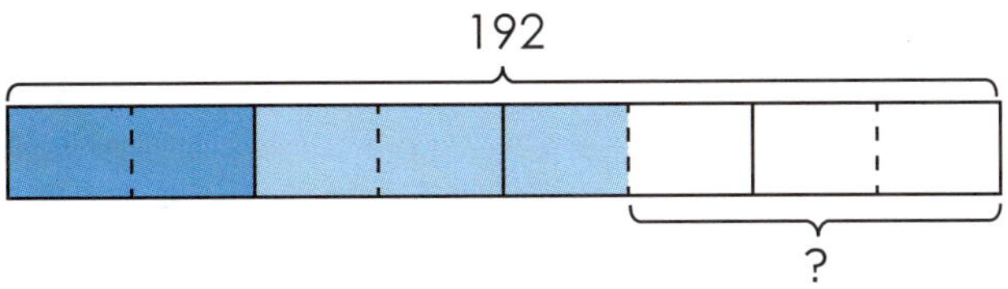

- [ ] 1. **Understand**
- [ ] 2. **Plan**
- [ ] 3. **Answer**
- [ ] 4. **Check**

8 units → 192

3 units → ______

P/B Chapter 3: Exercise 21, pages 82–85

Let's Learn

Mr. Shah had 360 eggs. He sold $\frac{1}{3}$ of them on Monday and $\frac{1}{4}$ of the remainder on Tuesday. How many eggs did he sell on Tuesday?

Method 1

$$1 - \frac{1}{3} = \frac{2}{3}$$

First, I find the fraction of eggs left on Monday.

He had $\frac{2}{3}$ of the eggs left on Monday.

$$\frac{2}{\cancel{3}_{1}} \times \cancel{360}^{120} = 2 \times 120$$
$$= 240$$

Then, I find the number of eggs left on Monday.

He had 240 eggs left on Monday.

$$\frac{1}{\cancel{4}_{1}} \times \cancel{240}^{60} = 1 \times 60$$
$$= 60$$

Lastly, I find the number of eggs sold on Tuesday.

He sold 60 eggs on Tuesday.

ISBN 978-93-5103-033-1

Method 2

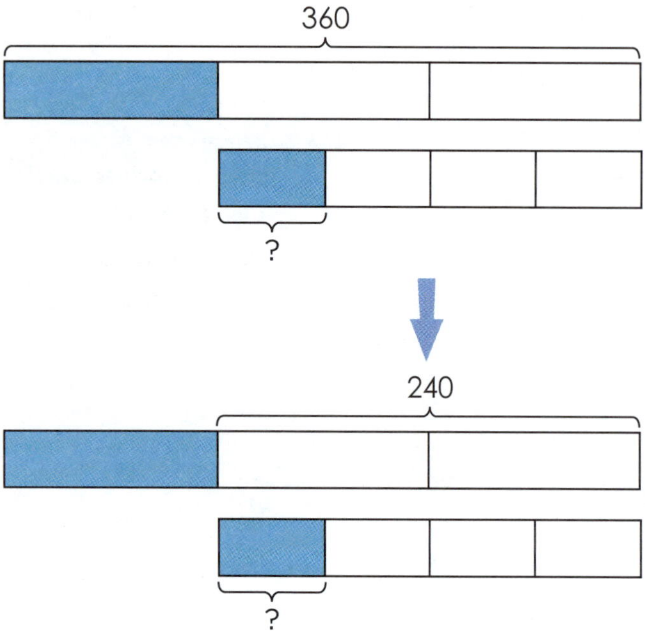

There are 4 equal parts in the remainder.

$$4 \text{ units} \rightarrow \frac{2}{{}_{1}\cancel{3}} \times \overset{120}{\cancel{360}}$$
$$= 2 \times 120$$
$$= 240$$
$$1 \text{ unit} \rightarrow 240 \div 4 = 60$$

He sold 60 eggs on Tuesday.

- ☑ 1. Understand
- ☑ 2. Plan
- ☑ 3. Answer
- ☑ 4. Check

Let's Do

1. Mrs. Singh made 300 samosas. She sold $\frac{3}{4}$ of them and gave $\frac{1}{3}$ of the remainder to her neighbour. How many samosas did she have left?

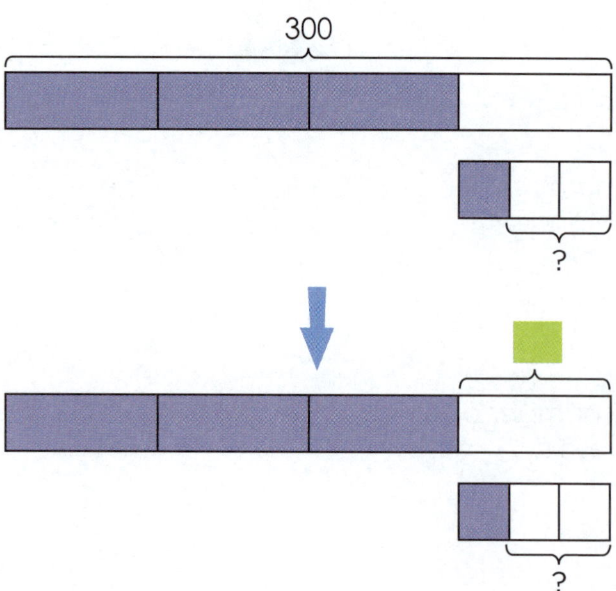

4 units → 300
1 unit → 300 ÷ 4 = ______

- ☐ 1. Understand
- ☐ 2. Plan
- ☐ 3. Answer
- ☐ 4. Check

 ISBN 978-93-5103-033-1

2. Mr. Manny gave $\frac{2}{5}$ of his money to his wife and spent $\frac{1}{2}$ of the remainder. If he had ₹ 300 left, how much money did he have at first?

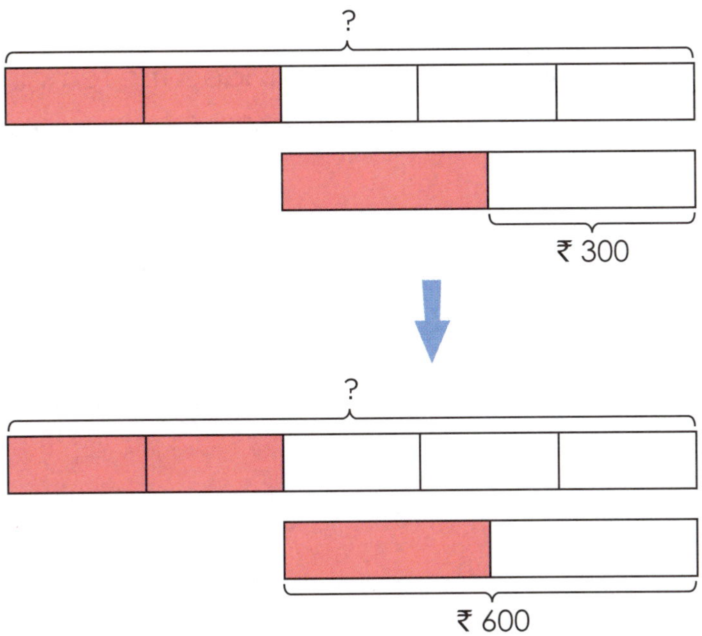

- ☐ 1. Understand
- ☐ 2. Plan
- ☐ 3. Answer
- ☐ 4. Check

P/B Chapter 3: Exercise 22, pages 86–89

Practice 8

Solve the word problems. Show your work clearly.

1. There are 42 red and green apples in a box. $\frac{3}{7}$ of the apples are red. How many green apples are there?

2. After spending $\frac{2}{5}$ of her money on a toy aeroplane, Sita had ₹ 42 left. How much money did she have at first?

3. Mr. Satish had ₹ 400. He spent $\frac{2}{5}$ of it on a bouquet of flowers and $\frac{1}{4}$ of the remainder on a card. How much money did he have left?

4. A cafe sold 210 sandwiches. $\frac{2}{3}$ of the sandwiches were sold in the morning, $\frac{1}{6}$ of them in the afternoon and the remainder in the evening. How many sandwiches were sold in the evening?

 ISBN 978-93-5103-033-1

5. Anil bought some stamps. He used $\frac{1}{2}$ of them to send some postcards and gave $\frac{1}{4}$ of the remainder to his sister. He had 9 stamps left. How many stamps did he buy?

6. Mr. Lal gave $\frac{1}{4}$ of a sum of money to his wife. Then, he divided the remainder equally between his 4 children. If each child received ₹ 600, find the sum of money he had at first.

7. Pearl read 10 pages of a book on Monday. She read $\frac{1}{3}$ of the remainder on Tuesday. If she still had 24 pages to read, how many pages were there in the book?

Mind stretcher

Let's Learn

$$\frac{C}{D} \div \frac{A}{B} = \frac{15}{14}$$

A, B, C and D represent different whole numbers. Each number is greater than 1 but smaller than 10. The only factors of each number are 1 and the number itself. A < B and C < D.
Find a possible group of whole numbers that represent the letters, A, B, C and D.

1 Understand the problem.

How are A, B, C and D related to one another?

2 Plan what to do.

First, I list the possible numbers.
Then, I use **guess and check** to solve the problem.

 ISBN 978-93-5103-033-1

3 Work out the **Answer**.

Each number is greater than 1 but smaller than 10.
The numbers can be 2, 3, 4, 5, 6, 7, 8, 9.

The only factors of each number are 1 and the number itself.
The numbers 4, 6, 8 and 9 have more than two factors each.

So, the possible numbers are 2, 3, 5 and 7.

Since $A < B$, I guess $A = 2$ and $B = 7$.
$C < D$, $C = 3$ and $D = 5$.

$$\frac{C}{D} \div \frac{A}{B} = \frac{3}{5} \div \frac{2}{7}$$
$$= \frac{3}{5} \times \frac{7}{2}$$
$$= \frac{21}{10}$$

4 **Check**
Did you answer the question?
Is your answer correct?

$\frac{C}{D} \div \frac{A}{B}$ is not equal to $\frac{15}{14}$.

My guess is incorrect. I have to guess again.

3 Work out the **Answer**.

Since $A < B$, I guess $A = 2$ and $B = 5$.
$C < D$, $C = 3$ and $D = 7$.

$$\frac{C}{D} \div \frac{A}{B} = \frac{3}{7} \div \frac{2}{5}$$
$$= \frac{3}{7} \times \frac{5}{2}$$
$$= \frac{15}{14}$$

So, $A = 2$, $B = 5$, $C = 3$ and $D = 7$.

4 **Check**
Did you answer the question?
Is your answer correct?

$A = 2$, $B = 5$, $C = 3$ and $D = 7$.

Each number is greater than 1 but smaller than 10.

$A < B \quad 2 < 5$
$C < D \quad 3 < 7$

My answer is correct.

☑ **1. Understand**
☑ **2. Plan**
☑ **3. Answer**
☑ **4. Check**

 ISBN 978-93-5103-033-1

4 Angles

Lesson 1 Angle Properties

Sum of angle measures on a line

Let's Learn

a) $\angle AOB$ and $\angle BOC$ are **angles on a line**.
We write measures of $\angle AOB$ and $\angle BOC$ as $m\angle AOB$ and $m\angle BOC$.

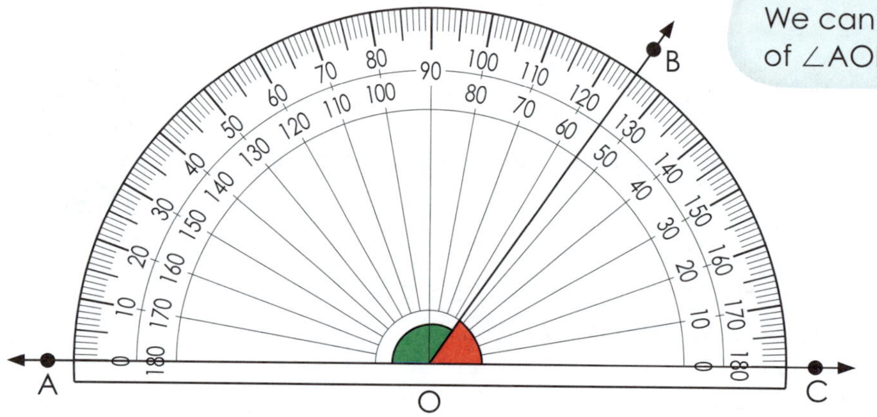

We can also write measure of $\angle AOB$ as $m\angle AOB$.

$m\angle AOB + m\angle BOC = 180°$

b) $\angle p$, $\angle q$ and $\angle r$ are angles on Line AOB.
Use a protractor to measure $\angle p$, $\angle q$ and $\angle r$.

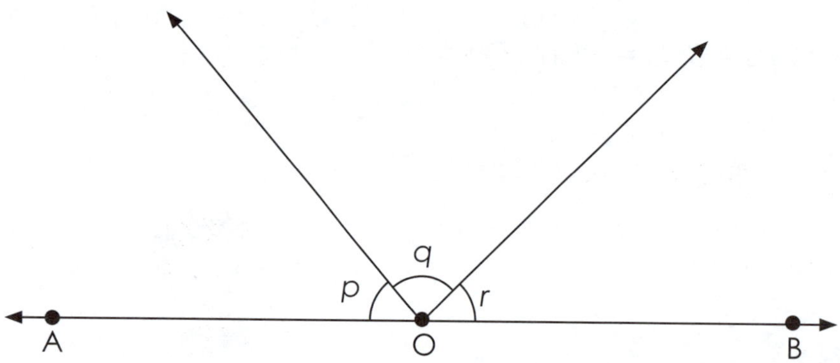

$m\angle p = 50°$

$m\angle q =$ ____

$m\angle r =$ ____

$m\angle p + m\angle q + m\angle r =$ ____

AOB is a line.

The sum of the angle measures on a line is 180°.

 ISBN 978-93-5103-033-1

Let's Do

1. Use a protractor to find the measures of the angles.

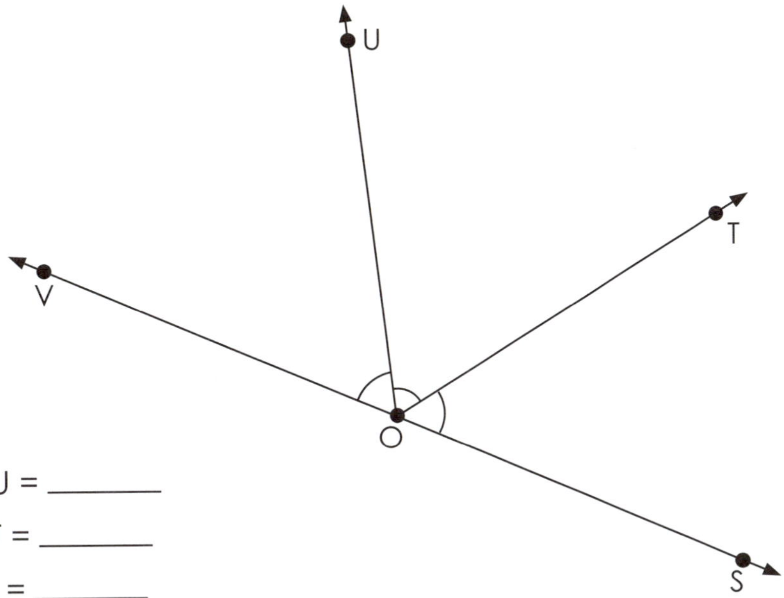

m∠VOU = ______

m∠UOT = ______

m∠TOS = ______

m∠VOU + m∠UOT + m∠TOS = ______ + ______ + ______

= ______

Are these angles on a line? Explain why.

______

Sum of angle measures at a point

Let's Learn

OA, OB and OC are rays that meet at Point O.
∠*x*, ∠*y* and ∠*z* are **angles at a point**.

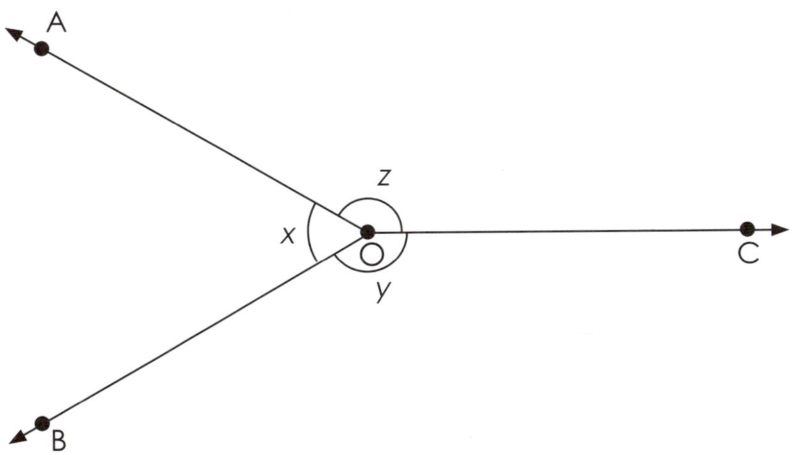

Use a protractor to measure ∠*x*, ∠*y* and ∠*z*.

m∠*x* = 60°
m∠*y* = ▢
m∠*z* = ▢

m∠*x* + m∠*y* + m∠*z* = ▢

The sum of the angle measures at a point is 360°.

ISBN 978-93-5103-033-1

Let's Do

1. Use a protractor to find the measures of the angles.

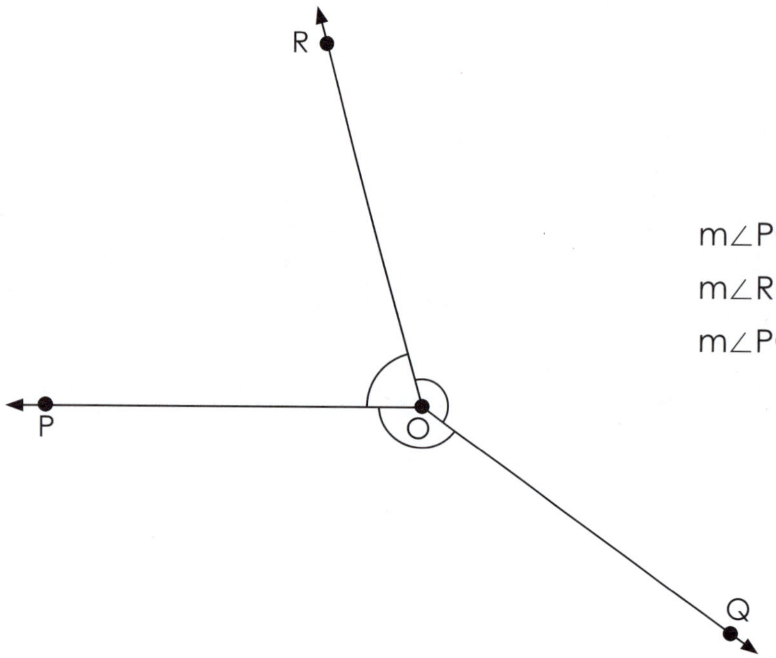

m∠POR = ______

m∠ROQ = ______

m∠POQ = ______

m∠POR + m∠ROQ + m∠POQ = ______ + ______ + ______

= ______

Are these angles at a point? Explain why.

____

Vertically opposite angles

Let's Learn

WX and YZ are two lines that cross each other to form ∠*a*, ∠*b*, ∠*c* and ∠*d*.

∠*a* and ∠*c* are **vertically opposite angles**.
∠*b* and ∠*d* are also vertically opposite angles.

Maths Lab

Picture It

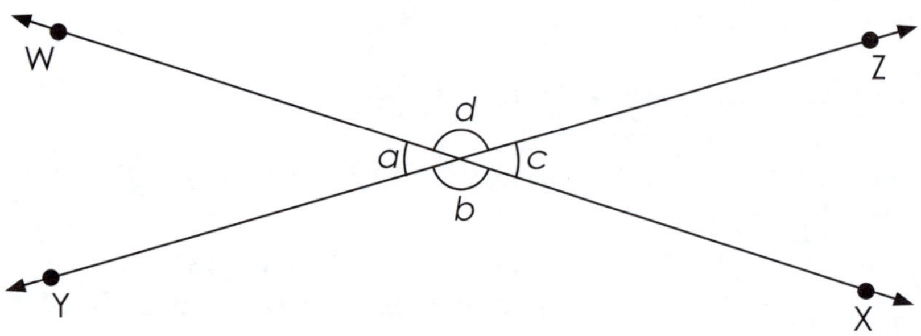

 ISBN 978-93-5103-033-1

Use a protractor to measure ∠a, ∠b, ∠c and ∠d.

m∠a = 34°   m∠c = ____

m∠a = m∠ ____

m∠b = ____   m∠d = ____

m∠ ____ = m∠ ____

Vertically opposite angles have equal measures.

Let's Do

1. The figure shows the four angles formed when two lines cross. Use a protractor to find the measures of the angles.

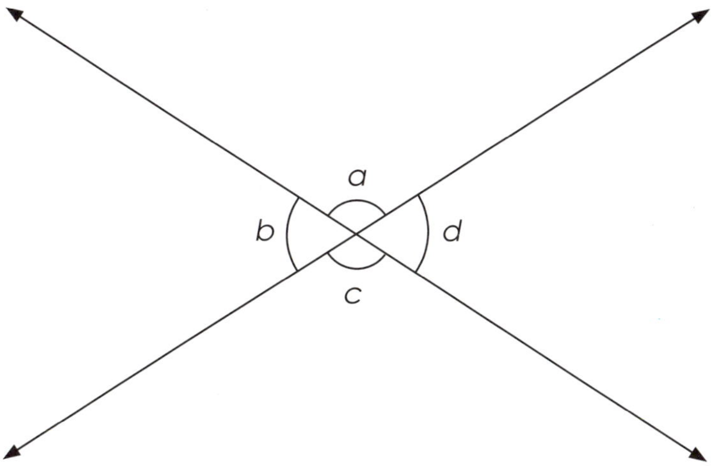

m∠a = ______

m∠b = ______

m∠c = ______

m∠d = ______

Which are the two pairs of vertically opposite angles?

____

Chapter 4: Exercise 1, pages 90–92

 ISBN 978-93-5103-033-1

Practice 1

1. What is the sum of the measures of angles

   a) on a line? b) at a point?

2. What is the sum of the marked angle measures in each figure?

   a) AB is a line.

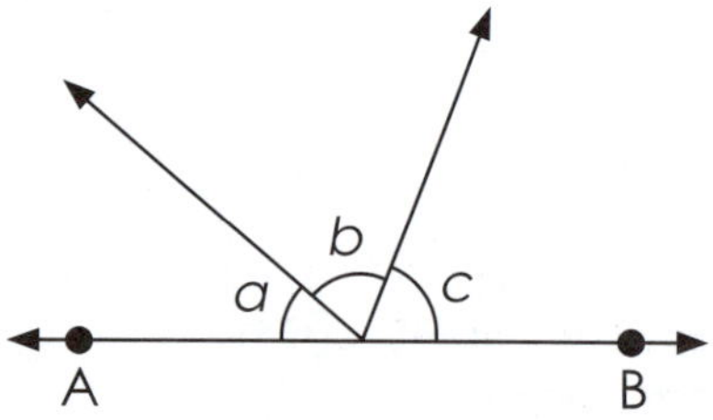

$m\angle a + m\angle b + m\angle c =$ _____

   b)

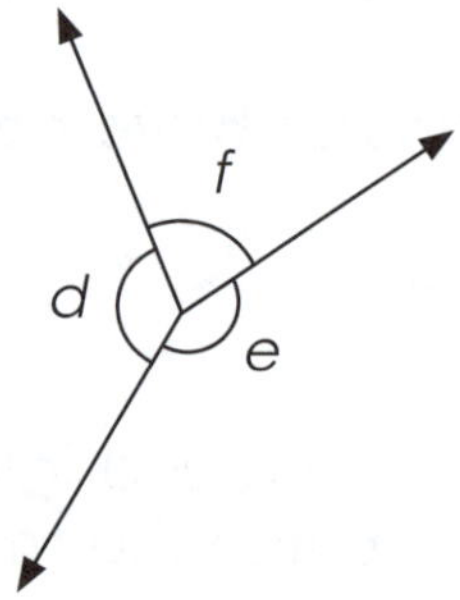

$m\angle d + m\angle e + m\angle f =$ _____

3. COD and EOF are lines.
   Name the pairs of vertically opposite angles.

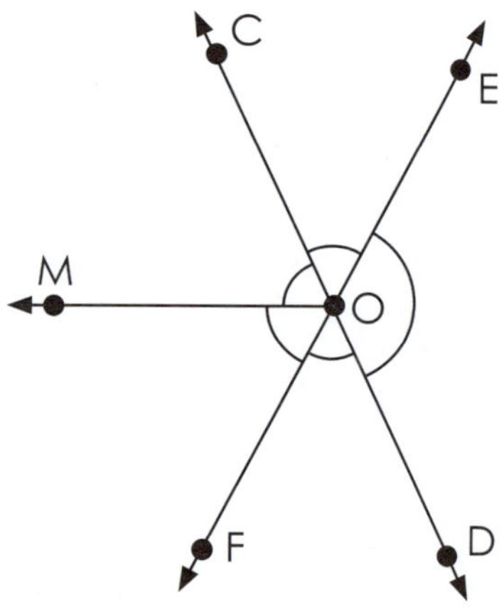

Lesson 2 Finding Unknown Measures of Angles

Finding unknown measures of angles

Let's Learn

a) AOB is a line. Find $m\angle AOC$.

Picture It

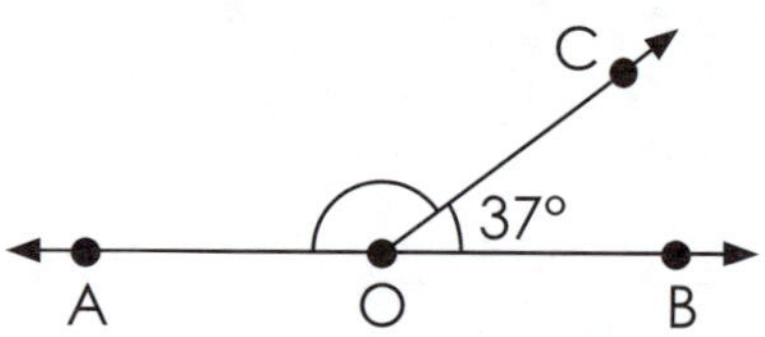

$m\angle AOC = 180° - 37°$
$= 143°$

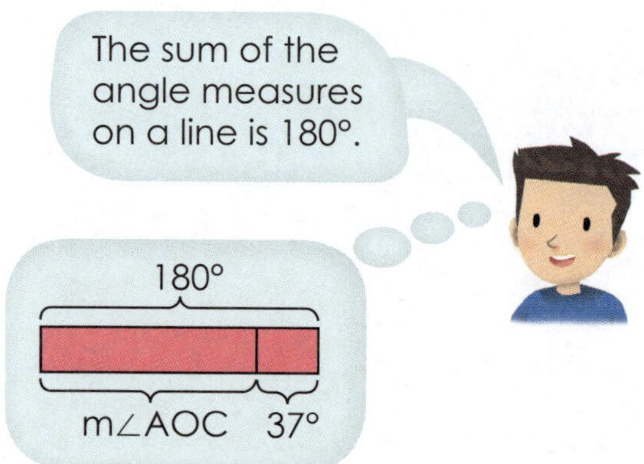

 ISBN 978-93-5103-033-1

b) Find m∠DOE.

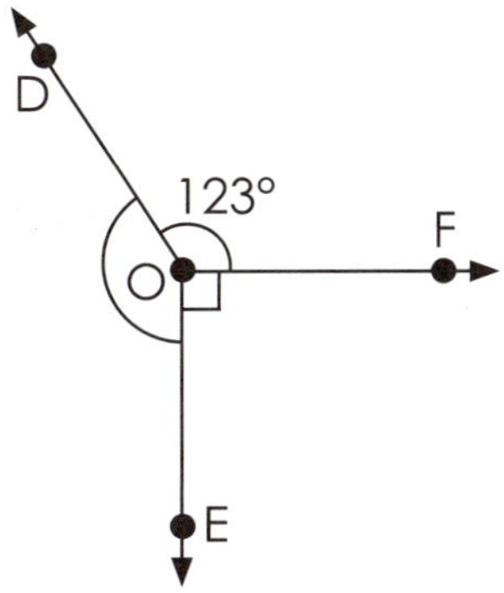

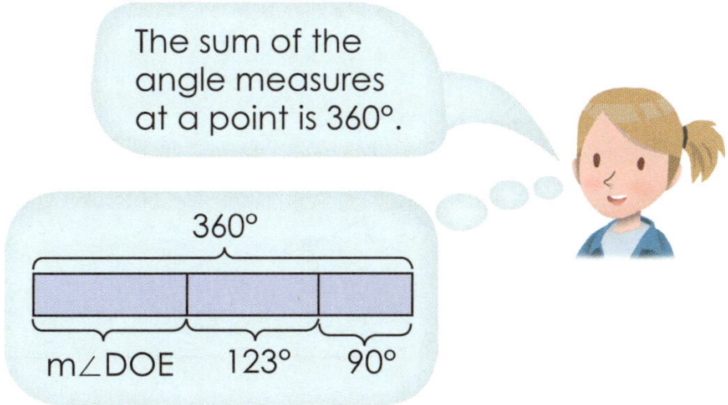

m∠DOE = 360° – 123° – 90°

= ____

c) GOH and IOJ are lines. Find m∠JOH.

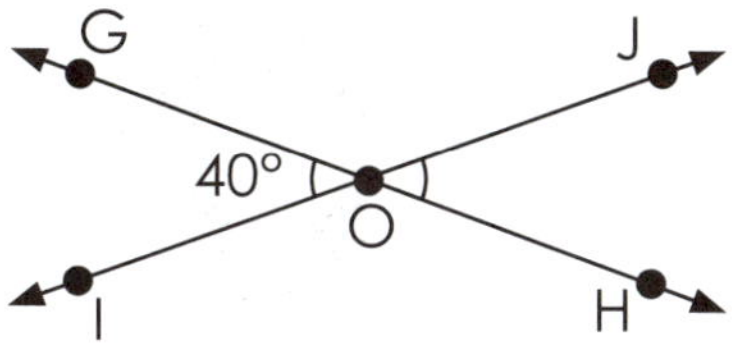

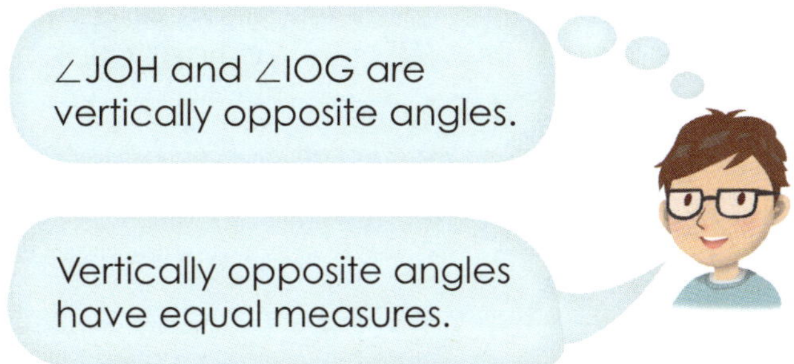

m∠JOH = ____

Let's Do

The figures in this section are not drawn to scale.

1. In the figure, AOB is a line. Find the measure of ∠DOC.

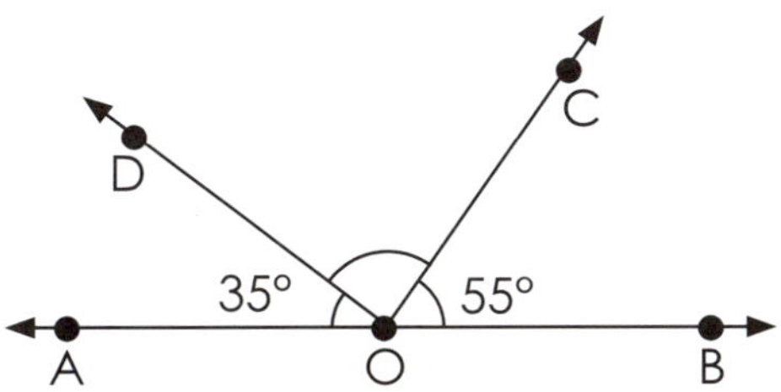

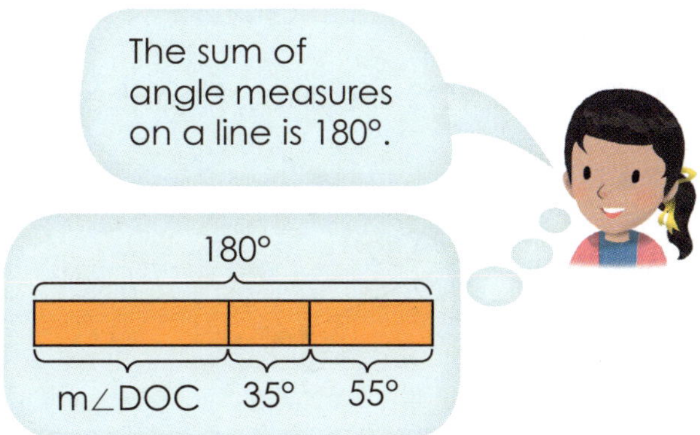

m∠DOC = 180° – ________ – ________

= ________

 ISBN 978-93-5103-033-1

2. Find the measure of ∠GOF.

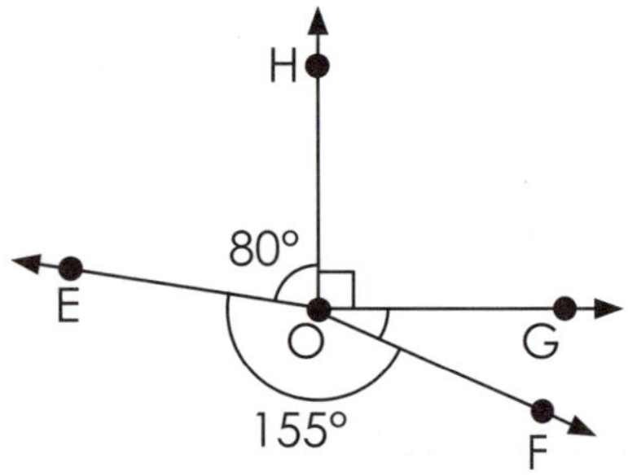

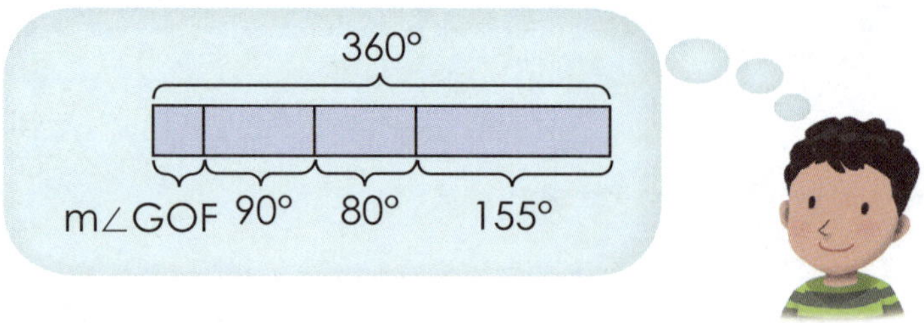

m∠GOF = 360° – _______ – _______ – _______

= _______

3. POQ and ROS are lines. Find the measure of ∠QOS.

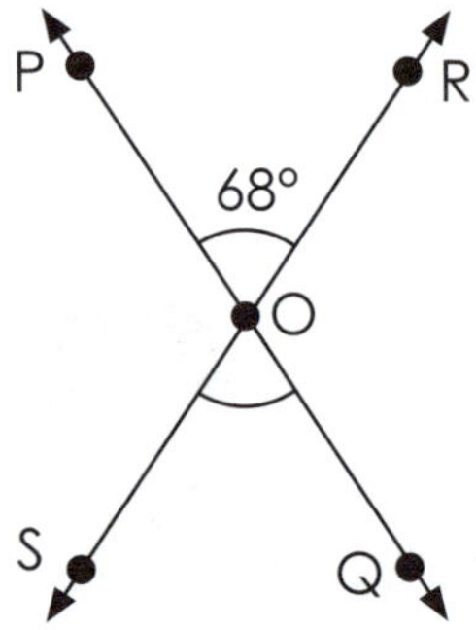

∠POR and ∠_____ are vertically opposite angles.

m∠QOS = _______

P/B Chapter 4: Exercise 2, pages 93–95

Let's Learn

POQ and ROS are lines. Find the measures of ∠QOR and ∠POS.

Picture It

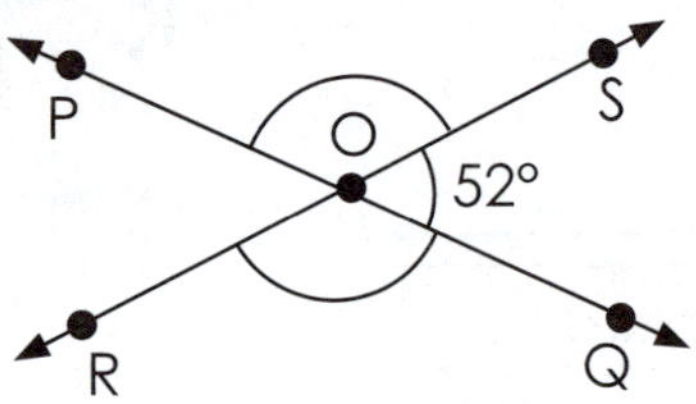

m∠QOR = 180° – 52°
= 128°
m∠POS = m∠QOR
= ▇

The sum of the angle measures on a line is 180°.

Vertically opposite angles have equal measures.

 ISBN 978-93-5103-033-1

Let's Do

1. The figure is not drawn to scale. It shows four angles formed by two lines. If m∠a = 46°, find m∠b, m∠c and m∠d.

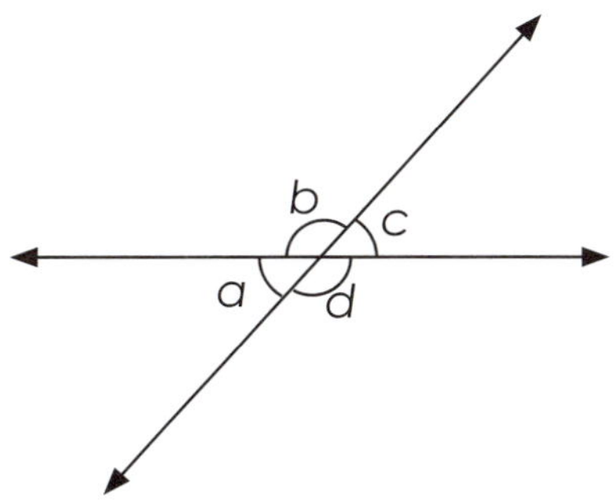

m∠b = _______ – _______

= _______

m∠c = m∠a

= _______

m∠d = m∠b

= _______

P/B Chapter 4: Exercise 3, pages 96–97

Practice 2

In this practice, the figures are not drawn to scale.

1. AB and CD are lines. Find the unknown angle measures.

a)

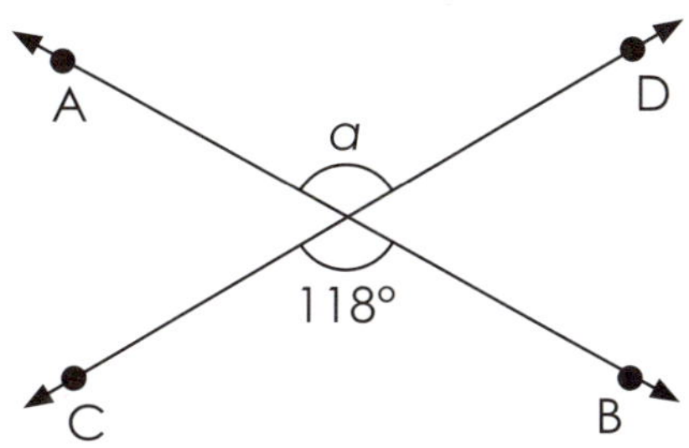

b)

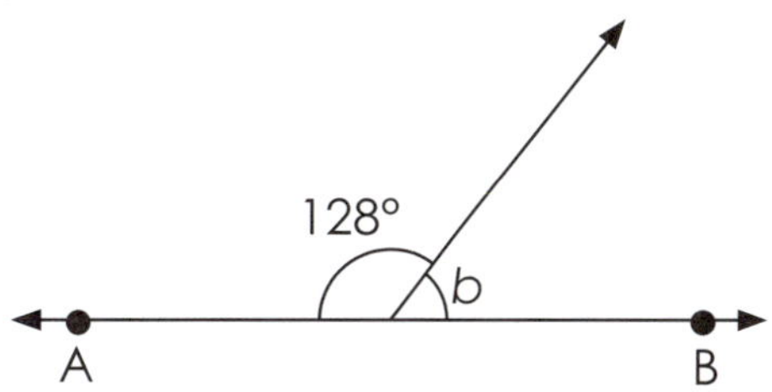

c)

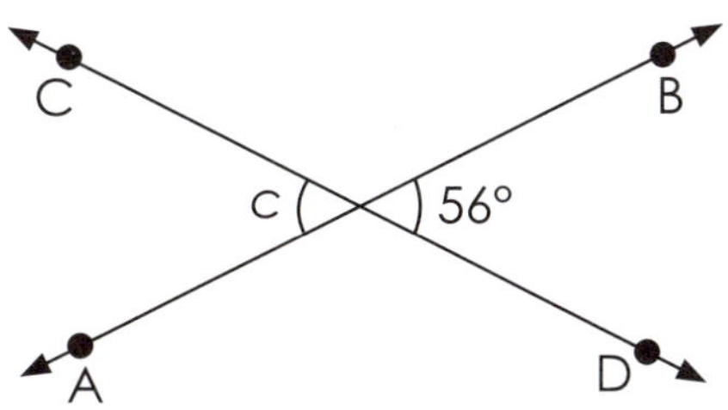

d)

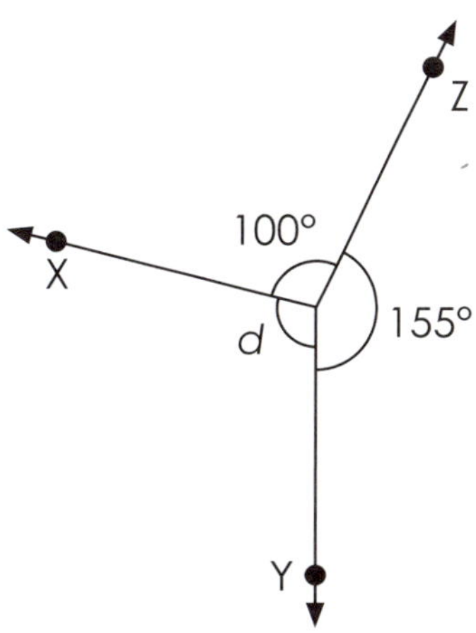

 ISBN 978-93-5103-033-1

e)

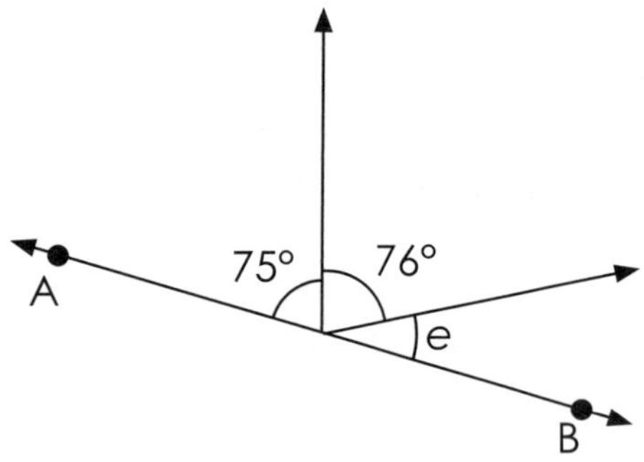

f)

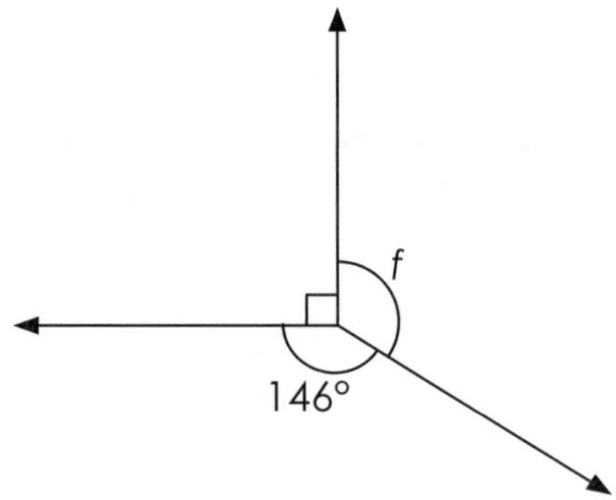

2. POQ and ROS are lines. Find the measure of ∠ROQ.

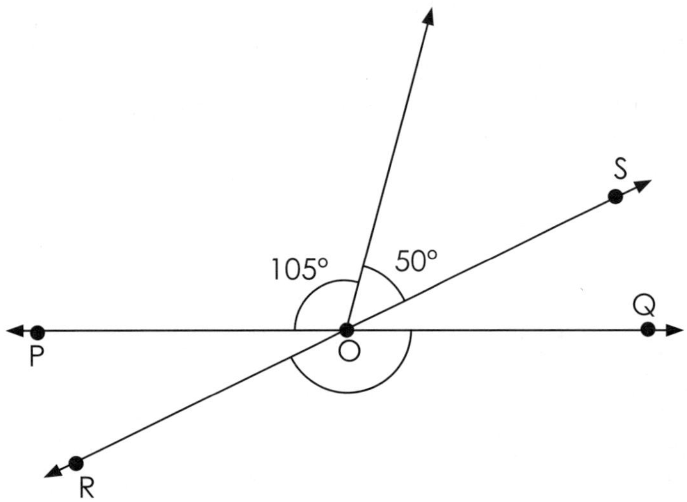

3. AOB and COD are lines. Find the measures of ∠COA and ∠DOB.

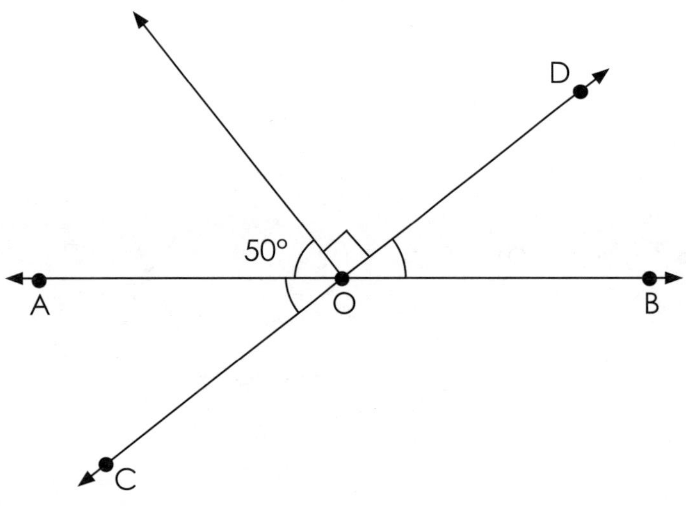

 ISBN 978-93-5103-033-1

4. PQ is a line. The measures of $\angle r$ and $\angle s$ are equal. Find the measure of $\angle r$.

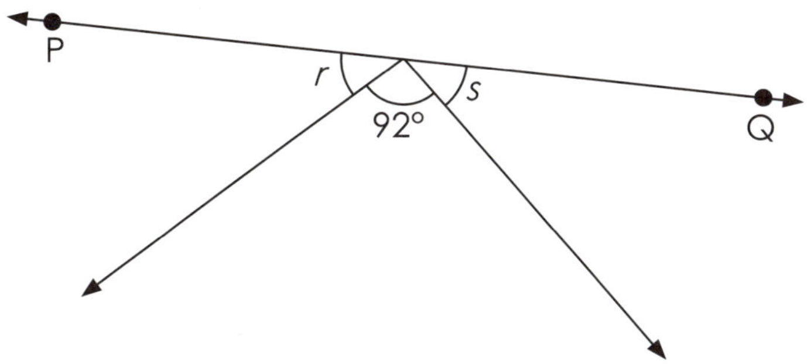

Lesson 3 Problem Solving

Mind stretcher

Let's Learn

In the figure, AB, CD, EF and GH are lines.
The measure of $\angle a$ is equal to the measure of $\angle c$.
What is the fewest number of angle measures you need to know to find every angle measure in the figure?

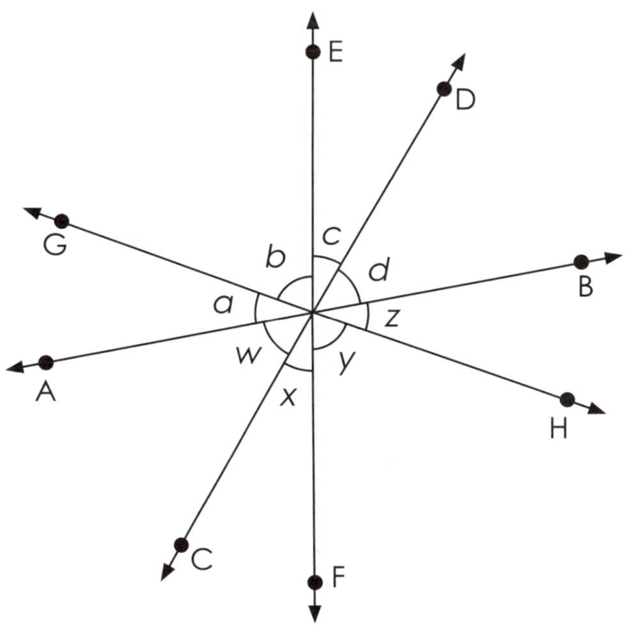

1 Understand the problem.

How many angles are there?
How many lines are there?
Which angle measures are equal?
What do I have to find?

 ISBN 978-93-5103-033-1

2 Plan
what to do.

I **make a supposition** about the number of angle measures I need to know to find the other angle measures.

3 Work out the **Answer**.

Supposition 1: I know the measure of $\angle a$.

$m\angle c = m\angle a$

I can use the property of vertically opposite angles to find $m\angle z$ and $m\angle x$.

I cannot find the measures of $\angle b$, $\angle d$, $\angle w$ and $\angle y$.

Supposition 2: I also know the measure of $\angle b$.

$\angle b$ and $\angle y$ are vertically opposite angles.
So, $m\angle y = m\angle b$.

I can use the property of angles on a line to find $m\angle d$ and $m\angle w$.

If I know 2 angle measures, I can find every angle measure in the figure.

4 Check
Did you answer the question?
Is your answer correct?

Suppose $m\angle a = 40°$ and $m\angle b = 60°$.

$m\angle c = 40°$
$m\angle z = 40°$
$m\angle x = 40°$
$m\angle y = 60°$
$m\angle d = 180° - 40° - 60° - 40°$
$= 40°$
$m\angle w = 40°$

When I know 2 angle measures, I can find every angle measure in the figure.
My answer is correct.

☑ 1. Understand
☑ 2. Plan
☑ 3. Answer
☑ 4. Check

 ISBN 978-93-5103-033-1

5 Decimals

Lesson 1 Approximation

Rounding decimals to 2 decimal places

Let's Learn

a) The weight of the watermelon is 4.728 kilograms.

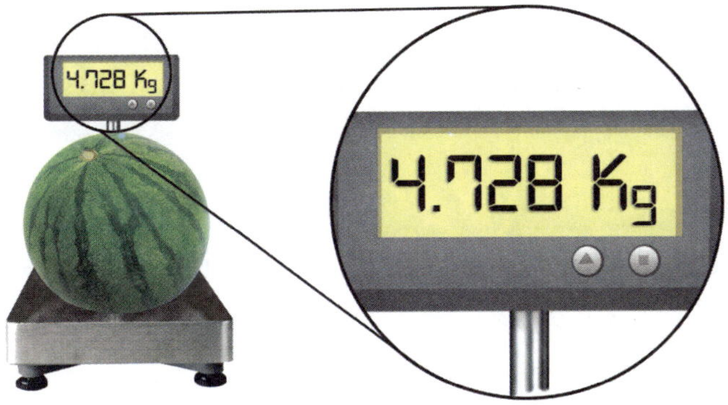

Picture It

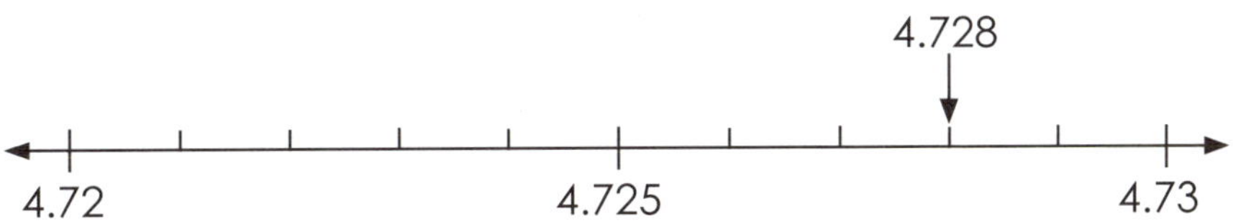

4.728 is more than halfway between 4.72 and 4.73.
4.728 is nearer to 4.73 than to 4.72.

4.728 is 4.73 when rounded to 2 decimal places.
$4.728 \approx 4.73$

The weight of the watermelon is about 4.73 kilograms.

b) Round 4.132 to 2 decimal places.

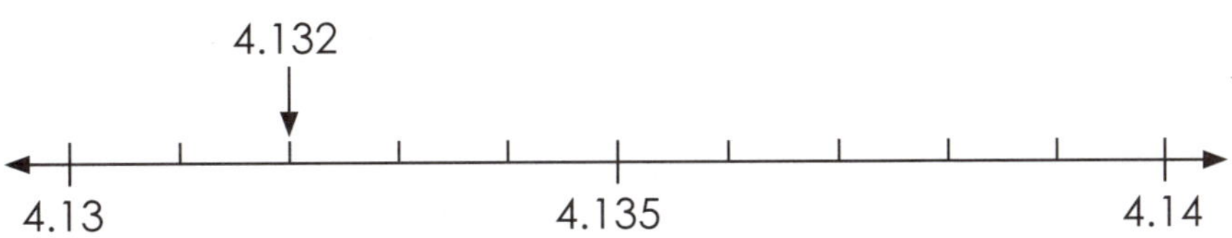

4.132 is less than halfway between 4.13 and 4.14.
4.132 is nearer to 4.13 than to 4.14.

4.132 is 4.13 when rounded to 2 decimal places.
$4.132 \approx 4.13$

 ISBN 978-93-5103-033-1

c) Round 10.805 to 2 decimal places.

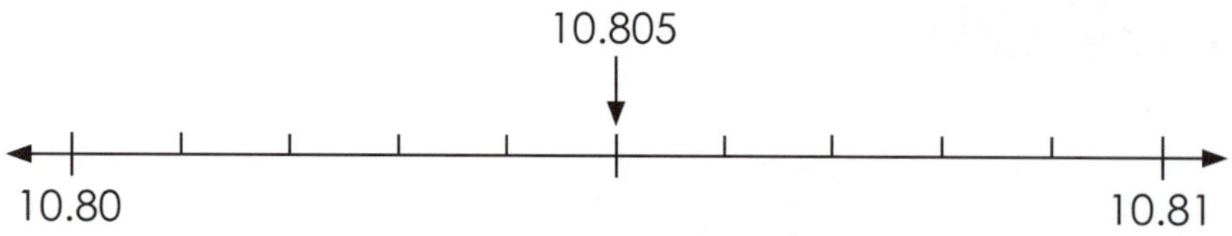

10.805 is halfway between 10.80 and 10.81.

10.805 is 10.81 when rounded to 2 decimal places.
$10.805 \approx 10.81$

To round a number to 2 decimal places, look at the digit in the thousandths place. If it is 5 or greater than 5, we round up. If it is smaller than 5, we round down.

Let's Do

1. Round each decimal to 2 decimal places.

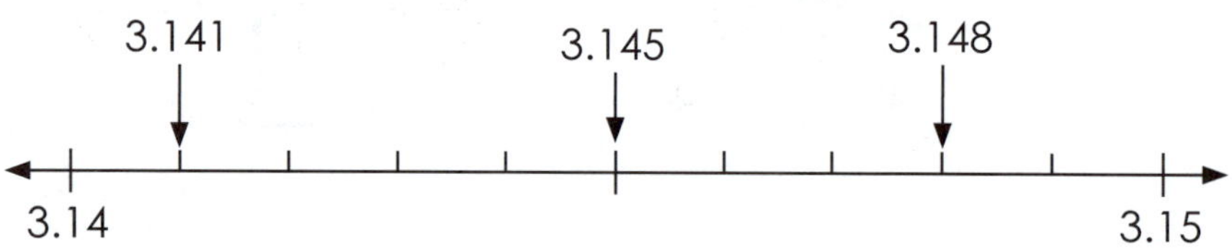

a) $3.148 \approx$ ______

b) $3.141 \approx$ ______

c) $3.145 \approx$ ______

2. Round 6.997 to 2 decimal places.

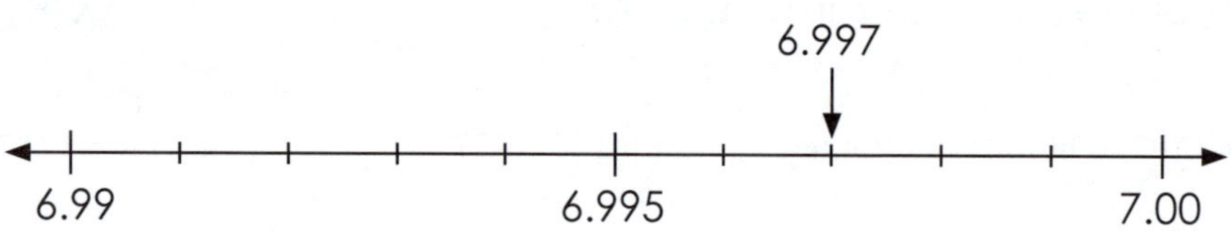

6.997 is more than halfway between ______ and ______.

6.997 is nearer to ______ than to ______.

6.997 is ______ when rounded to 2 decimal places.

$6.997 \approx$ ______

Chapter 5: Exercise 1, page 98

 ISBN 978-93-5103-033-1

Rounding quotients to 2 decimal places

Let's Learn

Find the value of $24.65 \div 8$ correct to 2 decimal places.

```
      3.0 8 1 ≈ 3.08
8 ) 2 4.6 5 0
    2 4
    -------
        6
        0
      -----
        6 5
        6 4
      -------
          1 0
            8
         -----
            2
```

$24.65 \div 8 \approx$ ☐

Let's Do

1. Find the value of each of the following correct to 2 decimal places.

   a) $0.77 \div 9 \approx$ ______ b) $9.65 \div 8 \approx$ ______ c) $27.69 \div 4 \approx$ ______

   $9 \overline{)\,0.7\,7}$ $8 \overline{)\,9.6\,5}$ $4 \overline{)\,2\,7.6\,9}$

P/B Chapter 5: Exercise 2, page 99

Expressing mixed numbers as decimals correct to 2 decimal places

Let's Learn

Express $4\frac{2}{3}$ as a decimal correct to 2 decimal places.

$4\frac{2}{3} = 4 + \frac{2}{3}$

≈ 4.67

$\frac{2}{3} = 2 \div 3$

≈ 0.67

```
    0.6 6 6 ≈ 0.67
3 ) 2.0 0 0
    1 8
    -------
      2 0
      1 8
      -----
        2 0
        1 8
        ---
          2
```

 ISBN 978-93-5103-033-1

Let's Do

1. Express each mixed number as a decimal correct to 2 decimal places.

a) $5\frac{7}{9} \approx$ ______   b) $4\frac{5}{7} \approx$ ______   c) $8\frac{3}{8} \approx$ ______

$9\overline{)7}$ $7\overline{)5}$ $8\overline{)3}$

P/B Chapter 5: Exercise 3, page 100

Practice 1

1. Round each decimal to 2 decimal places.

a) 0.119   b) 7.508

c) 40.082   d) 81.143

e) 0.725   f) 3.123

g) 59.005   h) 18.607

2. Round each measure to 2 decimal places.

a) 6.265 km   b) 4.083 kg

c) 0.189 L   d) 20.245 L

3. Find the value of each of the following correct to 2 decimal places.

a) $0.66 \div 9$ b) $1.8 \div 7$

c) $2.74 \div 6$ d) $62.7 \div 7$

e) $41.51 \div 6$ f) $20.93 \div 3$

4. Express each mixed number as a decimal correct to 2 decimal places.

a) $1\frac{1}{3}$ b) $2\frac{4}{7}$

c) $2\frac{5}{9}$ d) $5\frac{2}{3}$

 ISBN 978-93-5103-033-1

Lesson 2 Multiplication by Tens, Hundreds or Thousands

Multiplying tenths, hundredths or thousandths by 10

Let's Learn

Maths Lab

Picture It

a) 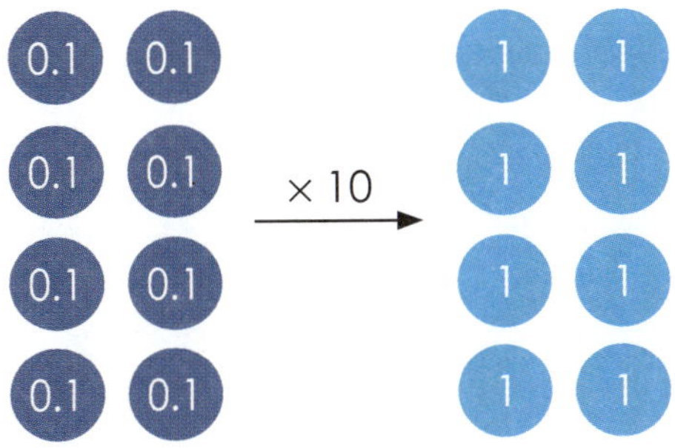

8 tenths 8 ones

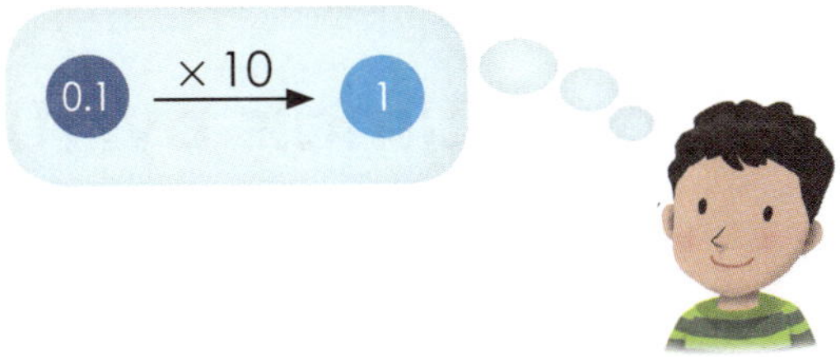

$0.8 \times 10 = 8$

b) 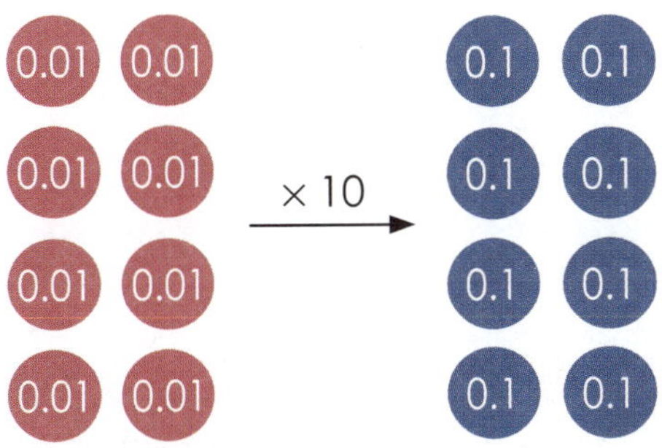

8 hundredths 8 tenths

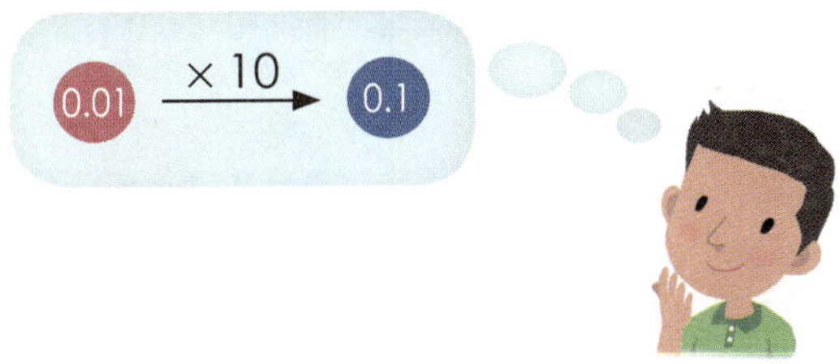

$0.08 \times 10 = 0.8$

c) 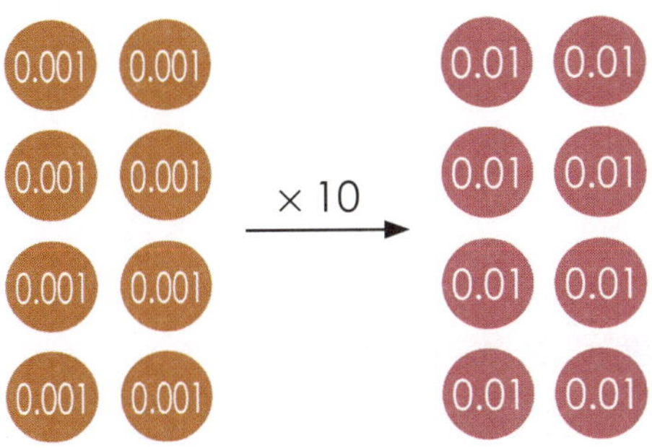

8 thousandths 8 hundredths

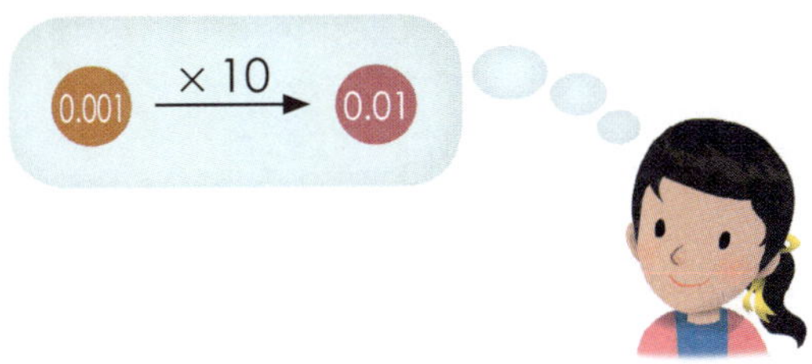

$0.008 \times 10 = 0.08$

 ISBN 978-93-5103-033-1

Let's Do

1. Multiply.

   a) $0.6 \times 10 =$ ______

      $0.06 \times 10 =$ ______

      $0.006 \times 10 =$ ______

   b) $0.9 \times 10 =$ ______

      $0.09 \times 10 =$ ______

      $0.009 \times 10 =$ ______

Multiplying decimals by 10

Let's Learn

a) Multiply 0.035 by 10.

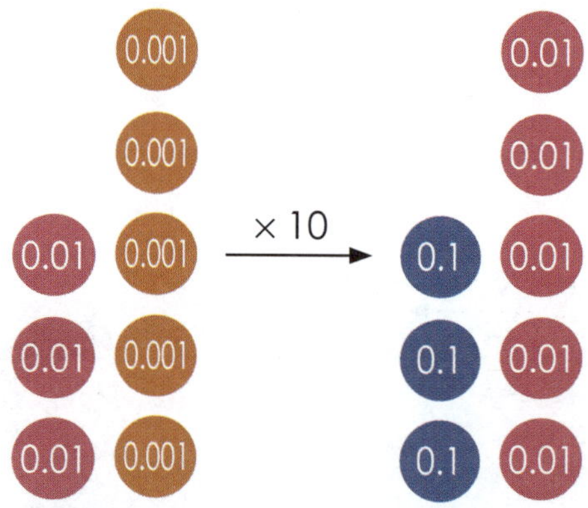

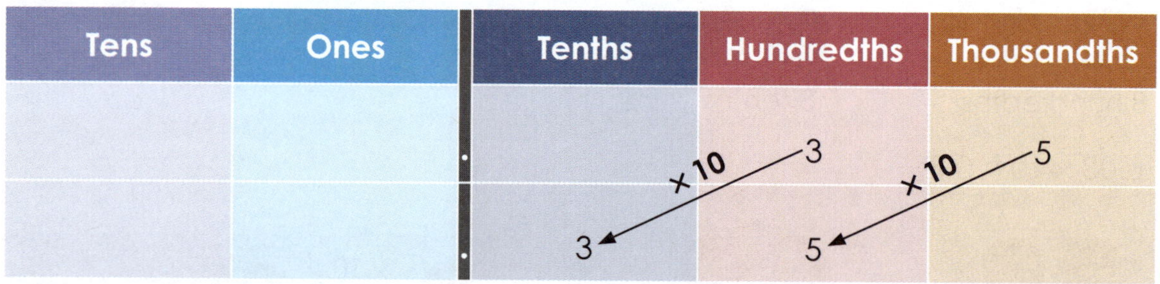

$0.035 \times 10 = 0.35$

b) Multiply 3.42 by 10.

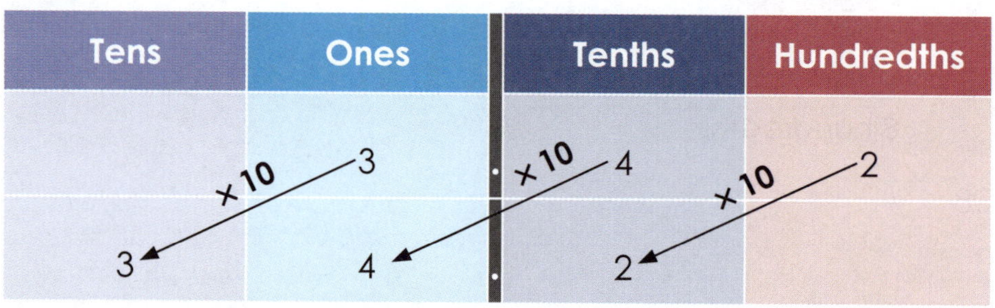

$3.42 \times 10 =$ ▢

When multiplying a decimal by 10, move the decimal point 1 place to the right.

 ISBN 978-93-5103-033-1

Let's Do

1. Multiply.
   a) $0.12 \times 10 =$ ______
   b) $0.068 \times 10 =$ ______
   c) $0.345 \times 10 =$ ______

Multiplying decimals by tens

Let's Learn

a) Multiply 0.006 by 30.

$$0.006 \times 30 = 0.006 \times 3 \times 10$$
$$= 0.018 \times 10$$
$$= \square$$

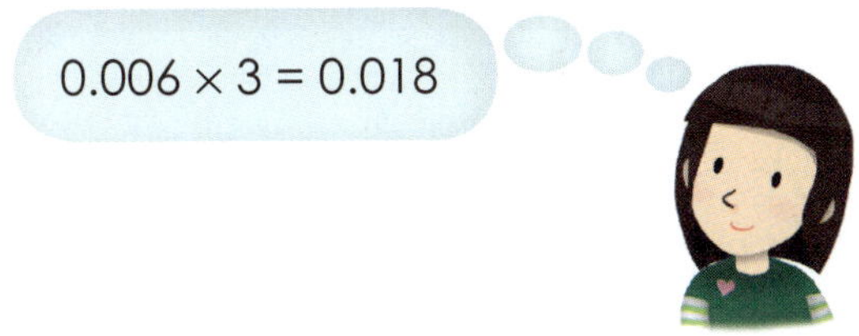

b) Multiply 0.53 by 40.

$$0.53 \times 40 = 0.53 \times 4 \times 10$$
$$= 2.12 \times 10$$
$$= \square$$

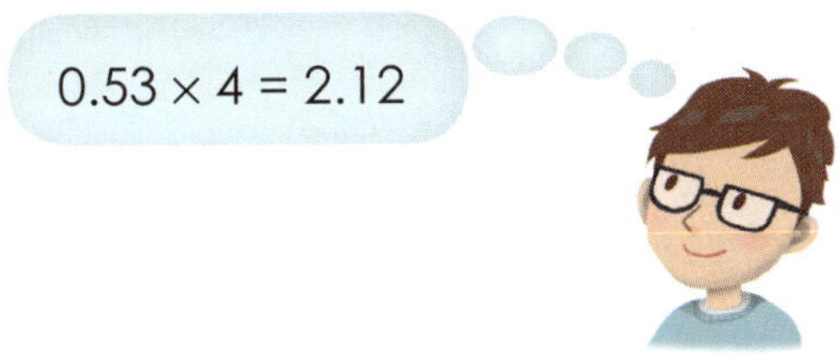

Let's Do

1. Multiply.
   a) $0.9 \times 50 = 0.9 \times 5 \times 10$
      $=$ ______ $\times 10$
      $=$ ______
   b) $0.08 \times 40 = 0.08 \times$ ______ $\times$ ______
      $=$ ______ $\times$ ______
      $=$ ______
   c) $6.81 \times 70 = 6.81 \times$ ______ $\times$ ______
      $=$ ______ $\times$ ______
      $=$ ______

P/B Chapter 5: Exercise 4, page 101

 ISBN 978-93-5103-033-1

Multiplying decimals by 100

Let's Learn

a) Multiply 0.007×100.

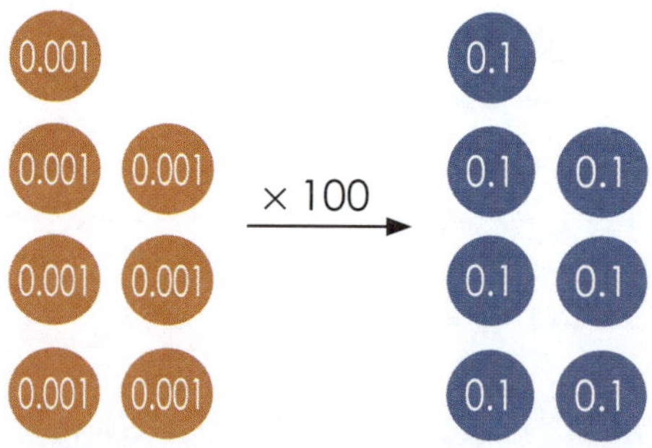

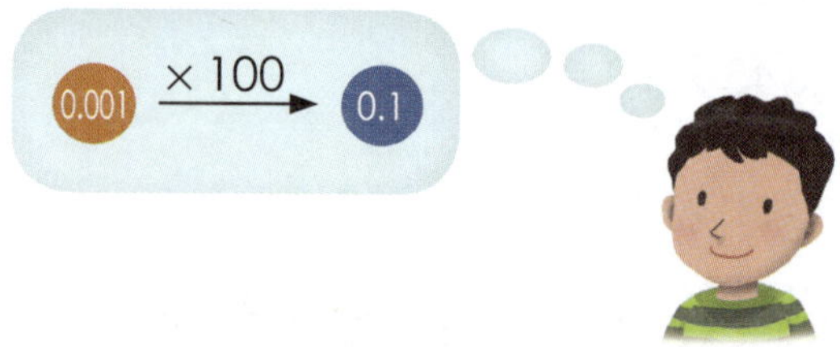

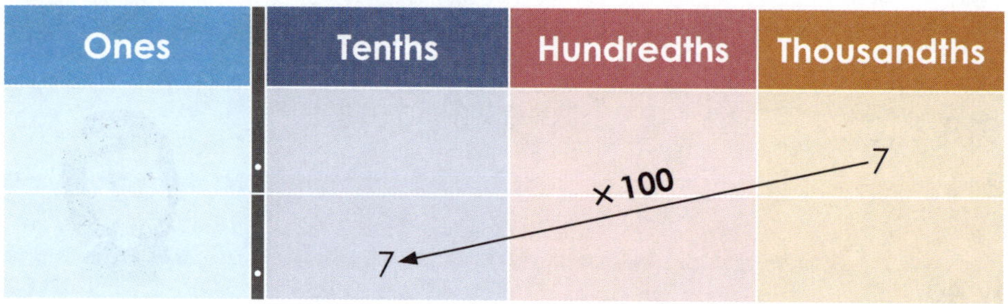

$0.007 \times 100 = 0.7$

b) Multiply 4.23 by 100.

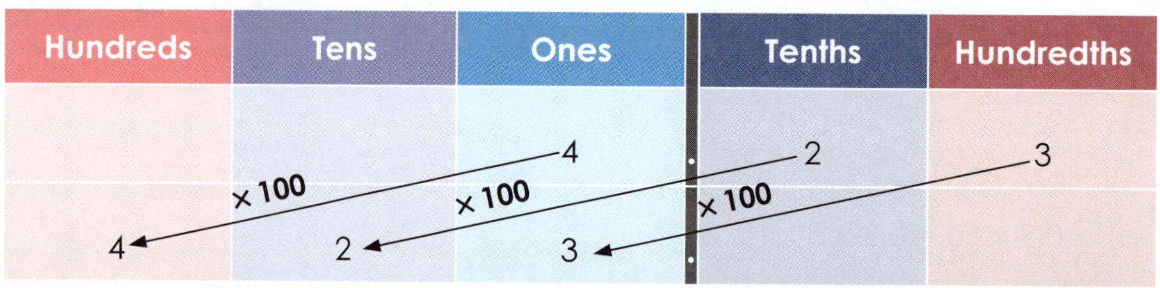

$4.23 \times 100 =$ ______

When multiplying a decimal by 100, move the decimal point 2 places to the right.

Let's Do

1. Multiply.

   a) $0.003 \times 100 =$ ______

   b) $3.2 \times 100 =$ ______

   c) $1.325 \times 100 =$ ______

  ISBN 978-93-5103-033-1

Multiplying decimals by 1000

Let's Learn

a) Multiply 0.006 by 1000.

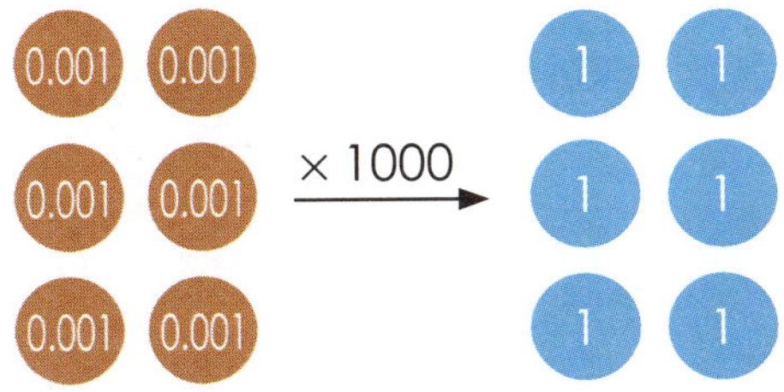

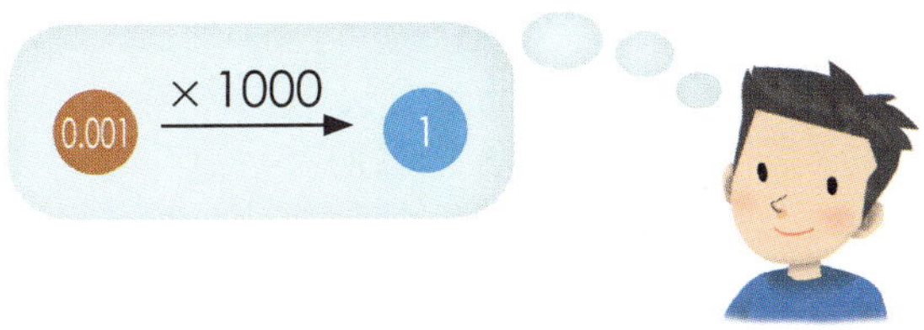

Ones	Tenths	Hundredths	Thousandths
			6
6			

× 1000

0.006 × 1000 = 6

b) Multiply 0.054 by 1000.

Tens	Ones	Tenths	Hundredths	Thousandths
			5	4
5	4			

× 1000

× 1000

0.054 × 1000 = ☐

When multiplying a decimal by 1000, move the decimal point 3 places to the right.

Let's Do

1. Multiply.

   a) 0.09 × 1000 = ______

   b) 3.62 × 1000 = ______

   c) 13.4 × 1000 = ______

Chapter 5: Exercise 5, page 102

ISBN 978-93-5103-033-1

Multiplying decimals by hundreds or thousands

Let's Learn

a) Multiply 4.203 by 200.

$$\begin{aligned} 4.203 \times 200 &= 4.203 \times 2 \times 100 \\ &= 8.406 \times 100 \\ &= \square \end{aligned}$$

4.203 × 2 = 8.406

8.406

b) Multiply 4.203 by 2000.

$$\begin{aligned} 4.203 \times 2000 &= 4.203 \times 2 \times 1000 \\ &= 8.406 \times 1000 \\ &= \square \end{aligned}$$

8.406

Let's Do

1. Multiply.

a) $0.12 \times 600 = 0.12 \times 6 \times 100$

$= \_\_\_\_\_\_ \times 100$

$= \_\_\_\_\_\_$

b) $1.54 \times 400 = 1.54 \times \_\_\_\_\_\_ \times \_\_\_\_\_\_$

$= \_\_\_\_\_\_ \times \_\_\_\_\_\_$

$= \_\_\_\_\_\_$

c) $0.03 \times 5000 = 0.03 \times 5 \times 1000$

$= \_\_\_\_\_\_ \times 1000$

$= \_\_\_\_\_\_$

d) $5.12 \times 4000 = 5.12 \times \_\_\_\_\_\_ \times \_\_\_\_\_\_$

$= \_\_\_\_\_\_ \times \_\_\_\_\_\_$

$= \_\_\_\_\_\_$

P/B Chapter 5: Exercise 6, page 103

 ISBN 978-93-5103-033-1

Practice 2

1. Multiply.
   a) 0.2×10
   b) 0.02×10
   c) 0.002×10
   d) 0.8×10
   e) 0.08×10
   f) 0.008×10

2. Multiply.
   a) 7.5×10
   b) 10×5.7
   c) 2.05×10
   d) 3.21×10
   e) 1.439×10
   f) 5.076×10

3. Multiply.
   a) 0.004×20
   b) 0.32×20
   c) 5.72×60
   d) 30×0.002
   e) 40×6.48
   f) 60×3.248

4. Multiply.
   a) 0.02×100
   b) 0.4×100
   c) 100×1.508
   d) 0.05×1000
   e) 7.25×1000
   f) 32.4×1000

5. Multiply.
   a) 0.007×400
   b) 0.03×600
   c) 500×1.45
   d) 400×3.29
   e) 2.23×600
   f) 5.19×200

6. Multiply.
   a) 6.8×3000
   b) 0.25×6000
   c) 6.23×5000
   d) 7000×2.25
   e) 5000×3.29
   f) 8000×1.508

 ISBN 978-93-5103-033-1

Lesson 3 Division by Tens, Hundreds or Thousands

Dividing ones, tenths or hundredths by 10

Let's Learn

a)

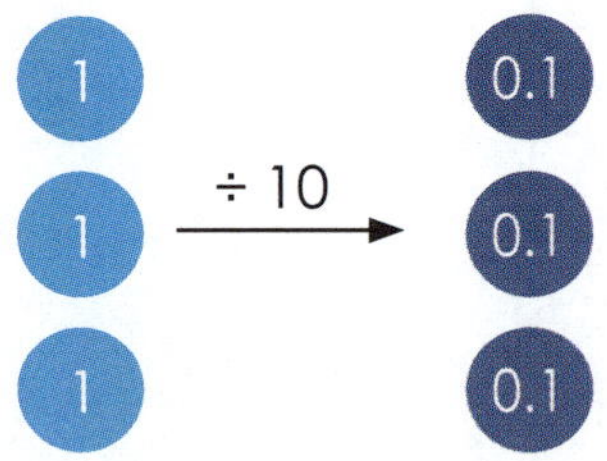

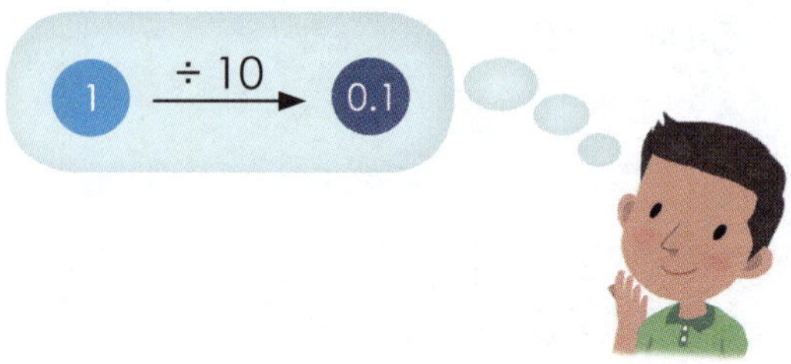

3 ones 3 tenths

3 ÷ 10 = 0.3

b)

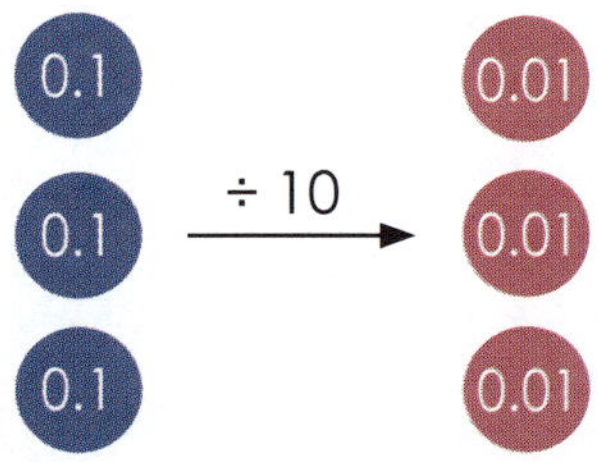

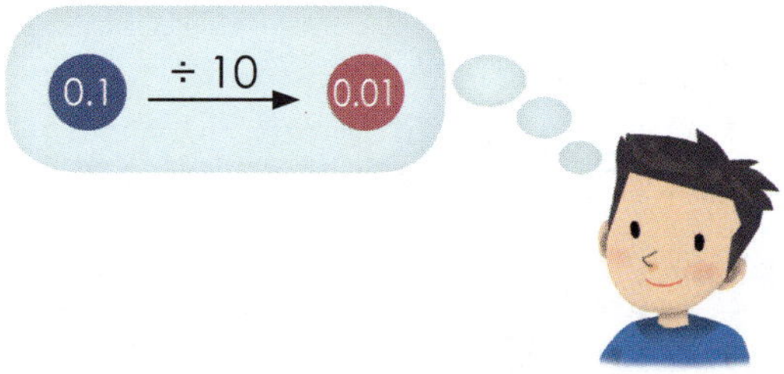

3 tenths 3 hundredths

0.3 ÷ 10 = 0.03

c)

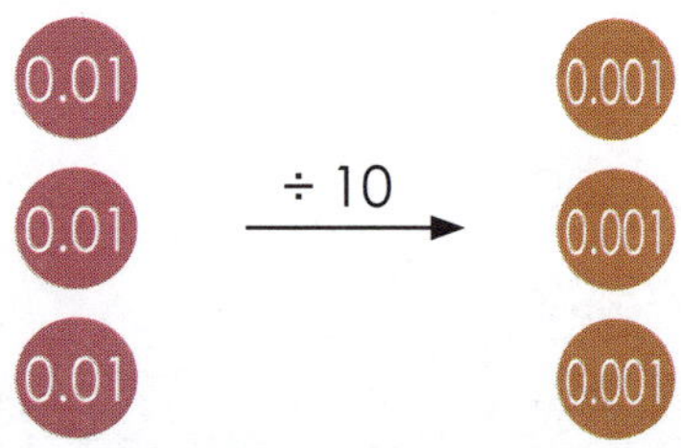

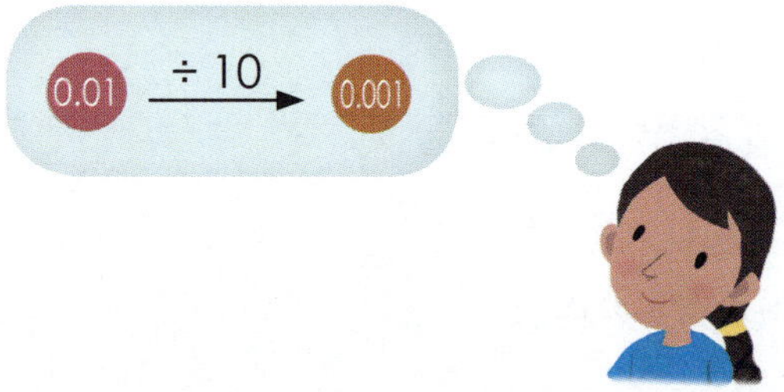

3 hundredths 3 thousandths

0.03 ÷ 10 = 0.003

 ISBN 978-93-5103-033-1

Let's Do

1. Divide.

   a) 8 ÷ 10 = ______

   0.8 ÷ 10 = ______

   0.08 ÷ 10 = ______

   b) 6 ÷ 10 = ______

   0.6 ÷ 10 = ______

   0.06 ÷ 10 = ______

Dividing whole numbers or decimals by 10

Let's Learn

a) Divide 0.46 by 10.

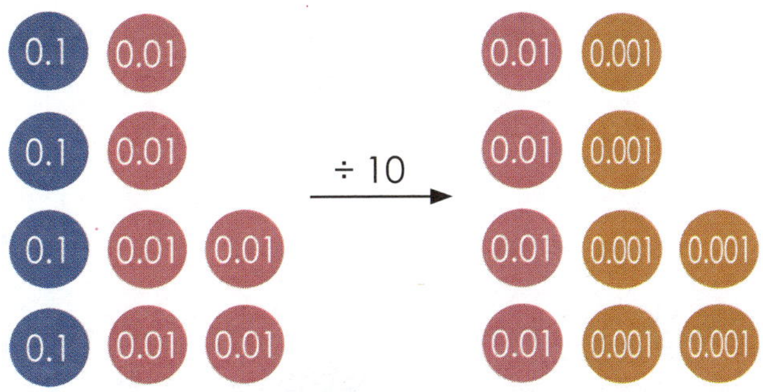

Ones	Tenths	Hundredths	Thousandths
	4 ÷ 10	6 ÷ 10	
		4	6

0.46 ÷ 10 = 0.046

b) Divide 5.3 by 10.

Ones	Tenths	Hundredths
5 ÷ 10	3 ÷ 10	
	5	3

5.3 ÷ 10 = ▢

When dividing a decimal by 10, move the decimal point 1 place to the left.

ISBN 978-93-5103-033-1

Let's Do

1. Divide.

   a) 0.23 ÷ 10 = ______

   b) 0.45 ÷ 10 = ______

   c) 12 ÷ 10 = ______

Dividing whole numbers or decimals by tens

Let's Learn

a) Divide 4.2 by 60.

4.2 ÷ 60 = 4.2 ÷ 6 ÷ 10
= 0.7 ÷ 10
= ______

b) Divide 0.45 by 50.

0.45 ÷ 50 = 0.45 ÷ 5 ÷ 10
= ______ ÷ 10
= ______

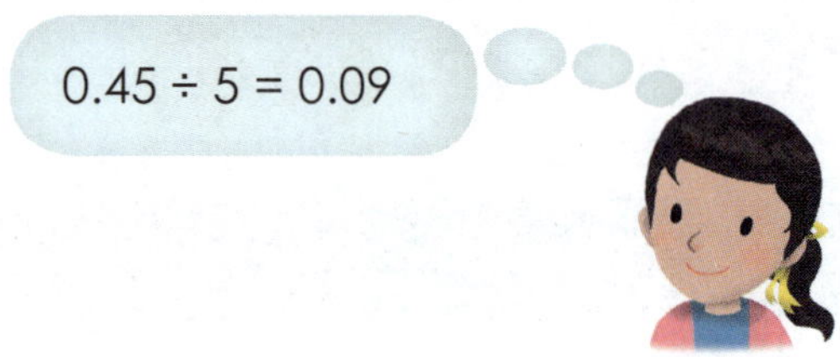

Let's Do

1. Divide.

   a) 8 ÷ 40 = 8 ÷ 4 ÷ 10
   = ______ ÷ 10
   = ______

   b) 4.8 ÷ 60 = 4.8 ÷ ______ ÷ ______
   = ______ ÷ ______
   = ______

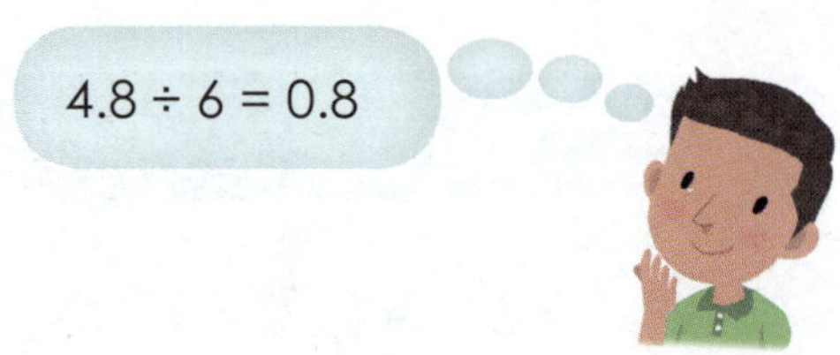

   c) 3.44 ÷ 80 = 3.44 ÷ ______ ÷ ______
   = ______ ÷ ______
   = ______

PB Chapter 5: Exercise 7, page 104

 ISBN 978-93-5103-033-1

Dividing whole numbers or decimals by 100

Let's Learn

a) Divide 4 by 100.

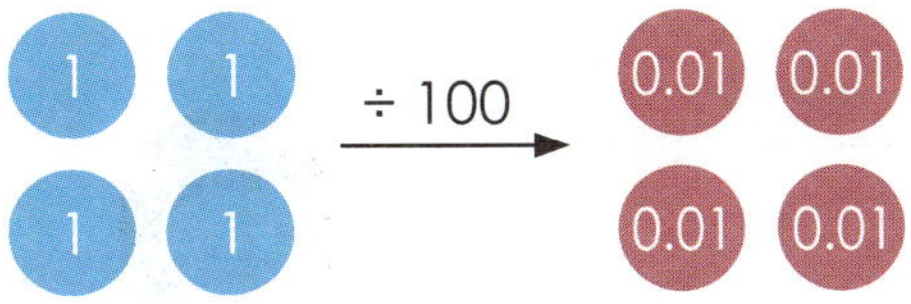

Ones	Tenths	Hundredths
4	÷ 100	
		4

4 ÷ 100 = 0.04

b) Divide 52.8 by 100.

Tens	Ones	Tenths	Hundredths	Thousandths
5	÷ 100 2	÷ 100 8	÷ 100	
		5	2	8

52.8 ÷ 100 = ▭

When dividing a decimal by 100, move the decimal point 2 places to the left.

Let's Do

1. Divide.
   a) 8 ÷ 100 = ______
   b) 90 ÷ 100 = ______
   c) 1.5 ÷ 100 = ______

 ISBN 978-93-5103-033-1

Dividing whole numbers by 1000

Let's Learn

a) Divide 5 by 1000.

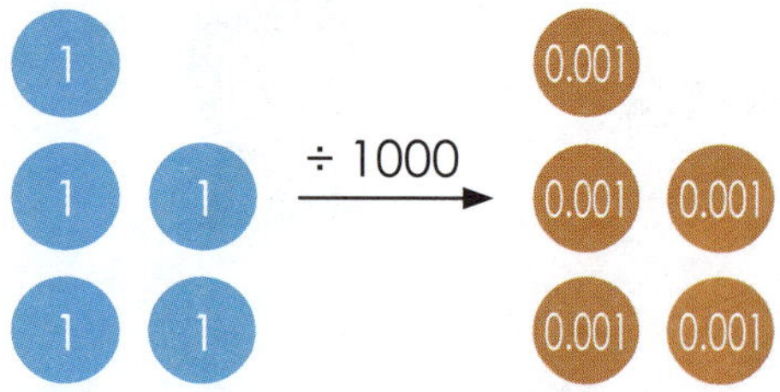

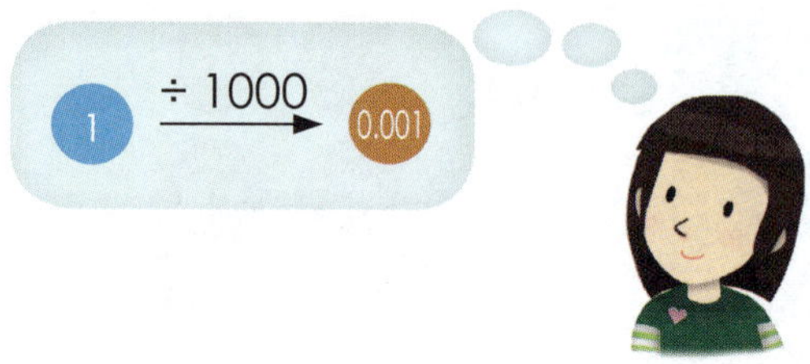

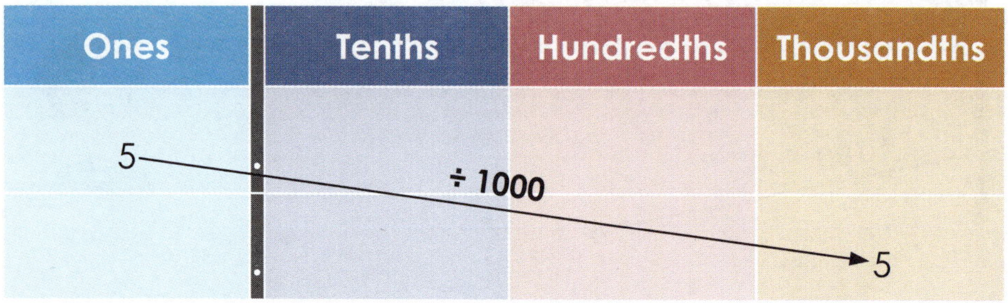

5 ÷ 1000 = 0.005

b) Divide 62 by 1000.

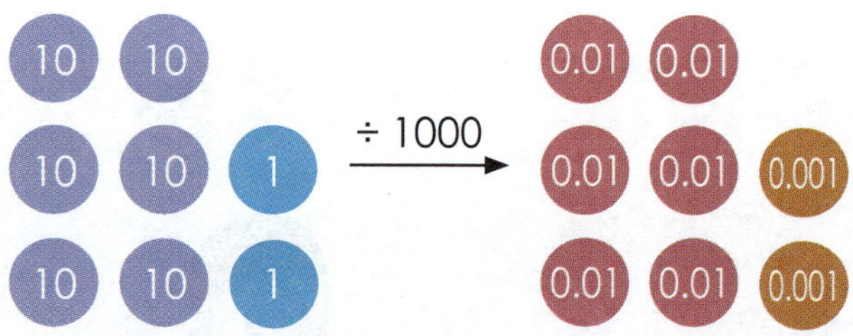

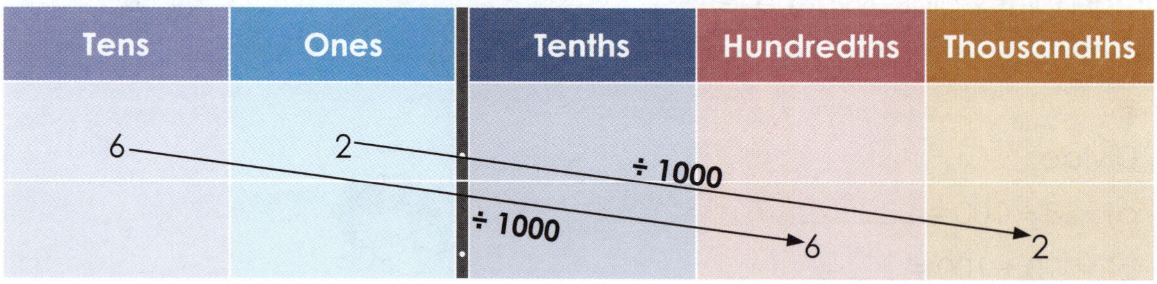

62 ÷ 1000 = ▭

When dividing a whole number by 1000, move the decimal point 3 places to the left.

 ISBN 978-93-5103-033-1

Let's Do

1. Divide.

   a) 4 ÷ 1000 = ______

   b) 200 ÷ 1000 = ______

   c) 324 ÷ 1000 = ______

Chapter 5: Exercise 8, page 105

Dividing whole numbers or decimals by hundreds or thousands

Let's Learn

a) Divide 46 by 200.

46 ÷ 200 = 46 ÷ 2 ÷ 100
= 23 ÷ 100
= ____

b) Divide 46 by 2000.

46 ÷ 2000 = 46 ÷ 2 ÷ 1000
= 23 ÷ 1000
= ____

Let's Do

1. Divide.

   a) 0.8 ÷ 200 = 0.8 ÷ 2 ÷ 100
   = ______ ÷ 100
   = ______

   b) 4.8 ÷ 300 = 4.8 ÷ ______ ÷ ______
   = ______ ÷ ______
   = ______

   c) 12 ÷ 6000 = 12 ÷ ______ ÷ ______
   = ______ ÷ ______
   = ______

 ISBN 978-93-5103-033-1

d) $714 \div 7000 = 714 \div$ ______ $\div$ ______

$=$ ______ $\div$ ______

$=$ ______

P/B Chapter 5: Exercise 9, page 106

Practice 3

1. Divide.

a)	$2 \div 10$	b)	$0.2 \div 10$	c)	$0.02 \div 10$
d)	$5 \div 10$	e)	$0.5 \div 10$	f)	$0.05 \div 10$

2. Divide.

a)	$0.12 \div 10$	b)	$0.36 \div 10$	c)	$4.7 \div 10$
d)	$5.3 \div 10$	e)	$39 \div 10$	f)	$103 \div 10$

3. Divide.

a)	$9 \div 30$	b)	$16 \div 80$	c)	$63 \div 90$
d)	$2.5 \div 20$	e)	$0.64 \div 40$	f)	$6.05 \div 50$

4. Divide.

a)	$7 \div 100$	b)	$0.7 \div 100$	c)	$34.2 \div 100$
d)	$9 \div 1000$	e)	$43 \div 1000$	f)	$506 \div 1000$

5. Divide.

a)	$0.6 \div 300$	b)	$1.6 \div 400$	c)	$5.4 \div 300$
d)	$12 \div 400$	e)	$648 \div 300$	f)	$413 \div 200$

6. Divide.

a)	$60 \div 2000$	b)	$84 \div 7000$	c)	$75 \div 5000$
d)	$99 \div 3000$	e)	$824 \div 8000$	f)	$117 \div 9000$

 ISBN 978-93-5103-033-1

Lesson 4 Conversion of Measurements

Converting a measurement from a larger unit to a smaller unit

Let's Learn

a) Express 0.75 metre in centimetres.

0.75 m = 0.75 × 100 cm
= 75 cm

0.75 m = 0.75 of 1 m
= 0.75 × 100 cm

0.75

b) Express 3.75 metres in centimetres.

Method 1

3.75 m = 3 m + 0.75 m
= 300 cm + 75 cm
= 375 cm

Method 2

3.75 m = 3.75 × 100 cm
= $\square$ cm

1 m = 100 cm
3.75

Let's Do

1. Find the equivalent measures.

a) 0.3 kg = 0.3 × 1000 g
= ______ g

1 kg = 1000 g
1 L = 1000 ml
1 km = 1000 m

b) 0.615 km = 0.615 × ______ m
= ______ m

c) 4.2 L = ______ L + ______ L
= ______ ml + ______ ml
= ______ ml

d) 1.85 m = 1.85 × ______ cm
= ______ cm

 ISBN 978-93-5103-033-1

Converting a measurement from a larger unit to compound units

Let's Learn

Express 4.2 kilograms in kilograms and grams.

4.2 kg = 4 kg + 0.2 kg
= 4 kg 200 g

0.2 kg = 0.2 × 1000 g
= 200 g

Let's Do

1. Find the equivalent measures.

   a) 7.4 km = 7 km + 0.4 km
   = 7 km ______ m

   0.4 km = 0.4 × 1000 m

   b) 2.06 m = 2 m + ______ m
   = 2 m ______ cm

Chapter 5: Exercise 10, page 107

Converting a measurement from a smaller unit to a larger unit

Let's Learn

a) Express 145 millilitres in litres.

145 ml = 145 ÷ 1000 L
= 0.145 L

145.0

b) Express 3080 grams in kilograms.

Method 1

3080 g = 3000 g + 80 g
= 3 kg + 0.08 kg
= 3.08 kg

80 g = 80 ÷ 1000 kg
= 0.08 kg

Method 2

3080 g = 3080 ÷ 1000 kg
= [ ] kg

3080.0

 ISBN 978-93-5103-033-1

Let's Do

1. Find the equivalent measures. Express each answer as a decimal.

a) 350 m = ______ ÷ 1000 km

= ______ km

b) 625 g = ______ ÷ ______ kg

= ______ kg

c) 4070 m = ______ m + ______ m

= ______ km + ______ km

= ______ km

d) 605 cm = ______ ÷ ______ m

= ______ m

Chapter 5: Exercise 11, page 108

Converting a measurement from compound units to a larger unit

Let's Learn

Express 3 kilograms 500 grams in kilograms.

3 kg 500 g = 3 kg + 500 g
= 3 kg + 0.5 kg
= 3.5 kg

500 g = 500 ÷ 1000 kg
= 0.5 kg

Let's Do

1. Find the equivalent measures. Express each answer as a decimal.

a) 4 m 35 cm = 4 m + 35 cm

= 4 m + ______ m

= ______ m

b) 5 km 90 m = 5 km + ______ m

= 5 km + ______ km

= ______ km

Chapter 5: Exercise 12, page 109

 ISBN 978-93-5103-033-1

Practice 4

1. Find the equivalent measures.

   a) 0.285 L = ____ ml b) 2.75 L = ____ ml c) 0.085 km = ____ m

   d) 0.706 kg = ____ g e) 1.54 m = ____ cm f) 3.825 kg = ____ g

2. Find the equivalent measures.

   a) 20.08 km = ____ km ____ m b) 16.5 L = ____ L ____ ml

   c) 2.08 kg = ____ kg ____ g d) 40.006 L = ____ L ____ ml

   e) 56.075 km = ____ km ____ m f) 64.104 kg = ____ kg ____ g

3. Find the equivalent measures. Express each answer as a decimal.

   a) 670 ml = ____ L b) 105 m = ____ km c) 69 g = ____ kg

   d) 2870 g = ____ kg e) 3500 ml = ____ L f) 4060 m = ____ km

4. Find the equivalent measures. Express each answer as a decimal.

   a) 9 m 60 cm = ____ m b) 4 L 705 ml = ____ L

   c) 20 kg 400 g = ____ kg d) 54 L 60 ml = ____ L

   e) 120 m 4 cm = ____ m f) 63 km 80 m = ____ km

Lesson 5 Multiplication by 2-digit Whole Numbers

Estimating products

Let's Learn

a) Multiply 2187 by 32.

Estimate:
$2187 \times 32 \approx 2000 \times 30$
$= 60{,}000$
My answer should be about 60,000.

❶ Multiply 2187 by 2.

$$\begin{array}{r} {\scriptstyle 1\;1\;\;} \\ 2187 \\ \times \quad 32 \\ \hline 4374 \end{array}$$

❷ Multiply 2187 by 30.

$$\begin{array}{r} {\scriptstyle 2\;2\;\;} \\ {\scriptstyle 1\;1\;\;} \\ 2187 \\ \times \quad 32 \\ \hline 4374 \\ 65610 \\ \hline \end{array}$$

❸ Add.

$$\begin{array}{r} {\scriptstyle 2\;2\;\;} \\ {\scriptstyle 1\;1\;\;} \\ 2187 \\ \times \quad 32 \\ \hline 4374 \\ 65610 \\ \hline 69984 \\ \hline \end{array}$$

 ISBN 978-93-5103-033-1

b) Multiply 21.87 by 32.

Estimate:
$21.87 \times 32 \approx 20 \times 30$
$= 600$
My answer should be about 600.

$$\begin{array}{r} {}^{2}\,{}^{2} \\ {}^{1}\,{}^{1} \\ 21.87 \\ \times \quad 32 \\ \hline 4374 \\ 65610 \\ \hline 69984 \\ \hline \end{array} \qquad \rightarrow \qquad \begin{array}{r} {}^{2}\,{}^{2} \\ {}^{1}\,{}^{1} \\ 21.87 \\ \times \quad 32 \\ \hline 4374 \\ 65610 \\ \hline 699.84 \\ \hline \end{array}$$

Align the decimal points.

Let's Do

1. Estimate the value of each of the following.

a) 3267×28

$3267 \times 28 \approx 3000 \times 30$

$= $ ______

b) 326.7×28

$326.7 \times 28 \approx$ ______ $\times$ ______

$= $ ______

c) 32.67×28

$32.67 \times 28 \approx$ ______ $\times$ ______

$= $ ______

$3267 \approx 3000$

$326.7 \approx 300$

$32.67 \approx 30$

P/B Chapter 5: Exercise 13, page 110

ISBN 978-93-5103-033-1

Multiplying decimals by 2-digit whole numbers

Let's Learn

Estimate and then find the value of 0.23×59.

$0.23 \times 59 \approx 0.2 \times 60$
$= 12$

Round 0.23 to 1 decimal place.
Round 59 to the nearest ten.

My answer should be about 12.

1 Multiply 0.23 by 9.

$$\begin{array}{r} {\scriptstyle 2\ \ 2} \\ 0.23 \\ \times\ \ 59 \\ \hline 2\ 07 \end{array}$$

2 Multiply 0.23 by 5.

$$\begin{array}{r} {\scriptstyle 1\ \ 1} \\ {\scriptstyle 2\ \ 2} \\ 0.23 \\ \times\ \ 59 \\ \hline 2\ 07 \\ 11\ 50 \\ \hline \end{array}$$

3 Add.

$$\begin{array}{r} {\scriptstyle 1\ \ 1} \\ {\scriptstyle 2\ \ 2} \\ 0.23 \\ \times\ \ 59 \\ \hline 2\ 07 \\ 11\ 50 \\ \hline 13.57 \\ \hline \end{array}$$

13.57 is about 12.
My answer is reasonable.

Let's Do

1. Estimate and then multiply.

   a) 0.78×43

   $0.78 \times 43 \approx$ ______ $\times$ ______

   $=$ ______

$$\begin{array}{r} 0.78 \\ \times\ \ 43 \\ \hline \end{array}$$

 ISBN 978-93-5103-033-1

b) 40.6×45

$40.6 \times 45 \approx$ ______ $\times$ ______

$=$ ______

$$\begin{array}{r} 40.6 \\ \times \quad 45 \\ \hline \end{array}$$

P/B Chapter 5: Exercise 14, pages 111–113

Think About It

$12.34 \times 25 = ?$

Sam: The answer should have 2 decimal places.

Ria: $12.34 \times 25 \approx 12 \times 30$
$= 360$

Ria: The answer should be about 360.

Who is correct? Explain why.

Solving word problems

Let's Learn

Mr. Jones sold 19 booklets at ₹ 7.95 each. How much money did he collect altogether?

₹ $7.95 \times 19 =$ ₹ 151.05

He collected ₹ 151.05 altogether.

₹ $7.95 \times 19 \approx$ ₹ 8×20
$=$ ₹ 160
My answer is close to ₹ 160.
It is reasonable.

 ISBN 978-93-5103-033-1

Let's Do

1. An apple juice box contains 0.25 litre of apple juice.
   How much apple juice is there in 32 such apple juice boxes?

   _______ × _______ = _______

   There are _______ litres of apple juice in 32 such apple juice boxes.

Check your answer.
Is it reasonable?

P/B Chapter 5: Exercise 15, page 114

Practice 5

1. Estimate the value of each of the following.

   a) 37×4.9 b) 23.7×26 c) 18×132.4

   d) 43×3.58 e) 15.09×26 f) 27.8×34

2. Multiply.

   a) 56×2.07 b) 1.29×29 c) 72×1.57

   d) 84×0.13 e) 143.2×87 f) 24.05×53

Solve the word problems. Show your work clearly.

3. Lata bought 18 bags of flour for a bake sale. Each bag contained 1.75 kilograms of flour. How many kilograms of flour did she buy?

4. Kunal spends ₹ 2.75 for a bus ticket every day. How much money does he spend on bus tickets in 31 days?

5. Jane's handspan is 18.3 centimetres long. She measures a table and finds that it is 12 handspans long. What is the length of the table?

  ISBN 978-93-5103-033-1

Lesson 6 Multiplication of Decimals

Multiplying tenths by tenths or hundredths

Let's Learn

a) Multiply 0.2 by 0.4.

$$0.2 \times 0.4 = \frac{2}{10} \times \frac{4}{10}$$
$$= \frac{8}{100}$$
$$= 0.08$$

First, express the decimals as fractions. Then, multiply the fractions. Lastly, express the fraction as a decimal.

b) Multiply 0.3 by 0.05.

$$0.3 \times 0.05 = \frac{3}{10} \times \frac{5}{100}$$
$$= \frac{15}{1000}$$
$$= \square$$

Let's Do

1. Multiply.

a) $0.3 \times 0.5 = \frac{\square}{10} \times \frac{\square}{10}$

$= \frac{\square}{\square}$

$=$ ______

b) $0.4 \times 0.08 = \frac{\square}{10} \times \frac{\square}{100}$

$= \frac{\square}{\square}$

$=$ ______

 ISBN 978-93-5103-033-1

Multiplying decimals

Let's Learn

a) Multiply 215 by 25.

Estimate:
$215 \times 25 \approx 200 \times 30$
$= 6000$
My answer should be about 6000.

❶ Multiply 215 by 5.

$$\begin{array}{r} {}^{2} \\ 215 \\ \times \quad 25 \\ \hline 1075 \end{array}$$

❷ Multiply 215 by 20.

$$\begin{array}{r} {}^{1} \\ {}^{2} \\ 215 \\ \times \quad 25 \\ \hline 1075 \\ 4300 \\ \hline \end{array}$$

❸ Add.

$$\begin{array}{r} {}^{1} \\ {}^{2} \\ 215 \\ \times \quad 25 \\ \hline 1075 \\ 4300 \\ \hline 5375 \\ \hline \end{array}$$

b) Multiply 2.15 by 2.5.

Estimate:
$2.15 \times 2.5 \approx 2 \times 3$
$= 6$
My answer should be about 6.

$$\begin{array}{r} {}^{1} \\ {}^{2} \\ 2.15 \\ \times \quad 2.5 \\ \hline 1075 \\ 4300 \\ \hline 5375 \\ \hline \end{array}$$

$$\begin{array}{rl} {}^{1} & \\ {}^{2} & \\ 2.15 & \text{2 decimal places} \\ \times \quad 2.5 & \text{1 decimal place} \\ \hline 1075 & \\ 4300 & \\ \hline 5.375 & \text{3 decimal places} \\ \hline \end{array}$$

When multiplying two decimals, the number of decimal places in the product is equal to the sum of the decimal places in both decimals.

 ISBN 978-93-5103-033-1

Let's Do

1. Estimate and then multiply.

   a) 18×79

   $18 \times 79 \approx 20 \times 80$

   $= \_\_\_\_\_\_\_$

   $$\begin{array}{r} 1\ 8 \\ \times\ 7\ 9 \\ \hline \end{array}$$

   b) 1.8×7.9

   $1.8 \times 7.9 \approx \_\_\_\_\_\_\_ \times \_\_\_\_\_\_\_$

   $= \_\_\_\_\_\_\_$

   $$\begin{array}{r} 1\ .\ 8 \\ \times\ 7\ .\ 9 \\ \hline \end{array}$$

   c) 0.18×7.9

   $0.18 \times 7.9 \approx \_\_\_\_\_\_\_ \times \_\_\_\_\_\_\_$

   $= \_\_\_\_\_\_\_$

   $$\begin{array}{r} 0\ .\ 1\ \ 8 \\ \times\ \ \ 7\ .\ 9 \\ \hline \end{array}$$

P/B Chapter 5: Exercise 16, pages 115–116

Solving word problems

Let's Learn

Sunil's remote-controlled toy car can travel 9.7 kilometres every hour. How far can his toy car travel in 1.5 hours?

$9.7 \times 1.5 = 14.55$

His toy car can travel 14.55 kilometres in 1.5 hours.

$9.7 \times 1.5 \approx 10 \times 2$
$= 20$
My answer is close to 20.
It is reasonable.

ISBN 978-93-5103-033-1

Let's Do

1. Arup earns ₹ 11.70 in one hour for delivering newspapers. If he works 2.5 hours, how much does he earn?

   ₹ ______ × ______ = ₹ ______

   He earns ₹ ______.

P/B Chapter 5: Exercise 17, page 117

Practice 6

1. Estimate the value of each of the following.

   a) 1.08×2.3 b) 3.7×4.8

   c) 9.2×4.1 d) 2.12×4.3

   e) 5.17×5.7 f) 0.82×8.6

2. Multiply.

   a) 2.9×2.4 b) 3.4×6.6

   c) 7.7×8.9 d) 71.16×3.2

   e) 19.09×1.3 f) 39.87×3.4

Solve the word problems. Show your work clearly.

3. Mrs. Bal bought 4.6 kilograms of sugar. Each kilogram of sugar cost ₹ 34.50. How much did she pay for the sugar?

4. A contractor bought 7.5 metres of wire. Each metre of wire cost ₹ 6.20. How much did he pay for the wire?

5. Mr. Rao has a rectangular plot of land measuring 25.74 kilometres by 6.8 kilometres. What is the area of the plot of land? Round the area to the nearest square kilometre.

  ISBN 978-93-5103-033-1

Lesson 7 Division by 2-digit Whole Numbers

Estimating quotients

Let's Learn

a) Divide 3358 by 23.

Estimate:
3358 ÷ 23 ≈ 3000 ÷ 20
= 150
My answer should be about 150.

❶ Divide 33 hundreds by 23.

```
          1
23 ) 3 3 5 8
     2 3
     ---
     1 0
```

❷ Divide 105 tens by 23.

```
          1 4
23 ) 3 3 5 8
     2 3
     -----
     1 0 5
       9 2
       ---
       1 3
```

❸ Divide 138 ones by 23.

```
          1 4 6
23 ) 3 3 5 8
     2 3
     -----
     1 0 5
       9 2
       -----
       1 3 8
       1 3 8
       -----
           0
```

146 is about 150.
My answer is reasonable.

 ISBN 978-93-5103-033-1

b) Divide 33.58 by 23.

Estimate:
$33.58 \div 23 \approx 30 \div 20$
$= 1.5$
My answer should be about 1.5.

```
        1
23 ) 3 3 . 5 8
     2 3
     1 0
```

```
        1 . 4
23 ) 3 3 . 5 8
     2 3
     1 0   5
         9 2
         1 3
```

```
        1 . 4 6
23 ) 3 3 . 5 8
     2 3
     1 0   5
         9 2
         1 3 8
         1 3 8
             0
```

1.46 is about 1.5.
My answer is reasonable.

Let's Do

1. Estimate the value of each of the following.

a) $6496 \div 32$

$6496 \div 32 \approx 6000 \div 30$

$= \_\_\_\_\_\_$

b) $649.6 \div 32$

$649.6 \div 32 \approx \_\_\_\_\_\_ \div \_\_\_\_\_\_$

$= \_\_\_\_\_\_$

649.6 ≈ 600

c) $64.96 \div 32$

$64.96 \div 32 \approx \_\_\_\_\_\_ \div \_\_\_\_\_\_$

$= \_\_\_\_\_\_$

64.96 ≈ 60

 ISBN 978-93-5103-033-1

Dividing decimals by 2-digit whole numbers

Let's Learn

Estimate and then find the value of 8.19 ÷ 39.

$$\begin{aligned} 8.19 \div 39 &\approx 8 \div 40 \\ &= 8 \div 4 \div 10 \\ &= 2 \div 10 \\ &= 0.2 \end{aligned}$$

Round 8.19 to the nearest whole number.
Round 39 to the nearest ten.

My answer should be about 0.2.

1 Divide 8 ones by 39.

```
      0 .
39 ) 8 . 1 9
     0
     -
     8
```

2 Divide 81 tenths by 39.

```
      0 . 2
39 ) 8 . 1 9
     0
     -----
     8   1
     7   8
     -----
         3
```

3 Divide 39 hundredths by 39.

```
      0 . 2 1
39 ) 8 . 1 9
     0
     -----
     8   1
     7   8
     -------
         3 9
         3 9
         ---
           0
```

0.21 is about 0.2.
My answer is reasonable.

Let's Do

1. Estimate and then divide.

a) 26.88 ÷ 42

26.88 ÷ 42 ≈ ________ ÷ ________

= ________

```
42 ) 2 6 . 8 8
```

b) 95.58 ÷ 54

95.58 ÷ 54 ≈ ________ ÷ ________

= ________

```
54 ) 9 5 . 5 8
```

PB Chapter 5: Exercise 18, pages 118–119

 ISBN 978-93-5103-033-1

Dividing decimals by 2-digit whole numbers with zero as a place holder

Let's Learn

Find the value of 5.4 ÷ 42. Express your answer correct to 2 decimal places.

```
      0 . 1 2 8
42 ) 5 . 4 0 0
     0
     5   4
     4   2
     1   2 0
         8 4
         3 6 0
         3 3 6
           2 4
```

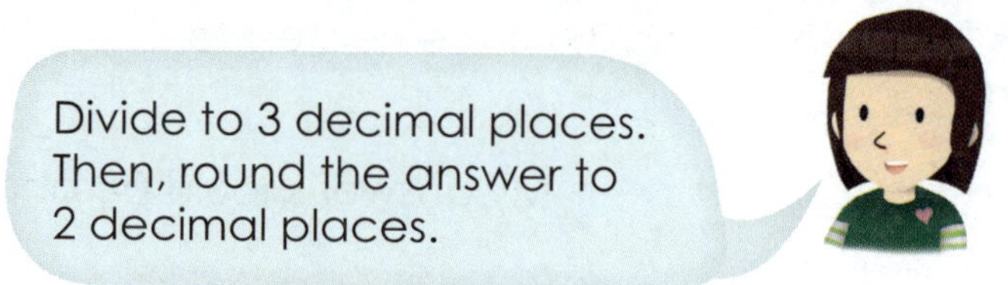

0.128 is ____ when rounded to 2 decimal places.

So, 5.4 ÷ 42 ≈ ____.

Let's Do

1. Find the value of each of the following. Express your answer correct to 2 decimal places.

   a) 16.3 ÷ 13 ≈ ______

   ```
         1 . □ □ □
   13 ) 1 6 . 3 □ □
        1 3
          □ □
          □ □
            □ □
            □ □
              □ □
              □ □
              □ □
   ```

   b) 6.3 ÷ 28 ≈ ______

   ```
   28 ) 6 . 3
   ```

P/B Chapter 5: Exercise 19, pages 120–121

 ISBN 978-93-5103-033-1

Solving word problems

Let's Learn

Eric bought 36 pencils for ₹ 25.20. How much did each pencil cost?

₹ 25.20 ÷ 36 = ₹ 0.70

Each pencil cost ₹ 0.70.

25.20 ÷ 36 ≈ 24 ÷ 40
= 24 ÷ 4 ÷ 10
= 6 ÷ 10
= 0.6
My answer is close to the estimate.
It is reasonable.

Let's Do

1. A rectangular hall is 21 metres wide and has a floor area of 518.28 square metres. Find its length.

   518.28 m^2 ÷ ______ m = ______ m

   Its length is ______ metres.

   518.28 ÷ ______ ≈ 500 ÷ ______
   = ______

   My answer is close to the estimate.
   It is reasonable.

Chapter 5: Exercise 20, page 122

Practice 7

1. Estimate the value of each of the following.

   a) 43.2 ÷ 24 b) 28.2 ÷ 15 c) 44.1 ÷ 18

   d) 115.17 ÷ 33 e) 94.86 ÷ 34 f) 167.85 ÷ 45

2. Find the value of each of the following. Express your answer correct to 1 decimal place.

   a) 35.2 ÷ 56 b) 67.4 ÷ 18 c) 75.6 ÷ 26

 ISBN 978-93-5103-033-1

3. Find the value of each of the following. Express your answer correct to 2 decimal places.

   a) 4.43 ÷ 53 b) 36.09 ÷ 32 c) 9.27 ÷ 38

Solve the word problems. Show your work clearly.

4. A vendor collected ₹ 161.25 from the sale of 75 visiting cards. If all cards sold at the same price, what was the price of each card?

5. The capacity of a wooden barrel is 45 times as much as the capacity of a water tank. If the capacity of the barrel is 158.4 litres, find the capacity of the water tank.

6. Mr. Ghosh has 9.15 litres of ketchup. He divides the ketchup equally into 37 bottles. How much ketchup is there in each bottle? Express your answer in litres correct to 2 decimal places.

7. The thickness of a pile of 24 similar textbooks is 56.18 centimetres. How thick is each textbook? Express your answer in centimetres correct to 2 decimal places.

Lesson 8 Problem Solving

Word problems

Let's Learn

Rafi bought a library membership. He paid a deposit of ₹ 210 and 28 monthly instalments of ₹ 31.25 each. How much did he pay in all?

1 Understand the problem.

How much did Rafi pay for the deposit?
How many instalments did he pay?
How much was each instalment?
What do I have to find?

2 Plan what to do.

First, find the total amount paid for the instalments. Then, add the deposit to find the total amount Rafi paid.

3 Work out the **Answer**.

28 × ₹ 31.25 = ₹ 875

Rafi paid a total of ₹ 875 for the monthly instalments.

₹ 875 + ₹ 210 = ₹ 1085

Rafi paid ₹ 1085 in all.

 ISBN 978-93-5103-033-1

4 Check

Did you answer the question? Is your answer reasonable?

$28 \times ₹\,31.25 \approx 30 \times ₹\,30$
$= ₹\,900$

$₹\,900 + ₹\,210 = ₹\,1110$

My answer is close to ₹ 1110.
It is reasonable.

- ☑ 1. Understand
- ☑ 2. Plan
- ☑ 3. Answer
- ☑ 4. Check

Let's Do

1. Sue had 7.5 litres of water. She made 12 cups of tea and 1 cup of coffee. She used 325 millilitres of water to make each cup of tea and 415 millilitres of water to make the cup of coffee. How much water did she have left?

How many litres of water did Sue use to make the tea?
How many litres of water did she use altogether?

- ☐ 1. Understand
- ☐ 2. Plan
- ☐ 3. Answer
- ☐ 4. Check

PB Chapter 5: Exercise 21, pages 123–124

Practice 8

Solve the word problems. Show your work clearly.

1. Juhi is 1.64 metres tall. Her sister is 6 centimetres shorter than Juhi. Find their total height in metres.

2. Mrs. Lal bought 17 packets of needles and a box of buttons. Each packet of needles cost ₹ 2.45 and the box of buttons cost ₹ 3.85. How much did Mrs. Lal spend altogether?

3. Mrs. Gomez had 3.45 kilograms of flour. After baking 3 loaves of bread and some cupcakes, she had 1.45 kilograms of flour left. If she used 1.25 kilograms of flour to make the cupcakes, how many grams of flour did she use for each loaf of bread?

4. The total weight of 25 marbles is 31.75 grams. The weight of a tennis ball is 45.5 times the weight of a marble. If all the marbles have the same weight, find the total weight of one marble and one tennis ball.

 ISBN 978-93-5103-033-1

Mind stretcher

Let's Learn

Find the value of 0.1 + 0.2 + 0.3 + 0.4 + 0.5 + ... + 9.8 + 9.9 + 10.0.

1 Understand the problem.

How many decimals are there?
Is there a quick way to find the answer?

2 Plan what to do.

I **look for a pattern**.
0.1 + 10.0 = 10.1
9.9 + 0.2 = 10.1
First, I find pairs of decimals that add to 10.1.
Then, I multiply the number of such pairs by 10.1.

3 Work out the **Answer**.

From 0.1 to 1.0, there are 10 decimals.
From 1.1 to 2.0, there are 10 decimals and so on.
There are 100 decimals altogether.
Since the decimals are paired, there will be 50 pairs of decimals.

$$\begin{aligned}&0.1 + 0.2 + 0.3 + \dots + 9.8 + 9.9 + 10.0\\&= 50 \times 10.1\\&= 505\end{aligned}$$

4 Check
Did you answer the question?
Is your answer reasonable?

$$\begin{aligned}50 \times 10.1 &\approx 50 \times 10\\&= 500\end{aligned}$$

My answer is close to 500.
It is reasonable.

☑ 1. Understand
☑ 2. Plan
☑ 3. Answer
☑ 4. Check

 ISBN 978-93-5103-033-1

6 Per Cent

Lesson 1 Per Cent

Understanding per cent

Let's Learn

a) There are 100 seats in a cinema hall.
54 seats are occupied.

Picture It

54 out of 100 seats are occupied.
We can also say that **54%** of the seats are occupied.
We read 54% as **54 per cent**.

b) 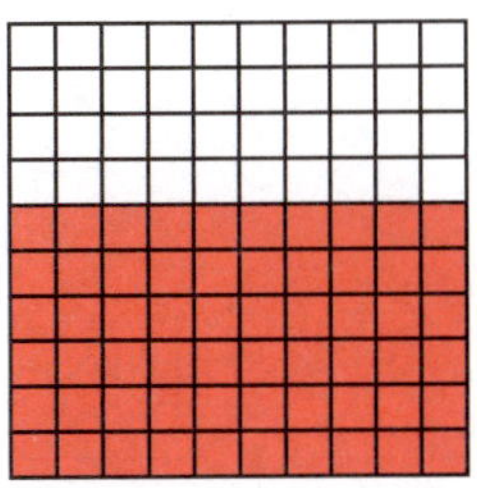

The whole is divided into 100 equal parts.
60 out of 100 parts are red.
60% of the whole is red.

40 out of 100 parts are not red.
40% of the whole is not red.

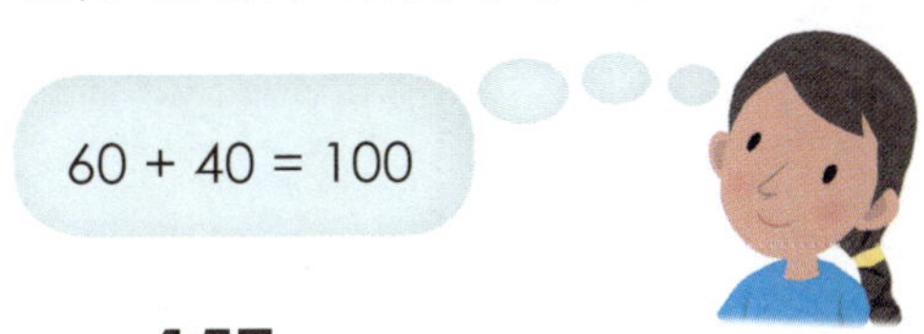

 ISBN 978-93-5103-033-1

c)

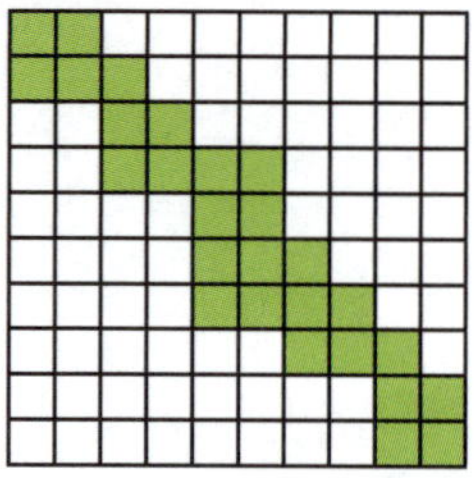

The whole is divided into 100 equal parts.
27 out of 100 parts are green.
____ % of the whole is green.

____ out of 100 parts are not green.
____ % of the whole is not green.

Let's Do

1. What percentage of the whole is shaded?

a)

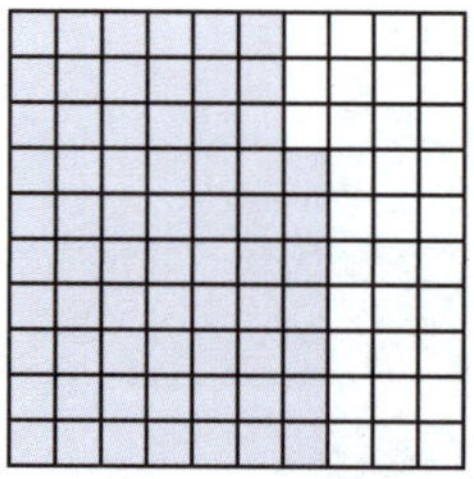

________%

b)

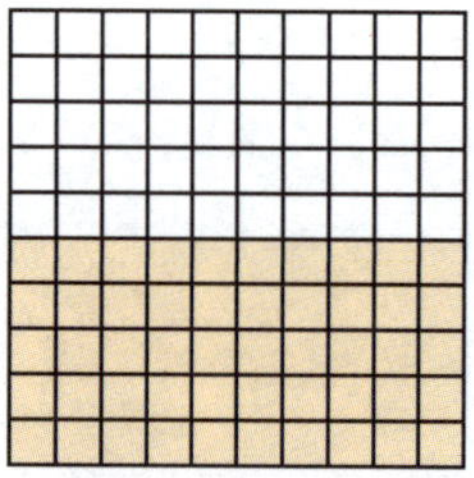

________%

c)

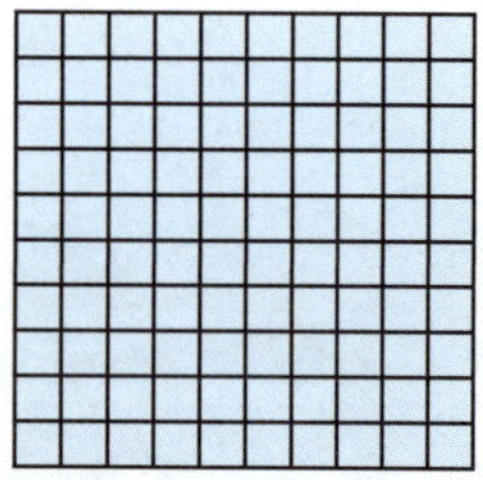

________%

2. Write each of the following as a per cent.

a) 33 out of 100 ________%

b) 20 out of 100 ________%

c) 5 out of 100 ________%

Expressing a fraction as a per cent

Let's Learn

Picture It

a)

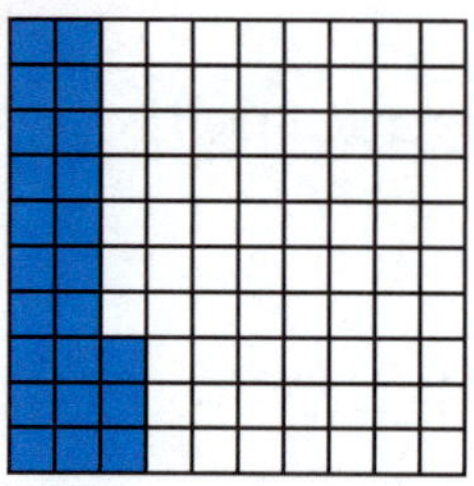

23 out of 100 equal parts are blue.

$\frac{23}{100}$ of the whole is blue.

23% of the whole is blue.

$\frac{23}{100} = 23\%$

 ISBN 978-93-5103-033-1

b) 

7 out of 10 equal parts are green.

$$\frac{7}{10} = \frac{70}{100} = 70\%$$

70% of the whole is green.

Let's Do

1. Express each fraction as a per cent.

a) $\frac{45}{100} =$ ______ %

b) $\frac{3}{10} = \frac{\square}{100} =$ ______ %

Chapter 6: Exercise 1, pages 125–126

Expressing a decimal as a per cent

Let's Learn

a) Express 0.35 as a per cent.

$$0.35 = \frac{35}{100}$$
$$= 35\%$$

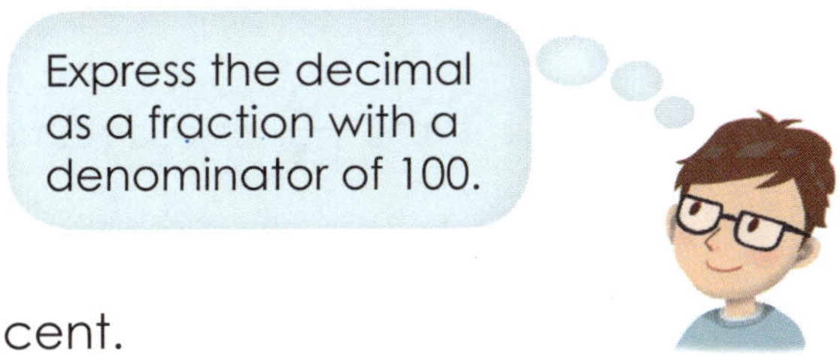

b) Express 0.07 as a per cent.

$$0.07 = \frac{7}{100}$$
$$= \square\%$$

 ISBN 978-93-5103-033-1

Let's Do

1. Express each decimal as a per cent.

a) $0.53 = \frac{\square}{100} = \_\_\_\_\_\_\%$

b) $0.85 = \frac{\square}{100} = \_\_\_\_\_\_\%$

c) $0.02 = \frac{\square}{\square} = \_\_\_\_\_\_\%$

d) $0.7 = \frac{\square}{\square} = \frac{\square}{\square} = \_\_\_\_\_\_\%$

Think About It

$\frac{9}{10} = 0.9 = 9\%$

Ria

Is Ria correct? Explain why.

Expressing a per cent as a decimal

Let's Learn

Express 43% as a decimal.

$$43\% = \frac{43}{100}$$
$$= 0.43$$

Write $\frac{43}{100}$ as a decimal.

Let's Do

1. Express each per cent as a decimal.

a) $28\% = \frac{\square}{100} = \_\_\_\_\_\_$

b) $88\% = \frac{\square}{100} = \_\_\_\_\_\_$

c) $30\% = \frac{\square}{\square} = \_\_\_\_\_\_$

d) $5\% = \frac{\square}{\square} = \_\_\_\_\_\_$

P/B Chapter 6: Exercise 2, pages 127–128

 ISBN 978-93-5103-033-1

Expressing a per cent as a fraction

Let's Learn

Picture It

40% of the flowers are yellow. What fraction of the flowers are yellow?

$40\% = \frac{40}{100}$

$= \square$

$\square$ of the flowers are yellow.

Let's Do

1. Express each per cent as a fraction in its simplest form.

a) $10\% = \frac{10}{100} = \_\_\_\_\_$

b) $75\% = \frac{\square}{100} = \_\_\_\_\_$

c) $5\% = \frac{\square}{100} = \_\_\_\_\_$

d) $8\% = \frac{\square}{100} = \_\_\_\_\_$

P/B Chapter 6: Exercise 3, page 129

 ISBN 978-93-5103-033-1

Practice 1

1. What percentage of the whole is shaded?

   a) 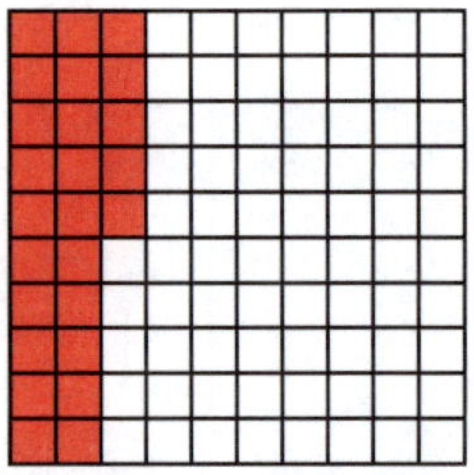

   b) 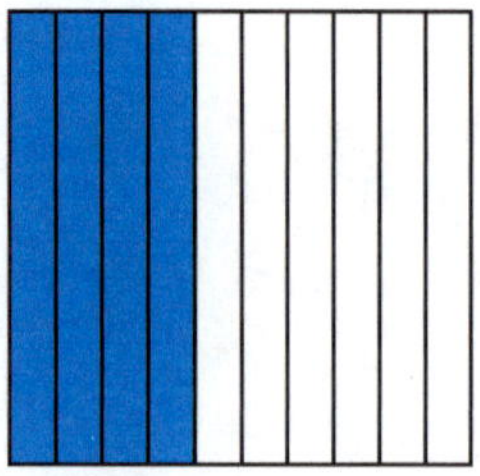

2. Write each of the following as a per cent.

   a) 46 out of 100 b) 80 out of 100 c) 8 out of 100

3. Express each fraction as a per cent.

   a) $\frac{70}{100}$ b) $\frac{25}{100}$ c) $\frac{9}{100}$ d) $\frac{5}{10}$

4. Express each decimal as a per cent.

   a) 0.63 b) 0.05 c) 0.2 d) 0.4

5. Express each per cent as a decimal.

   a) 15% b) 41% c) 9% d) 80%

6. Express each per cent as a fraction in its simplest form.

   a) 46% b) 40% c) 28% d) 6%

Solve the word problems. Show your work clearly.

7. 15 out of 100 oranges in a box are rotten. What percentage of the oranges are rotten?

8. There are 100 cups in a bag. 37 of them are green. The rest are red. What percentage of the cups are red?

9. A football team won 60% of its matches. What fraction of the matches did the football team win?

 ISBN 978-93-5103-033-1

Lesson 2 Expressing a Fraction as a Per Cent

Expressing a fraction with denominator smaller than 100 as a per cent

Let's Learn

a) Mr. Roy has painted $\frac{3}{4}$ of a wall. What percentage of the wall has he painted?

Method 1

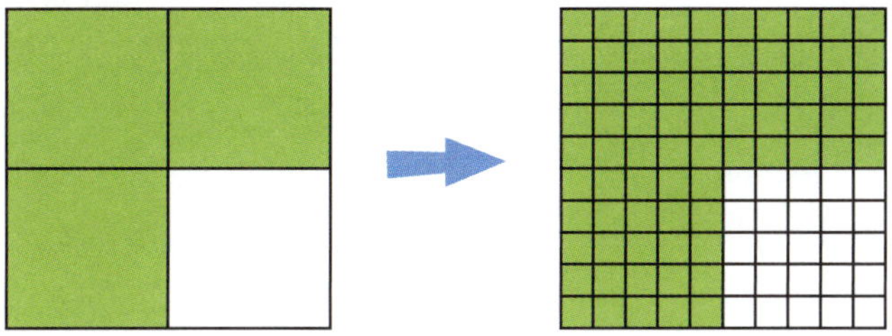

Find an equivalent fraction of $\frac{3}{4}$ with a denominator of 100.

$$\frac{3}{4} \underset{\times 25}{\overset{\times 25}{=}} \frac{75}{100}$$

$$\frac{3}{4} = \frac{75}{100}$$
$$= 75\%$$

He has painted ___ % of the wall.

Method 2

$$\frac{3}{4} = \frac{3}{4} \times 100\%$$
$$= \_\_\_\ \%$$

1 whole is 100%.

$\frac{3}{4}$ is $\frac{3}{4}$ of 100%.

$$\frac{3}{\cancel{4}_1} \times \cancel{100}^{25} = 3 \times 25$$
$$= \_\_\_$$

He has painted ___ % of the wall.

 ISBN 978-93-5103-033-1

b) Express $\frac{2}{5}$ as a per cent.

Method 1

$$\frac{2}{5} = \frac{4}{10} = \frac{\square}{100} = \square\%$$

Method 2

$$\frac{2}{5} = \frac{2}{5} \times 100\%$$
$$= \square\%$$

Let's Do

1. Express each fraction as a per cent.

Method 1

a) $\frac{9}{20} = \frac{\square}{100}$

$= \_\_\_\_\_\_\%$

b) $\frac{4}{5} = \frac{\square}{10}$

$= \frac{\square}{100}$

$= \_\_\_\_\_\_\%$

c) $\frac{14}{25} = \frac{\square}{100}$

$= \_\_\_\_\_\_\%$

Method 2

a) $\frac{9}{20} = \frac{9}{20} \times 100\%$

$= \_\_\_\_\_\_\%$

b) $\frac{4}{5} = \frac{4}{5} \times 100\%$

$= \_\_\_\_\_\_\%$

c) $\frac{14}{25} = \frac{14}{25} \times 100\%$

$= \_\_\_\_\_\_\%$

 ISBN 978-93-5103-033-1

Expressing a part of a whole as a per cent

Let's Learn

a) Express 7 out of 25 as a per cent.

Method 1

$$\frac{7}{25} \overset{\times 4}{=} \frac{28}{100} = 28\%$$

Method 2

$$\frac{7}{25} = \frac{7}{25} \times 100\%$$
$$= \square\%$$

b) Tara has 20 apples. 14 of them are red apples.
What percentage of the apples are red apples?

Method 1

$$\frac{14}{20} \overset{\times 5}{=} \frac{\square}{100} = \square\%$$

Method 2

$$\frac{14}{20} = \frac{14}{20} \times 100\%$$
$$= \square\%$$

$\square$% of the apples are red apples.

Let's Do

1. Express 2 out of 5 as a per cent.

Method 1

$$\frac{2}{5} = \frac{\square}{100} = \_\_\_\_\_\%$$

Method 2

$$\frac{2}{5} = \frac{2}{5} \times 100\% = \_\_\_\_\_\%$$

2. Jane has 20 roses. She gives 13 of them to her friends.
What percentage of the roses does she give away?

Method 1

$$\frac{13}{20} = \frac{\square}{100} = \_\_\_\_\_\%$$

Method 2

$$\frac{13}{20} = \frac{13}{20} \times 100\% = \_\_\_\_\_\%$$

She gives away _____% of the roses.

PB Chapter 6: Exercise 4, pages 130–132

 ISBN 978-93-5103-033-1

Expressing a fraction with denominator greater than 100 as a per cent

Let's Learn

a) Express 180 out of 300 as a per cent.

Method 1

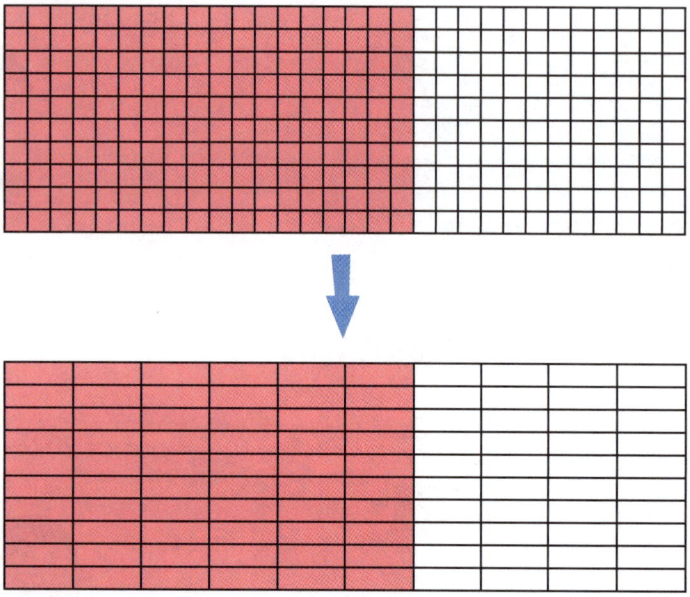

$$\frac{180}{300} = \frac{60}{100}$$
$$= 60\%$$

Find an equivalent fraction of $\frac{180}{300}$ with a denominator of 100.

$$\frac{180}{300} \overset{\div 3}{=} \frac{60}{100}$$

Method 2

$$\frac{180}{300} = \frac{180}{300} \times 100\%$$
$$= \_\_\_\%$$

b) 200 children are at a concert. 98 of them are boys.
What percentage of the children are boys?

Method 1

$$\frac{98}{200} \overset{\div 2}{=} \frac{\_\_\_}{100} = \_\_\_\%$$

___% of the children are boys.

Method 2

$$\frac{98}{200} = \frac{98}{200} \times 100\%$$
$$= \_\_\_\%$$

98 out of 200

 ISBN 978-93-5103-033-1

Let's Do

1. Express each fraction as a per cent.

Method 1

a) $\frac{8}{200} = \frac{\square}{100}$

$= \_\_\_\_\%$

b) $\frac{60}{300} = \frac{\square}{100}$

$= \_\_\_\_\%$

c) $\frac{128}{400} = \frac{\square}{100}$

$= \_\_\_\_\%$

Method 2

a) $\frac{8}{200} = \frac{8}{200} \times 100\%$

$= \_\_\_\_\%$

b) $\frac{60}{300} = \frac{60}{300} \times 100\%$

$= \_\_\_\_\%$

c) $\frac{128}{400} = \frac{128}{400} \times 100\%$

$= \_\_\_\_\%$

P/B Chapter 6: Exercise 5, pages 133–134

Relating 1 whole to 100%

Let's Learn

Find the percentage of each bar that is shaded.

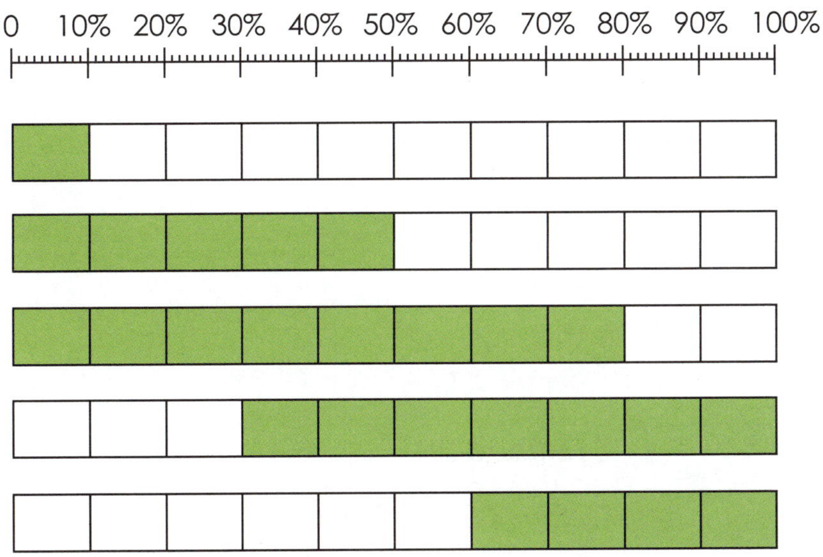

Shaded	Unshaded	Whole
10%	90%	100%
50%	50%	100%
□%	□%	□%
□%	□%	100%
□%	□%	□%

1 whole is 100%.

 ISBN 978-93-5103-033-1

Solving 2-step word problems

Let's Learn

$\frac{3}{4}$ of the sandwiches that Mrs. Gupta made were cheese sandwiches.

a) What percentage of the sandwiches were cheese sandwiches?
b) What percentage of the sandwiches were not cheese sandwiches?

a) $\frac{3}{4} = \frac{3}{4} \times 100\%$
$= 75\%$

75% of the sandwiches were cheese sandwiches.

b) $100\% - 75\% = 25\%$

___% of the sandwiches were not cheese sandwiches.

Let's Do

1. 7 out of 25 children are boys.

   a) What percentage of the children are boys?
   b) What percentage of the children are girls?

   a) $\frac{7}{25} = \frac{7}{25} \times 100\%$
   = _______%

   _______% of the children are boys.

   b) 100% – _______% = _______%

   _______% of the children are girls.

Let's Learn

Sam had ₹ 750. He spent ₹ 300 and saved the rest.
What percentage of the money did he save?

Method 1

$\frac{300}{750} = \frac{300}{750} \times 100\%$
$= 40\%$

Sam spent 40% of the money.

100% – 40% = ___%

He saved ___% of the money.

Method 2

₹ 750 – ₹ 300 = ₹ 450

Sam saved ₹ 450.

$\frac{450}{750} = \frac{450}{750} \times 100\%$
= ___%

He saved ___% of the money.

 ISBN 978-93-5103-033-1

Let's Do

1. Peter answered 18 out of 20 questions correctly.
What percentage of the questions did he answer incorrectly?

First, I find the percentage of questions he answered correctly. Then, I find the percentage of questions he answered incorrectly.

First, I find the number of questions he answered incorrectly. Then, I find the percentage of questions he answered incorrectly.

P/B Chapter 6: Exercise 6, pages 135–136

Practice 2

1. Express each fraction as a per cent.

a) $\frac{3}{10}$ b) $\frac{3}{5}$ c) $\frac{1}{4}$ d) $\frac{11}{20}$

e) $\frac{9}{25}$ f) $\frac{45}{300}$ g) $\frac{50}{250}$ h) $\frac{36}{180}$

2. Express each of the following as a per cent.

a) 4 out of 5 b) 15 out of 20 c) 18 out of 25

Solve the word problems. Show your work clearly.

3. If 70% of a tank is filled with water, what percentage of the tank is not filled?

4. $\frac{4}{5}$ of the books in a library are fiction books. What percentage of the books are fiction books?

5. There are 50 vehicles in a car park. 14 of them are motorcycles.
   a) What percentage of the vehicles are motorcycles?
   b) What percentage of the vehicles are not motorcycles?

6. 1500 people took part in a walkathon. 450 of them were children. The rest were adults. What percentage of the participants were adults?

7. Perry bought 5 metres of wire. He used 2 metres to make some photo frames and the rest to make some jewellery. What percentage of the wire did he use to make the jewellery?

 ISBN 978-93-5103-033-1

Lesson 3 Percentage of a Quantity

Finding the value of a percentage of a quantity

Let's Learn

a) There were 500 people at an exhibition. 30% of them were children.
How many children were there at the exhibition?

Method 1

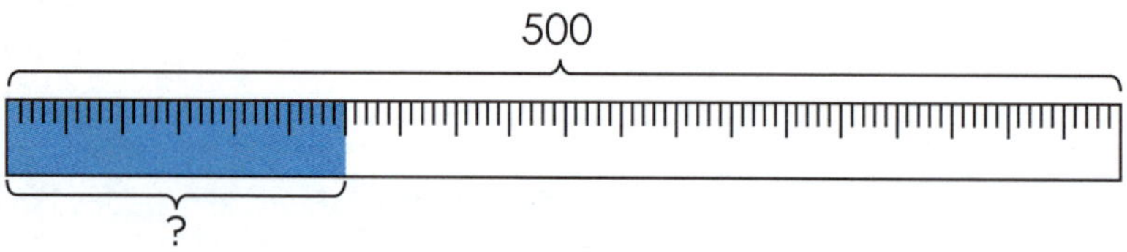

30% of the whole is shaded.

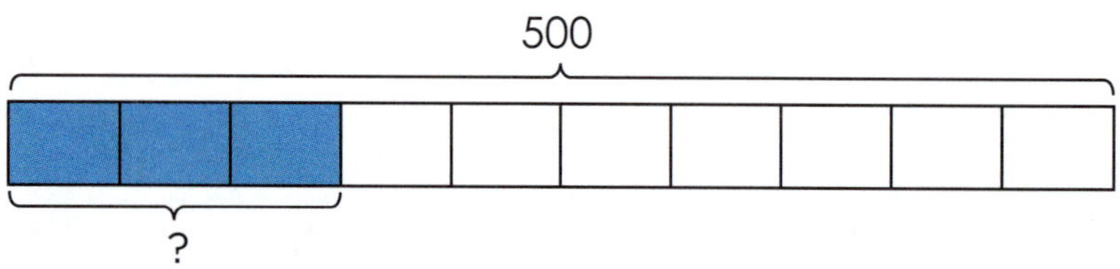

$100\% \rightarrow 500$

$1\% \rightarrow \frac{500}{100} = 5$

$30\% \rightarrow 30 \times 5 = 150$

There were 150 children at the exhibition.

Method 2

$$30\% \text{ of } 500 = \frac{30}{{}_1\cancel{100}} \times \cancel{500}^{5}$$
$$= 150$$

$30\% = \frac{30}{100}$

There were 150 children at the exhibition.

 ISBN 978-93-5103-033-1

b) Mrs. Mittal bought a refrigerator that cost ₹ 8000. She had to pay 5% **sales tax** on ₹ 8000. How much was the sales tax?

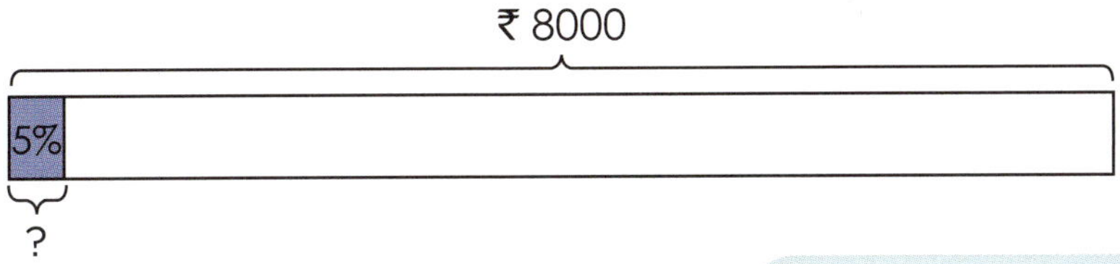

Method 1

100% → ₹ 8000

$1\% \rightarrow ₹\ \frac{8000}{100} = ₹\ 80$

5% → 5 × ₹ 80 = ₹ ____

The sales tax was ₹ ____.

Method 2

$5\% \text{ of } ₹\ 8000 = \frac{5}{\cancel{100}_{1}} \times ₹\ \cancel{8000}^{80}$

= ₹ ____

The sales tax was ₹ ____.

Let's Do

1. 120 students took a fitness test. 90% of them passed the test. How many students passed the test?

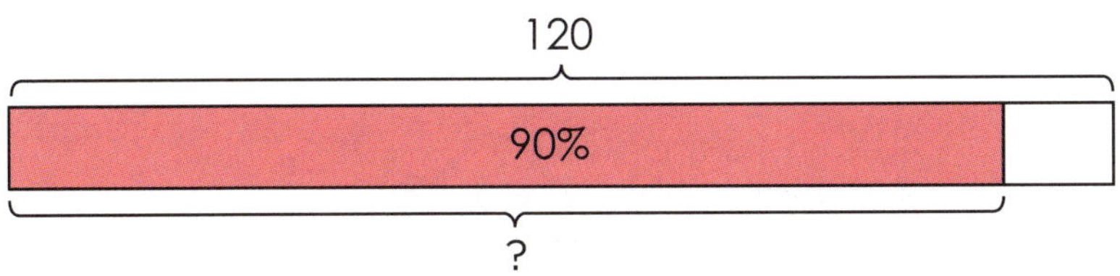

$90\% \text{ of } 120 = \frac{\square}{100} \times$ ______

= ______

______ students passed the test.

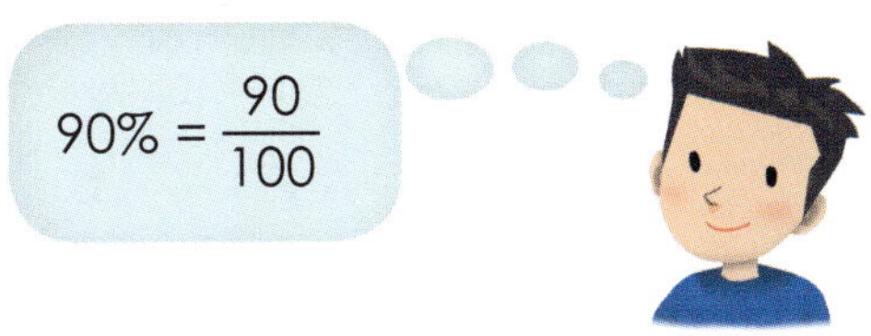

2. Fill in the blanks.

a) 5% of 300 is ______.

b) 8% of 200 is ______.

c) 25% of 40 metres is ______ metres.

Chapter 6: Exercise 7, pages 137–138

 ISBN 978-93-5103-033-1

Solving 2-step word problems

Let's Learn

Vinod had ₹ 500. He spent 24% of his money on transport and 36% on food.

a) What percentage of his money was left?
b) How much money was left?

a)

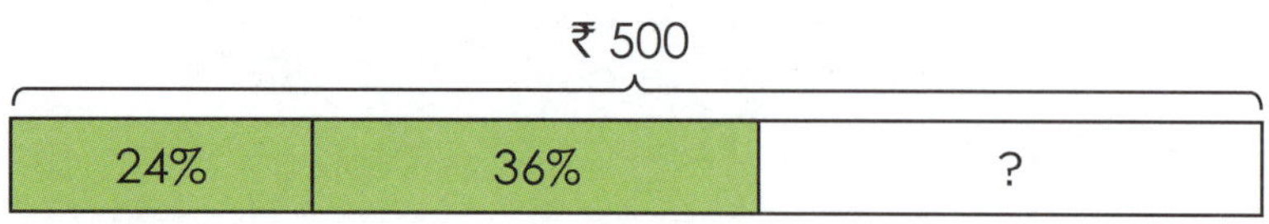

100% – 24% – 36% = 40%

____ % of his money was left.

b)

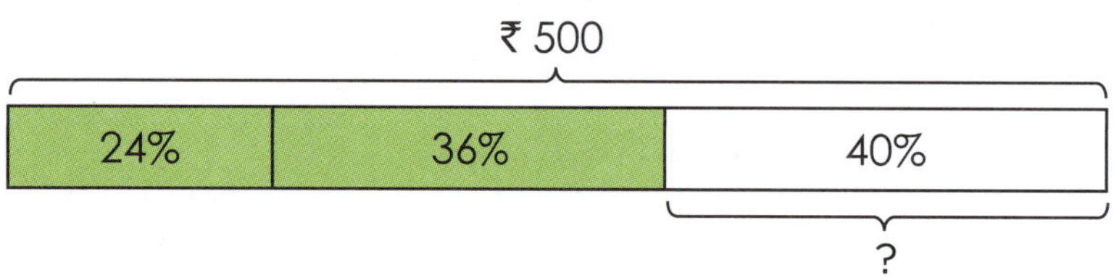

$$40\% \times ₹\,500 = \frac{40}{100} \times ₹\,500$$
$$= ₹\,200$$

₹ ____ was left.

1 whole is 100%. $\frac{1}{2}$ is 50%.

$$50\% \text{ of } ₹\,500 = \frac{1}{2} \times ₹\,500$$
$$= ₹\,250$$

40% is less than 50%.
₹ 200 is less than ₹ 250.
My answer is reasonable.

Let's Do

1. 600 people visited the museum last Sunday. 40% of the visitors were men, 35% were women and the rest were children. How many children visited the museum?

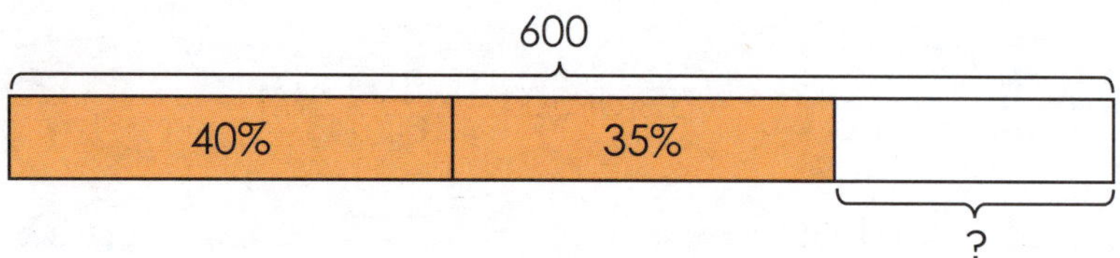

 ISBN 978-93-5103-033-1

Let's Learn

There were 400 members in a swimming club. 12% of the members were children. The rest were adults. How many adults were there?

Picture It

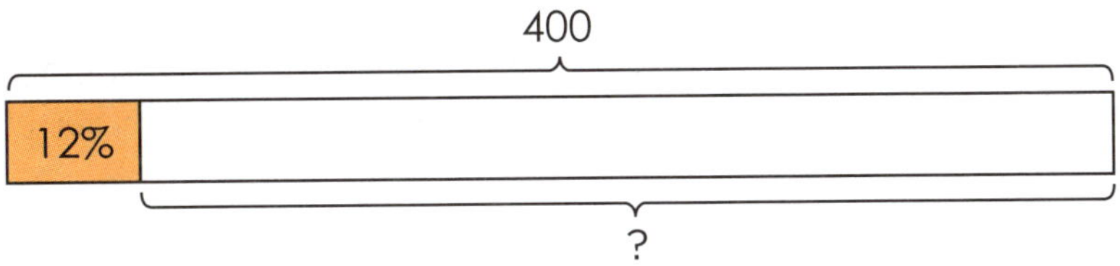

Method 1

$100\% - 12\% = 88\%$

88% of the members were adults.

$$88\% \times 400 = \frac{88}{100} \times 400$$

$$= \_\_\_$$

There were ____ adults.

Method 2

$12\% \times 400 = 48$

There were 48 children.

$400 - 48 =$ ____

There were ____ adults.

88% is close to 90%.
90% of 400 is 360.
____ is close to 360.
My answer is reasonable.

Let's Do

1. 150 students sat for an English test. 98% of them passed the test. How many students did not pass the test?

First, I find the percentage of students who did not pass the test. Then, I find the number of students who did not pass the test.

First, I find the number of students who passed the test. Then, I find the number of students who did not pass the test.

P/B Chapter 6: Exercise 8, pages 139–140

 ISBN 978-93-5103-033-1

Let's Learn

a) Ahmad has ₹ 6300 in a savings account that pays 3% **interest** per year. How much money will he have in the account after 1 year?

Interest = 3% of ₹ 6300

$= \frac{3}{100} \times ₹\ 6300$

= ₹ 189

Interest is the amount of money the bank pays you for depositing money with them.

Amount of money in the account after 1 year
= ₹ 6300 + Interest
= ₹ 6300 + ₹ 189
= ₹ 6489

He will have ₹ ____ in the account after 1 year.

3% of ₹ 6300 ≈ 3% × ₹ 6000
= ₹ 180
₹ 189 is close to ₹ 180.
My answer is reasonable.

b) Mr. Basu bought a jacket at a **discount** of 12%. Its usual price was ₹ 900. How much did he pay for the jacket?

Method 1

Discount = 12% of ₹ 900

$= \frac{12}{100} \times ₹\ 900$

= ₹ 108

Discount is the amount of money you save when buying things.

Discount = Usual price – Selling price

Amount of money paid = ₹ 900 – Discount
= ₹ 900 – ₹ 108
= ₹ ____

He paid ₹ ____ for the jacket.

12% of ₹ 900 ≈ 10% × ₹ 900
= ₹ 90

₹ ____ is close to ₹ 90.
My answer is reasonable.

Method 2

100% – 12% = ____%

____% × ₹ 900 = ₹ ____

He paid ₹ ____ for the jacket.

 ISBN 978-93-5103-033-1

Let's Do

1. A bicycle costs ₹ 9500. There is a 3% sales tax on the bicycle.
   What is the cost of the bicycle with the tax?

How much is the sales tax?

2. The usual price of a pair of earrings was ₹ 94. It was sold at a discount of 20%.
   Find the selling price of the pair of earrings.

How much was the discount?

PB Chapter 6: Exercise 9, pages 141–143

Let's Learn

a) Ramu's monthly salary in May was ₹ 2500. It was increased by 8% in June.
What was his salary in June?

Increase in salary = 8% of ₹ 2500

$$= \frac{8}{100} \times ₹\ 2500$$

$$= ₹\ 200$$

Salary in June = ₹ 2500 + Increase

= ₹ 2500 + ₹ 200

= ₹ [ ]

His salary in June was ₹ [ ].

8% is close to 10%.
10% of ₹ 2500 is ₹ 250.
₹ 200 is close to ₹ 250.
My answer is reasonable.

b) There were 400 members in a chess club last year. The membership was decreased by 5% this year. How many members are there this year?

Decrease = 5% of 400 members

$$= \frac{5}{100} \times 400$$

$$= \square$$

Number of members this year = 400 – Decrease

$$= 400 - \square$$

$$= \square$$

There are $\square$ members this year.

Let's Do

1. In a school, there were 500 boys and 450 girls in Class Five last year. The number of boys decreased by 10% and the number of girls increased by 8% this year.

   a) Find the number of boys this year.

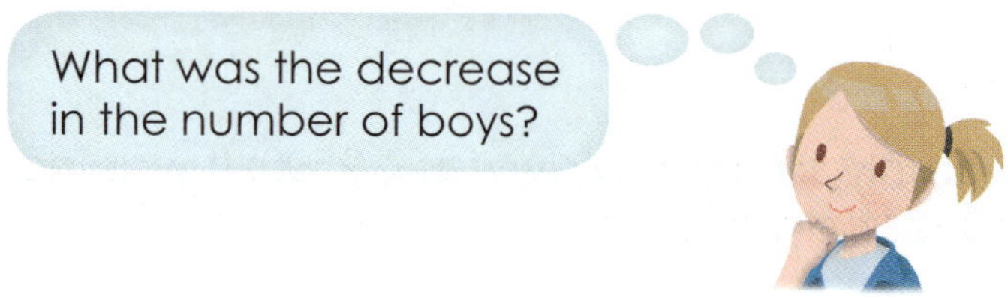

   b) Find the number of girls this year.

P/B Chapter 6: Exercise 10, pages 144–145

 ISBN 978-93-5103-033-1

Practice 3

1. Find the value of each of the following.

a)	8% of 75	b)	27% of ₹ 450	c)	33% of 100
d)	40% of 308	e)	75% of 148 kg	f)	62% of 520 m

Solve the word problems. Show your work clearly.

2. There are 1200 people living in a block of flats. 45% of them are children. How many children are there?

3. The area of a garden is 60 square metres. 7% of it is taken up by a pond. What is the area of the pond?

4. There were 50 words in a spelling test. Shobha spelt 90% of them correctly. How many words did she spell correctly?

5. Sana earns ₹ 1350 weekly. She saves 30% of the money. How much does she save each week?

6. There are 20 staff members in a library. 55% of them are females. How many male staff members are there?

7. A swimming club had 720 members last year. This year, the membership increased by 5%. Find the number of members this year.

8. Mary bought a comic which cost ₹ 50. In addition, she had to pay 10% sales tax. How much did she pay for the comic?

9. The usual price of a vase was ₹ 190. At a sale, it was sold at a discount of 30%. What was the sale price?

10. Vipul shot 15 arrows. 40% of the arrows hit the target. How many arrows did not hit the target?

11. A library has a reading club. 30% of the members of the club are boys, 40% are girls and the rest are adults. If there are 280 members, how many of them are adults?

12. There are 200 parking spaces in a car park. 10% are for trucks, 75% are for cars and the rest are for motorcycles. How many parking spaces are for motorcycles?

 ISBN 978-93-5103-033-1

Lesson 4 Problem Solving

Mind stretcher

Let's Learn

I think of a 2-digit number smaller than 20. The digit in the tens place is smaller than the digit in the ones place. When this number is increased by 50%, I get another whole number in which the digit in the tens place is greater than the digit in the ones place. What is the original 2-digit number?

1 Understand the problem.

How many digits are there in the original number?
By what per cent is the number increased?
What do I have to find?

2 Plan what to do.

I can only increase an even number by 50% to get a whole number. The original 2-digit number must be even. I can **make a list** to find the original number.

3 Work out the **Answer**.

2-digit even numbers smaller than 20 are 12, 14, 16 and 18.

Number	Increase	New number	Correct?
12	6	18	✗
14	7	21	✓
16	8	24	✗
18	9	27	✗

4 Check
Did you answer the question?
Is your answer correct?

14 is smaller than 20 and 1 < 4.
When 14 is increased by 50%, I get 21.
21 is a whole number and 2 > 1.
My answer is correct.

- ☑ 1. Understand
- ☑ 2. Plan
- ☑ 3. Answer
- ☑ 4. Check

ISBN 978-93-5103-033-1

7 Average

Lesson 1 Understanding Average

Finding the average of a group of data

Let's Learn

a) There is a different number of tomatoes on each plate.

If the tomatoes are rearranged so that each plate has the same number of tomatoes, how many tomatoes will there be on each plate?

4 + 9 + 5 = 18

There are 18 tomatoes altogether.

18 ÷ 3 = 6

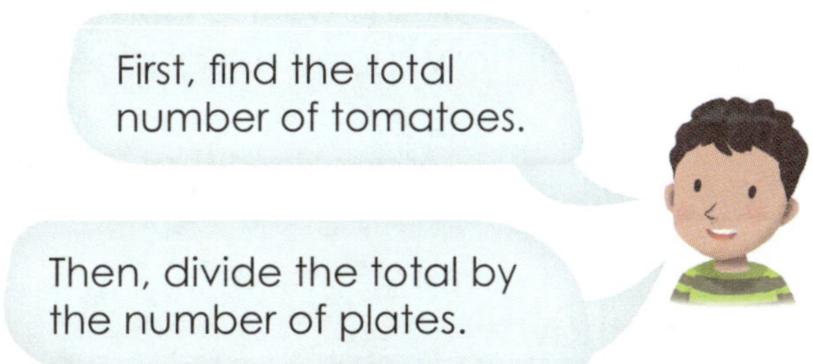

There will be 6 tomatoes on each plate.

The **average** of 4, 9 and 5 is 6.

 ISBN 978-93-5103-033-1

b) What is the average of 7, 3, 4 and 6?

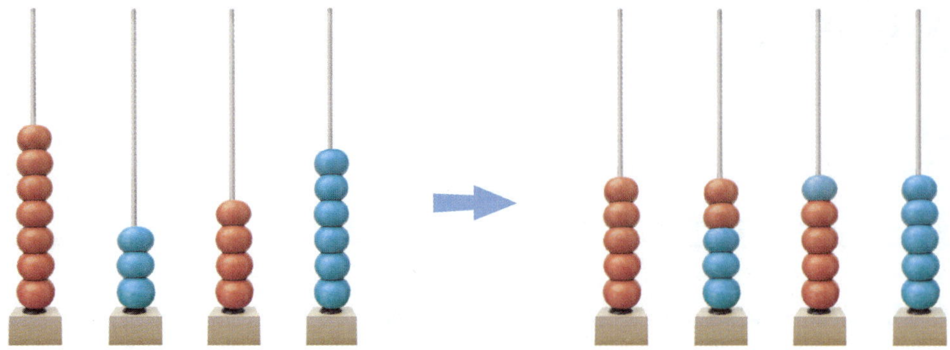

$7 + 3 + 4 + 6 = 20$

The sum is 20.

$20 \div 4 =$ ___

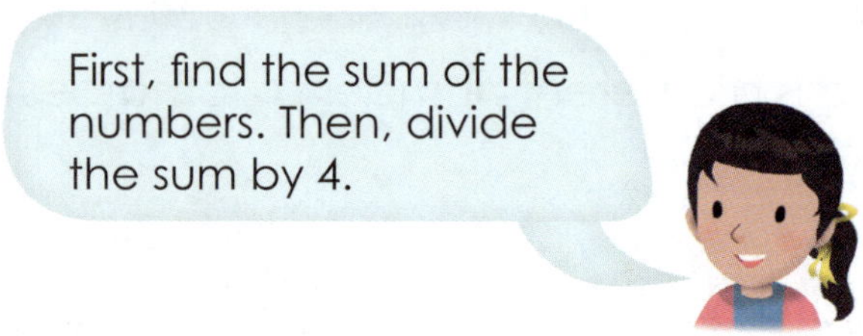

The average of 7, 3, 4 and 6 is ___.

$$\text{Average} = \frac{\text{Sum of data}}{\text{Number of data}}$$

Let's Do

1. The picture graph shows the number of magazines that 3 children bought. On average, how many magazines did each child buy?

Magazines that 3 children bought

  ISBN 978-93-5103-033-1

5 + 7 + 3 = _______

The 3 children bought _______ magazines altogether.

_______ ÷ 3 = _______

On average, each child bought _______ magazines.

2. Sophia collected 36 stickers, Nitin collected 38 stickers and Lily collected 40 stickers. What was the average number of stickers each child collected?

   36 + 38 + 40 = _______

   The total number of stickers collected was _______.

   _______ ÷ 3 = _______

   The average number of stickers each child collected was _______.

P/B Chapter 7: Exercise 1, pages 146–147

Finding average in the form of a decimal

Let's Learn

The lengths of 5 strings are 1.4 metres, 1.8 metres, 2 metres, 2.6 metres and 3.2 metres. What is their average length?

1.4 + 1.8 + 2 + 2.6 + 3.2 = 11

The total length of the strings is 11 metres.

11 m ÷ 5 = ▢ m

Their average length is ▢ metres.

 ISBN 978-93-5103-033-1

Let's Do

1. The table shows Gaurav's scores for 4 games.

Game	A	B	C	D
Score	68	76	78	88

What is his average score?

68 + 76 + 78 + 88 = ______

The sum of his scores is ______.

______ ÷ 4 = ______

His average score is ______.

P/B Chapter 7: Exercise 2, pages 148–149

Finding the average given the total amount and the number of items

Let's Learn

A taxi driver drove a total distance of 1659 kilometres in 7 days.
Find the average distance he drove each day.

1659 km ÷ 7 = 237 km

$$\text{Average distance} = \frac{\text{Total distance}}{\text{Number of days}}$$

The average distance he drove each day was 237 kilometres.

Let's Do

1. The total height of a group of 4 children is 572 centimetres.
Find the average height of the group.

572 cm ÷ ______ = ______ cm

The average height of the group is ______ centimetres.

  ISBN 978-93-5103-033-1

Finding the total amount given the average and the number of items

Let's Learn

Koyel's average score for 5 tests is 74.6 marks.
Find her total score.

$74.6 \times 5 = 373$

Total score = Average score × Number of tests

Her total score is 373 marks.

Let's Do

1. William spent an average of ₹ 4.65 each day for 8 days.
   How much did he spend altogether?

   ₹ ______ × ______ = ₹ ______

   He spent ₹ ______ altogether.

P/B Chapter 7: Exercise 3, pages 150–151

Finding the total amount given the average in compound units and the number of items

Let's Learn

The average weight of 3 parcels is 1 kilogram 400 grams.
Find their total weight.

1 kg 400 g × 3 → 1 kg × 3 = 3 kg; 400 g × 3 = 1200 g

1 kg 400 g → 1 kg; 400 g

1 kg 400 g × 3 = 3 kg 1200 g
= ☐ kg ☐ g

1200 g = 1000 g + 200 g
= 1 kg 200 g

Their total weight is ☐ kilograms ☐ grams.

 ISBN 978-93-5103-033-1

Let's Do

1. The average length of 3 ribbons is 2 metres 45 centimetres.
   What is the total length of the ribbons?

   2 m 45 cm × 3
   - 2 m × 3 = ______ m
   - 45 cm × 3 = ______ cm

   2 m 45 cm × 3 = ______ m ______ cm
   = ______ m ______ cm

   The total length of the ribbons is
   ______ metres ______ centimetres.

Finding the average given the total amount in compound units and the number of items

Let's Learn

The total weight of 4 bags of apples is 5 kilograms 200 grams.
Find their average weight.

5 kg 200 g = 4 kg 1200 g

4 kg 1200 g ÷ 4
- 4 kg ÷ 4 = 1 kg
- 1200 g ÷ 4 = 300 g

5 kg 200 g ÷ 4 = ____ kg ____ g

Their average weight is ____ kilogram ____ grams.

 ISBN 978-93-5103-033-1

Let's Do

1. The total volume of 5 buckets of water is 11 litres 150 millilitres. Find their average volume.

11 L 150 ml = 10 L 1150 ml

10 L 1150 ml ÷ 5 → 10 L ÷ 5 = ______ L

10 L 1150 ml ÷ 5 → 1150 ml ÷ 5 = ______ ml

11 L 150 ml ÷ 5 = ______ L ______ ml

Their average volume is ______ litres ______ millilitres.

PB Chapter 7: Exercises 4–5, pages 152–154

Practice 1

1. Find the average of each of the following.

   a) 185, 103, 127 and 165
   b) 12.5, 36.2, 30.4 and 26.1
   c) 2.62 m, 2.08 m, 3.9 m and 0.96 m

Solve the word problems. Show your work clearly.

2. Mr. Davis travelled 5460 kilometres in 3 months. What was the average distance he travelled each month?

3. There are 6 crates of pears. The average weight of the crates is 18 kilograms. What is the total weight of the 6 crates of pears?

4. A family of four went to a fair. They spent an average of ₹ 23.75 on game stalls. What was the total amount they spent?

5. The average length of 4 wooden planks is 2 metres 30 centimetres. What is the total length of the planks?

6. Mr. Thomas used 10 litres 275 millilitres of petrol in 3 days. On average, how much petrol did he use each day?

 ISBN 978-93-5103-033-1

Lesson 2 Problem Solving

Word problems

Let's Learn

The average height of two boys is 1.55 metres.
The height of one of the boys is 1.62 metres.
What is the height of the other boy?

1 Understand the problem.

What is the average height of the two boys?
What is the height of one of the boys?
What do I have to find?

2 Plan what to do.

First, I find the total height of the boys.
Then, I subtract the height of one boy from the total height.

3 Work out the **Answer**.

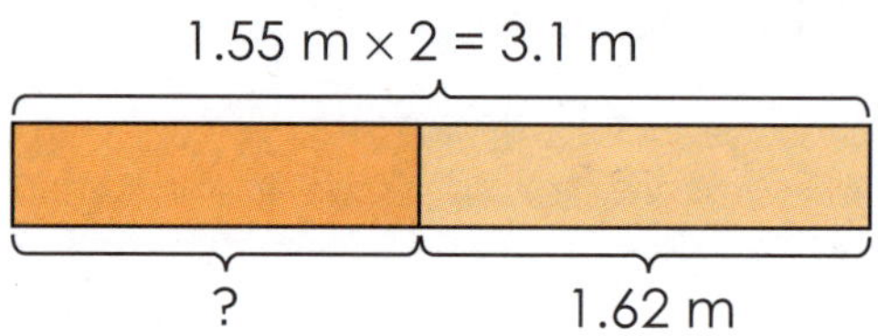

1.55 m × 2 = 3.1 m
The total height of the boys is 3.1 metres.

3.1 – 1.62 = 1.48 m
The height of the other boy is 1.48 metres.

4 Check
Did you answer the question?
Is your answer correct?

1.48 + 1.62 = 3.1
3.1 ÷ 2 = 1.55
The average of 1.48 and 1.62 is 1.55.

My answer is correct.

☑ 1. Understand
☑ 2. Plan
☑ 3. Answer
☑ 4. Check

ISBN 978-93-5103-033-1

Let's Do

1. The average cost of 3 gel pens is ₹ 4.50.
   The average cost of 2 of the pens is ₹ 3.90.
   Find the cost of the third pen.

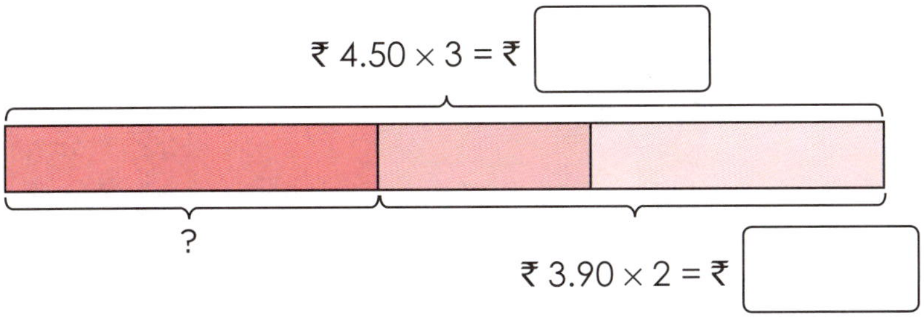

- ☐ 1. Understand
- ☐ 2. Plan
- ☐ 3. Answer
- ☐ 4. Check

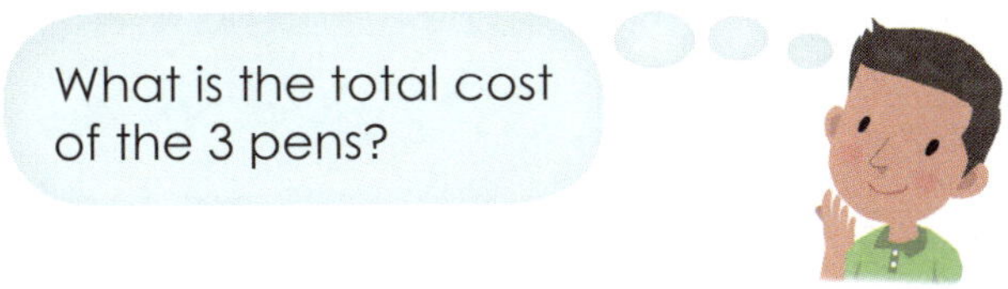

Let's Learn

During the first 3 days of an exhibition, there was an average of 145 visitors. Another 205 visitors went to the exhibition on the fourth day. What was the average number of visitors each day?

$145 \times 3 = 435$

There was a total of 435 visitors for the first 3 days.

$435 + 205 = 640$

There was a total of 640 visitors for 4 days.

$640 \div 4 =$ ☐

The average number of visitors each day was ☐.

- ☑ 1. Understand
- ☑ 2. Plan
- ☑ 3. Answer
- ☑ 4. Check

ISBN 978-93-5103-033-1

Let's Do

1. An average of 387 eggs were laid by the hens on a farm in the first 4 weeks. They laid 157 eggs in the fifth week.
What was the average number of eggs laid each week?

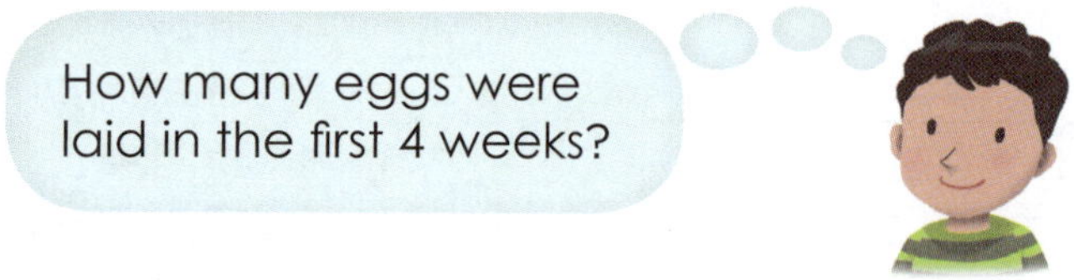

- ☐ 1. Understand
- ☐ 2. Plan
- ☐ 3. Answer
- ☐ 4. Check

Let's Learn

The average weight of 2 deer is 90 kilograms. If one deer is 20 kilograms heavier than the other, find the weight of the lighter deer.

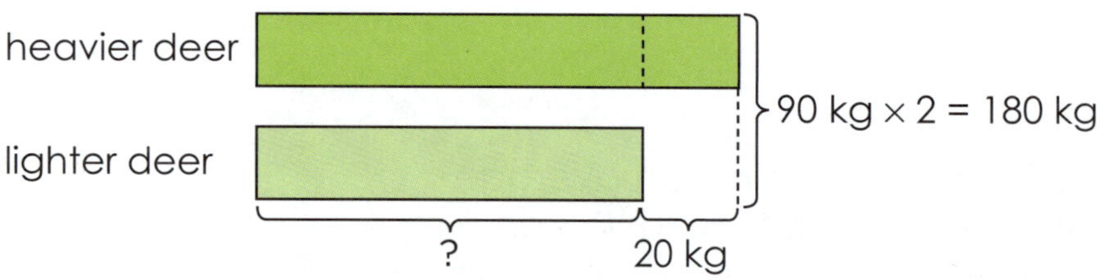

$90 \text{ kg} \times 2 = 180 \text{ kg}$

The total weight of the two deer is 180 kilograms.

2 units $\rightarrow$ $180 - 20 = 160$ kg

1 unit $\rightarrow$ $160 \text{ kg} \div 2 =$ ▢ kg

The weight of the lighter deer is ▢ kilograms.

- ☑ 1. Understand
- ☑ 2. Plan
- ☑ 3. Answer
- ☑ 4. Check

 ISBN 978-93-5103-033-1

Let's Do

1. The average of 2 numbers is 72. If the greater number is 8 times the smaller number, what is the greater number?

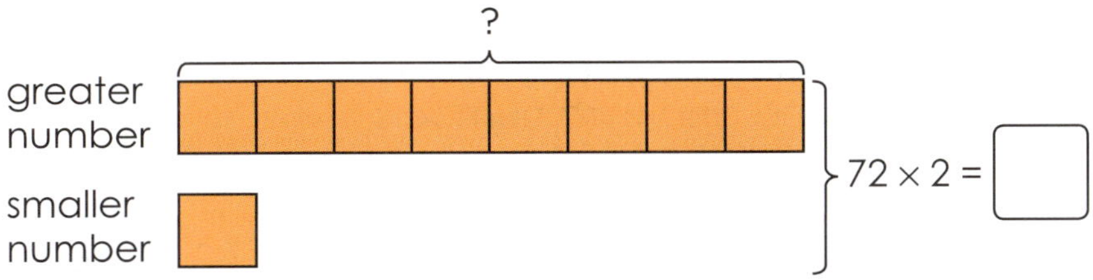

- ☐ 1. Understand
- ☐ 2. Plan
- ☐ 3. Answer
- ☐ 4. Check

P/B Chapter 7: Exercise 6, pages 155–156

Practice 2

Solve the word problems. Show your work clearly.

1. The average weight of these 4 packages is 33 kilograms. Find the weight of the fourth package.

18 kg   27 kg   37 kg   ? kg

2. To win a prize in an archery contest, Kenny must score an average of 70 points or above after 3 rounds. Kenny scores 76 points and 65 points in the first two rounds. To win a prize, what is the minimum score Kenny must get in the third round?

3. The average weight of 3 packets of peanuts is 2.2 kilograms. The average weight of 2 of the packets is 1.8 kilograms. Find the weight of the third packet.

4. A dance company held auditions for new dancers. An average of 108 people came for the auditions during the first 3 days. Another 124 people came for the auditions on the fourth day. What was the average number of people who came each day?

5. Philip scored an average of 79 marks in 2 tests. The difference between the two scores is 28 marks. Find the lower score.

 ISBN 978-93-5103-033-1

Mind stretcher

Let's Learn

37, 3[ ], [ ]8

The average of the three 2-digit numbers shown above is 42.
What are the missing digits in the second and third numbers?

1 Understand the problem.

What is the average of the three numbers?
What do I have to find?

2 Plan what to do.

I can **simplify the problem** by solving part of it using the given information. First, I find the sum of the three numbers. Then, I subtract 37 from the sum. Lastly, I **work backwards** to find the missing digits.

3 Work out the **Answer**.

$42 \times 3 = 126$
The sum of the three numbers is 126.

$126 - 37 = 89$
The sum of the second and the third numbers is 89.

	3	[1]
+	[5]	8
	8	9

The missing digit in the second number is 1.
The missing digit in the third number is 5.

4 Check
Did you answer the question?
Is your answer correct?

$37 + 31 + 58 = 126$
$126 \div 3 = 42$
My answer is correct.

☑ 1. Understand
☑ 2. Plan
☑ 3. Answer
☑ 4. Check

 ISBN 978-93-5103-033-1

8 Triangles

Lesson 1 Parts of a Triangle

Identifying the sides, vertices and angles of a triangle

Let's Learn

A triangle is a closed figure with three **sides**. Any two sides meet to form a **vertex** and an **angle**. A triangle has three vertices and three angles.

Picture It

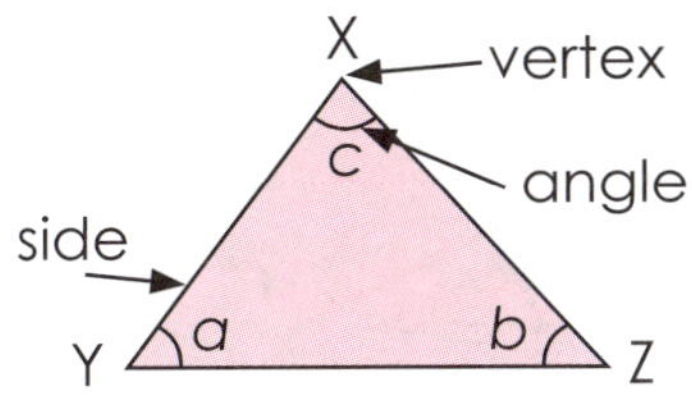

In Triangle XYZ shown,

- Points X, Y and Z are the vertices.
- XY, YZ and ZX are the sides.
- $\angle a$, $\angle b$ and $\angle c$ are the angles.

We can also name the angles as ∠XYZ, ∠YZX and ∠ZXY, respectively.

Let's Do

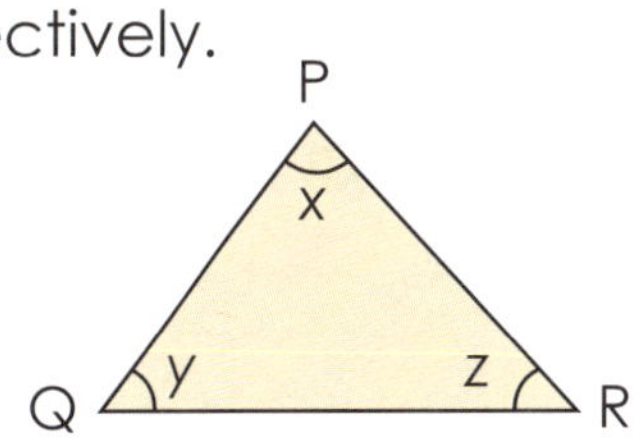

1. In Triangle PQR shown,
   a) Point R is a ________. b) PQ is a ________.
   c) ∠________ is formed by sides QR and RP.

Identifying the base and height of a triangle

Let's Learn

Sita made two triangles on a geoboard.

Maths Lab

a)

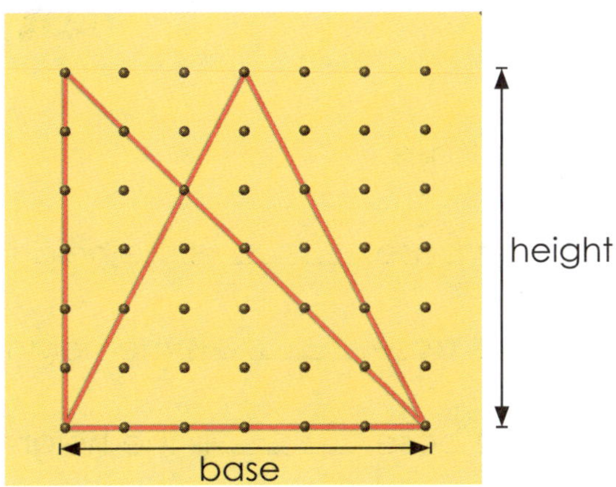

The two triangles have the same **base** and **height**.

 ISBN 978-93-5103-033-1

b) Any side of a triangle can be the base.
The height of a triangle is perpendicular to its base.

Picture It

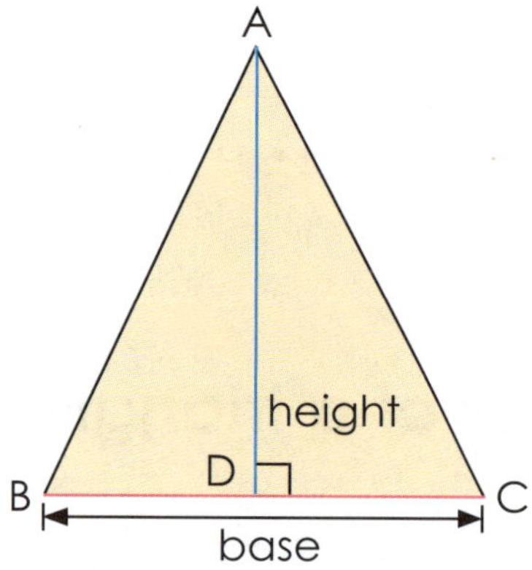

When BC is the base, AD is the height.
AD is perpendicular to BC.

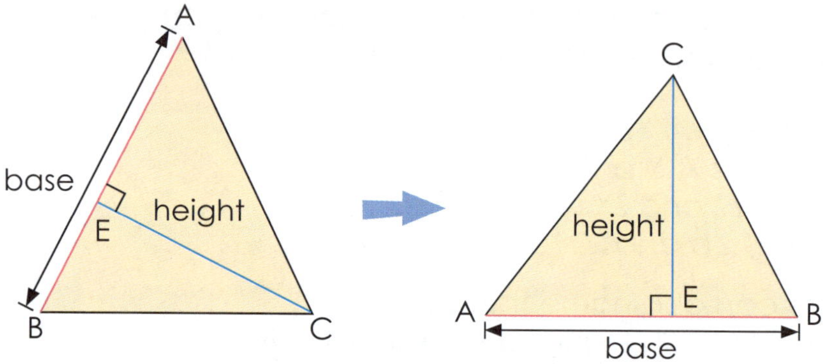

When AB is the base, CE is the height. AB is perpendicular to CE.

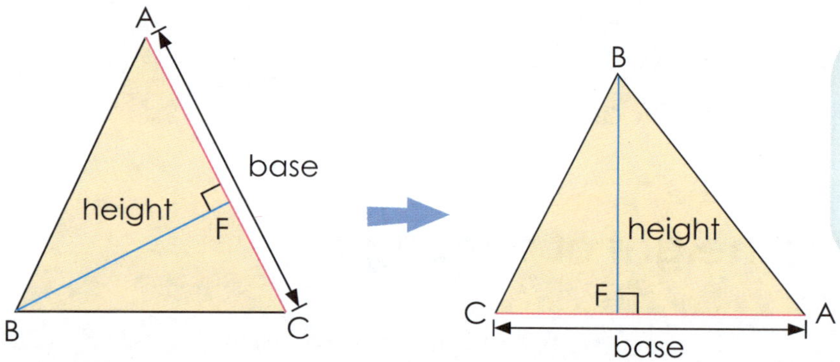

When AC is the base, BF is the height. AC is perpendicular to BF.

Let's Do

1. Name the height which is related to the given base.

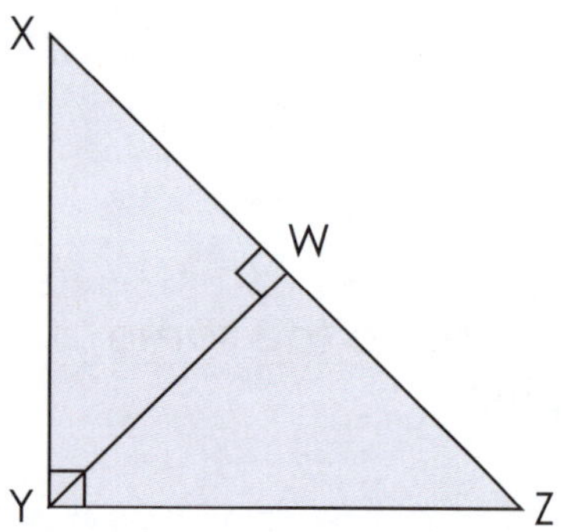

a) When YZ is the base, _______ is the height.

b) When XY is the base, _______ is the height.

c) When XZ is the base, _______ is the height.

  ISBN 978-93-5103-033-1

Identifying heights that are not within the triangles

Let's Learn

Picture It

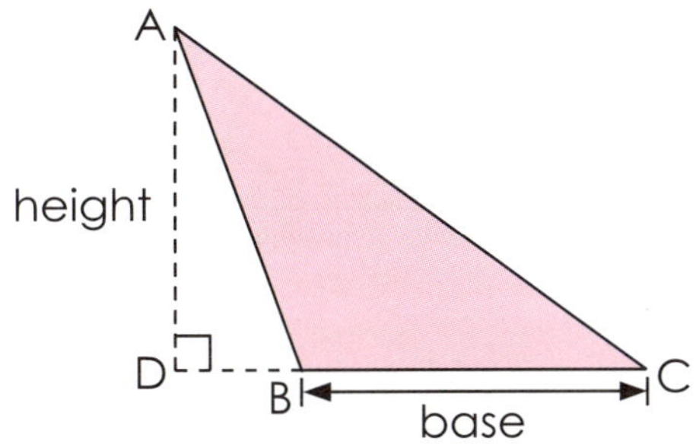

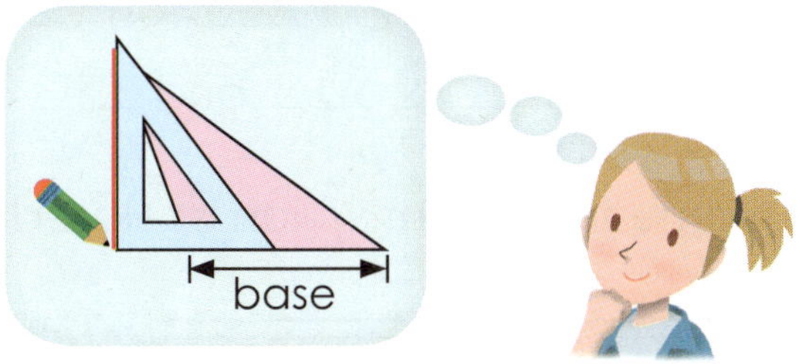

When BC is the base, AD is the height.

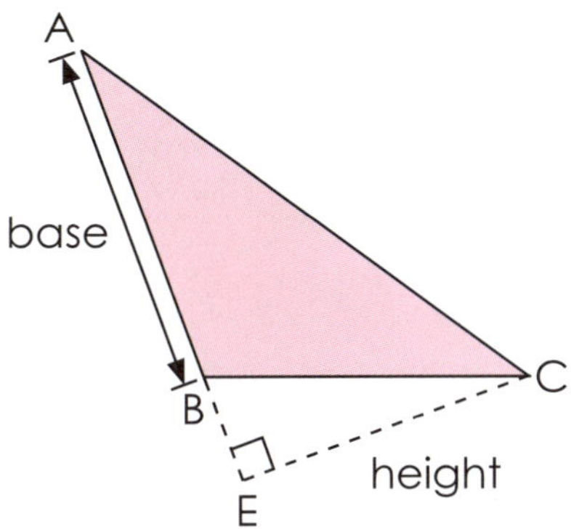

When AB is the base, CE is the height.

The height is the perpendicular distance from the base to the opposite vertex.

Let's Do

1. Name the height which is related to the given base.

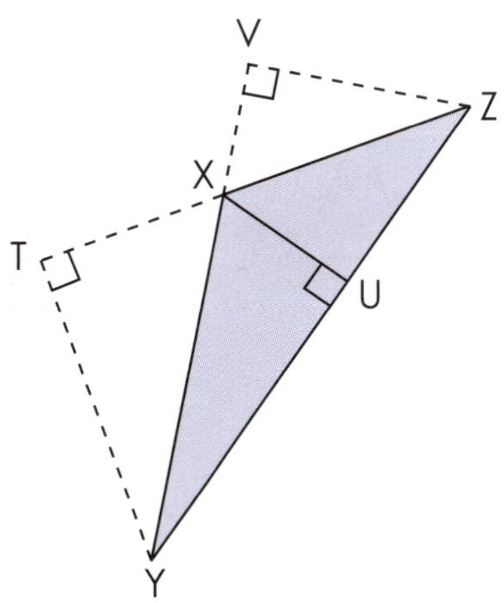

a) When YZ is the base, ______ is the height.

b) When XZ is the base, ______ is the height.

c) When XY is the base, ______ is the height.

PB Chapter 8: Exercise 1, pages 157–158

 ISBN 978-93-5103-033-1

Practice 1

1. In Triangle LMN,

   a) sides _____ and _____ form ∠NLM.

   b) points _____, _____ and _____ are the vertices.

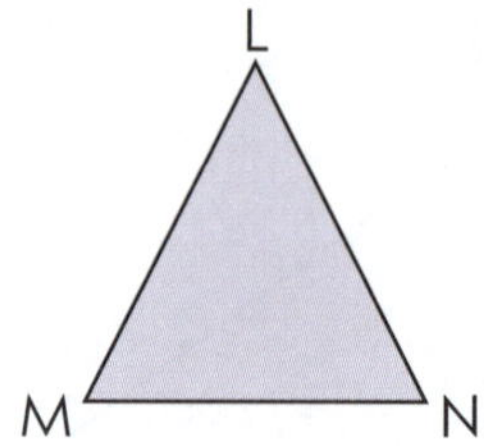

2. Name the height which is related to the given base.

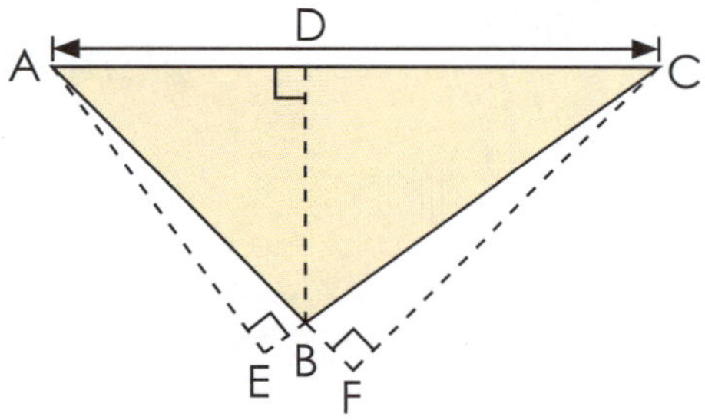

When AC is the base, _____ is the height.

When AB is the base, _____ is the height.

When BC is the base, _____ is the height.

Lesson 2 Types of Triangles

Identifying different types of triangles

Let's Learn

a)

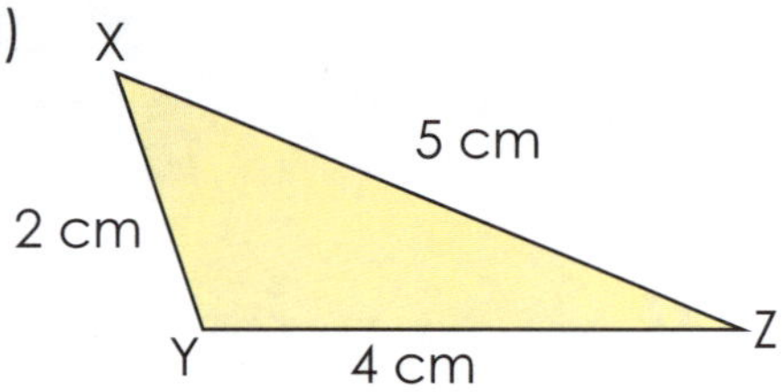

In Triangle XYZ, all three sides are of different lengths.

XY = 2 cm, YZ = 4 cm, ZX = 5 cm
XY ≠ YZ ≠ ZX

Such a triangle is known as a **scalene triangle**.

b)

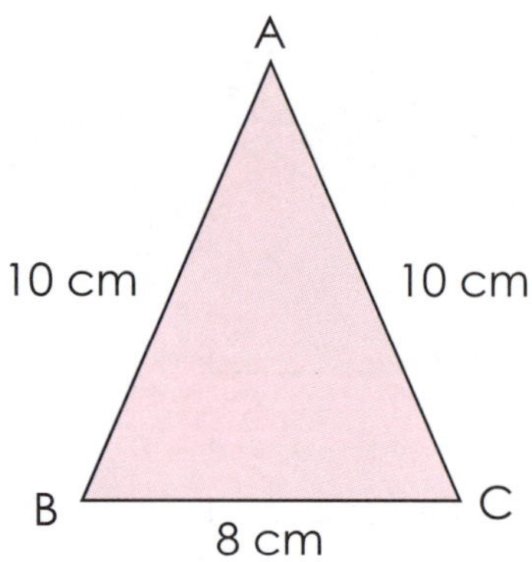

In Triangle ABC, two of the sides are of equal lengths.

AB = AC = 10 cm

Such a triangle is known as an **isosceles triangle**.

Mark equal sides of an isosceles triangle like this:

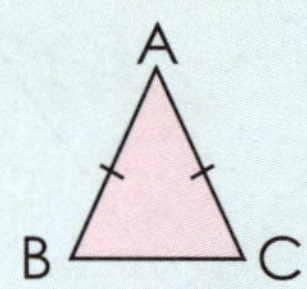

In an isosceles triangle, the measures of the angles opposite the equal sides are equal.

In Triangle ABC, m∠ABC = m∠ACB.

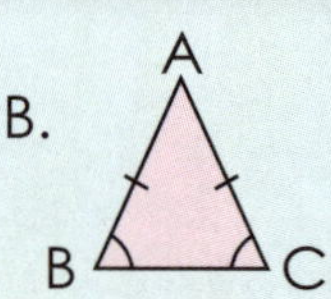

 ISBN 978-93-5103-033-1

c) In Triangle PQR, all three sides are of equal lengths.

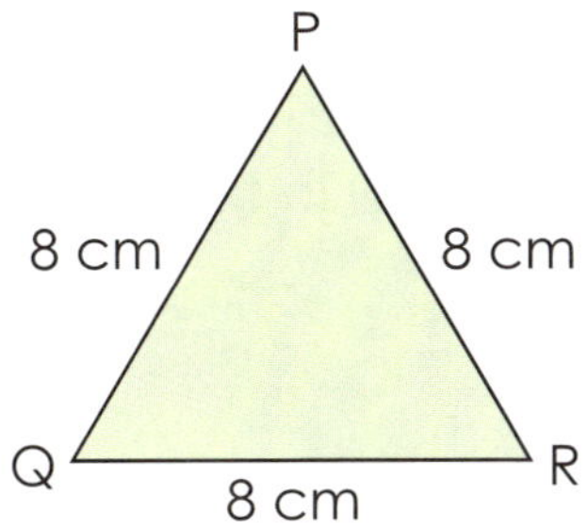

PQ = QR = RP = 8 cm

Such a triangle is known as an **equilateral triangle**.

Mark equal sides of an equilateral triangle like this:

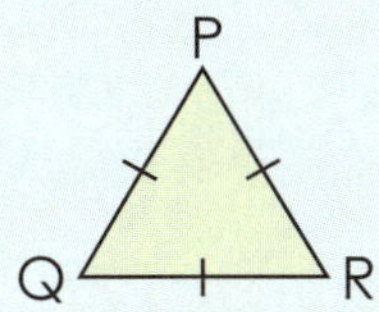

In an equilateral triangle, the measures of all three angles are equal.

The sum of angles in any triangle is 180°.

$180° \div 3 = 60°$

So, each angle in an equilateral triangle measures 60°.

$m\angle PQR = 60°$
$m\angle QRP = 60°$
$m\angle RPQ = 60°$

Let's Do

1. The following triangles are not drawn to scale.

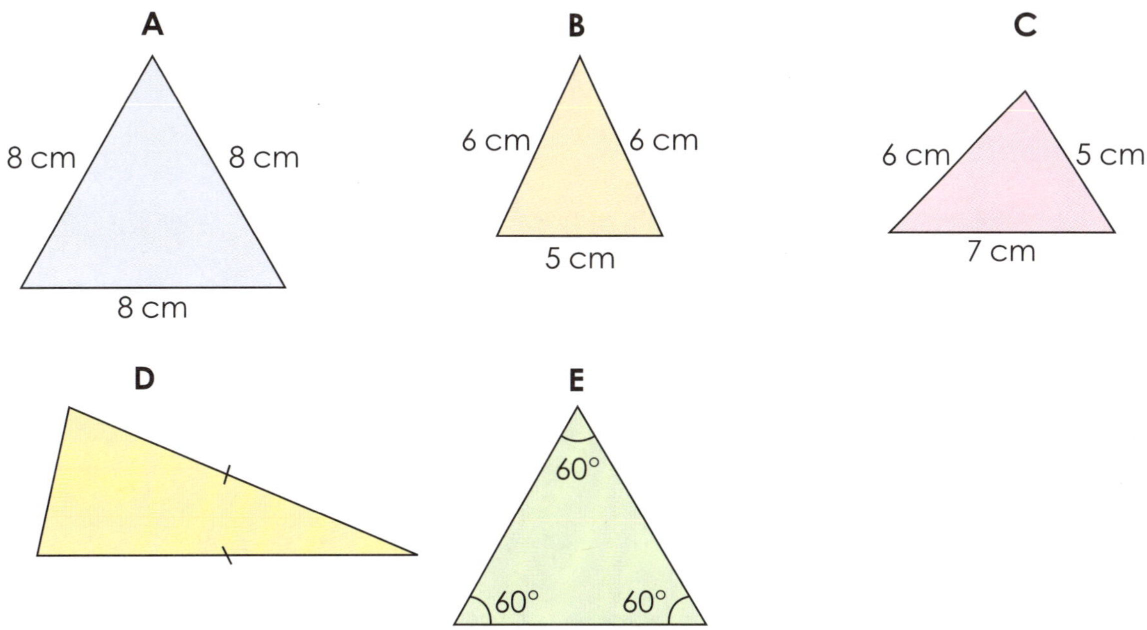

a) Triangle _____ is a scalene triangle.

b) Triangles _____ and _____ are isosceles triangles.

c) Triangles A and _____ are _______________ triangles.

d) The sides and angles of a _______________ triangle are all different.

P/B Chapter 8: Exercise 2, pages 159–160

 ISBN 978-93-5103-033-1

Practice 2

1. Measure the lengths of the sides and identify each triangle. Fill in the blanks with **scalene**, **isosceles** or **equilateral**.

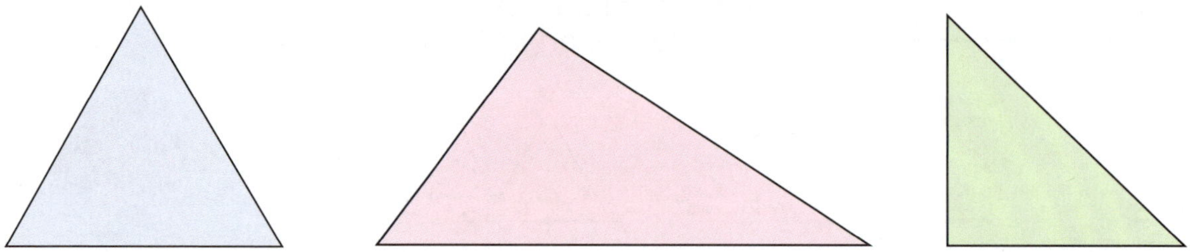

______________ ______________ ______________

2. Write down the measures of the unknown angles.

a)

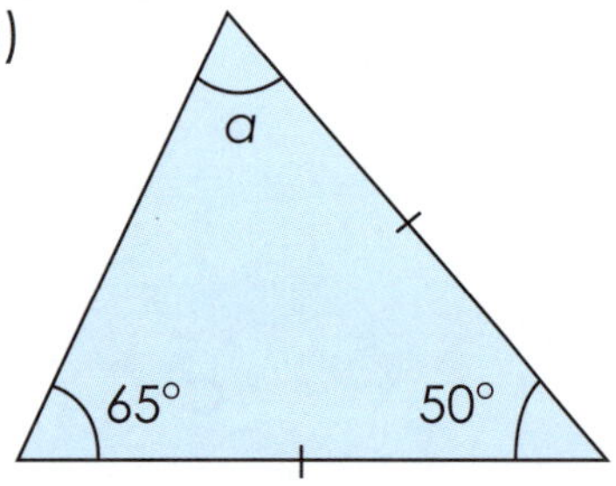

$m\angle a =$ ____°

b)

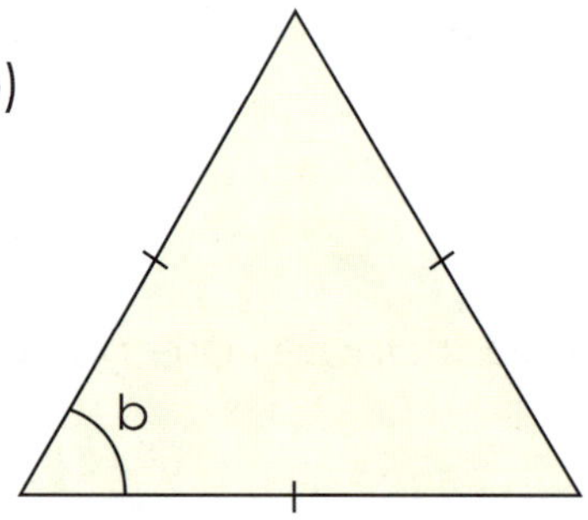

$m\angle b =$ ____°

Lesson 3 Area of Triangles

Finding area of triangles

Let's Learn

Maths Lab

Picture It

a)

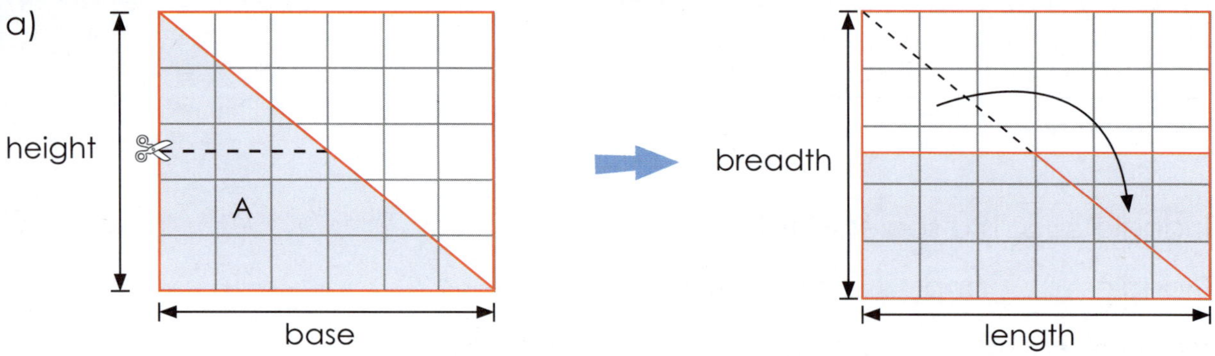

 ISBN 978-93-5103-033-1

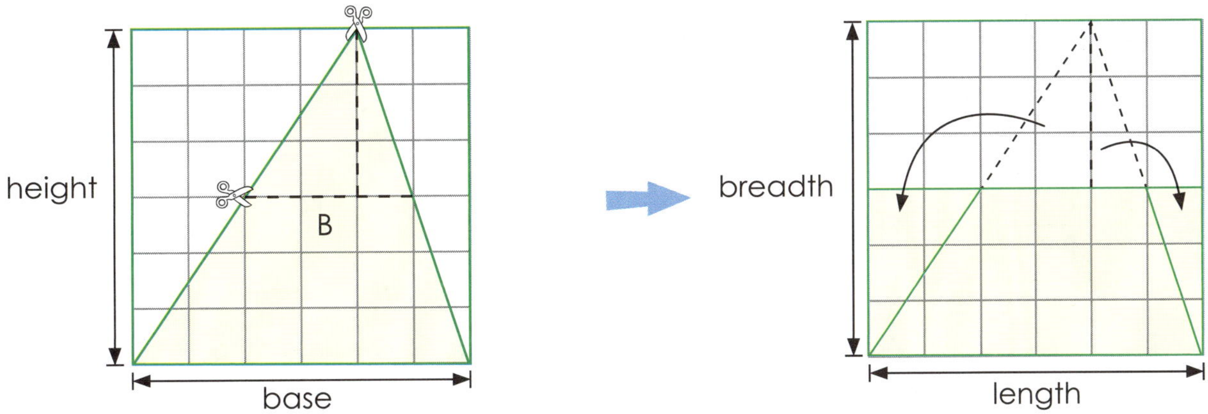

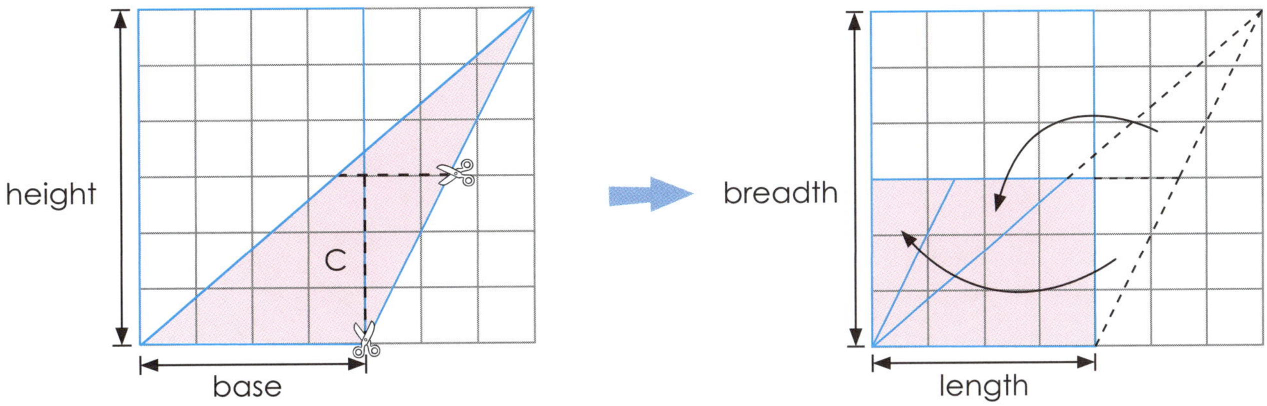

Each triangle has a related rectangle. The base of the triangle is the length of the rectangle. The height of the triangle is the breadth of the rectangle.

Each triangle can be cut up and rearranged to fit in half of the related rectangle.

$$\text{Area of triangle} = \frac{1}{2} \times \text{Area of related rectangle}$$

$$= \frac{1}{2} \times \text{Length} \times \text{Breadth}$$

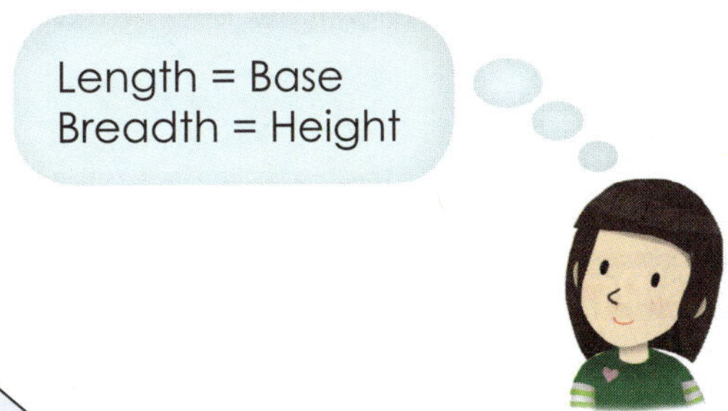

$$\textbf{Area of triangle} = \frac{1}{2} \times \textbf{Base} \times \textbf{Height}$$

b)

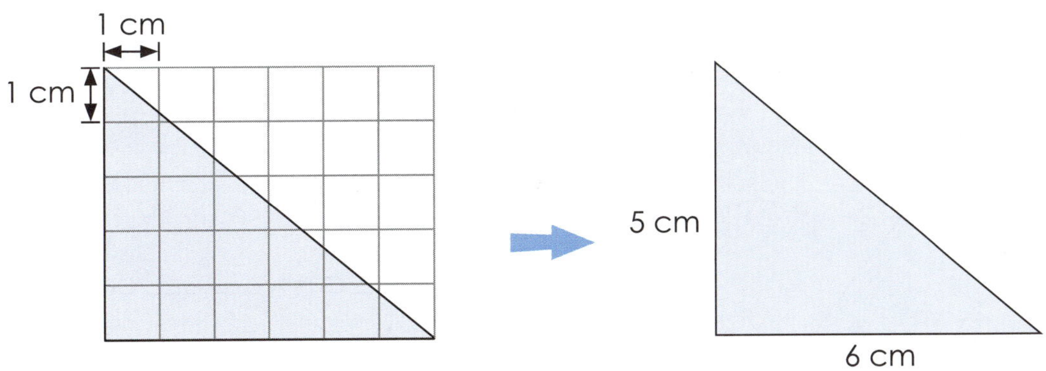

$$\text{Area of triangle} = \frac{1}{2} \times \text{Base} \times \text{Height} = \frac{1}{2} \times 6\text{ cm} \times 5\text{ cm}$$

$$= 15\text{ cm}^2$$

 ISBN 978-93-5103-033-1

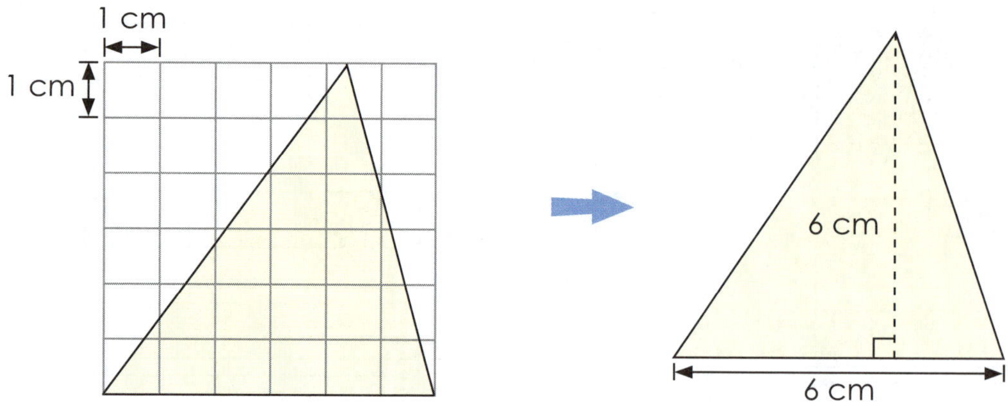

Area of triangle $= \frac{1}{2} \times \text{Base} \times \text{Height} = \frac{1}{2} \times \square \text{ cm} \times \square \text{ cm}$

$= \square \text{ cm}^2$

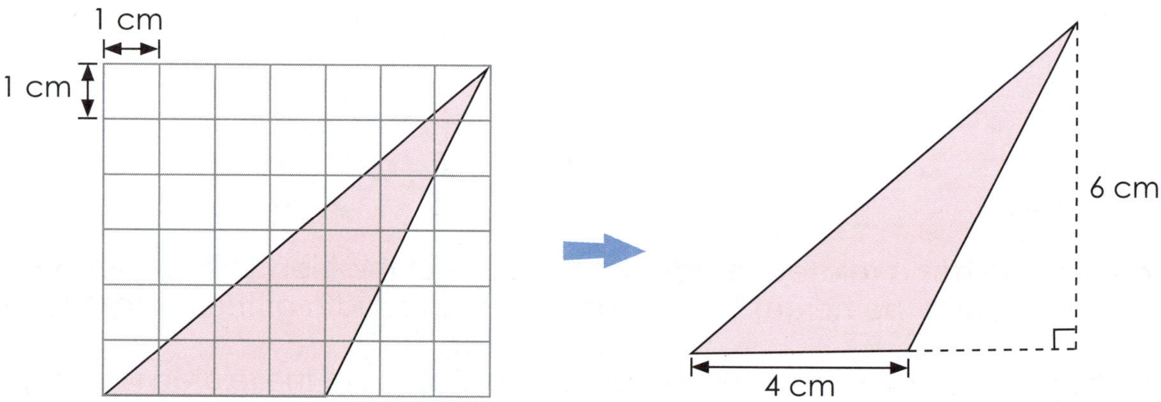

Area of triangle $= \frac{1}{2} \times \text{Base} \times \text{Height} = \frac{1}{2} \times \square \text{ cm} \times \square \text{ cm}$

$= \square \text{ cm}^2$

Let's Do

1. Find the area of each shaded triangle.

a)

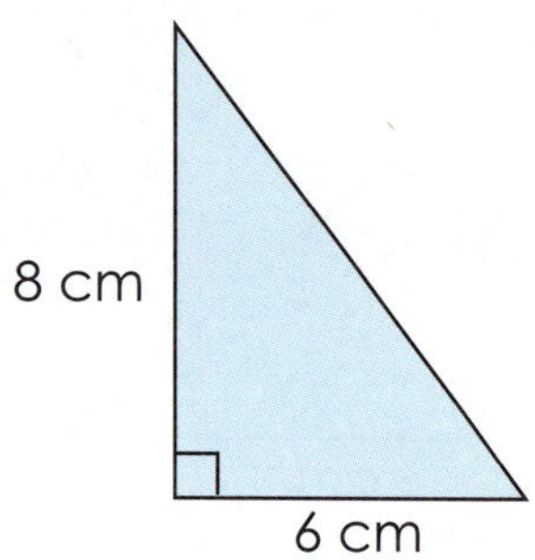

Area of triangle

$= \frac{1}{2} \times \text{Base} \times \text{Height}$

$= \frac{1}{2} \times$ ______ cm $\times$ ______ cm

$=$ ______ cm^2

 ISBN 978-93-5103-033-1

b)

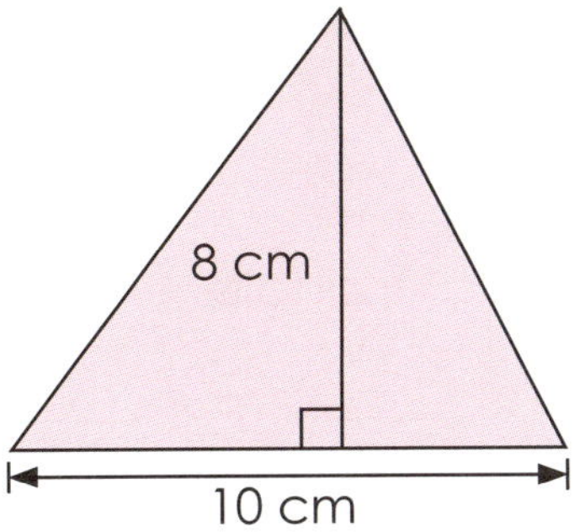

Area of triangle

$= \frac{1}{2} \times$ ______ cm $\times$ ______ cm

$=$ ______ cm^2

c)

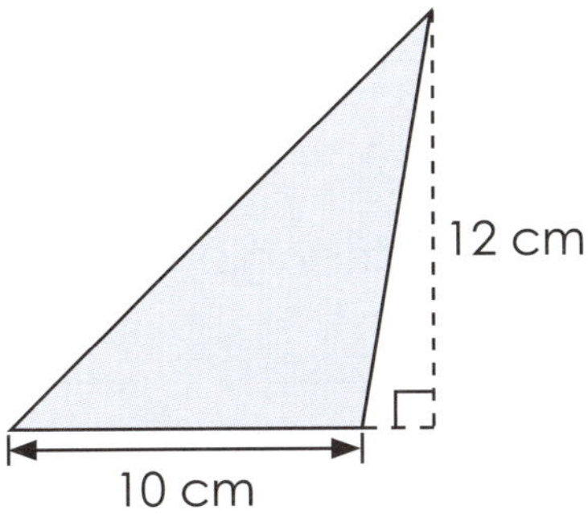

Area of triangle

$= \frac{1}{2} \times$ ______ cm $\times$ ______ cm

$=$ ______ cm^2

PB Chapter 8: Exercises 3–4, pages 161–165

Identifying bases and heights, then finding area of triangles

Let's Learn

Find the area of each triangle.

Picture It

a)

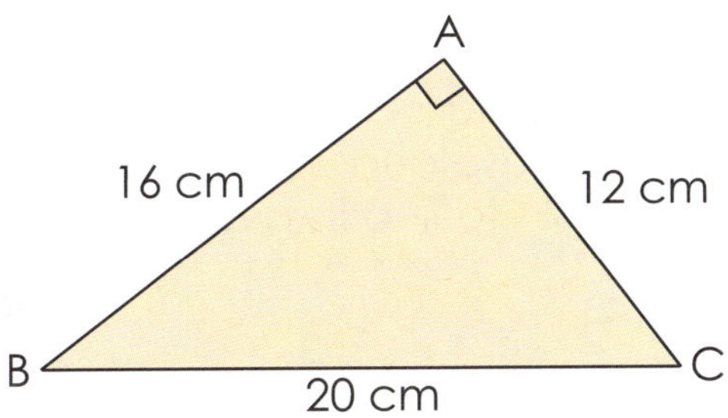

Area of triangle

$= \frac{1}{2} \times \text{Base} \times \text{Height}$

$= \frac{1}{2} \times 12 \text{ cm} \times 16 \text{ cm}$

$= 96 \text{ cm}^2$

b)

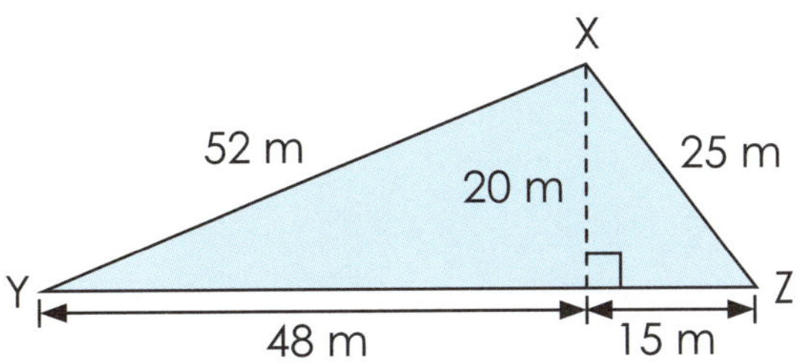

Area of triangle

$= \frac{1}{2} \times \text{Base} \times \text{Height}$

$= \frac{1}{2} \times$ ___ m $\times$ ___ m

$=$ ___ m^2

ISBN 978-93-5103-033-1

Let's Do

1. Find the area of each shaded triangle.

a)

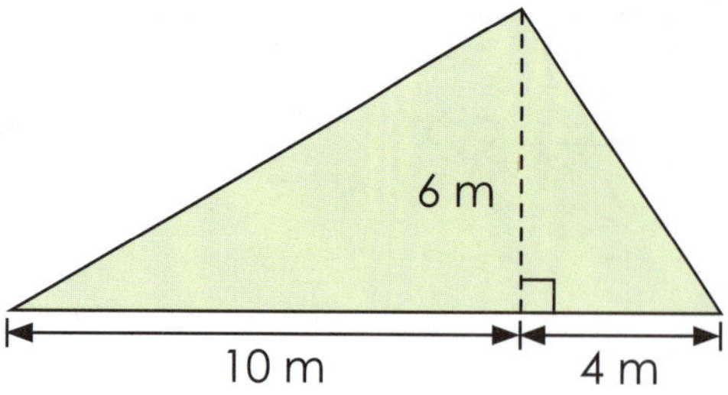

Area of triangle

$= \frac{1}{2} \times$ ______ m $\times$ ______ m

$=$ ______ m^2

b)

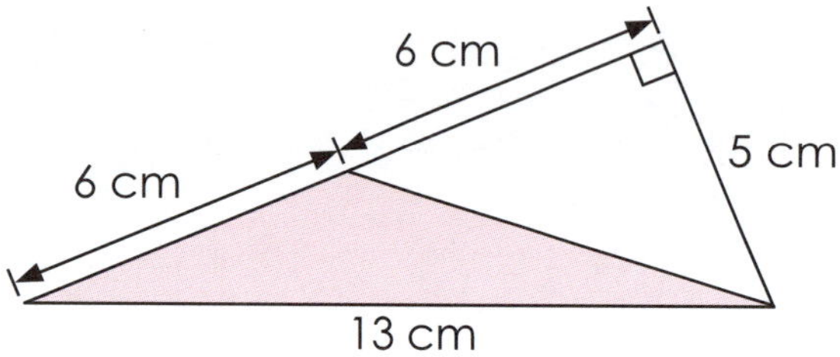

Area of triangle

$= \frac{1}{2} \times$ ______ cm $\times$ ______ cm

$=$ ______ cm^2

Chapter 8: Exercise 5, page 166

Finding the shaded area related to area of triangles

Let's Learn

Find the shaded area of each rectangle.

Picture It a)

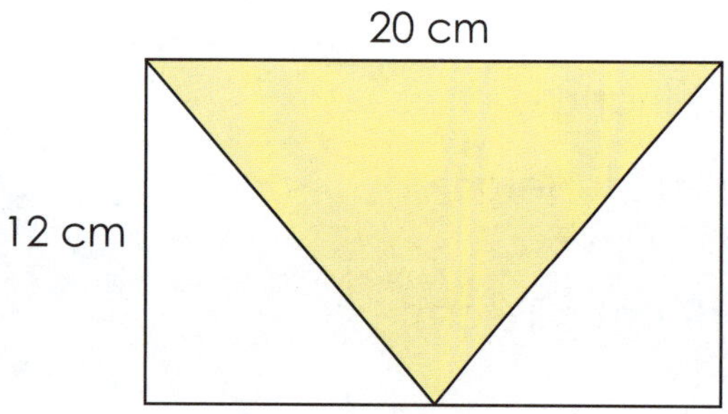

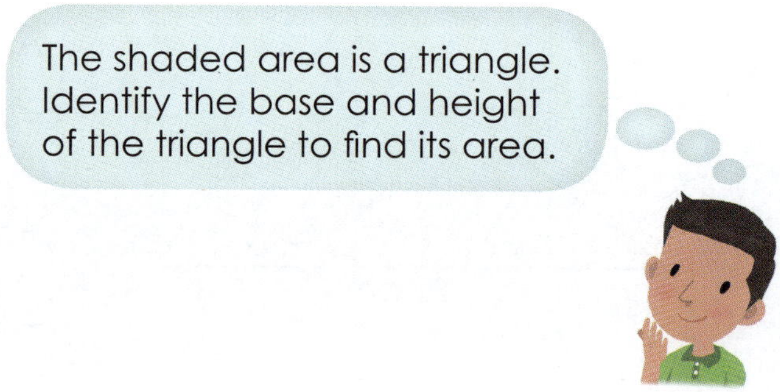

Shaded area = Area of triangle

$= \frac{1}{2} \times \text{Base} \times \text{Height}$

$= \frac{1}{2} \times 20 \text{ cm} \times 12 \text{ cm}$

$= 120 \text{ cm}^2$

  ISBN 978-93-5103-033-1

b)

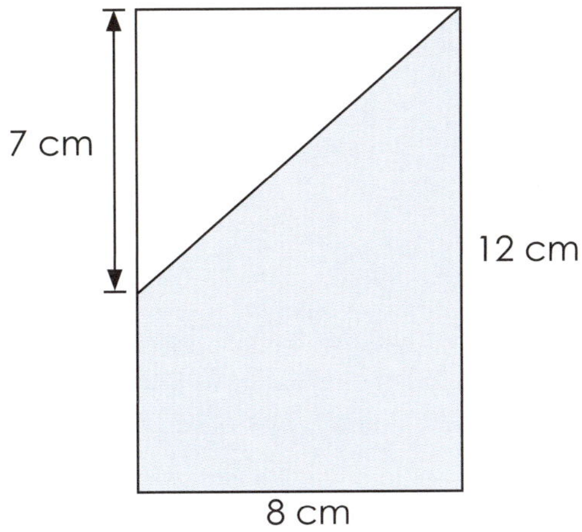

Shaded area
= Area of rectangle – Area of triangle

Area of rectangle = 8 cm × 12 cm
= 96 cm^2

Area of triangle = $\frac{1}{2} \times \square$ cm × $\square$ cm
= $\square$ cm^2

Shaded area = 96 – $\square$
= $\square$ cm^2

Let's Do

1. Find the shaded area of each rectangle.

a)

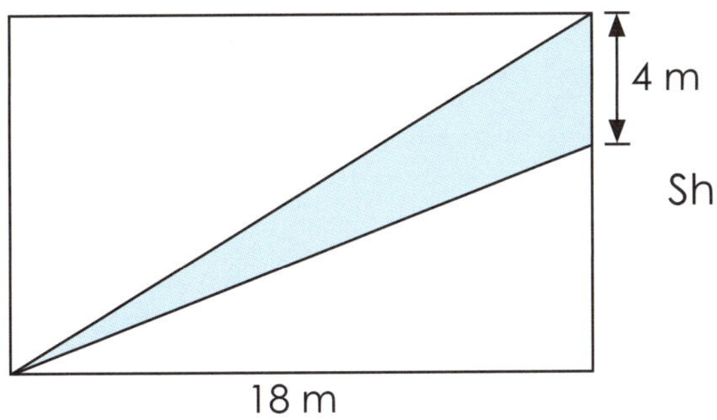

Shaded area = Area of triangle
= $\frac{1}{2}$ × ________ m × ________ m
= ________ m^2

b)

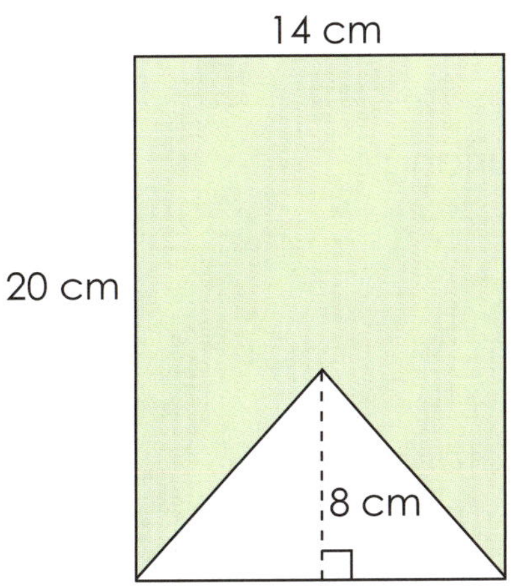

Shaded area
= Area of rectangle – Area of triangle

Chapter 8: Exercise 6, pages 167–169

 ISBN 978-93-5103-033-1

Finding area of composite figures

Let's Learn

a) The figure is made up of a square and a triangle.
Find the area of the figure.

Picture It

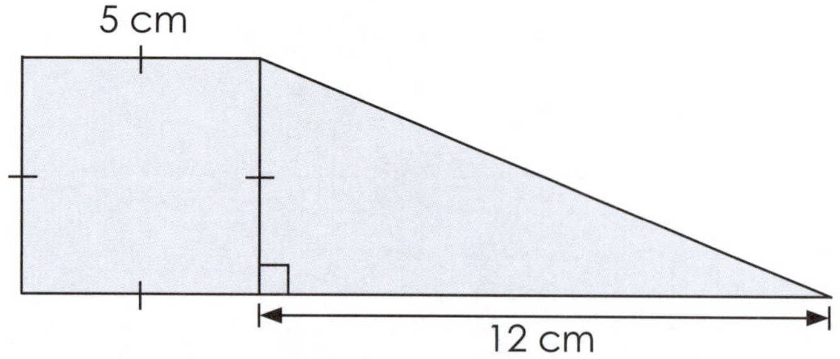

Area of square = Length × Length
= 5 cm × 5 cm
= 25 cm^2

Area of triangle = $\frac{1}{2}$ × Base × Height
= $\frac{1}{2}$ × 12 cm × 5 cm
= 30 cm^2

Area of figure = ☐ + ☐
= ☐ cm^2

Let's Do

1. The figure is made up of a rectangle and a triangle.
Find the area of the figure.

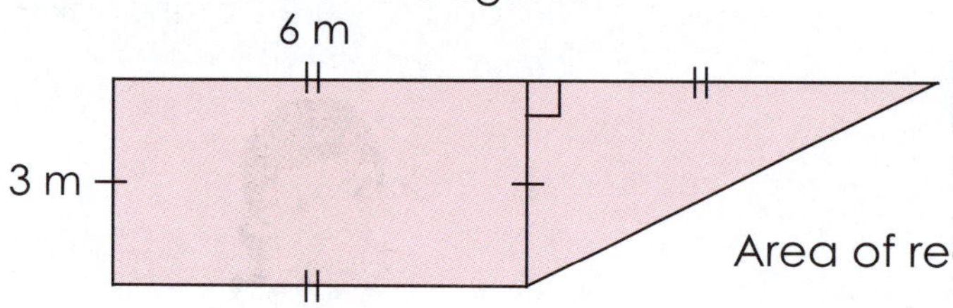

Area of rectangle = ______ m × ______ m
= ______ m^2

Area of triangle = $\frac{1}{2}$ × ______ m × ______ m
= ______ m^2

Area of figure = ______ + ______
= ______ m^2

P/B Chapter 8: Exercise 7, pages 170–171

 ISBN 978-93-5103-033-1

Practice 3

1. Find the area of each shaded triangle.

a)

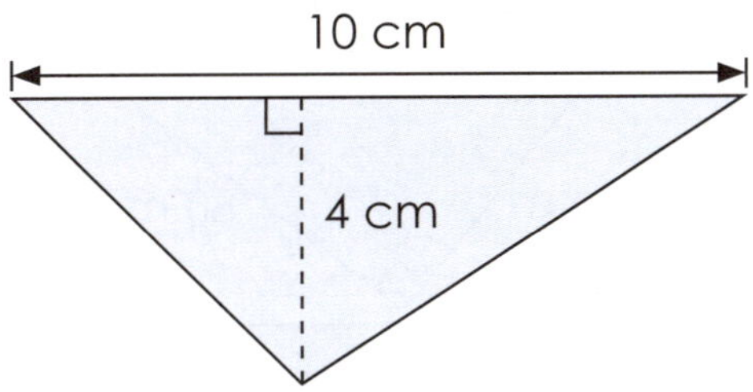

b)

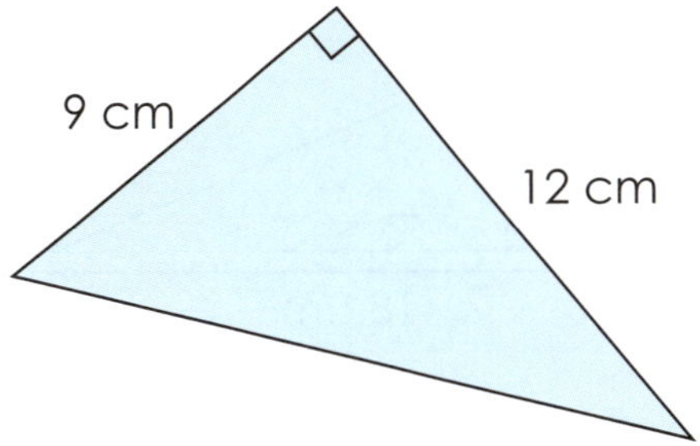

c)

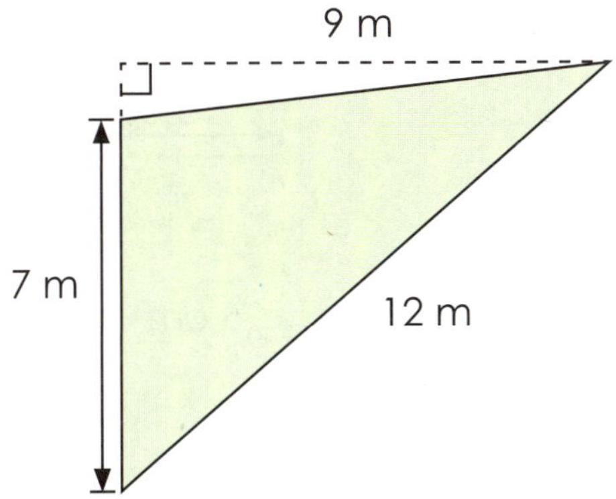

d)

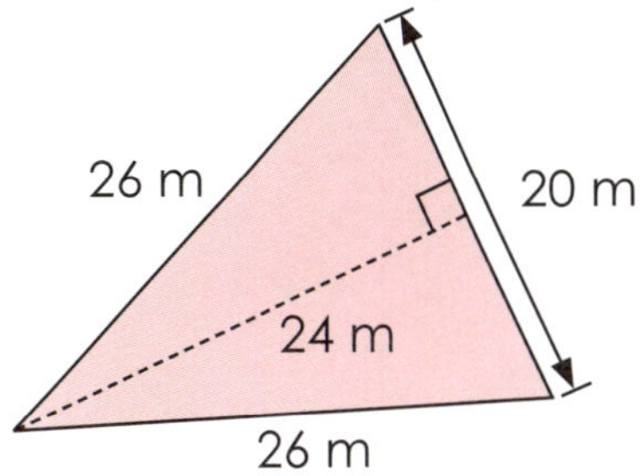

2. Find the shaded area of each rectangle.

a)

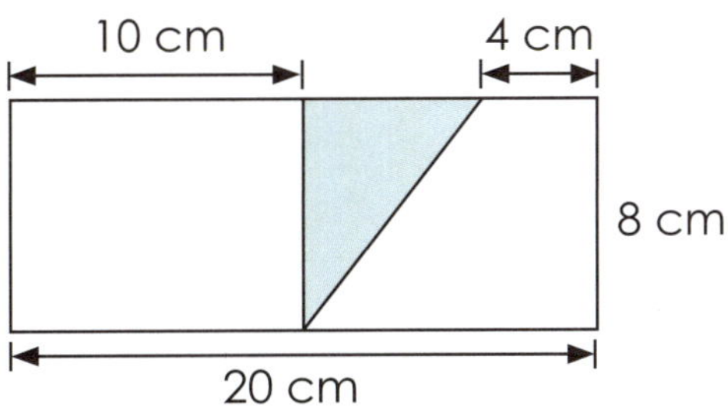

b)

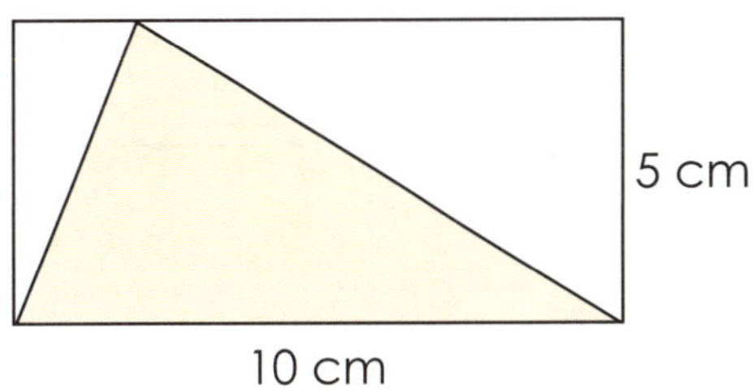

c)

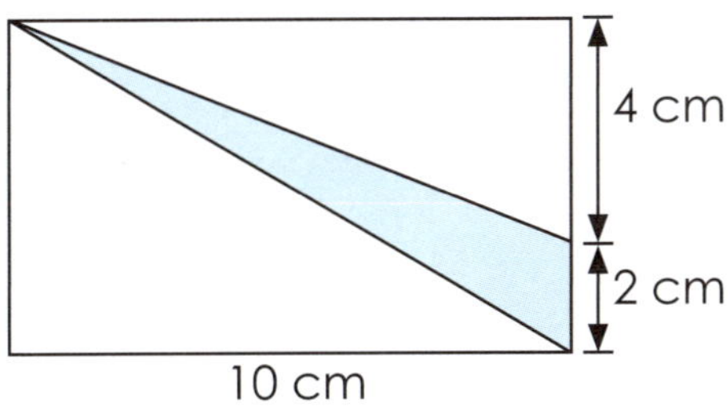

d)

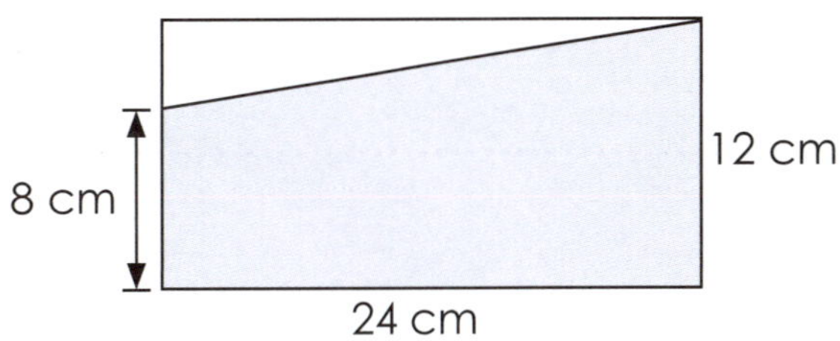

3. Find the shaded area of each figure.

a)

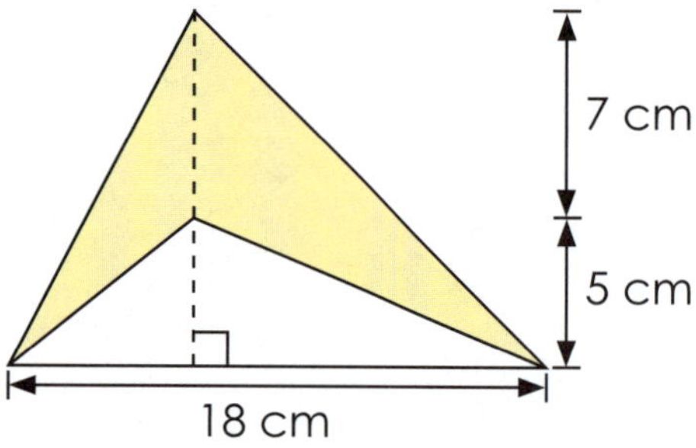

b)

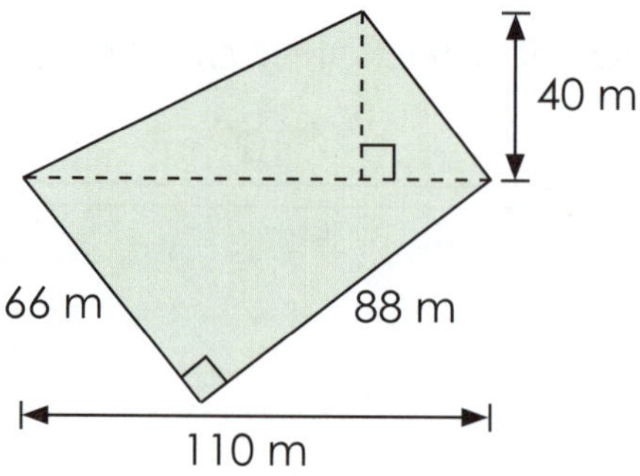

4. Find the area of each figure.

a)

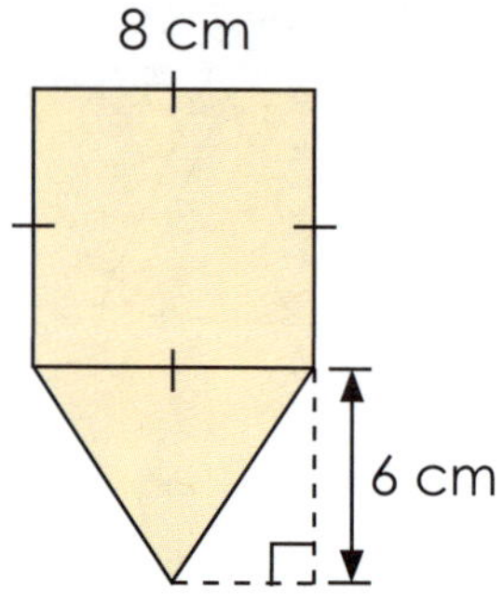

b)

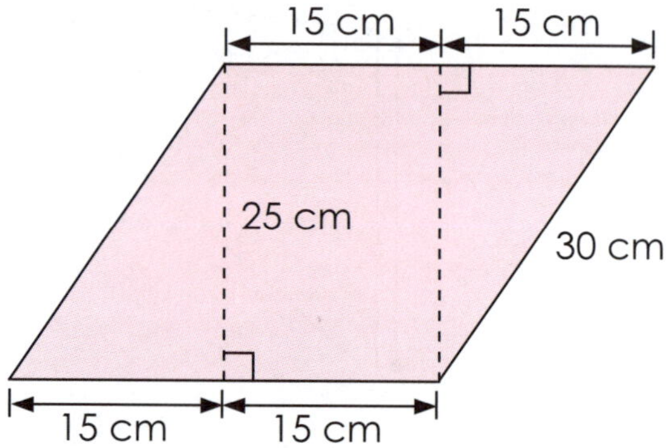

c)

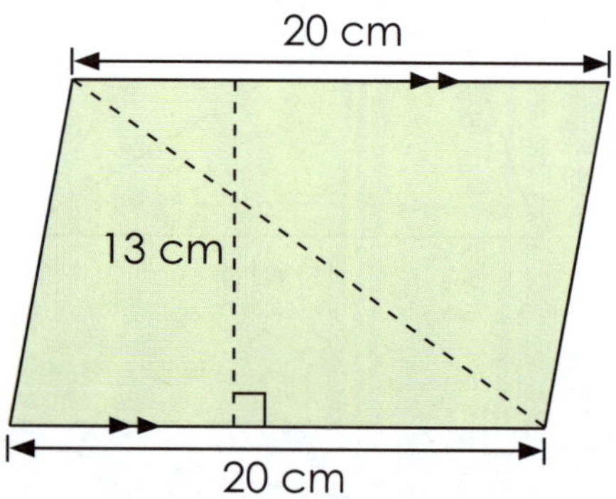

  ISBN 978-93-5103-033-1

9 Circles

Lesson 1 Parts of a Circle

Drawing circles

Let's Learn

Draw a circle of **radius** 2 centimetres with a pair of compasses.

Maths Lab

Picture It

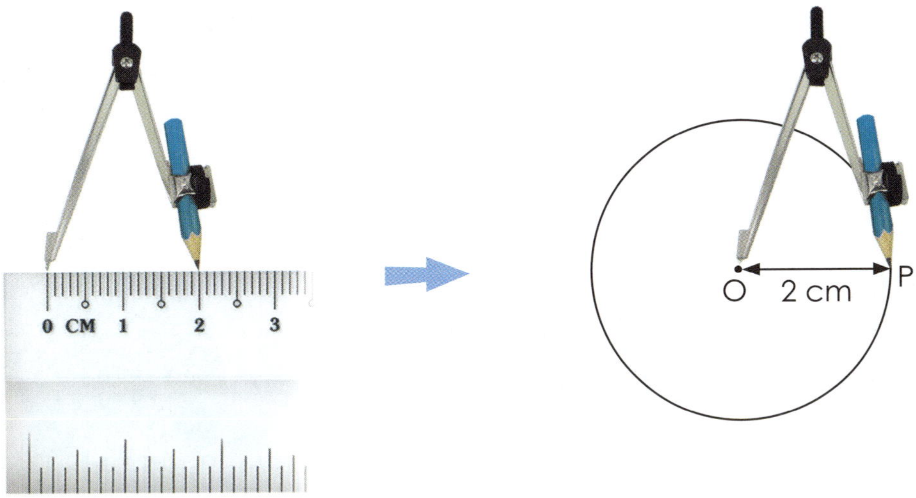

Point O is the centre of the circle. OP is a radius of the circle.

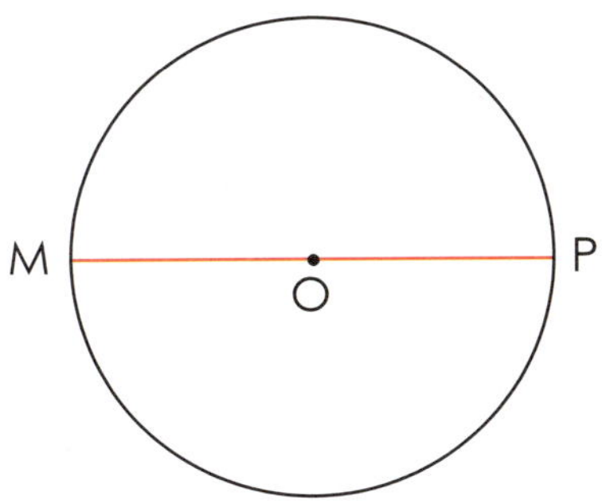

Then, draw a line segment MP which passes through the centre of the circle.

MP is a **diameter** of the circle.

Let's Do

1. a) Draw a circle of radius 3 centimetres.
   b) Draw a circle of radius 4 centimetres.

P/B Chapter 9: Exercise 1, pages 172–173

 ISBN 978-93-5103-033-1

Identifying parts of a circle

Let's Learn

a) Draw and cut out a circle on a piece of paper. Then, fold it into halves.

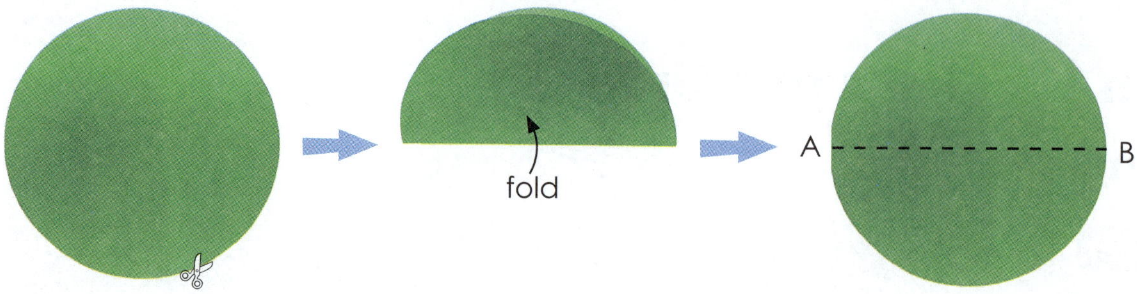

The fold line AB shows a diameter of the circle. It divides the circle into two half circles. Each half circle is known as a **semicircle**.

Next, fold the circle into **quadrants**.

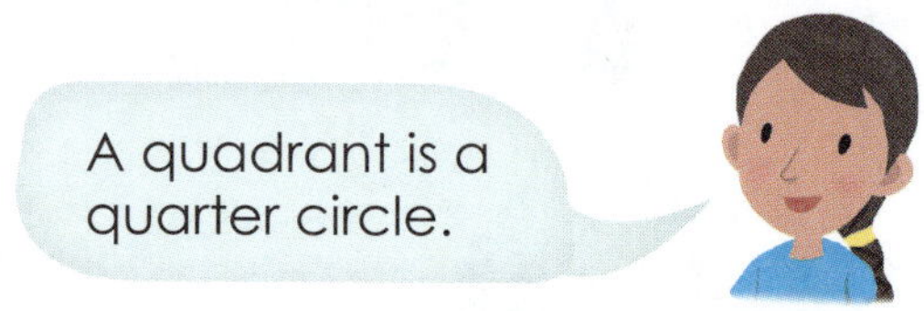

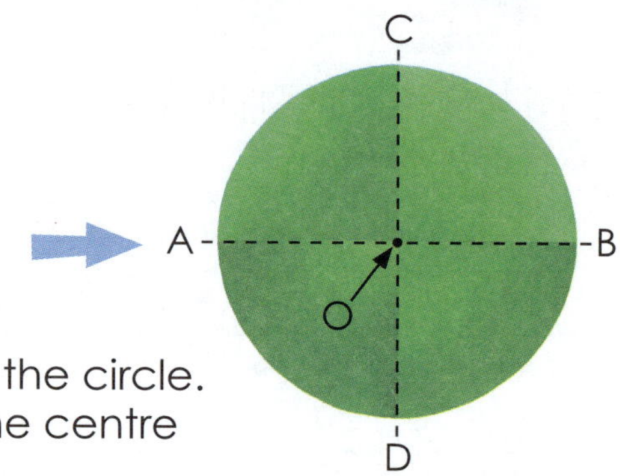

The new fold line CD is another diameter of the circle. Both diameters, AB and CD, pass through the centre of the circle, Point O.
The diameters of a circle pass through the centre of the circle.

Line segment AO is a radius of the circle.
Line segments OB, OC and OD are also **radii** of the circle.

b)

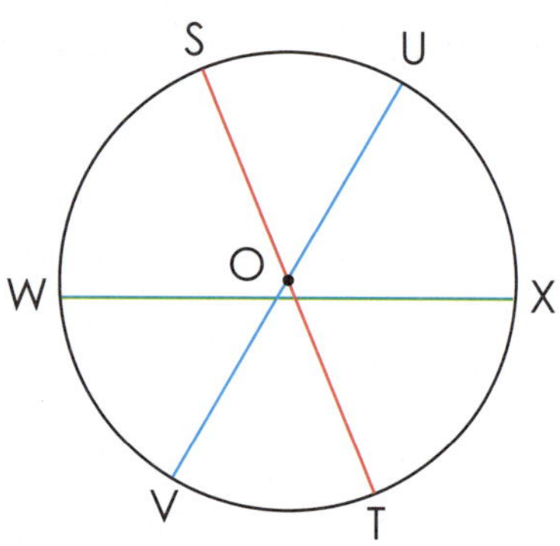

Point O is the centre of the circle.
ST, UV and WX are line segments.

ST and ☐ are diameters of the circle.

OS, OT, ☐ and ☐ are radii of the circle.

☐ does not pass through the centre of the circle. It is not a diameter of the circle.

 ISBN 978-93-5103-033-1

c)

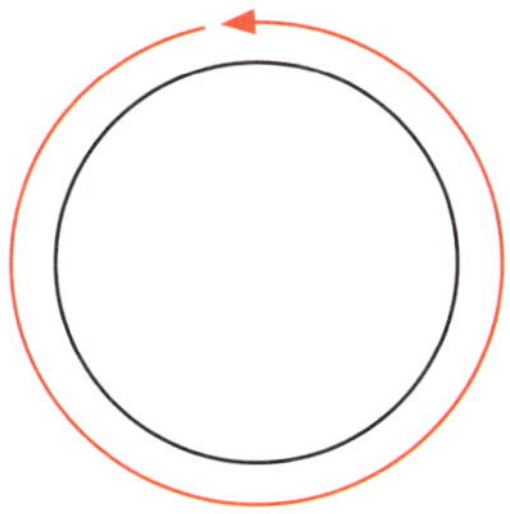

The perimeter of a circle, or the length around a circle, is known as its **circumference**.

d)

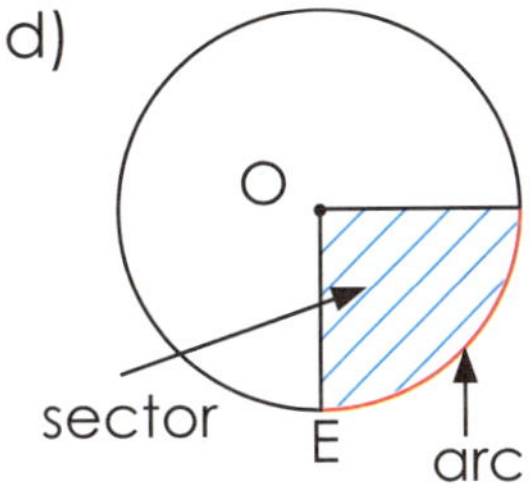

D and E are two points on the circle. The curved part of the circle from point D to point E is known as an **arc**.

OD and OE are two radii of the circle. The region between two radii and an arc is known as a **sector**.

e)

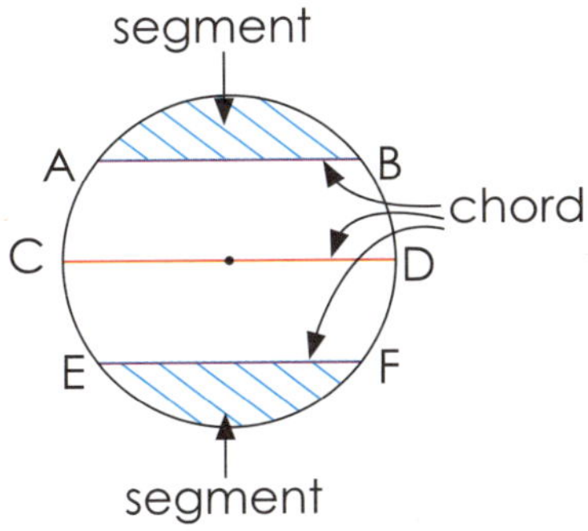

A line segment which has both its end points on a circle is known as a **chord** of the circle. AB, CD and EF are chords of this circle. CD is also the diameter of this circle.

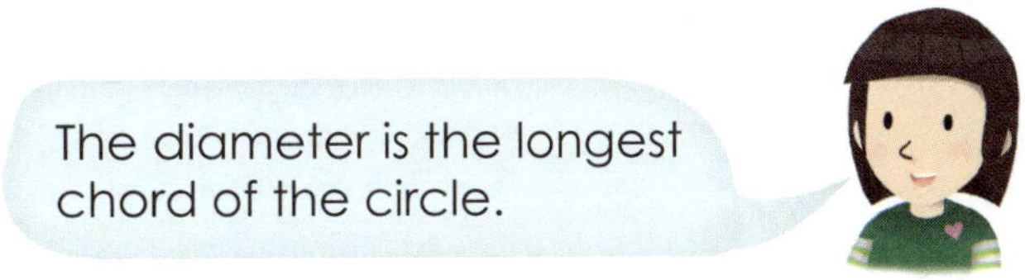

The region between a chord and an arc is known as a **segment**.

Let's Do

1. Point O is the centre of the circle. PQ, RS, TU and VW are line segments.

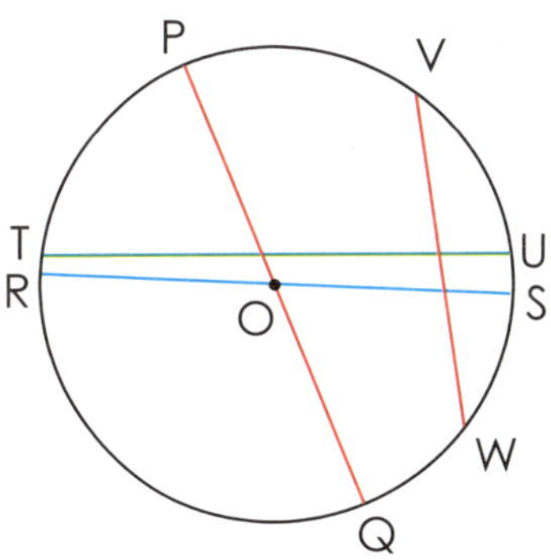

a) Name the diameters. ______________

b) Name the radii. ______________

c) Name two chords other than the diameters.

____

d) Mark and label an arc on the circle.

e) Shade and label a sector and a segment on the circle.

 ISBN 978-93-5103-033-1

Finding radii and diameters of circles

Let's Learn

Maths Lab a) Use a ruler to measure the diameters and radii of the circle you have cut out on page 206. What do you notice?

Diameter = 2 × Radius **Radius = Diameter ÷ 2**

b) Find the diameter of the circle.

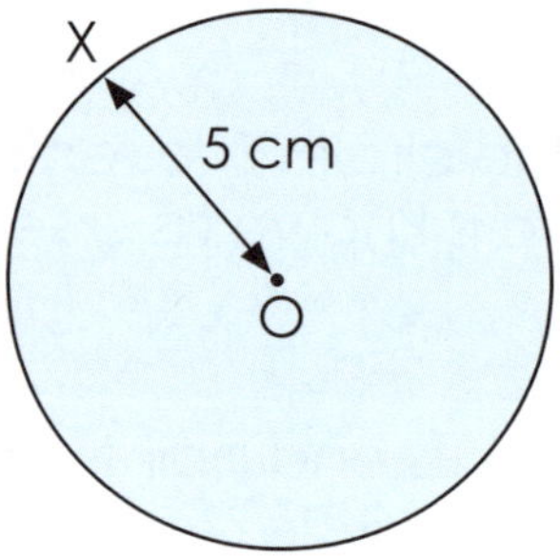

The radius of the circle is 5 centimetres.

Diameter = 2 × Radius
= 2 × 5 cm
= 10 cm

c) Find the radius of the circle.

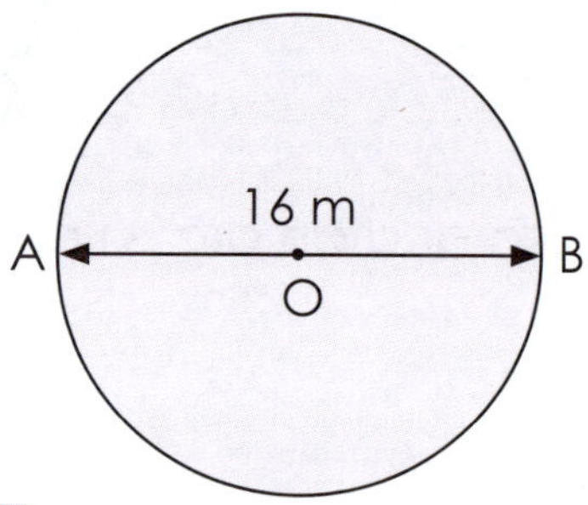

The diameter of the circle is 16 metres.

Radius = Diameter ÷ 2
= 16 m ÷ 2
= 8 m

OA = OB = 8 m

Let's Do

1. Find the radius of each circle.

a)

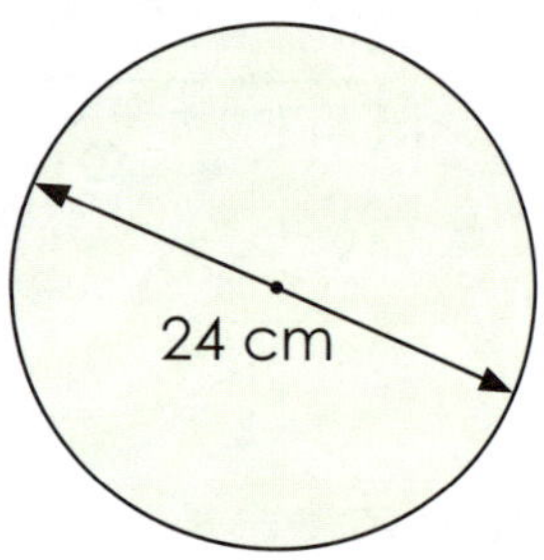

The diameter of the circle is 24 centimetres.

Radius = Diameter ÷ 2
= ______ cm ÷ 2
= ______ cm

b)

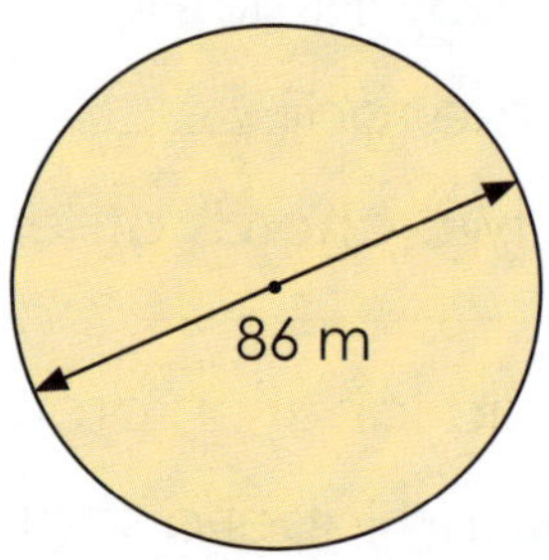

The diameter of the circle is 86 metres.

Radius = ______ m ÷ ______
= ______ m

 ISBN 978-93-5103-033-1

2. Measure the radius of each circle. Then, find the diameter.

a)

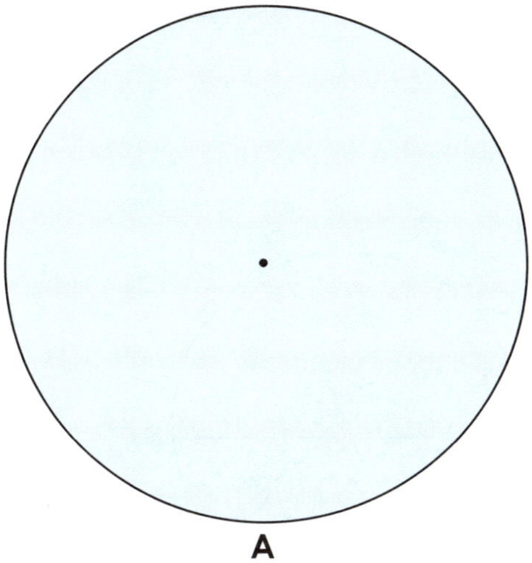

Radius: _______ cm

Diameter: _______ cm

b)

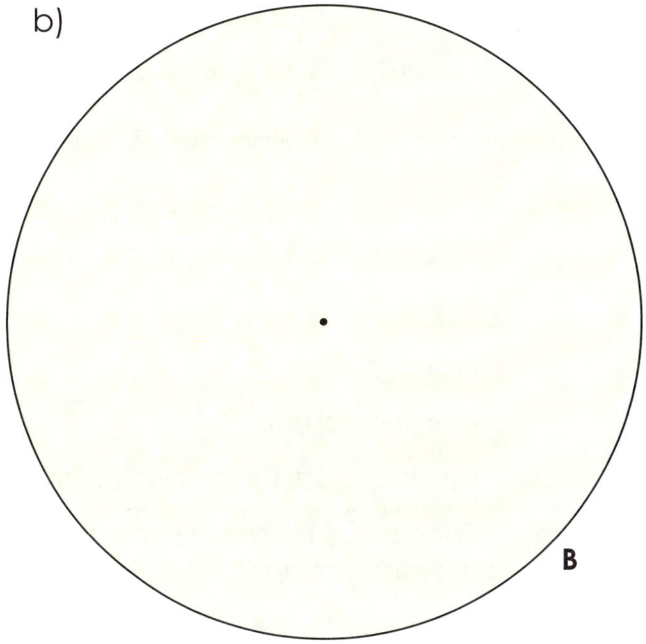

Radius: _______ cm

Diameter: _______ cm

c)

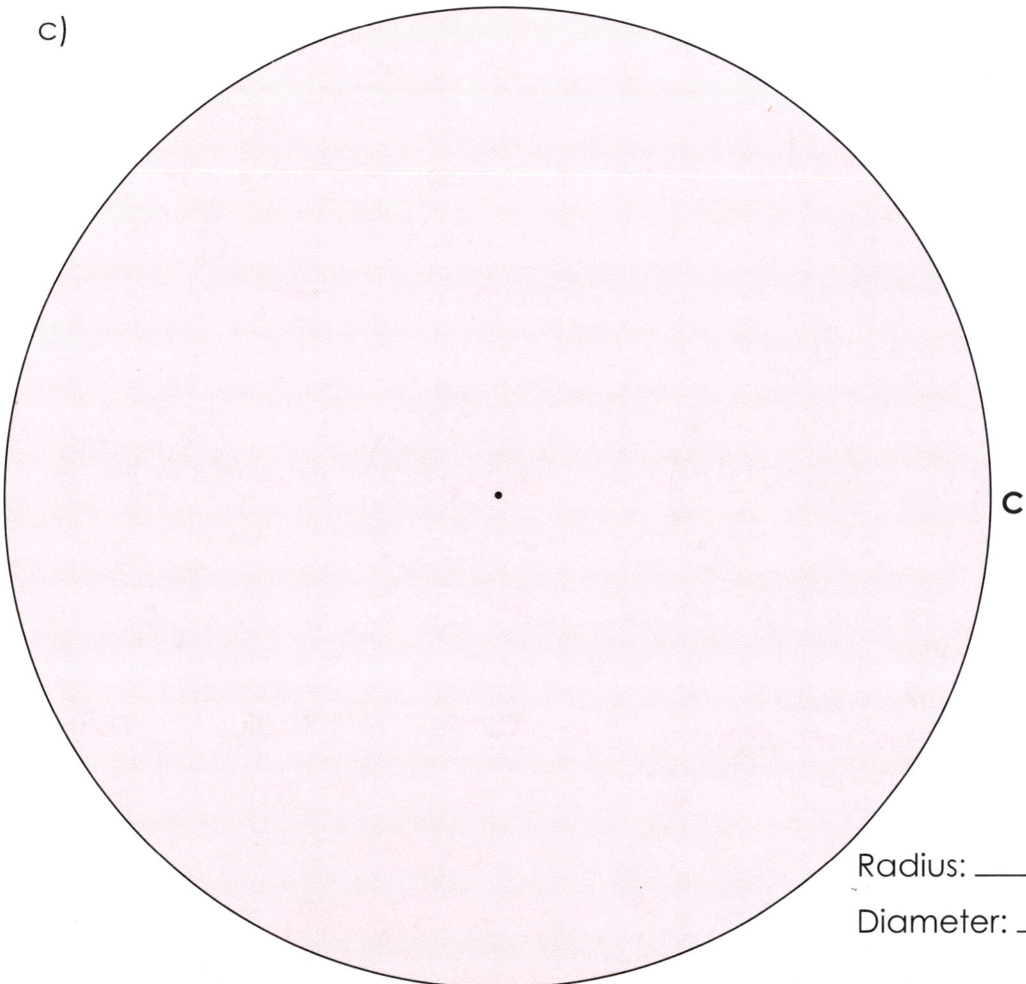

Radius: _______ cm

Diameter: _______ cm

PB Chapter 9: Exercise 2, pages 174–176

Practice 1

1. Draw a circle of radius 6 centimetres.

2. Draw a circle of diameter 7 centimetres.

3. Point O is the centre of the circle.
   AB, CD and EF are line segments.

   a) Name the diameters.

   b) Name the radii.

   c) Name a chord.

   d) Mark and label an arc on the circle.

   e) Shade and label a sector and a segment on the circle.

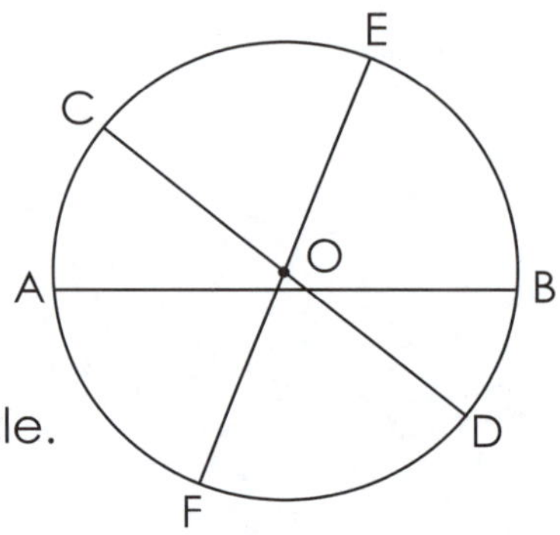

4. a) The radius of the circle is 4 centimetres. Find its diameter.

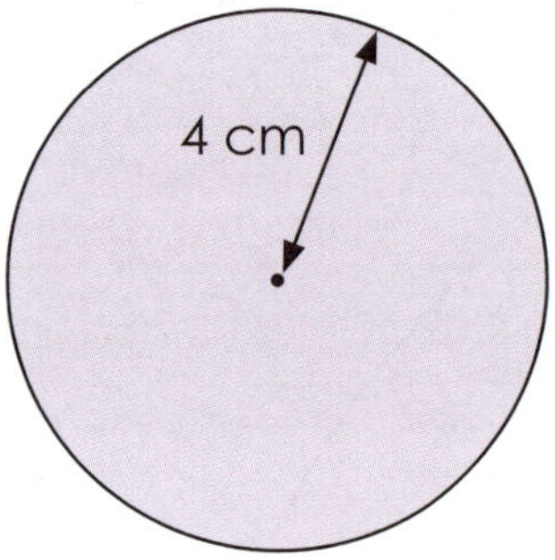

   b) The diameter of the circle is 18 centimetres. Find its radius.

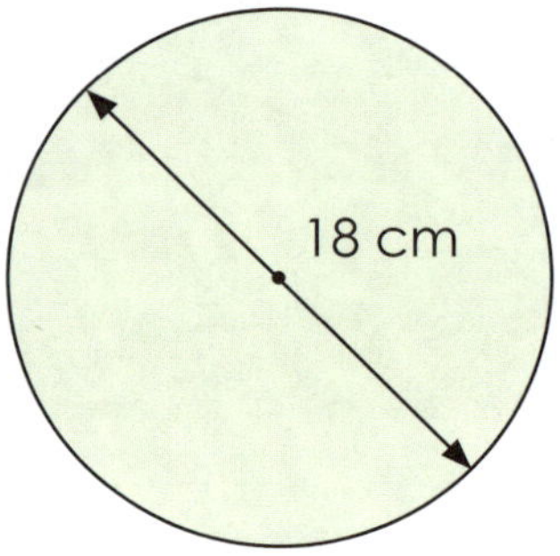

5. The following circles are not drawn to scale.

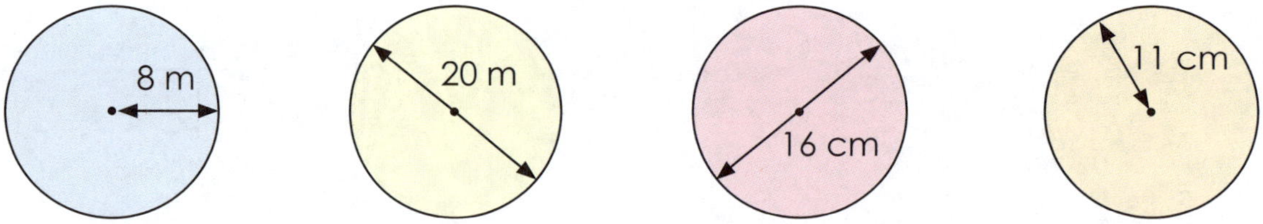

A **B** **C** **D**

   a) Complete the table.
   b) Which circle is the biggest?
   c) Which circle is the smallest?

Circle	Radius	Diameter
A	8 m	
B		20 m
C		16 cm
D	11 cm	

 ISBN 978-93-5103-033-1

10 Graphs

Lesson 1 Pie Charts

Making pie charts

Let's Learn

The table shows the number of T-shirts of different sizes sold in a shop on a certain day.

Size	S	M	L	XL
Number of T-shirts	9	18	6	3

There are 36 T-shirts altogether.

$\frac{1}{4}$ of them are of size S. $\frac{9}{36} = \frac{1}{4}$

$\frac{1}{2}$ of them are of size M. $\frac{18}{36} = \frac{1}{2}$

$\frac{1}{6}$ of them are of size L. $\frac{6}{36} = \frac{1}{6}$

$\frac{1}{12}$ of them are of size XL. $\frac{3}{36} = \frac{1}{12}$

The fractions can be presented in a **pie chart**. The pie chart below represents the number of T-shirts of different sizes sold in the shop.

Picture It

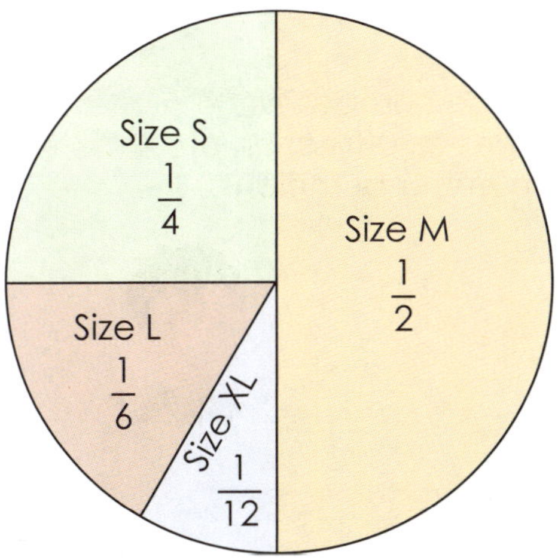

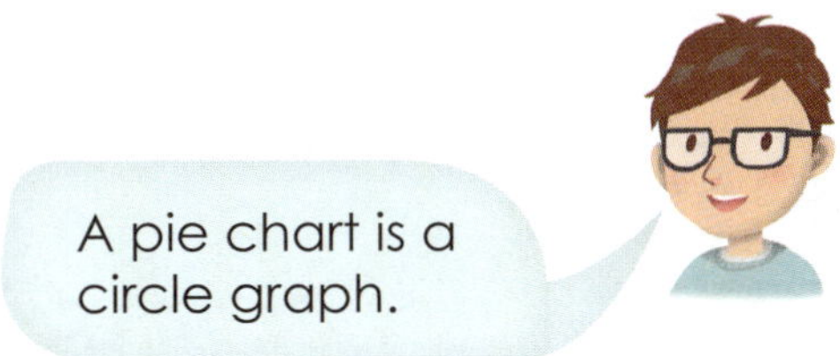

 ISBN 978-93-5103-033-1

Reading and interpreting pie charts which display whole numbers

Let's Learn

200 fruits were sold in a day at a supermarket. Of the fruits, 80 oranges, 40 melons and 30 pears were sold. The rest of the fruits sold were apples.

Picture It

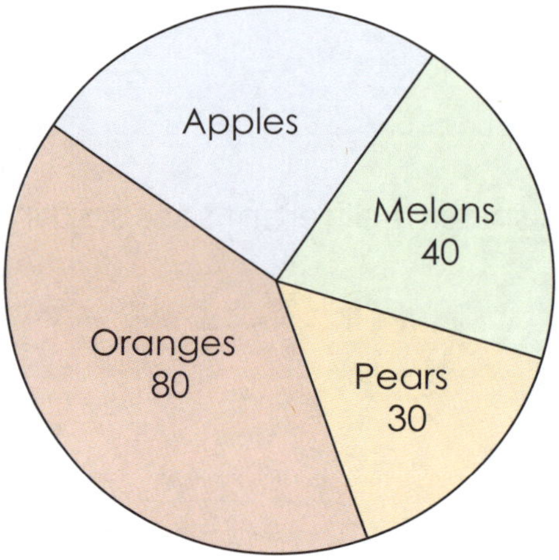

a) Which fruit was sold in the greatest quantity?

Oranges were sold in the greatest quantity.

b) How many apples were sold?

200 – 80 – 30 – 40 = 50

____ apples were sold.

c) What fraction of the fruits were oranges?

$$\frac{80}{200} = \frac{2}{5}$$

____ of the fruits were oranges.

d) How many times as many oranges as melons were sold?

$$\frac{80}{40} = \frac{2}{1} = 2$$

There were 2 times as many oranges as melons sold.

 ISBN 978-93-5103-033-1

Let's Do

1. The pie chart represents the amount of money collected by various stalls at a fair.

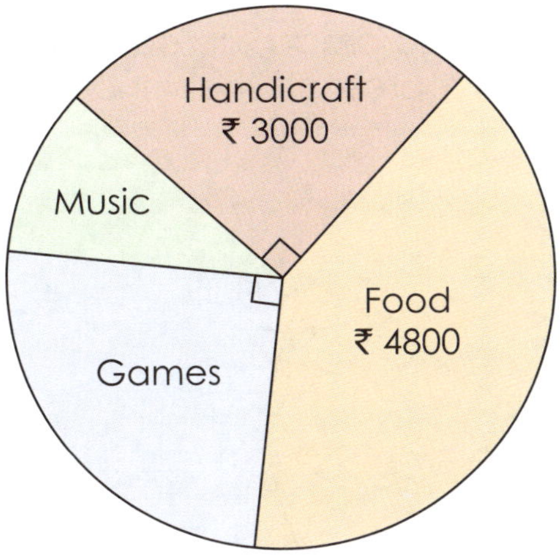

The amount collected by the handicraft stalls is $\frac{1}{4}$ of the total amount of money collected at the fair.

a) What fraction of the total amount of money was collected by the games stalls?

The games stalls collected _____ of the total amount of money.

The part of the pie chart that represents games stalls is the same size as that of handicraft stalls.

b) What was the total amount of money collected by the various stalls?

$4 \times$ ₹ 3000 = ₹ _______

The various stalls collected a total of ₹ _______.

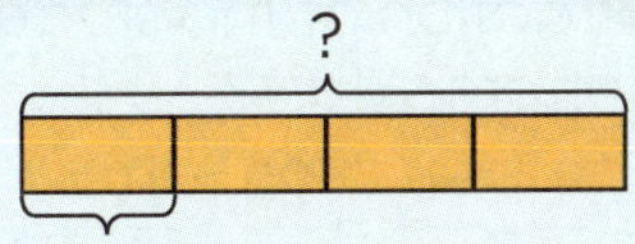

1 unit → ₹ 3000
4 units → ?

c) How much money was collected by the music stalls?

₹ _______ – ₹ 3000 – ₹ 3000 – ₹ 4800 = ₹ _______

The music stalls collected ₹ _______.

P/B Chapter 10: Exercise 1, pages 177–180

 ISBN 978-93-5103-033-1

Reading and interpreting pie charts which display fractions

Let's Learn

A group of 40 students were asked to choose bread, cereals, dosas or fruits for breakfast on a certain day. The pie chart represents their choices.

Picture It

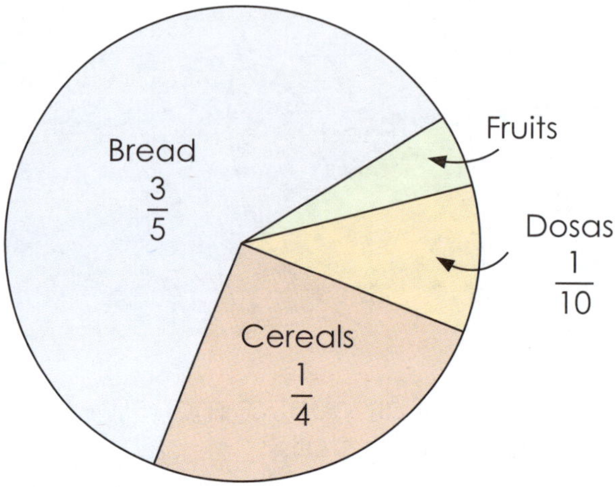

a) Which type of breakfast did most students have on that day?

Most students had bread on that day.

The biggest part of the pie chart represents bread.

b) What fraction of the students had fruits for breakfast?

$$1-\frac{3}{5}-\frac{1}{4}-\frac{1}{10}=\frac{20}{20}-\frac{12}{20}-\frac{5}{20}-\frac{2}{20}$$
$$=\frac{1}{20}$$

____ of the students had fruits for breakfast.

c) How many students had bread for breakfast?

$$\frac{3}{5}\text{ of }40=\frac{3}{5}\times 40$$
$$=\frac{3\times \cancel{40}^{8}}{\cancel{5}_{1}}$$
$$= \text{____}$$

$\frac{3}{5}$ of the 40 students had bread for breakfast.

____ students had bread for breakfast.

d) What percentage of the students had cereals for breakfast?

$$\frac{1}{4}\text{ of }100\%=\frac{1\times \cancel{100}^{25}}{\cancel{4}_{1}}$$
$$=25\%$$

Express $\frac{1}{4}$ as a percentage.

____ of the students had cereals for breakfast.

 ISBN 978-93-5103-033-1

Let's Do

1. The students in a school were asked to name their favourite colour. The pie chart represents their choices.

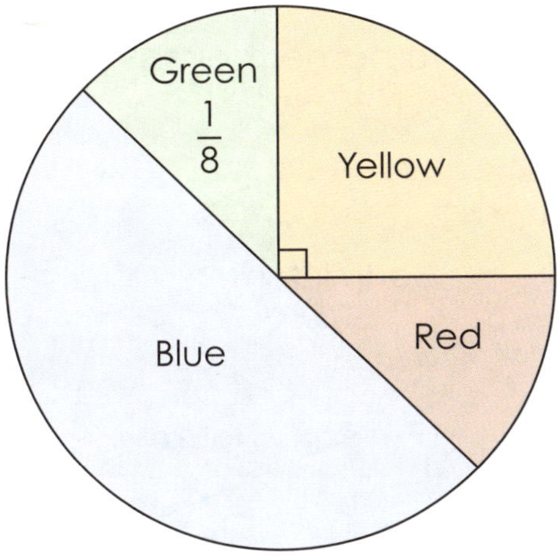

a) What fraction of the students liked blue?

_______ of the students liked blue.

b) What percentage of the students liked yellow?

$\frac{1}{4} \times 100\% = \frac{1 \times 100}{4}$

$= \_\_\_\_\_\_\_$

_______ of the students liked yellow.

c) What fraction of the students liked red?

$\frac{1}{2} - \frac{1}{8} - \frac{1}{4} = \frac{4}{8} - \frac{1}{8} - \frac{\square}{8}$

$= \_\_\_\_\_\_\_$

_______ of the students liked red.

d) If 1200 students liked blue, how many students liked yellow?

$1200 \div 2 = \_\_\_\_\_\_\_$

_______ students liked yellow.

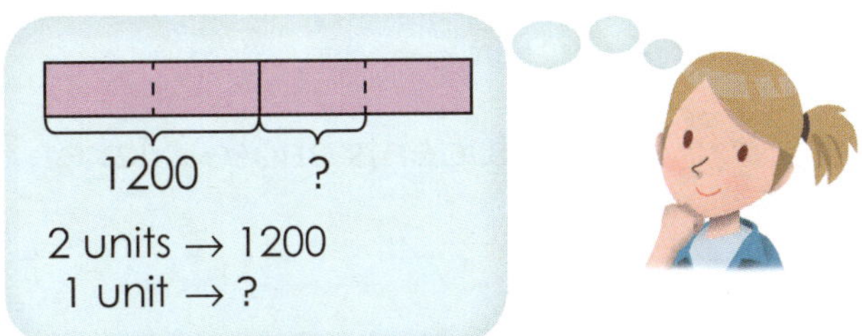

Chapter 10: Exercise 2, pages 181–184

Reading and interpreting pie charts which display percentages

Let's Learn

A group of 200 students were asked to name their favourite sport. The pie chart represents their choices.

Picture It

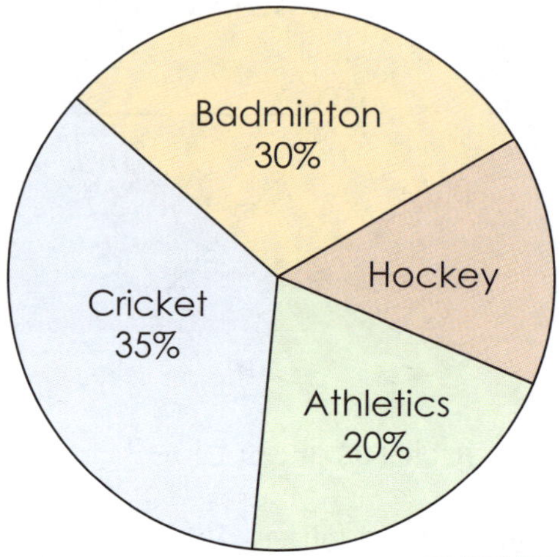

a) Which was the most popular sport?

Cricket was the most popular sport.

b) What percentage of the students chose hockey?

100% – 30% – 35% – 20% = ____

____ of the students chose hockey.

c) How many students chose badminton?

$30\% \text{ of } 200 = \frac{30}{\cancel{100}_1} \times \cancel{200}^2$

$= $ ____

____ students chose badminton.

d) What fraction of the students chose cricket?

$35\% = \frac{35}{100}$

$= $ ____

____ of the students chose cricket.

 ISBN 978-93-5103-033-1

Let's Do

1. The pie chart represents how Rati spent her allowance in a certain month.

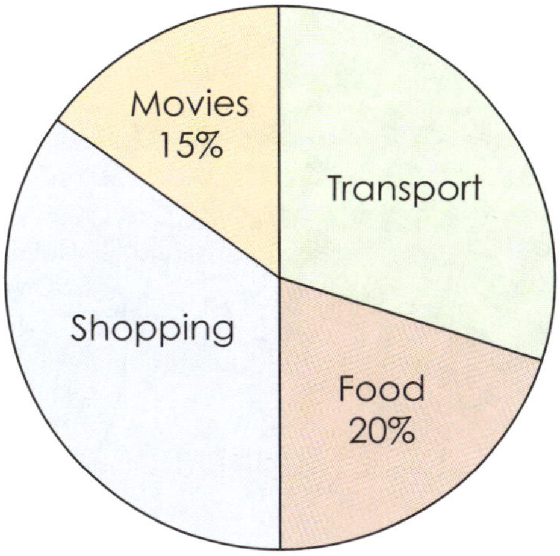

a) What did Rati spend the most money on?

She spent the most money on ________________.

b) What percentage of her allowance was spent on shopping?

50% – ________ = ________

$\frac{1}{2}$ of 100% = 50%

________ of her allowance was spent on shopping.

c) What percentage of her allowance was spent on transport?

________ – 20% = ________

________ of her allowance was spent on transport.

d) If Rati spent ₹ 600 on transport, how much did she spend altogether?

________% → ₹ 600

1% → ₹ ________

100% → ₹ ________

Total amount spent = 100%

She spent ₹ ________ altogether.

P/B Chapter 10: Exercise 3, pages 185–188

 ISBN 978-93-5103-033-1

Think About It

The pie charts represent how Ria and Sam used their allowance in a month.

Ria's pie chart

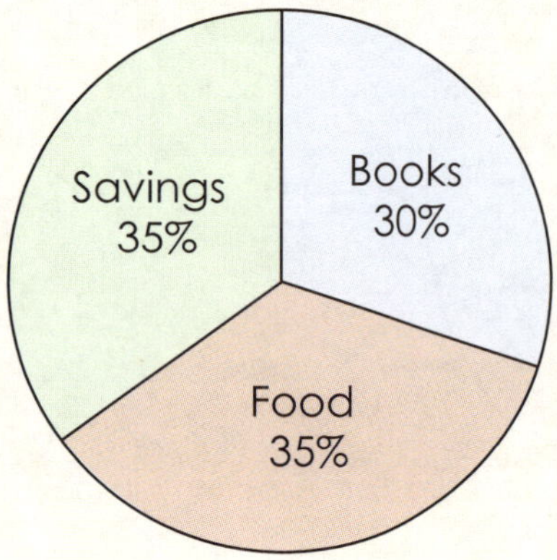

Sam's pie chart

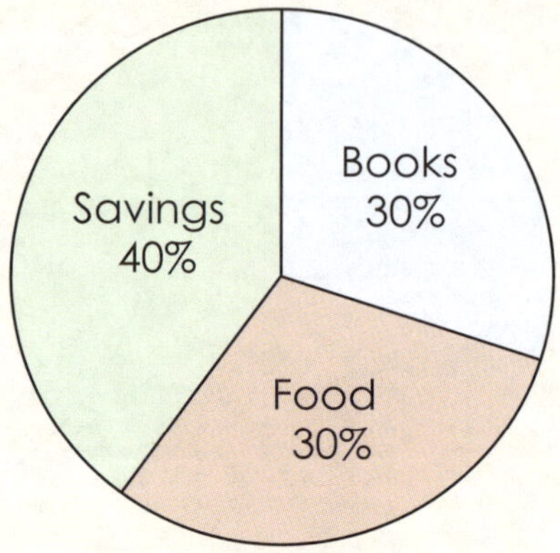

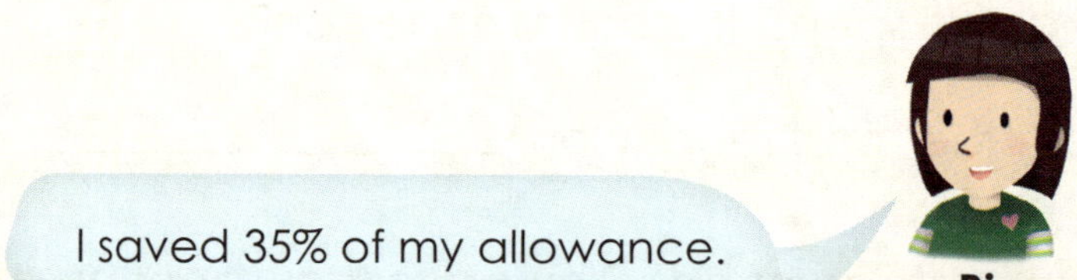

Ria

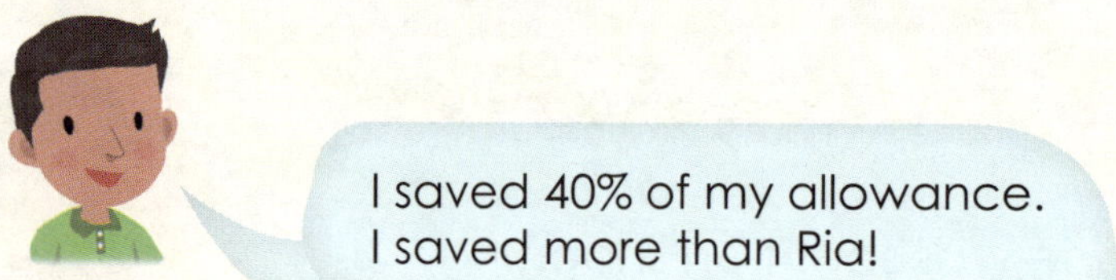

Sam

Is Sam correct? Explain why.

 ISBN 978-93-5103-033-1

Practice 1

1. A group of students was asked to choose the type of books they liked to read. The pie chart represents their choices.

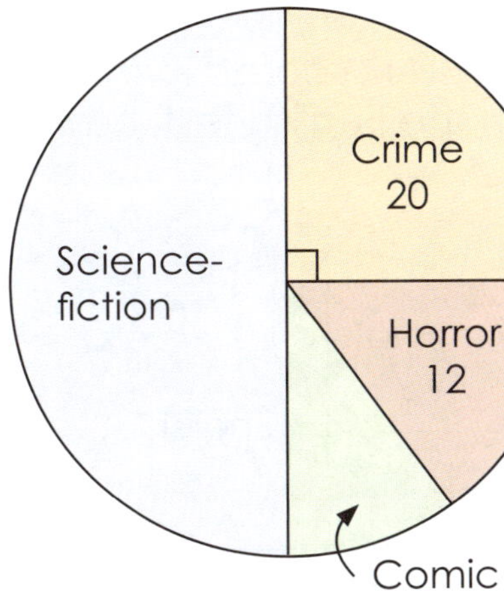

   a) How many students chose science-fiction books?

   b) What percentage of the students chose crime books?

   c) How many students chose comic books?

   d) How many students were there in the group?

2. A group of students was asked to name their favourite activity in school. The pie chart represents their choices.

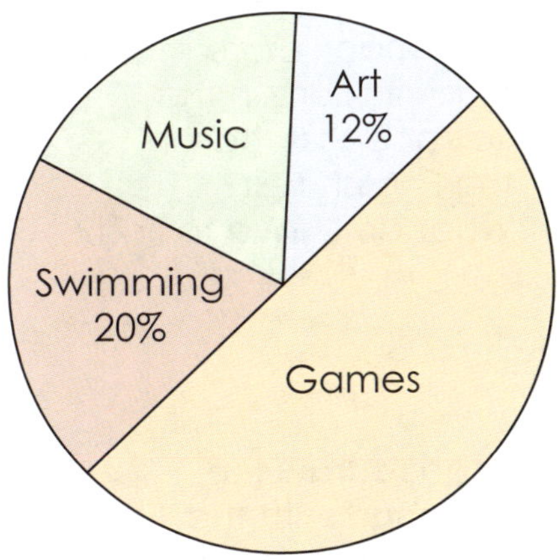

   a) Which was the most popular activity?

   b) What percentage of the students liked music?

   c) What fraction of the students liked swimming?

   d) If 18 students liked art, find the total number of students in the group.

 ISBN 978-93-5103-033-1

Lesson 2 Problem Solving

Mind stretcher

Let's Learn

The pie chart represents the marks Arif scored in three tests. If he scored 24 more marks in the Science test than in the English test, how many marks did he score in the Science test?

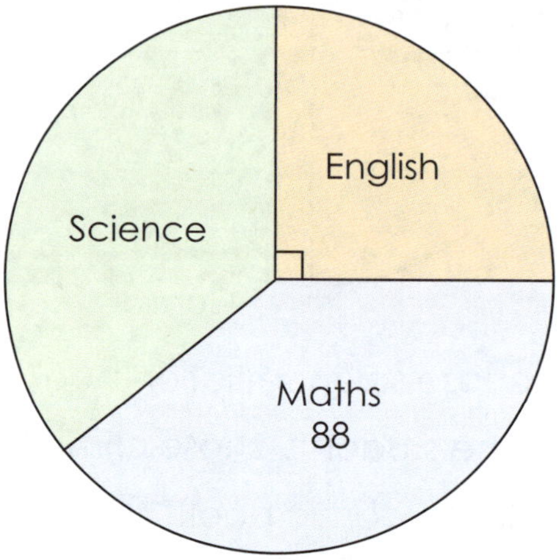

1 Understand the problem.

What does the pie chart represent?
What does '88' mean on the pie chart?
How many more marks did Arif score in the Science test than in the English test?
What do I have to find?

2 Plan what to do.

I can **redraw the pie chart** with the information given in the question.

 ISBN 978-93-5103-033-1

3 Work out the **Answer**.

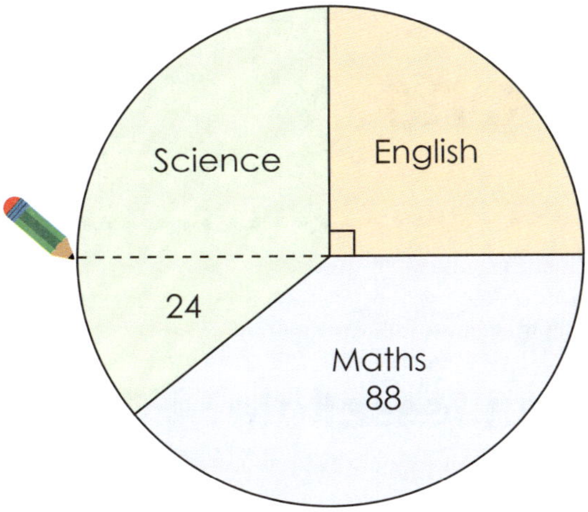

88 + 24 = 112
Half of his total score for the three tests is 112 marks.

112 ÷ 2 = 56
His score for the English test is 56 marks.

56 + 24 = 80
His score for the Science test is 80 marks.

4 **Check**

Did you answer the question?
Is your answer correct?

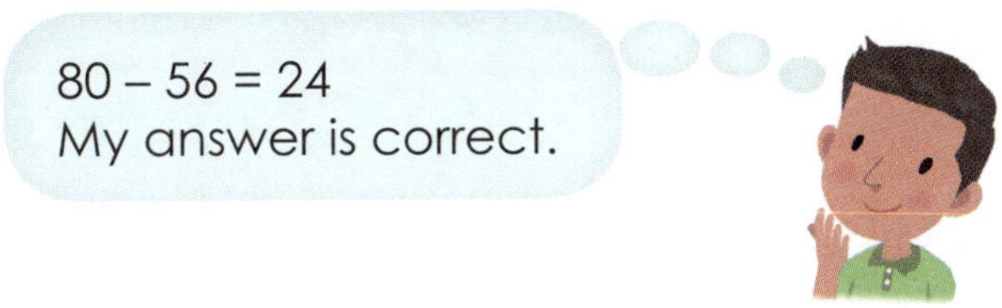

☑ 1. Understand
☑ 2. Plan
☑ 3. Answer
☑ 4. Check

 ISBN 978-93-5103-033-1

11 Tessellations

Lesson 1 Tiling Patterns

Recognising shapes that can tessellate

Let's Learn

a) These tiling patterns are **tessellations**. Each of them is made with one shape. The shape is called the **unit shape** of the tessellation.

Maths Lab

Picture It

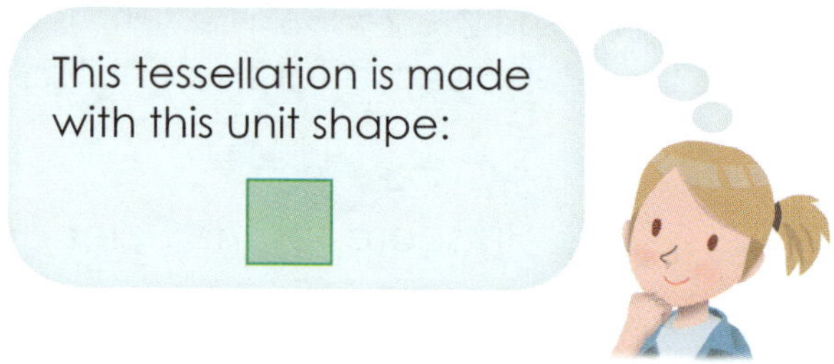

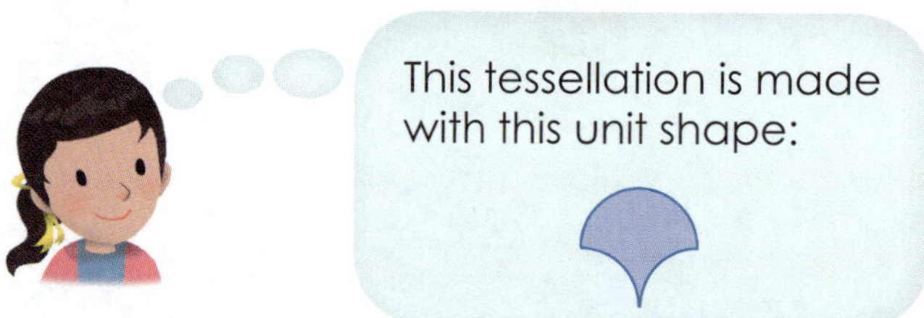

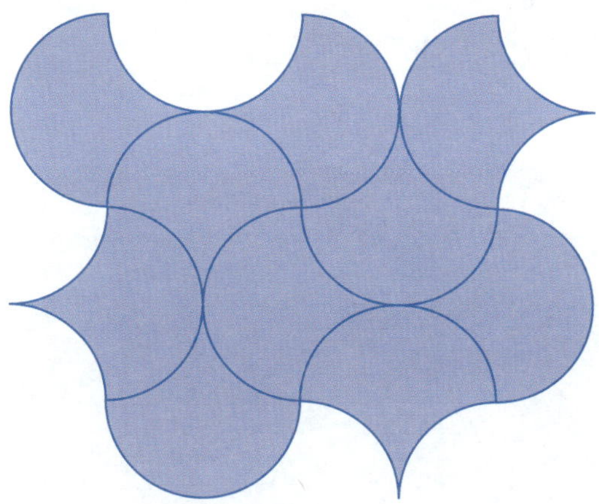

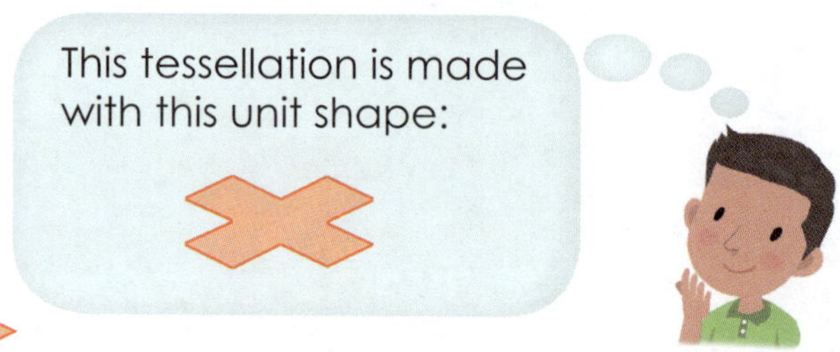

In a tessellation, the tiles fit together with no gaps or overlaps.

 ISBN 978-93-5103-033-1

b) In a tessellation, the unit shape can be repeated to extend the pattern in all directions.

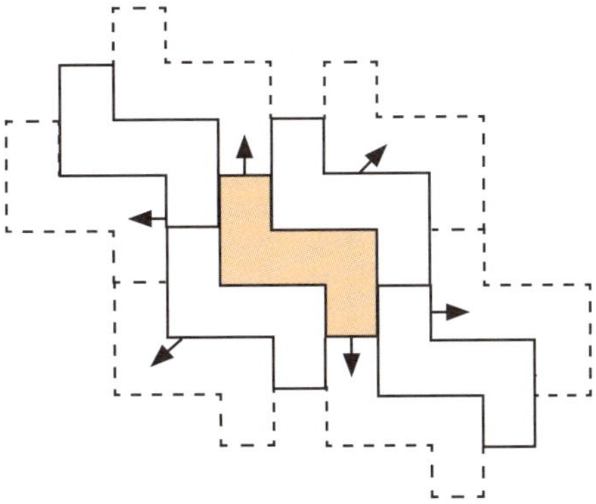

This tessellation is made with this unit shape:

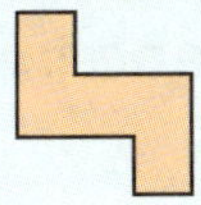

Let's Do

1. Colour the unit shape of each tessellation.

a)

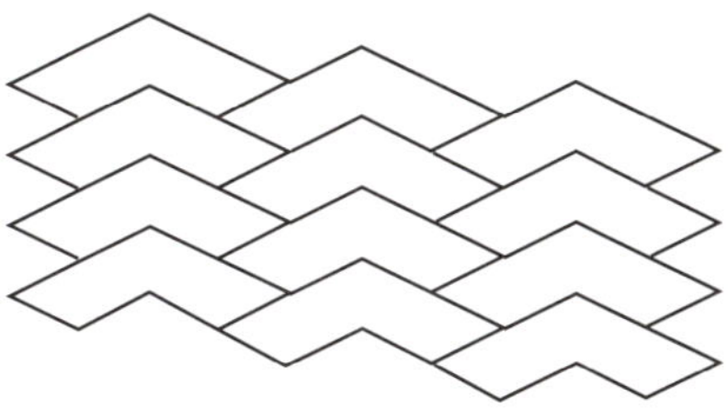

b)

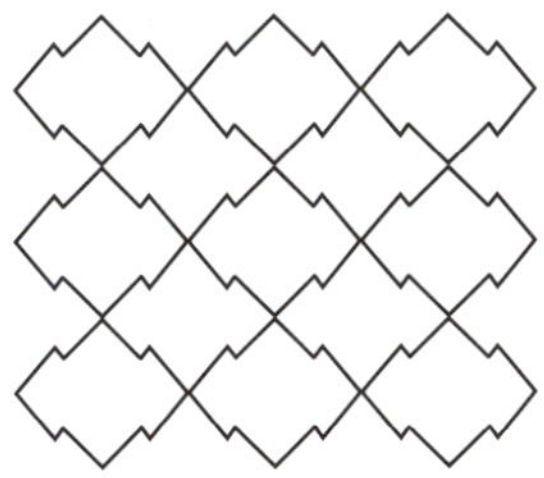

c)

d)

Chapter 11: Exercise 1, pages 189–191

Recognising shapes that cannot tessellate

Let's Learn

These are not tessellations.

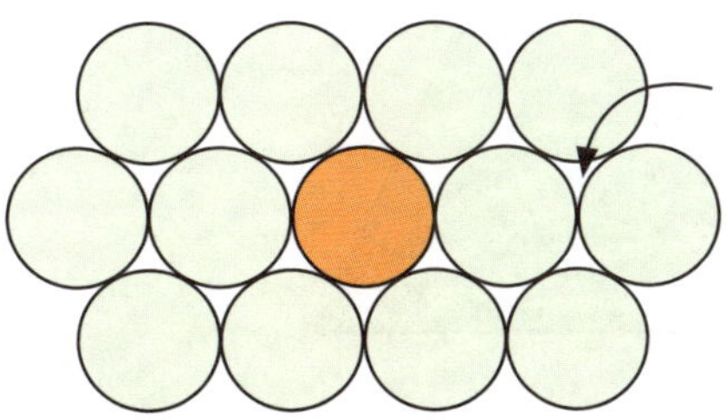

There are gaps between the shapes.

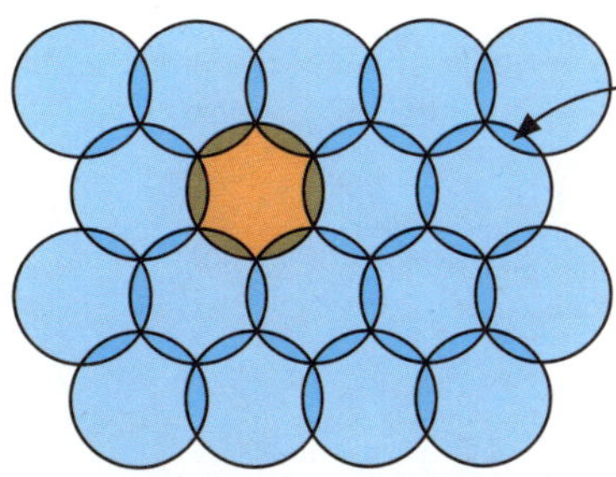

The shapes overlap.

 ISBN 978-93-5103-033-1

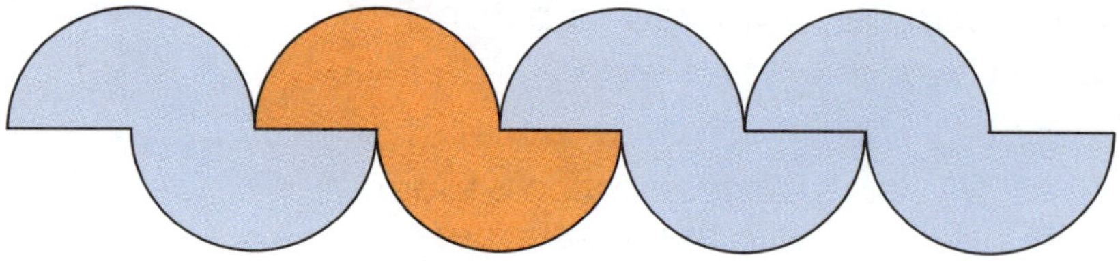

The pattern cannot extend in all directions.

Let's Do

1. Are the following figures tessellations?
   Fill in the blanks with **Yes** or **No**.

   a)

   ______

   b)

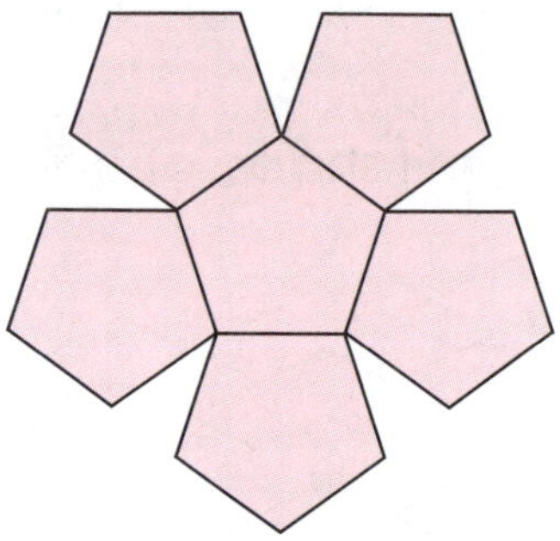

   ______

2. Trace and cut out each shape below. Then, make 12 copies of each shape to find out if the shape can tessellate.

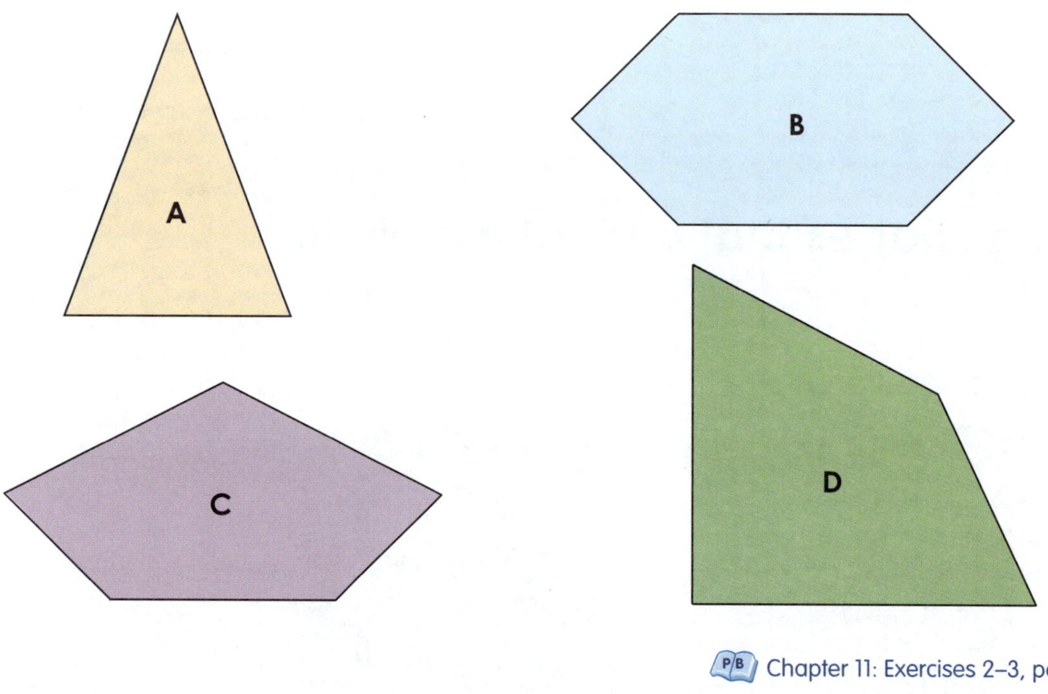

P/B Chapter 11: Exercises 2–3, pages 192–196

  ISBN 978-93-5103-033-1

Practice 1

1. Colour the unit shape of each tessellation.

a)

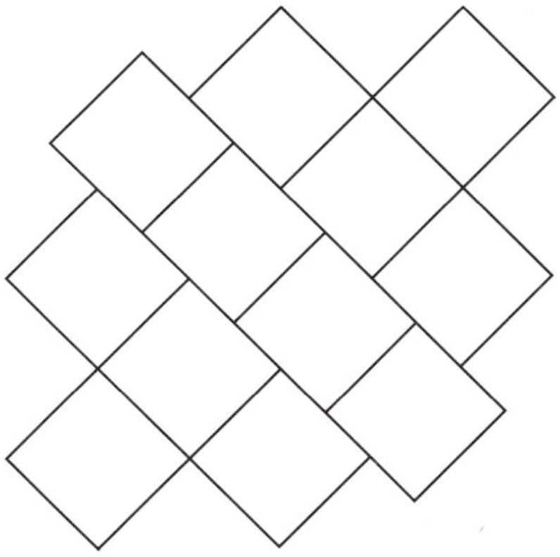

b)

c)

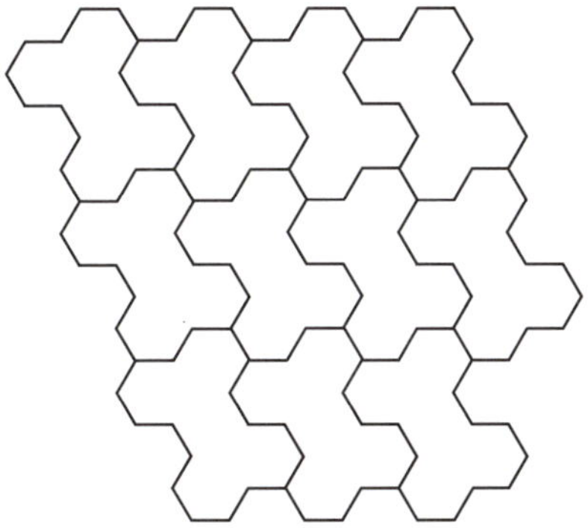

d)

2. Which of the following figures are tessellations made up of one unit shape each?

a)

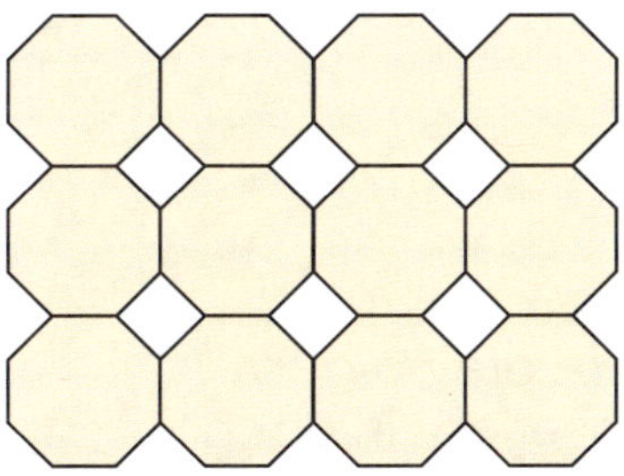

b)

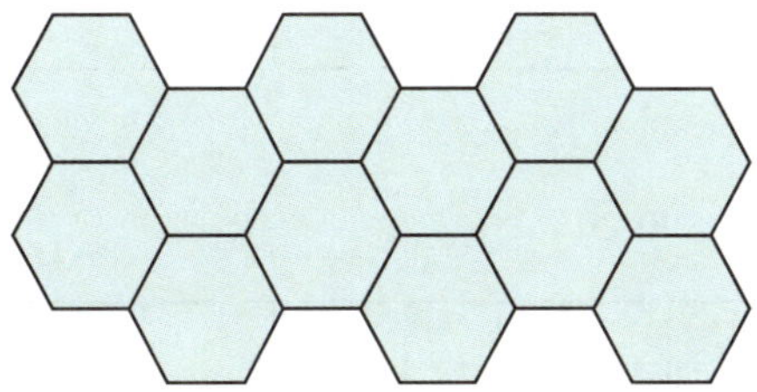

c)

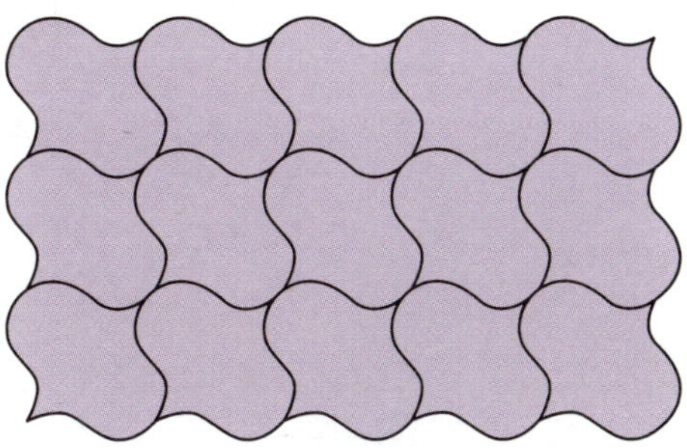

d)

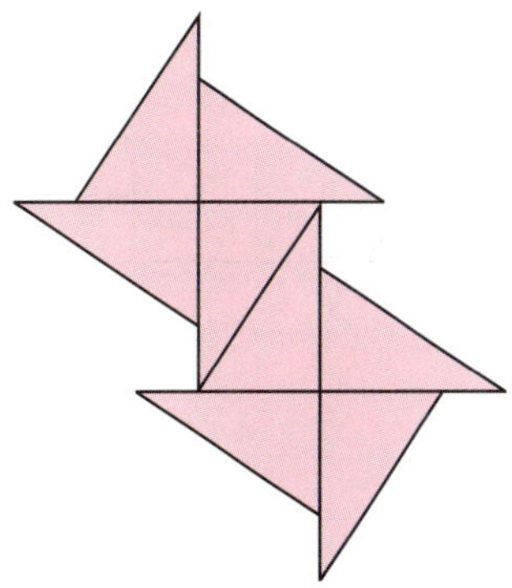

Lesson 2 Making More Tessellations

Making different tessellations with a unit shape

Let's Learn

A rectangle can tessellate in different ways.

Maths Lab

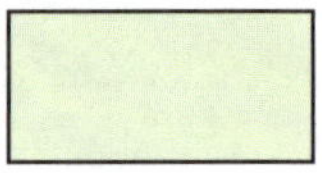

Picture It

Tessellation 1

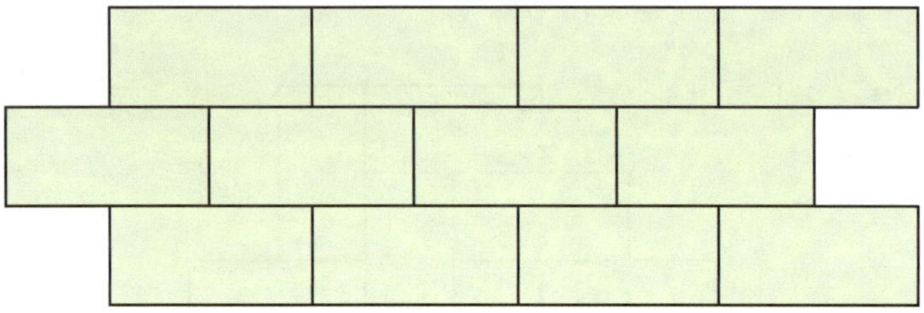

Tessellation 2

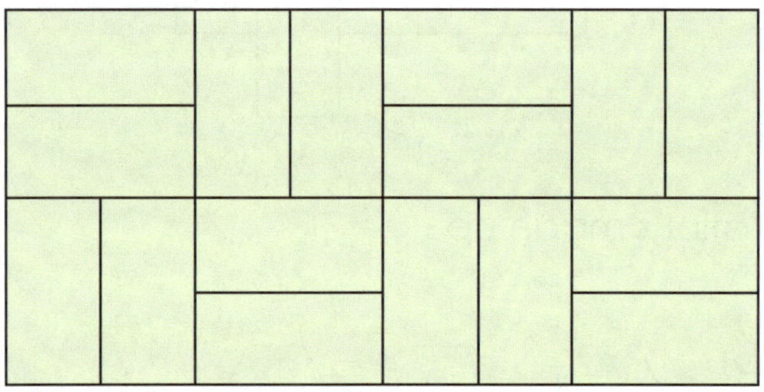

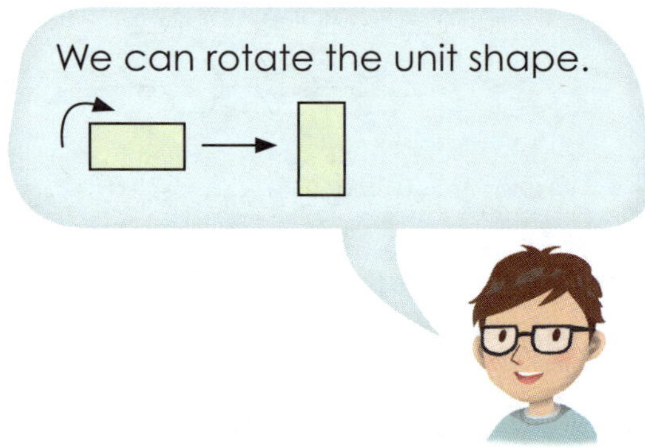

Tessellation 3

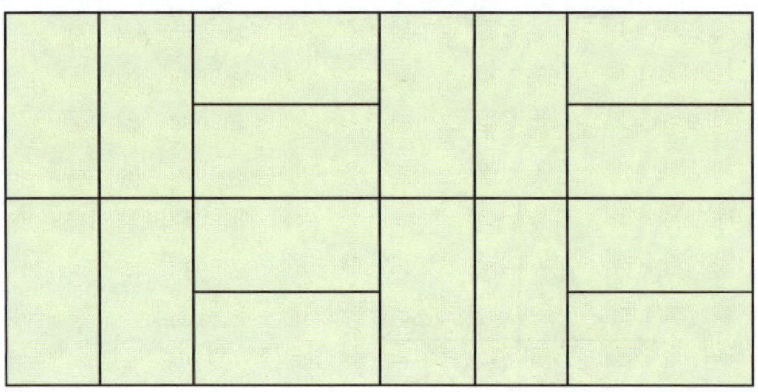

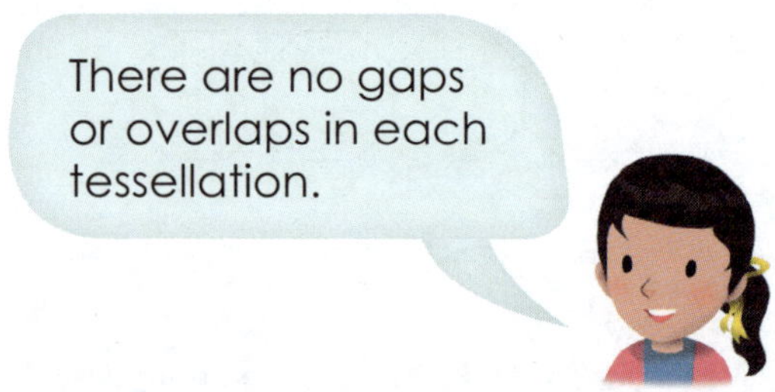

 ISBN 978-93-5103-033-1

Let's Do

1. Use the given shape to make two different tessellations.

Tessellation 1

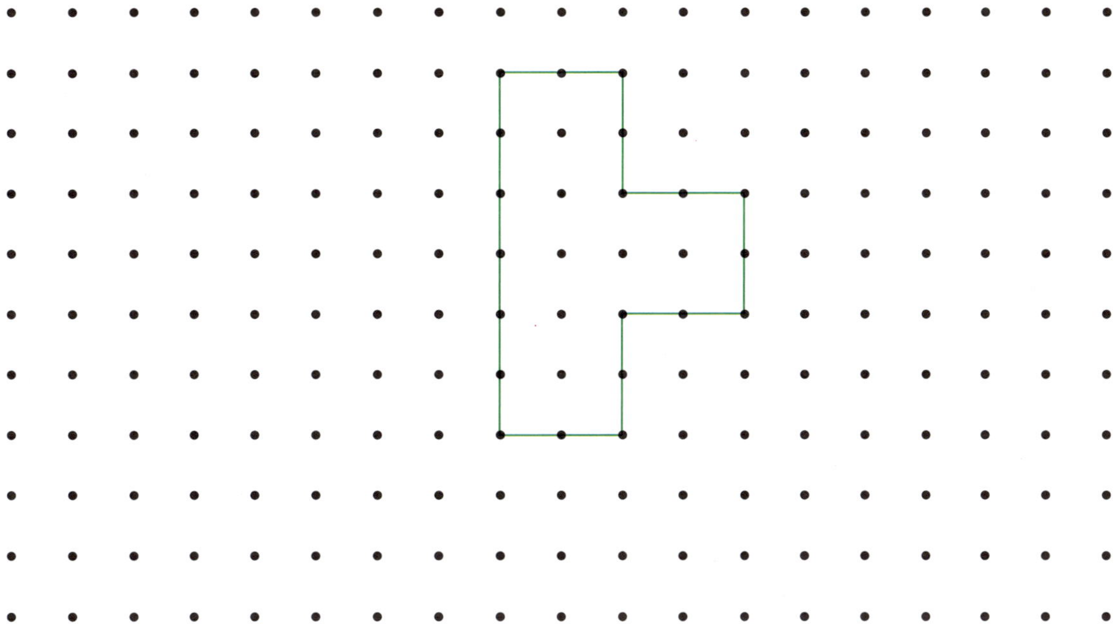

Tessellation 2

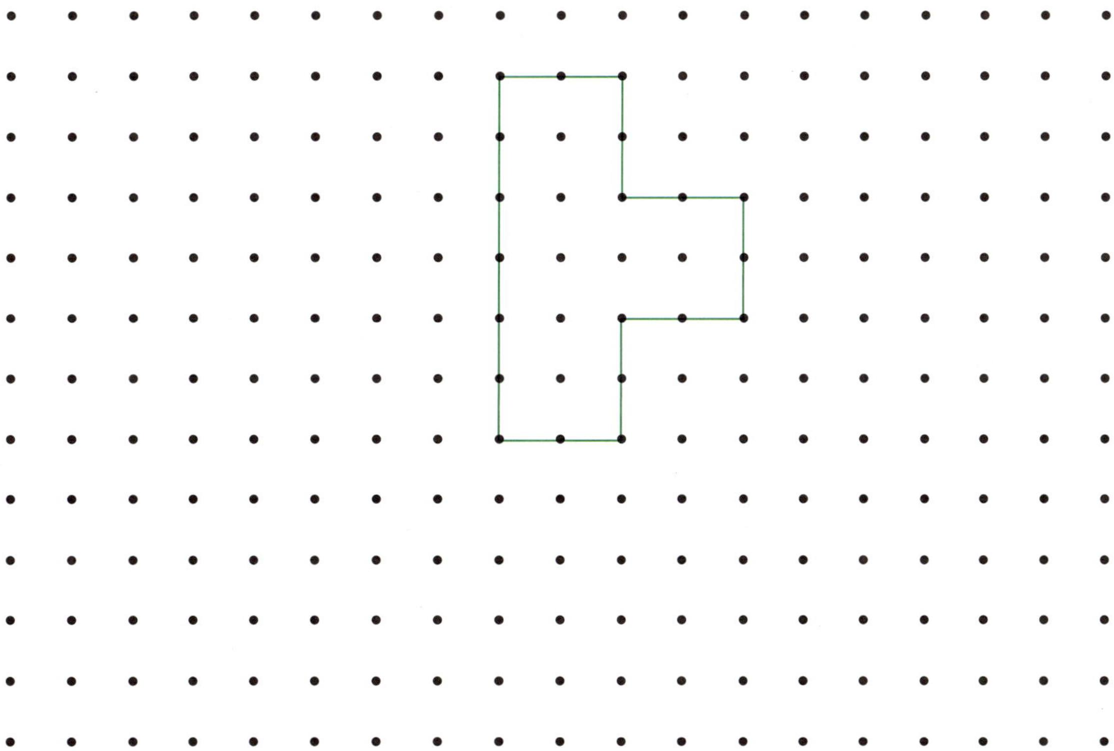

Chapter 11: Exercise 4, pages 197–198

ISBN 978-93-5103-033-1

Making a tessellation with two unit shapes

Let's Learn

We can make a tessellation with two different unit shapes.

Maths Lab

Picture It

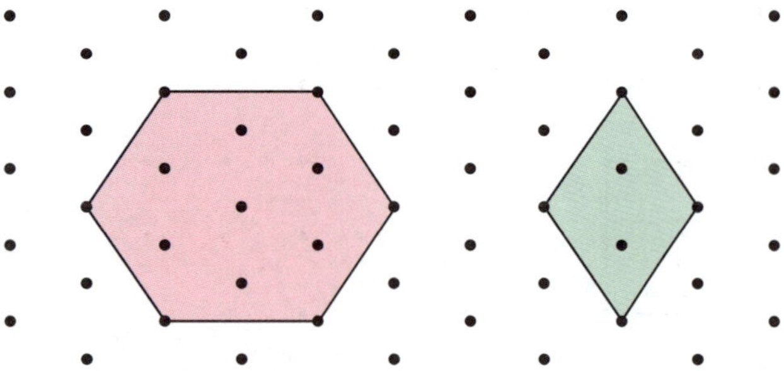

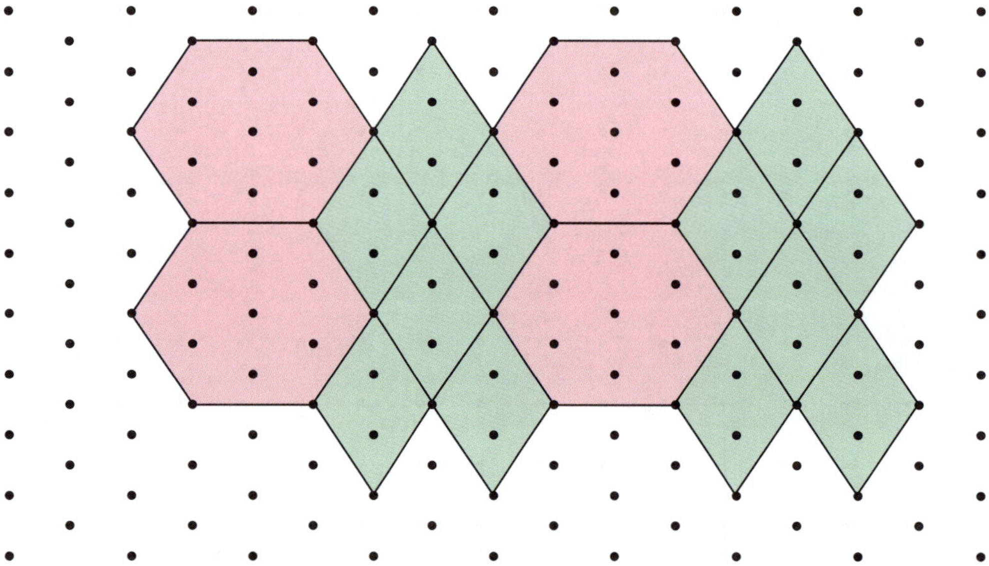

This is a tessellation of two unit shapes. The shapes fit together with no gaps between them.

 ISBN 978-93-5103-033-1

Let's Do

1. Use both shapes to make a tessellation.

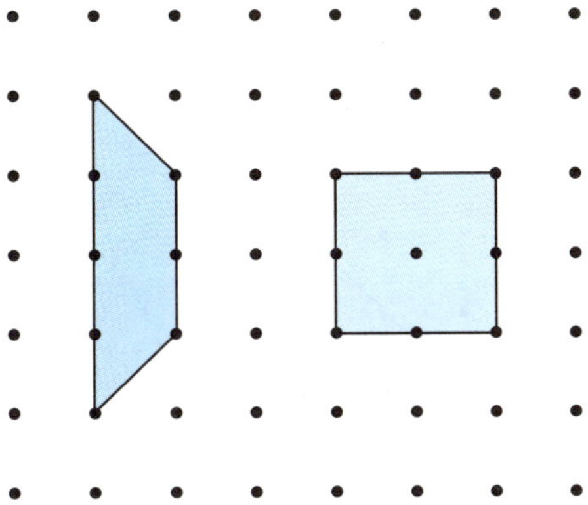

Chapter 11: Exercise 5, pages 199–200

 ISBN 978-93-5103-033-1

Practice 2

1. Copy the given shape on dot paper. Then, use each shape to make two different tessellations.

a)

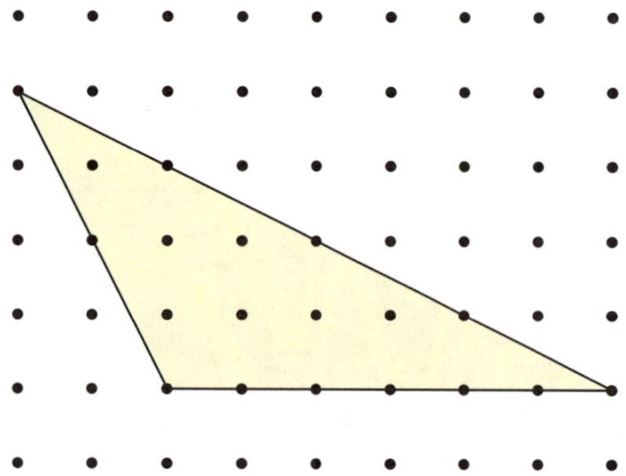

b)

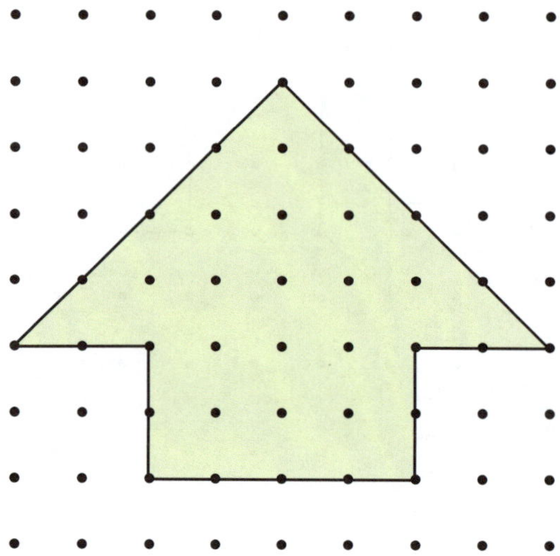

2. Copy the shapes on dot paper. Then, use each pair of shapes to make a tessellation.

a)

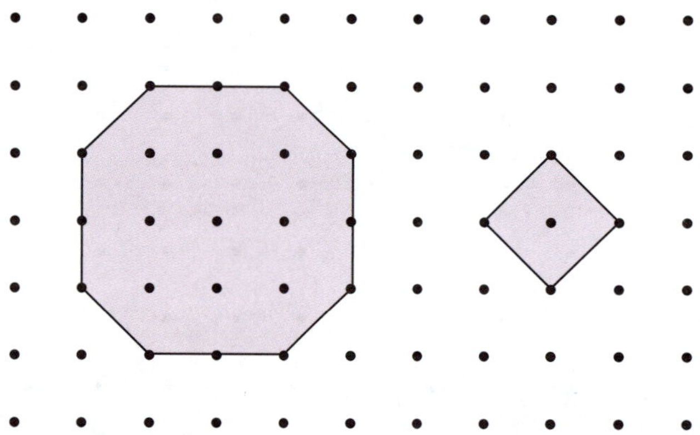

b)

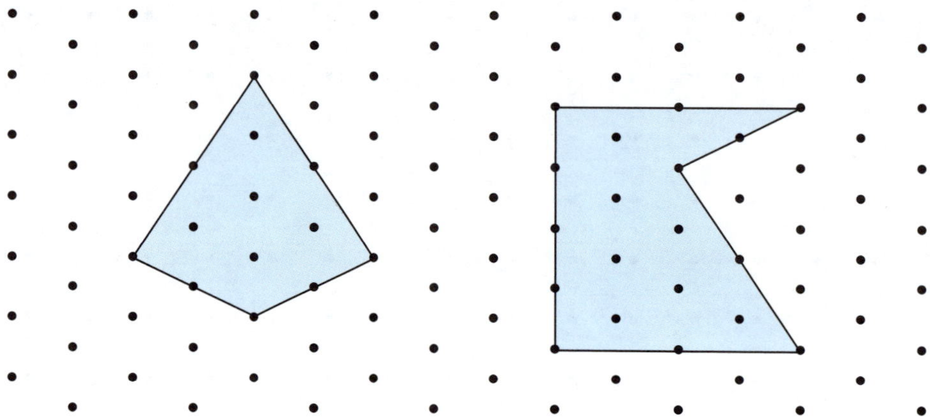

 ISBN 978-93-5103-033-1

Lesson 3 Problem Solving

Mind stretcher

Let's Learn

Jai wants to use the following shape to make a tessellation.

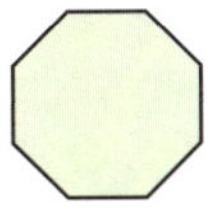

However, he realised the shape on its own cannot tessellate.
Find two other shapes he can use to form a tessellation with the given shape.

1 Understand the problem.

Can the given shape tessellate?
How do I find out what other shapes I can use to tessellate?
How many shapes do I need to find?

2 Plan what to do.

First, I tessellate the shape on its own to see where the gaps are. Then, I use the shapes that form the gaps to make tessellations.

3 Work out the **Answer**.

Tessellation 1

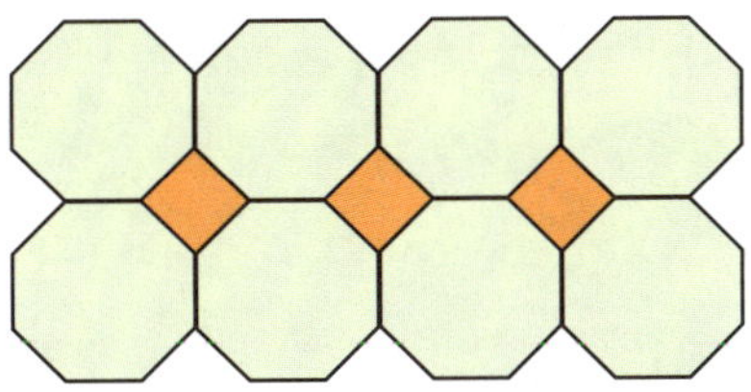

Tessellation 2

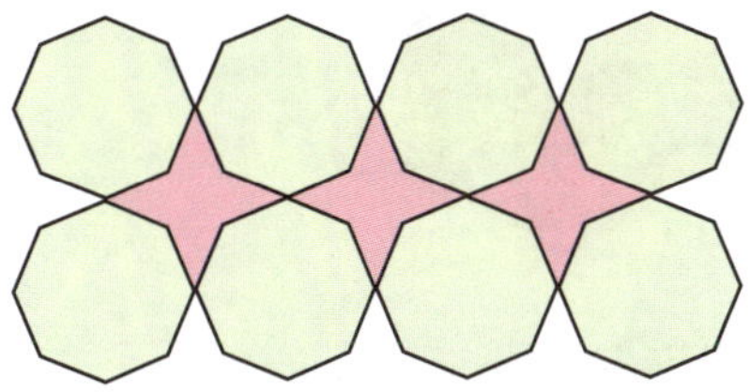

He can use  or  to form a tessellation with the given shape.

4 Check
Did you answer the question?
Is your answer correct?

When either  or  is used with 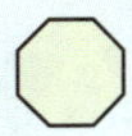 to form a tessellation, there are no gaps or overlaps in the pattern. My answer is correct.

☑ 1. Understand
☑ 2. Plan
☑ 3. Answer
☑ 4. Check

 ISBN 978-93-5103-033-1

12 Solids

Lesson 1 Identifying Solids

Building solids with unit cubes

Let's Learn

Maths Lab

Picture It

a)

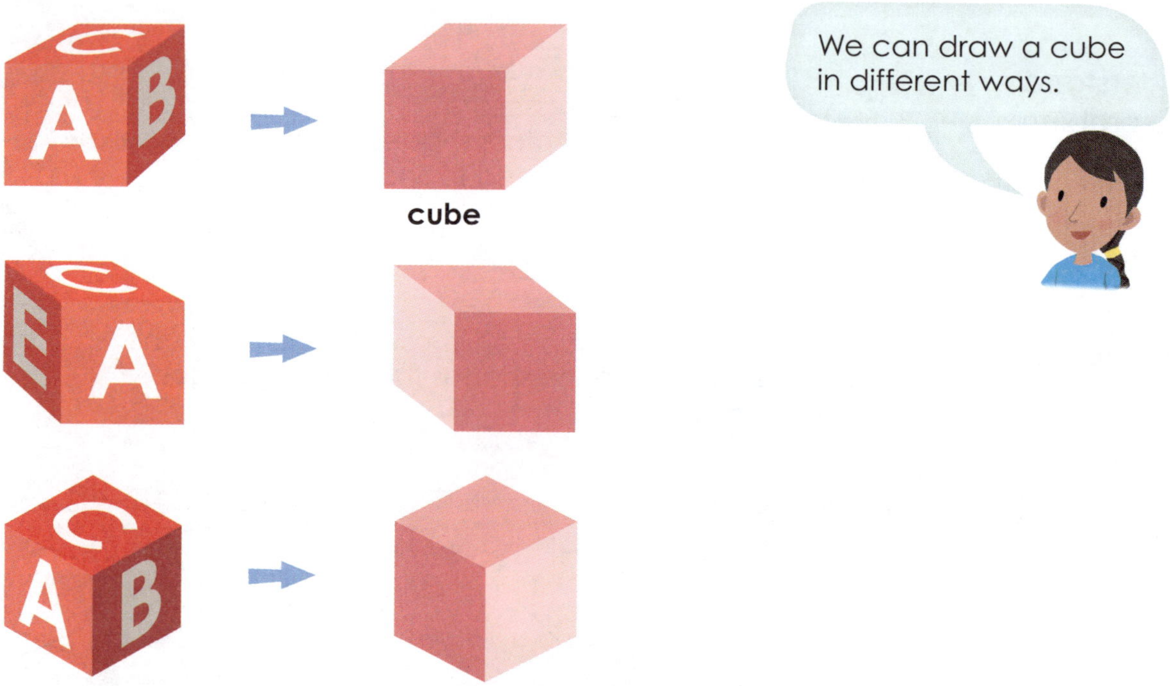

b) This is the drawing of a **unit cube** on dot paper.

Maths Lab

Picture It

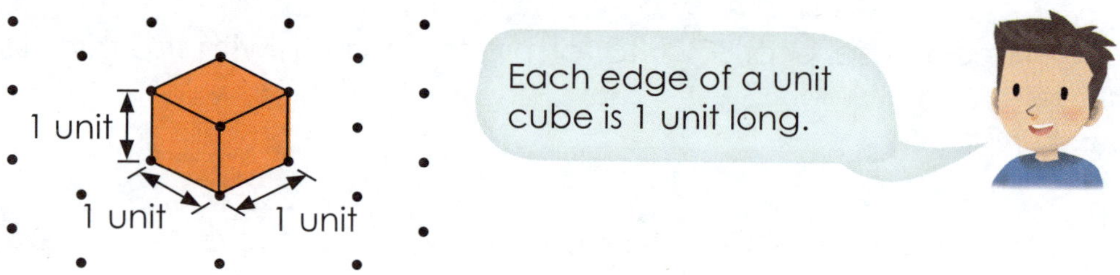

When another unit cube is added to it, we get:

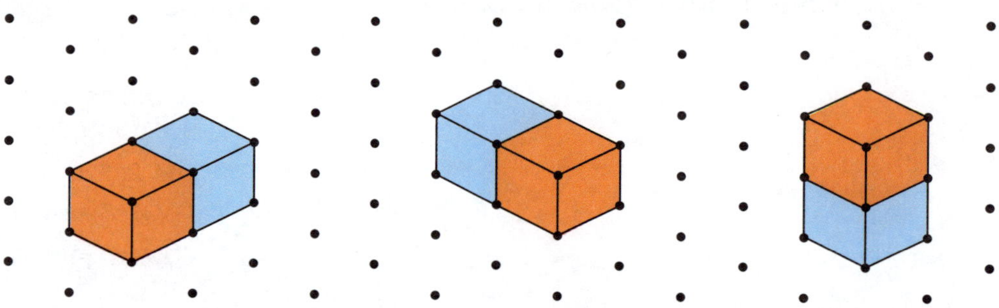

 ISBN 978-93-5103-033-1

Let's Do

1. a) Use 4 unit cubes to build a solid as shown.

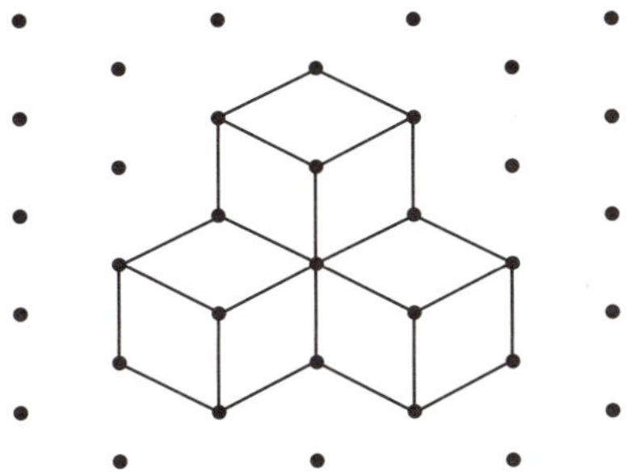

b) Build a different solid with 4 unit cubes.

2. Use 8 unit cubes to build a bigger cube.

P/B Chapter 12: Exercise 1, page 201

Counting unit cubes in a given solid

Let's Learn

The drawings of solids A and B are shown below. The solids have some hidden unit cubes. Use unit cubes to build these solids.

Maths Lab

Picture It

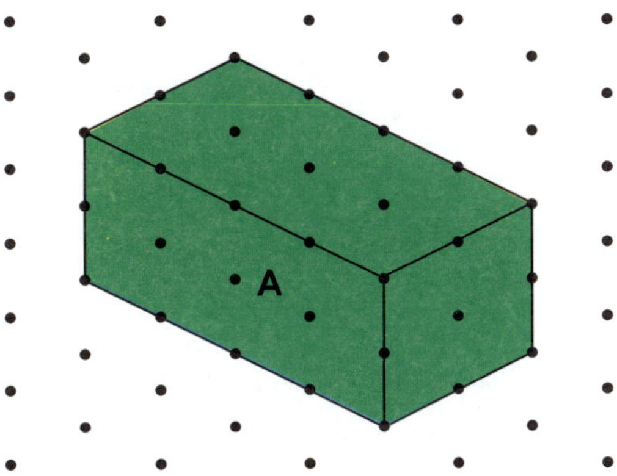

To build Solid A, ___ unit cubes are needed.

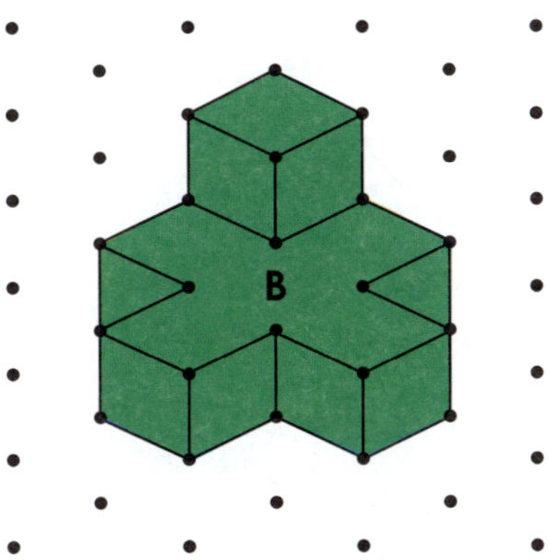

To build Solid B, ___ unit cubes are needed.

 ISBN 978-93-5103-033-1

Let's Do

1. Use unit cubes to build these solids. Then, complete the table.

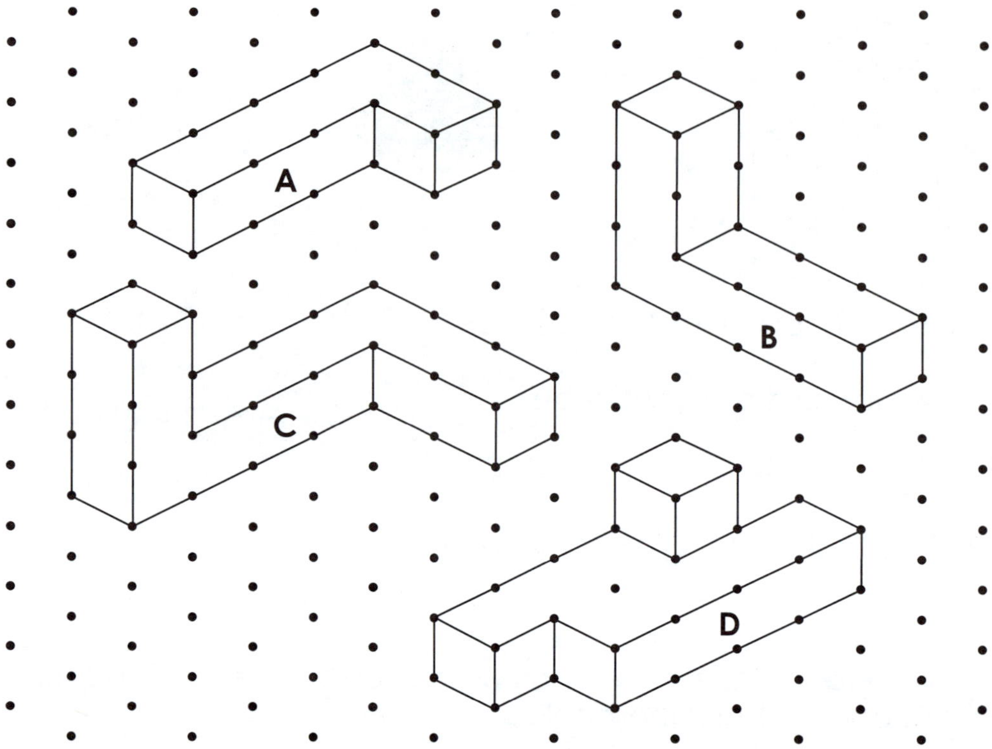

Solid	A	B	C	D
Number of unit cubes				

P/B Chapter 12: Exercise 2, pages 202–203

  ISBN 978-93-5103-033-1

Identifying different views of a solid

Let's Learn

A solid can be viewed from different angles.
We can view a solid from the front, top and side.

a)

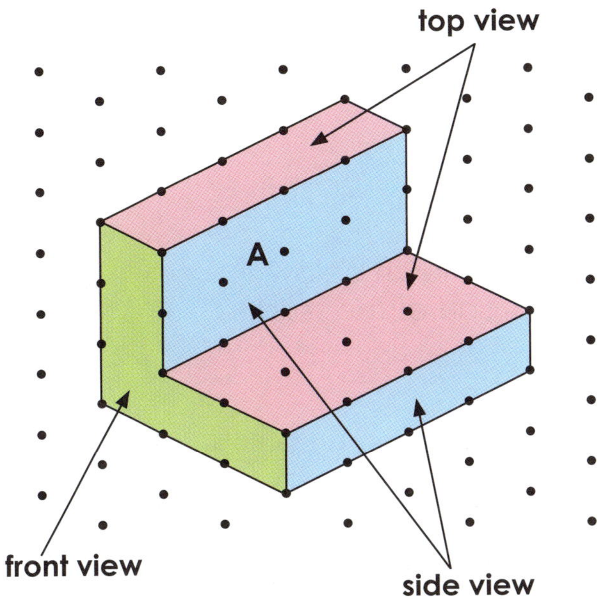

The different views of Solid A are shown below.

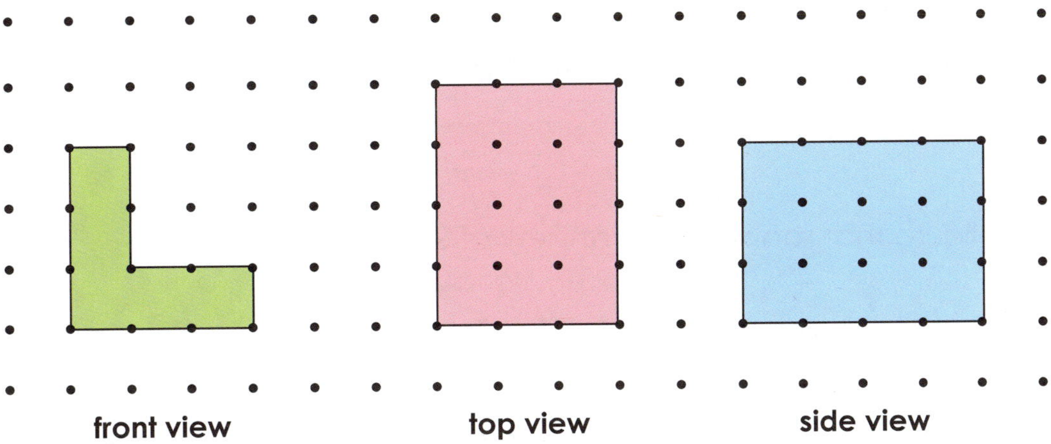

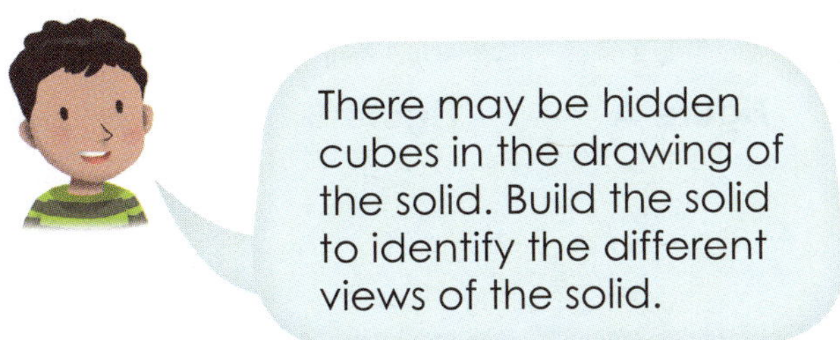

 ISBN 978-93-5103-033-1

b)

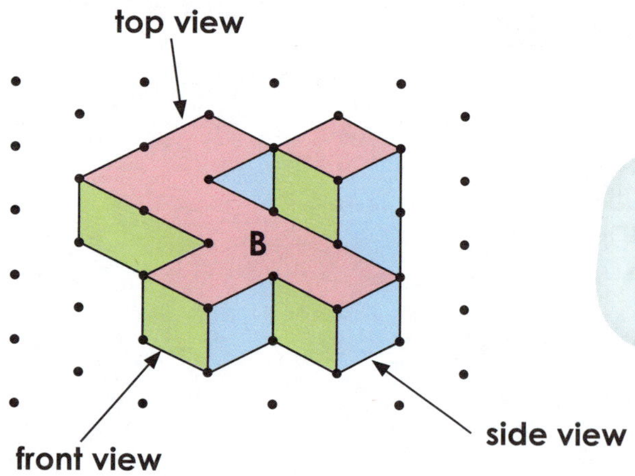

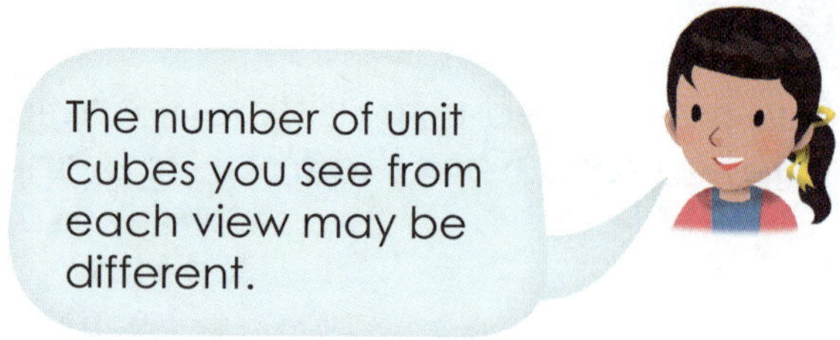

The front, top and side views of Solid B are shown below. Each view is different because we see a part of the solid from each view.

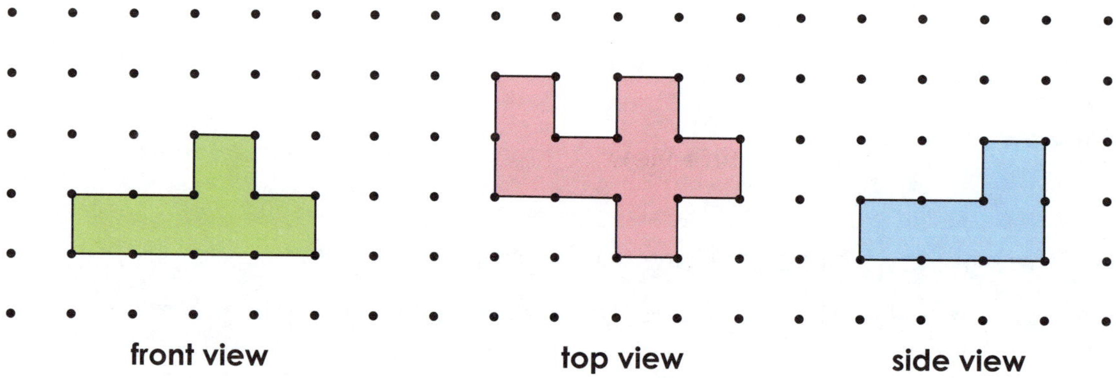

Let's Do

1. Circle the figure that shows the front view of Solid P.

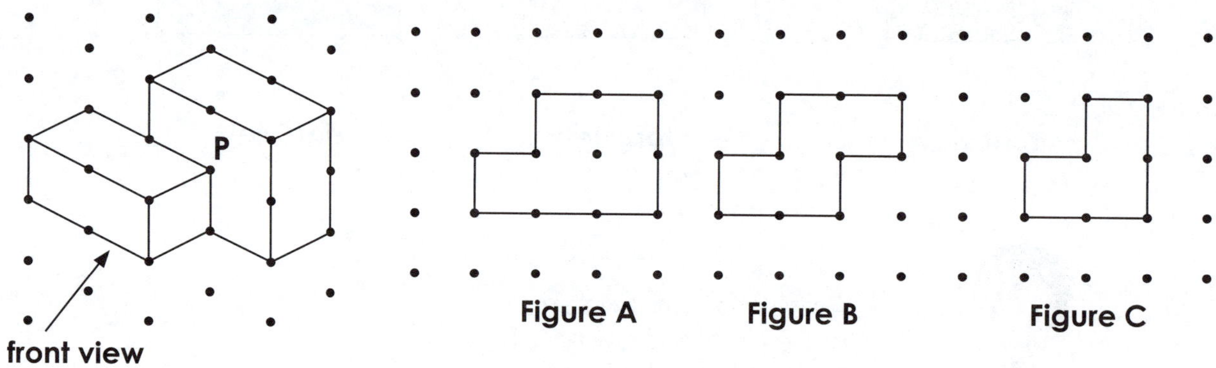

  ISBN 978-93-5103-033-1

2. Circle the figure that shows the top view of Solid Q.

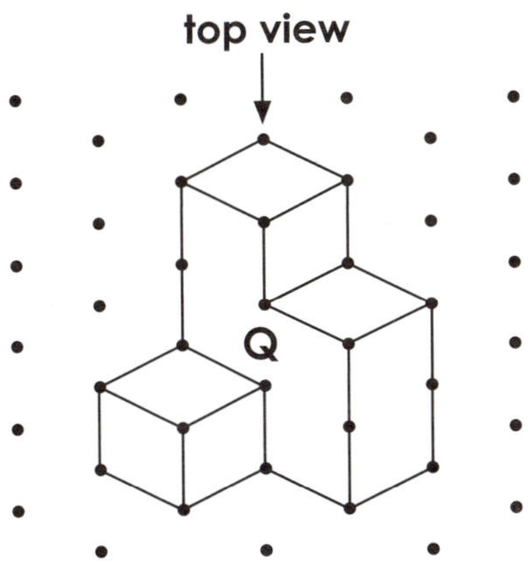

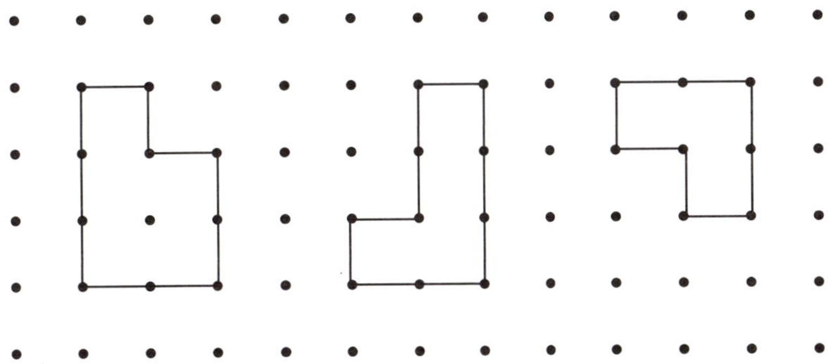

Figure A Figure B Figure C

Chapter 12: Exercise 3, pages 204–205

Adding or removing unit cubes to get a new solid

Let's Learn

a) Add unit cubes to form a new solid.

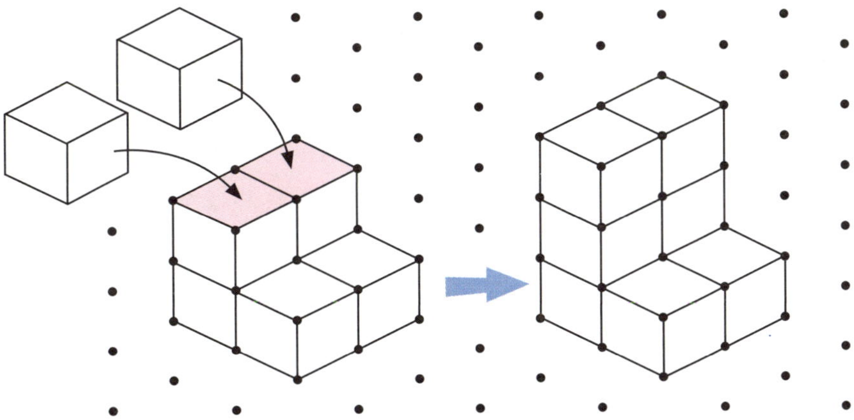

b) Remove unit cubes to form a new solid.

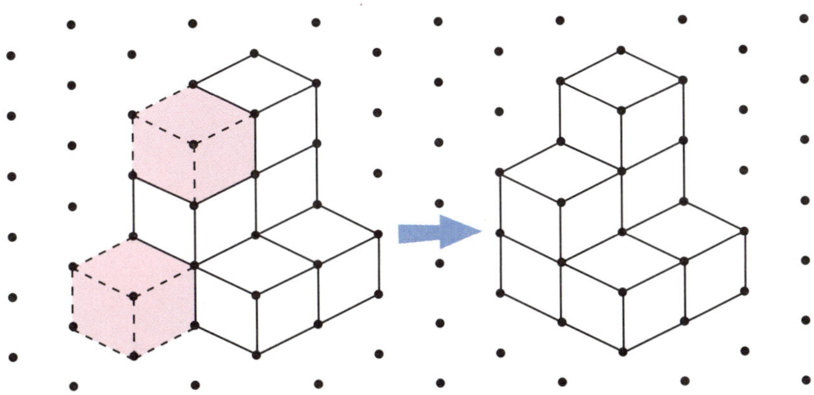

 ISBN 978-93-5103-033-1

Let's Do

1. Use unit cubes to build Solid A. Then, add some unit cubes to get Solid B. How many unit cubes are added?

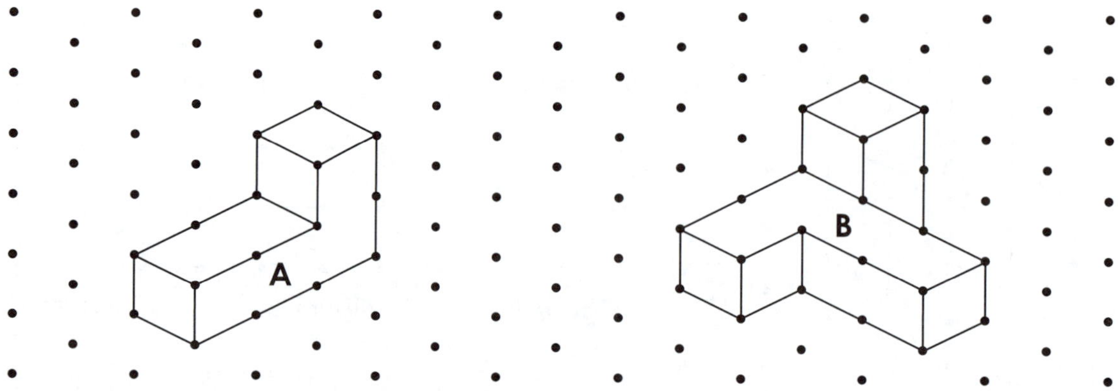

2. Use unit cubes to build Cuboid C. Then, remove some unit cubes to get Solid D. How many unit cubes are removed?

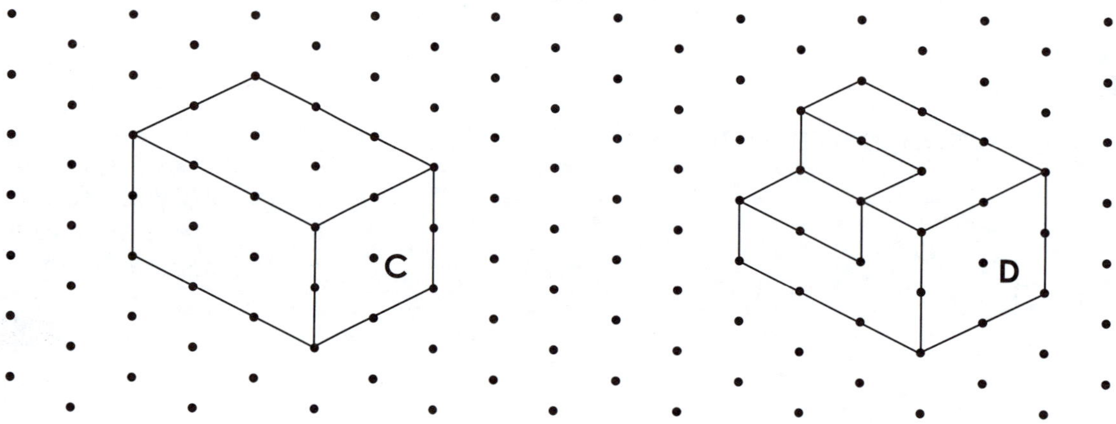

P/B Chapter 12: Exercise 4, pages 206–207

  ISBN 978-93-5103-033-1

Practice 1

1. How many unit cubes are needed to build each solid?
   Complete the table.

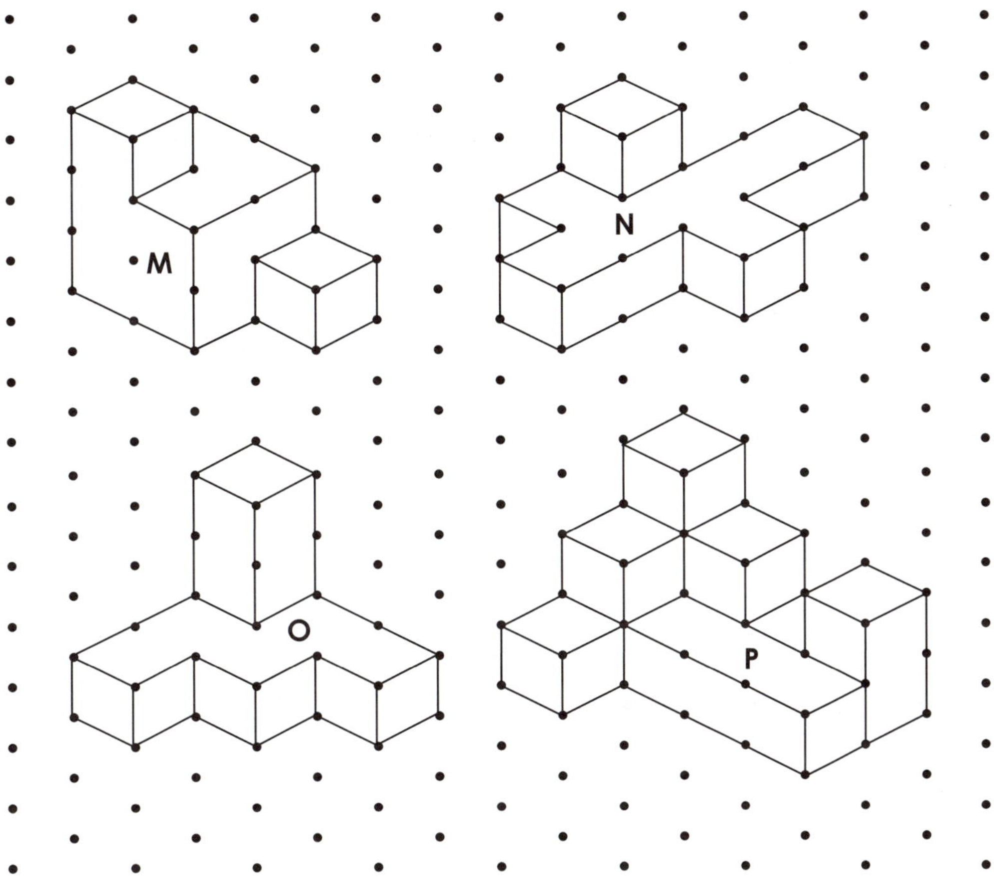

Solid	M	N	O	P
Number of unit cubes				

 ISBN 978-93-5103-033-1

2. Identify the figures that show the front, top and side views of Solid C.

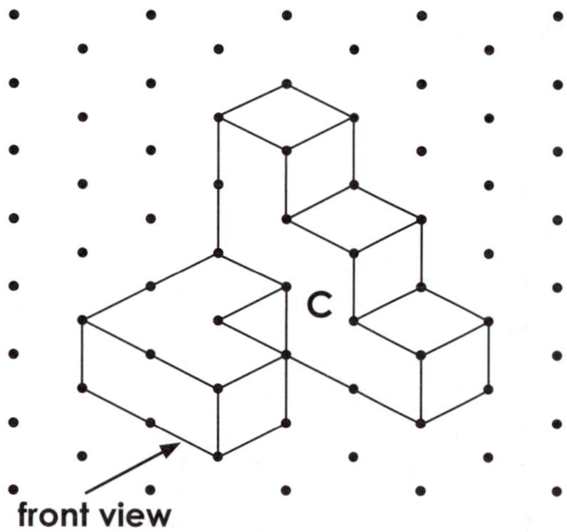

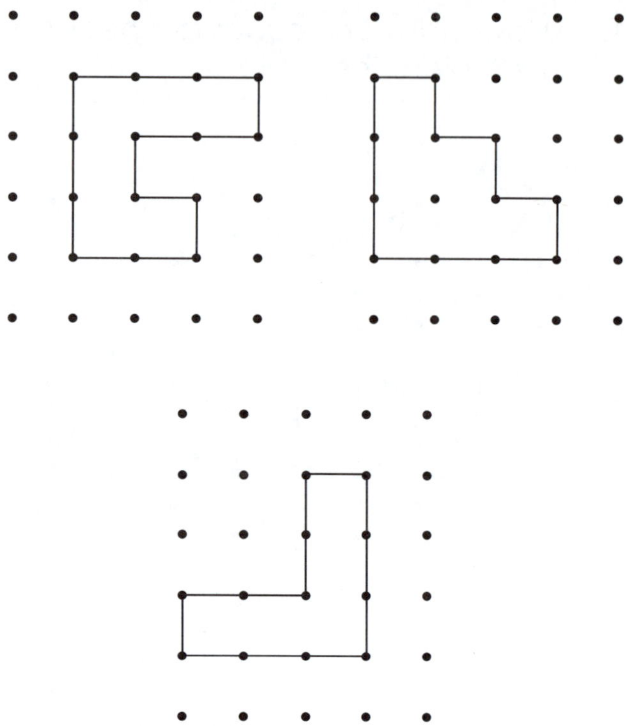

3. Some unit cubes are removed from Solid A to get Solid B. How many unit cubes are removed?

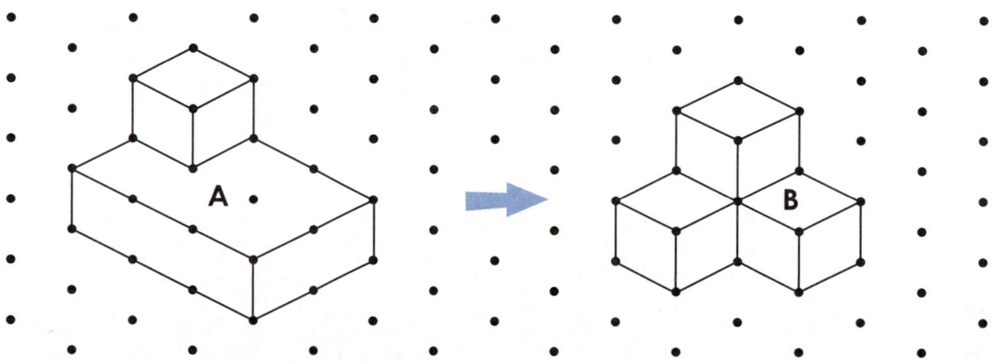

4. Some unit cubes are added to Solid X to get Solid Y. How many unit cubes are added?

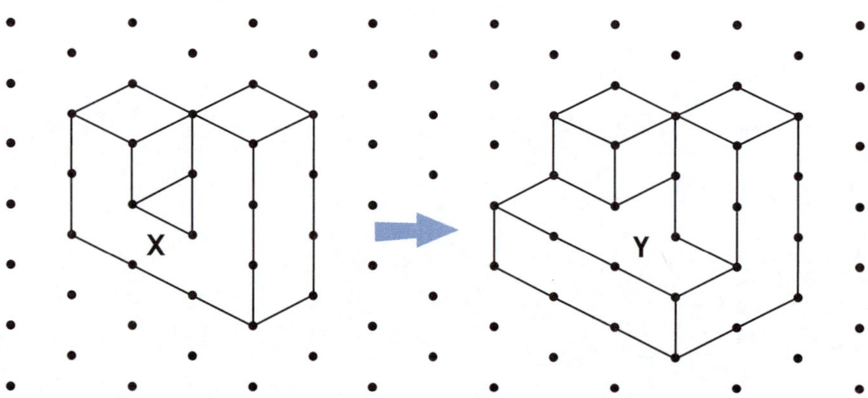

 ISBN 978-93-5103-033-1

Lesson 2 Prisms and Pyramids

Identifying different types of prisms

Let's Learn

A prism is a solid shape with two parallel identical faces joined by rectangular faces.

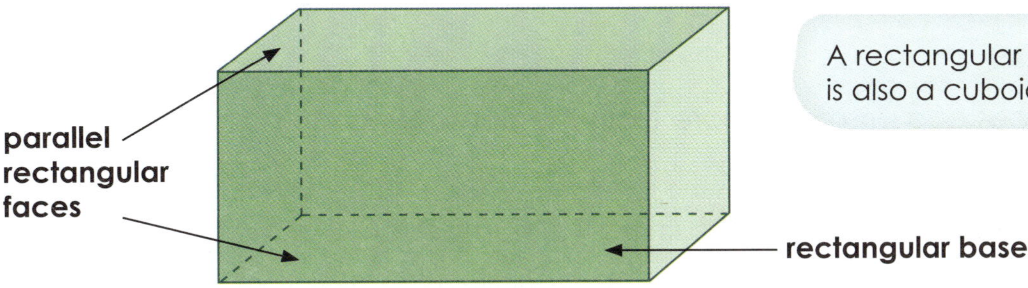

rectangular prism

A rectangular prism is also a cuboid.

A rectangular prism has 6 faces, 12 edges and 8 vertices.
The two rectangular faces that are parallel to each other are of the same size.

The solids below are also prisms.

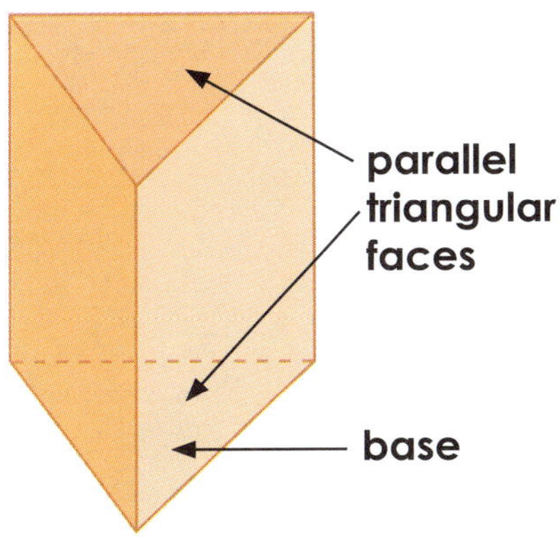

triangular prism

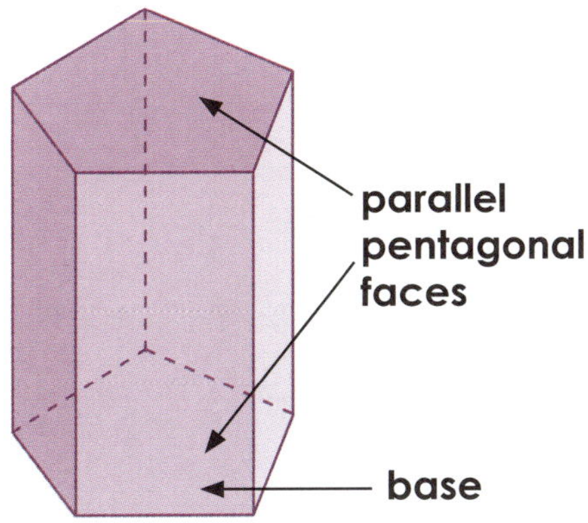

pentagonal prism

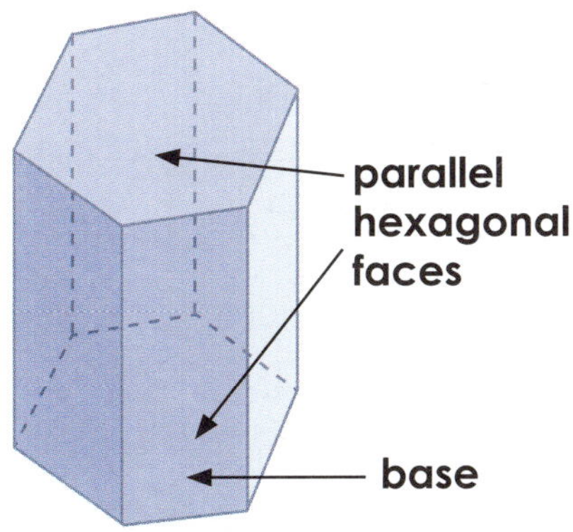

hexagonal prism

A **pentagon** is a shape with 5 sides.
A **hexagon** is a shape with 6 sides.

 ISBN 978-93-5103-033-1

Prism	Number of			
	sides of base	faces	vertices	edges
Triangular	3	5	6	9
Rectangular	4	6	8	12
Pentagonal	5	7	10	15
Hexagonal	6	8	12	18

The number of faces of a prism is 2 more than the number of sides of its base.

The number of vertices of a prism is ☐ times the number of sides of its base.

The number of edges of a prism is ☐ times the number of sides of its base.

Let's Do

1. Identify the solid that is not a prism.

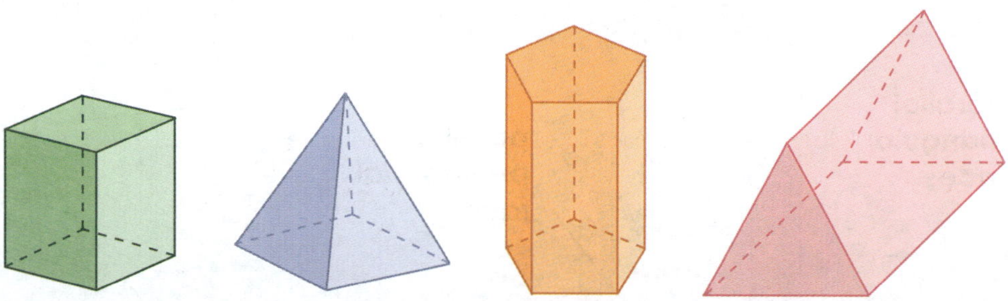

A B C D

 ISBN 978-93-5103-033-1

2. Look at the solid below.

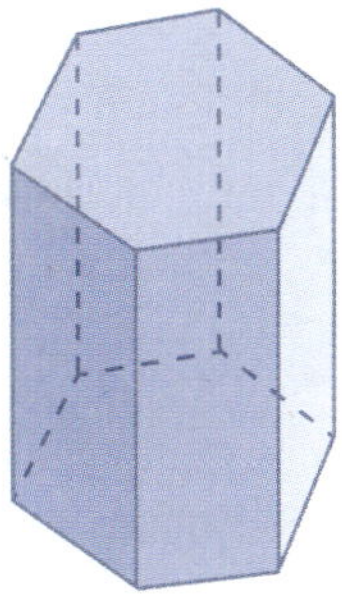

a) The shape of the two parallel faces of the solid is a ________________.
The solid is a ________________ prism.

b) The solid has ________ faces, ________ vertices and ________ edges.

Understanding cross sections of prisms

Let's Learn

a) Cut a triangular prism parallel to the triangular faces to get a **cross section** of the prism.

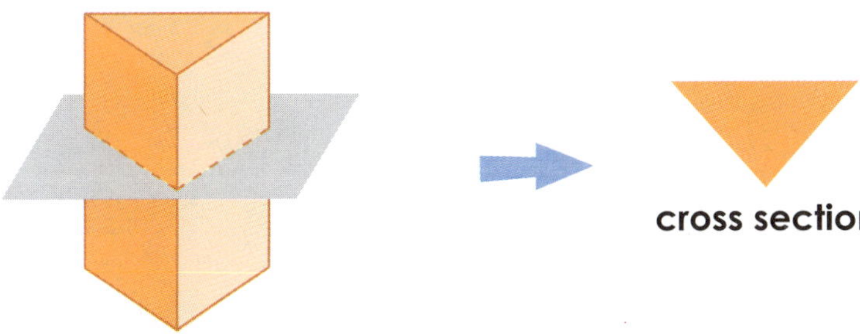

The cross section is a triangle with the same shape and size as the two parallel triangular faces of the prism.

Cut the triangular prism parallel to the triangular faces at a different position.
We get another triangle that is identical in shape and size to the first cross section.

We say that the triangular prism has a **uniform cross section**.

 ISBN 978-93-5103-033-1

b) Cut a pentagonal prism parallel to the pentagonal faces at two different positions.

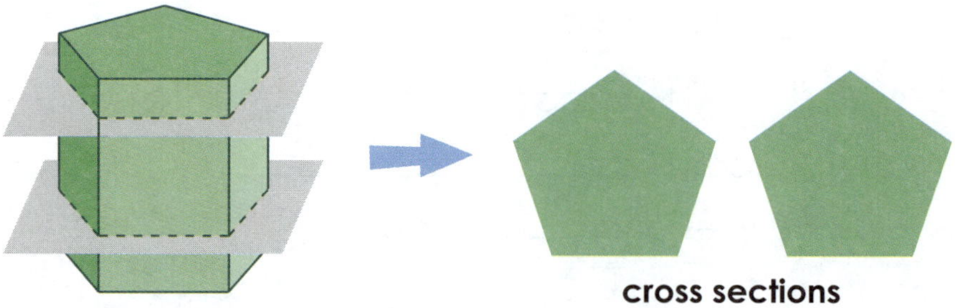

The cross sections are identical in shape and size to the parallel pentagonal faces of the prism. The pentagonal prism has a uniform cross section.

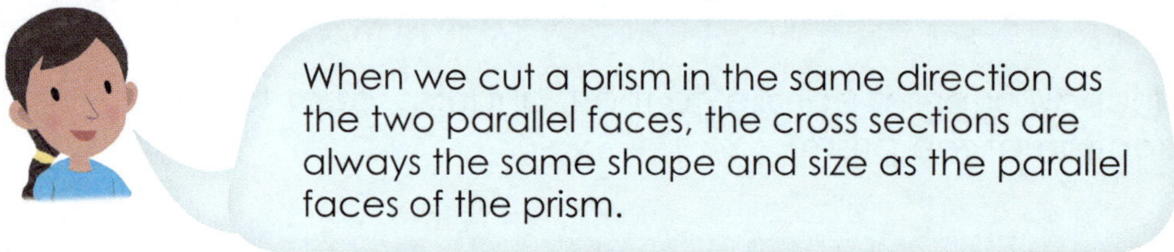

Let's Do

1. Match the cross section with the correct prism.

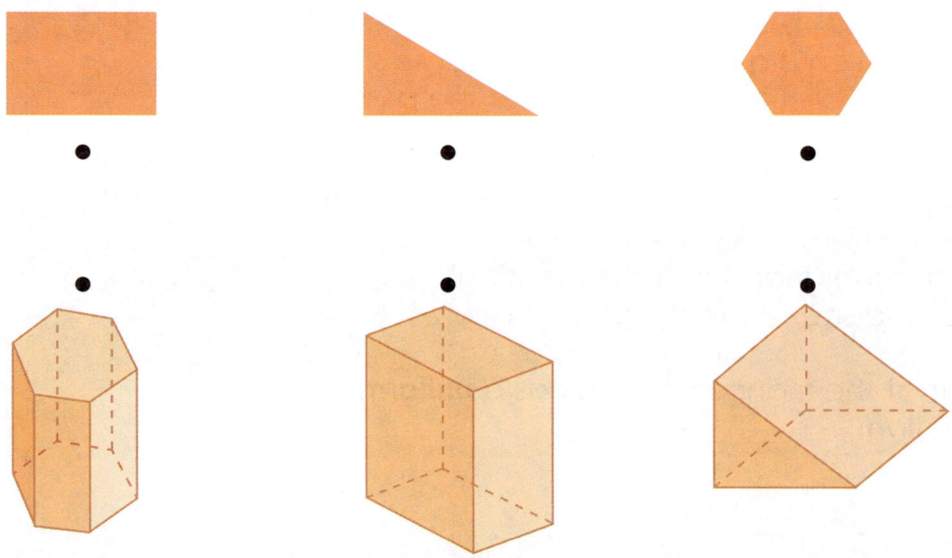

  ISBN 978-93-5103-033-1

Identifying different types of pyramids

Let's Learn

A pyramid has a base and three or more triangular faces that meet at a common vertex.
The base of a pyramid can be any shape.

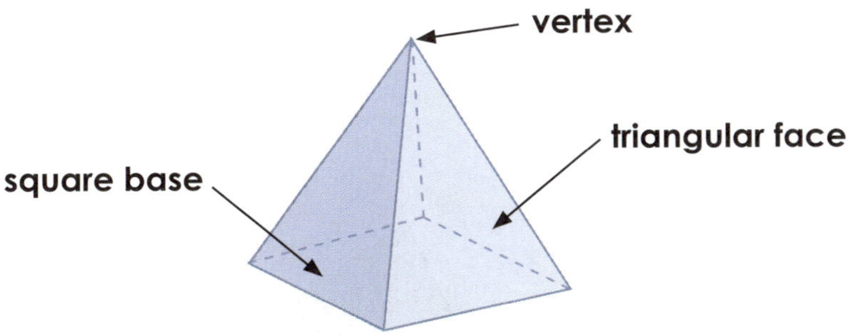

square pyramid

A square pyramid has 1 square face, 4 triangular faces, 8 edges and 5 vertices. The base of this pyramid is a square and the 4 triangular faces have a common vertex.

The solids below are also pyramids.

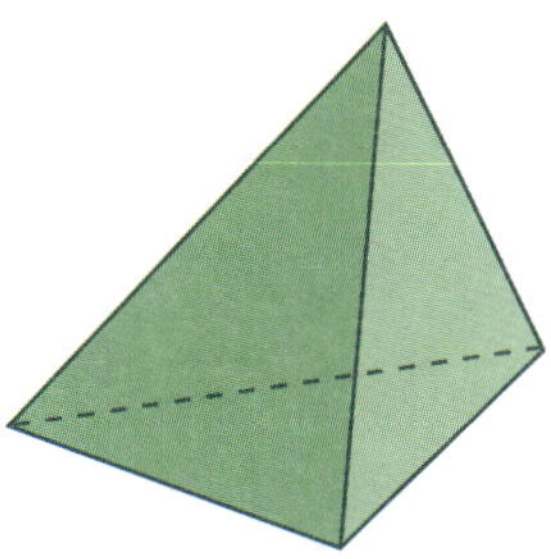

triangular pyramid

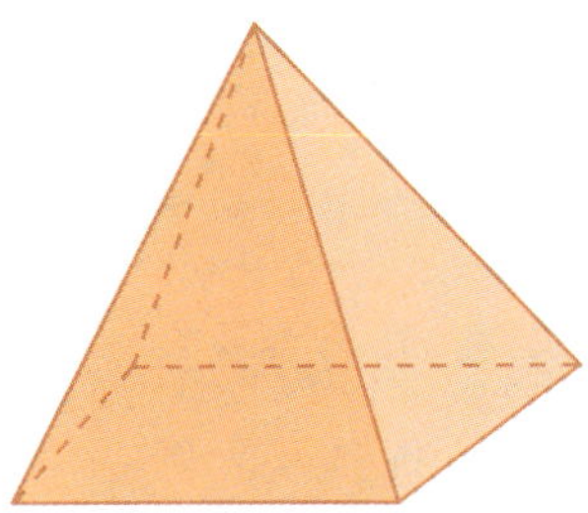

rectangular pyramid

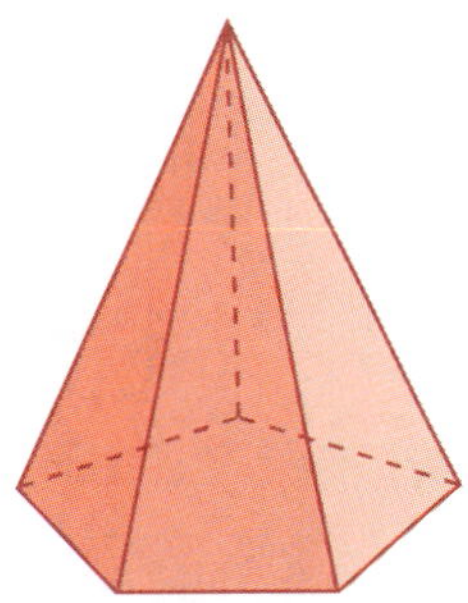

pentagonal pyramid

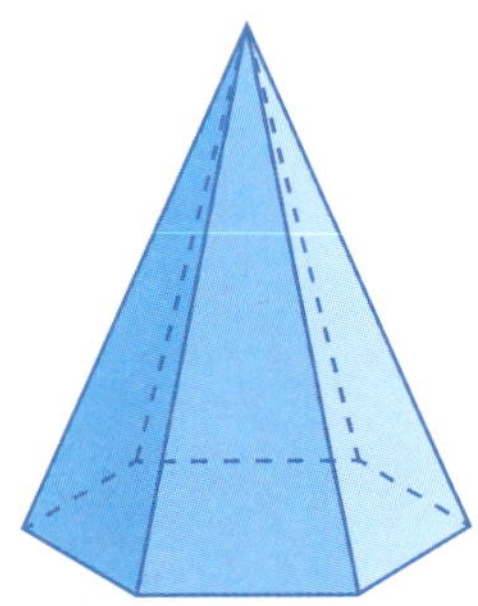

hexagonal pyramid

Pyramid	Number of			
	sides of base	**triangular faces with a common vertex**	**vertices**	**edges**
Triangular	3	3	4	6
Square	4	4	5	8
Rectangular	4			8
Pentagonal				
Hexagonal				

 ISBN 978-93-5103-033-1

The number of sides of the base of a pyramid is the same as the number of triangular faces with a common vertex.

The number of vertices of a pyramid is ____ more than the number of sides of its base.

The number of edges of a pyramid is ____ times the number of sides of its base.

Let's Do

1. Circle the pyramids.

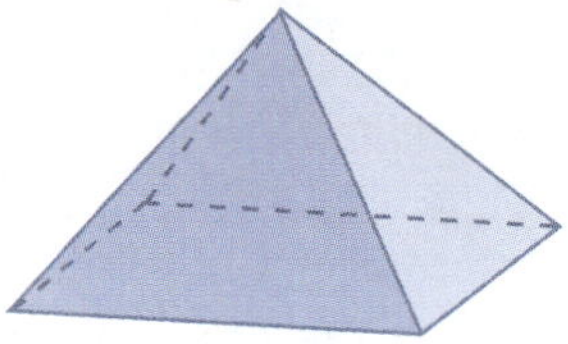
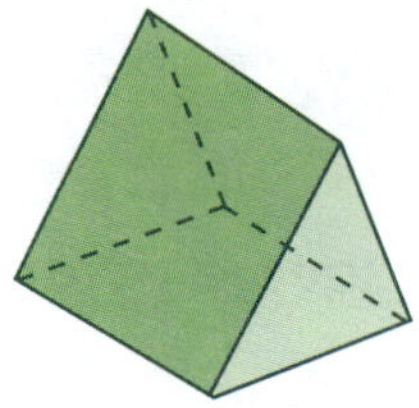
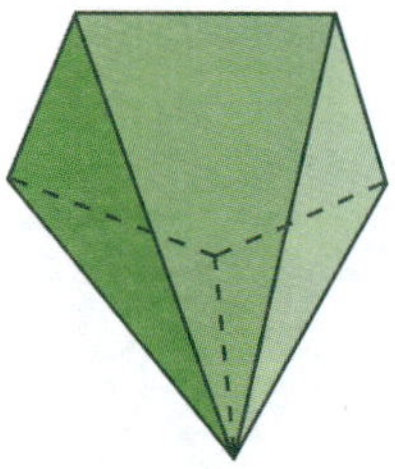
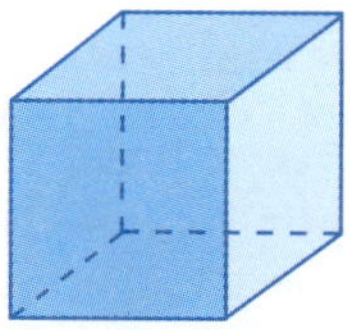
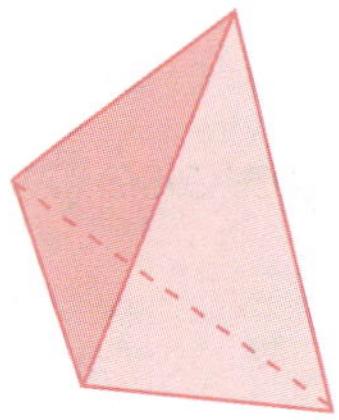

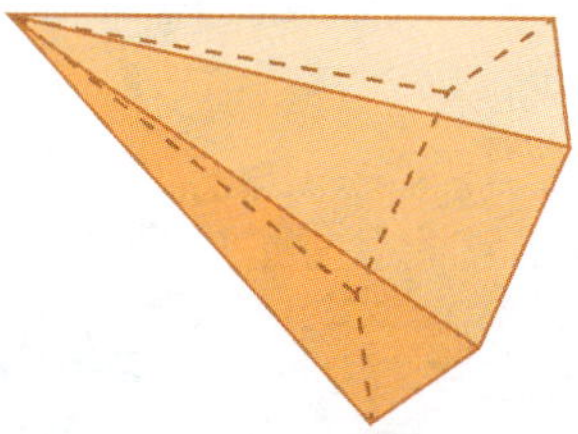

2. A pentagonal pyramid is shown below.

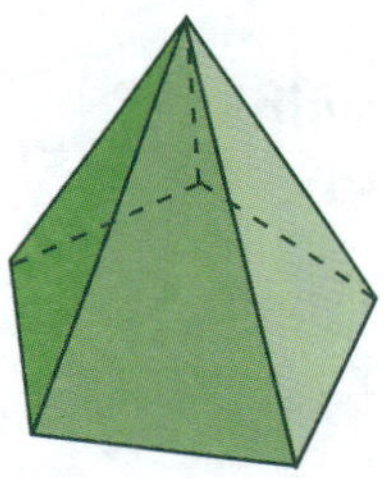

a) The base of the pyramid has ______ sides.

b) The pyramid has ______ triangular faces.

 ISBN 978-93-5103-033-1

Understanding cross sections of pyramids

Let's Learn

a) Cut a rectangular pyramid parallel to the base at two different positions.

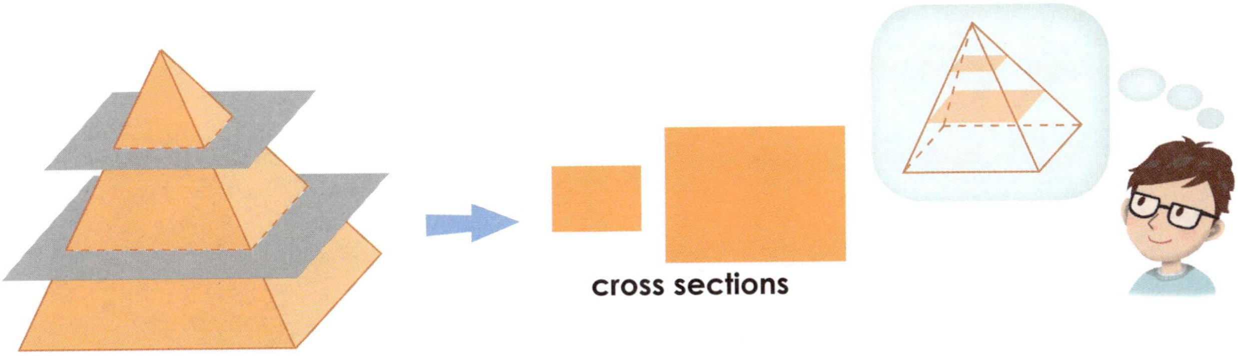

The two cross sections are of the same shape but of different sizes.
So, the rectangular pyramid does not have a **uniform cross section**.

b) Cut a hexagonal pyramid parallel to the base at two different positions.

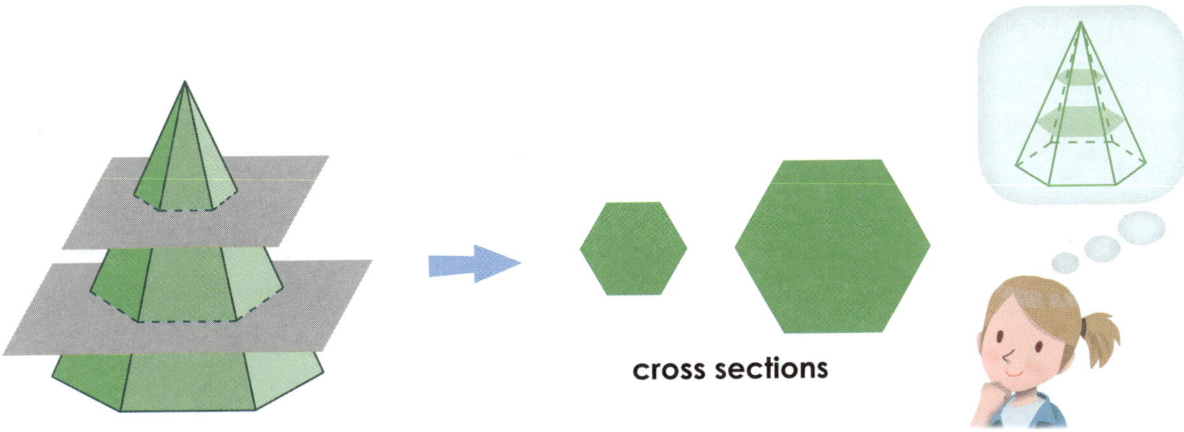

The two cross sections are of the same shape but of different sizes.
So, the hexagonal pyramid does not have a uniform cross section.

The cross sections parallel to the base of any pyramid will have the same shape as the base but they will not have the same size.

 ISBN 978-93-5103-033-1

Let's Do

1. A triangular pyramid is cut parallel to the base at two different positions.

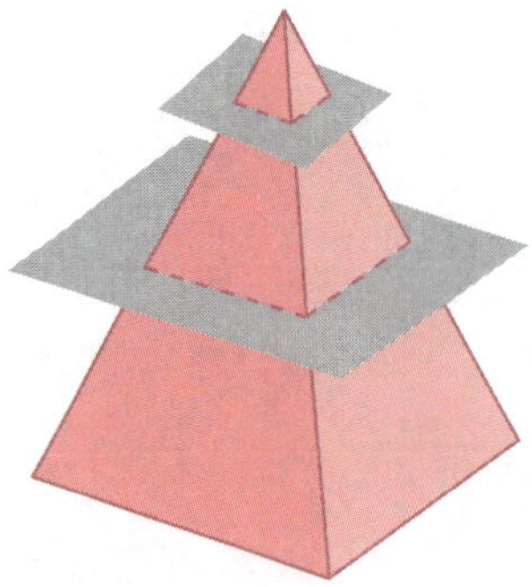

   a) Circle the shapes that show the cross sections.

   b) The sizes of the two cross sections are ________________.

Chapter 12: Exercises 5–6, pages 208–212

Think About It

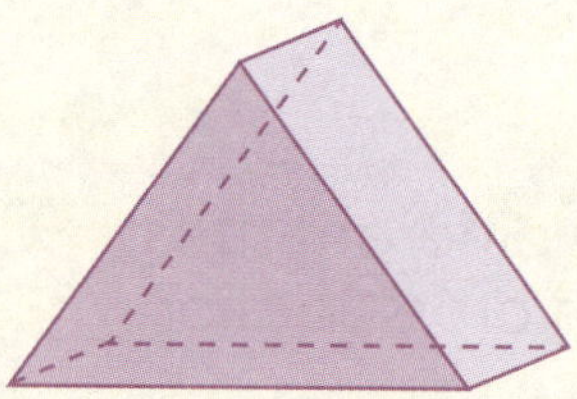

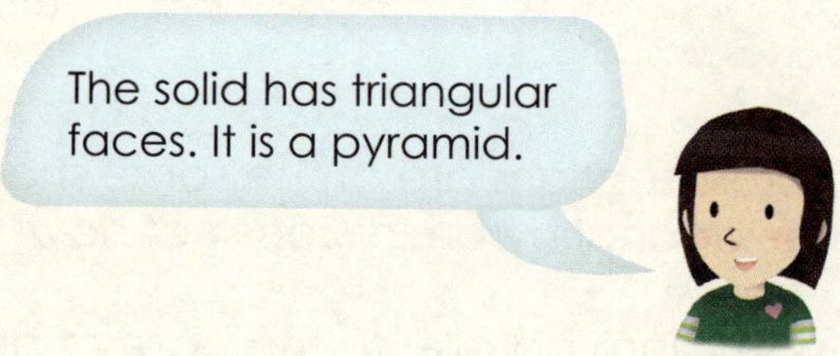

Is Ria correct? Explain why.

 ISBN 978-93-5103-033-1

Practice 2

1. Name each solid.

a)

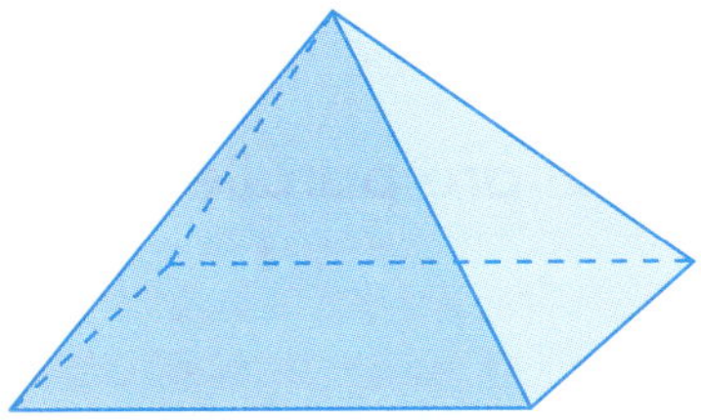

b)

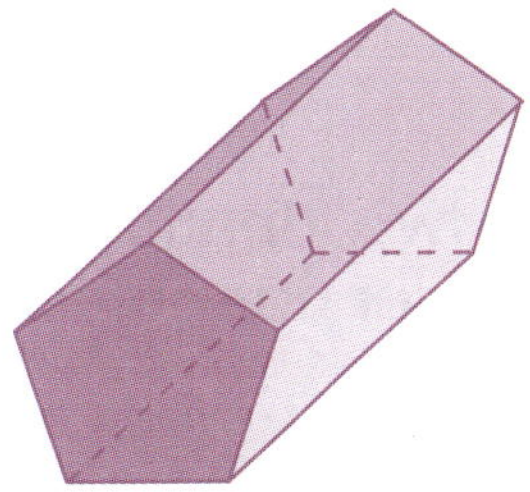

c)

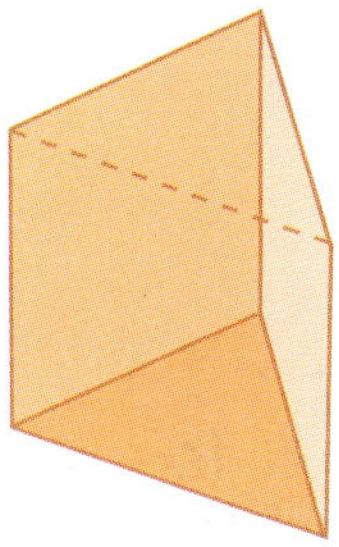

d)

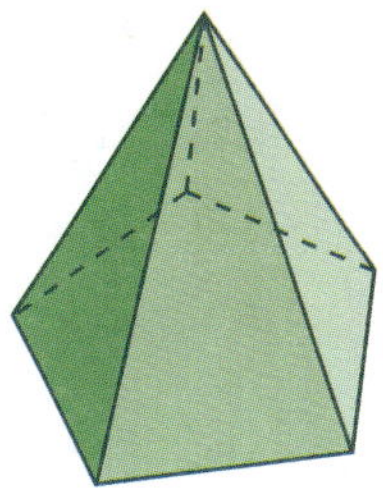

2. Look at the solids below.

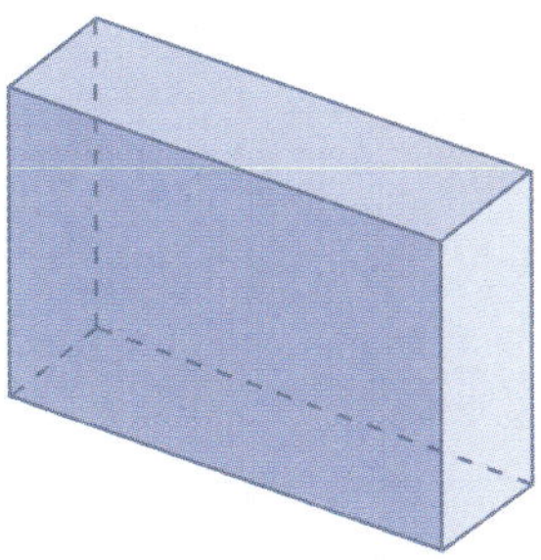

rectangular prism

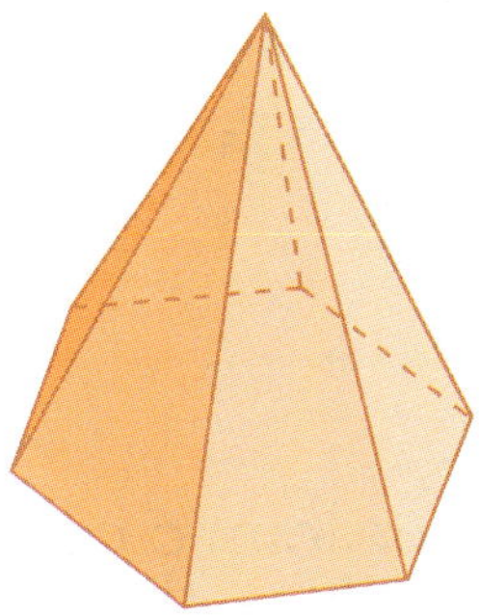

hexagonal pyramid

a) How many faces does each solid have?

b) How many edges does each solid have?

c) How many vertices does each solid have?

d) Which solid has a uniform cross section when it is cut parallel to the base?

e) The shape of the cross section of one of the solids above is a hexagon. Name the solid.

 ISBN 978-93-5103-033-1

Lesson 3 Cylinders and Cones

Understanding cylinders and cones

Let's Learn

a) **A cylinder has two identical circular flat faces that are parallel and a curved surface**. A cylinder has no edges or vertices.

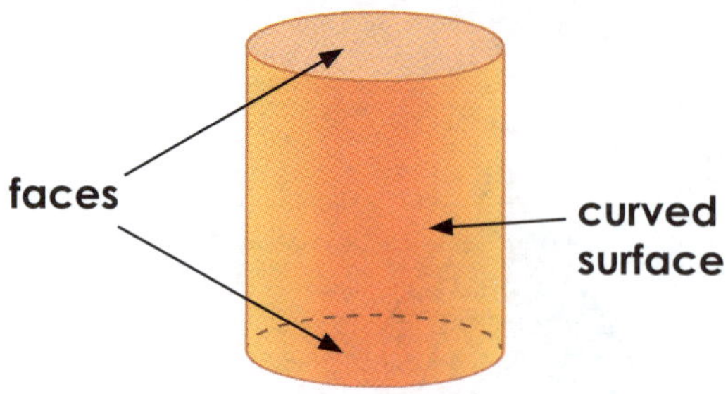

When a cylinder is cut parallel to the circular faces at two different positions, the two cross sections are of the same shape and size.

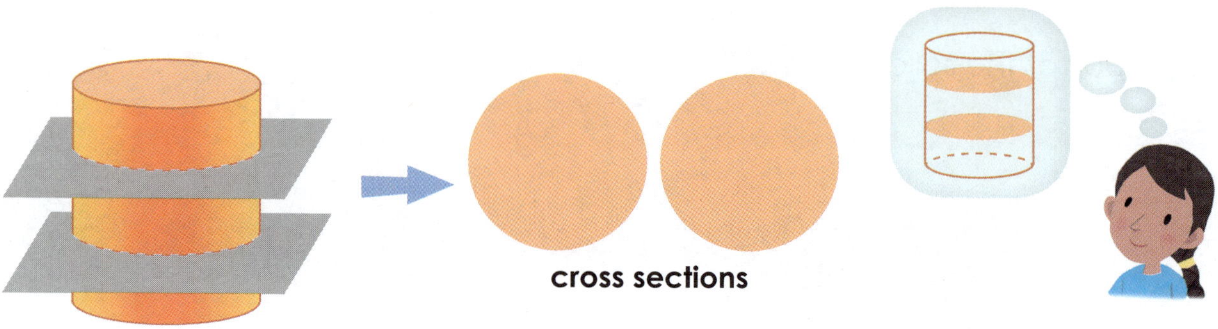

The cylinder has a uniform cross section.

b) **A cone has one circular flat face (or base) and a curved surface**. It has no vertices and no edges.

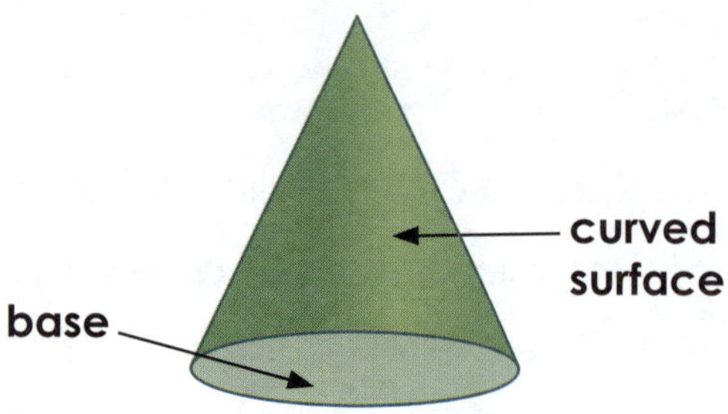

 ISBN 978-93-5103-033-1

When a cone is cut parallel to the base at two different positions, the two cross sections are of the same shape but of different sizes.

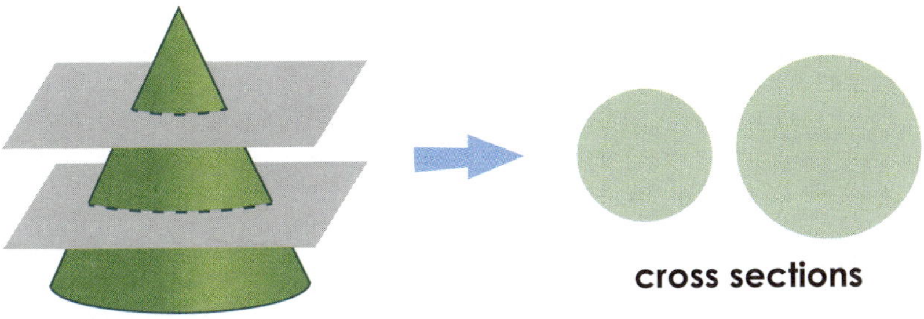

The cone does not have a uniform cross section.

Let's Do

1. Circle the cones.

2. The cross sections made by cutting a cylinder and a cone at two different positions are shown. Identify each solid.

a)

The solid is a

____________________.

b)

The solid is a

____________________.

 ISBN 978-93-5103-033-1

Understanding solids of revolution

Let's Learn

a) A rectangle is attached to a stick and spun around quickly as shown below.

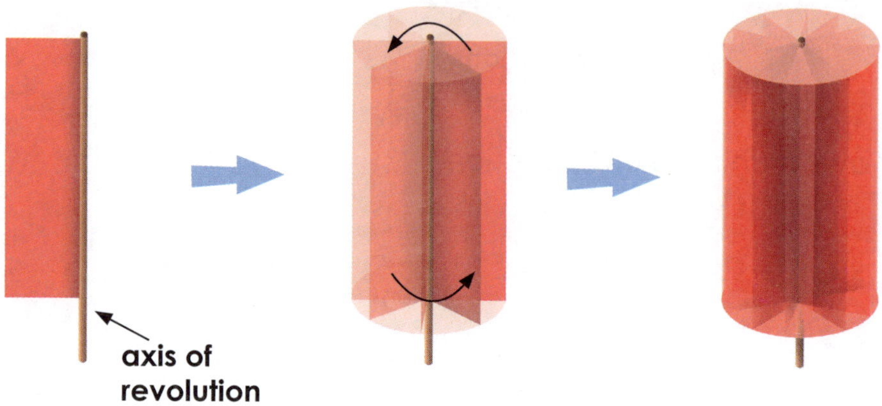

The stick is the **axis of revolution**. A cylindrical shape is formed when the rectangle revolves around this axis.

We say that a cylinder is a **solid of revolution**.

b) A right triangle is attached to a stick and spun around quickly as shown below.

The triangle revolves around the axis of revolution. A conical shape is formed when the triangle revolves around this axis.

A cone is another solid of revolution.

 ISBN 978-93-5103-033-1

Let's Do

1. Circle the correct solid of revolution that is formed when the figure is revolved around the axis.

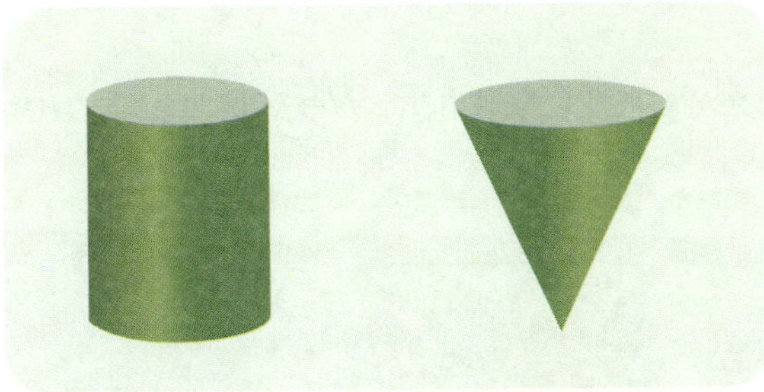

P/B Chapter 12: Exercise 7, pages 213–214

Practice 3

1. Name each solid.

a)

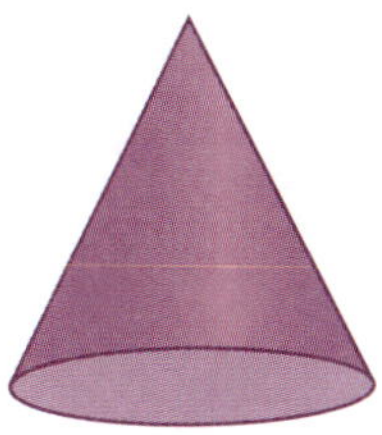

b)

2. Name each solid.

Solid	Number of		
	vertices	faces	curved surfaces
A	0	2	1
B	5	5	0
C	4	4	0

3. Which solid of revolution is formed when the figure is revolved around the axis?

a)

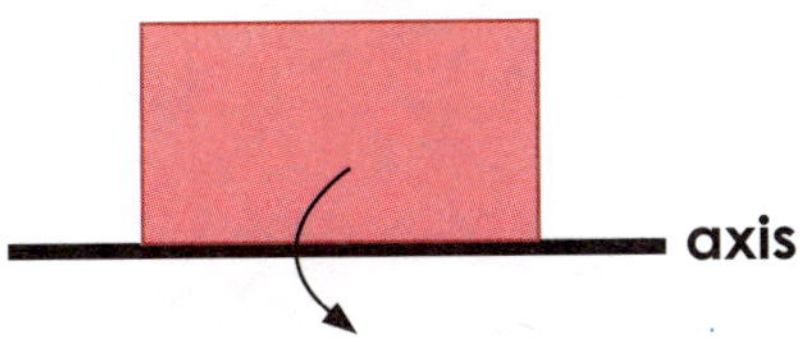

b)

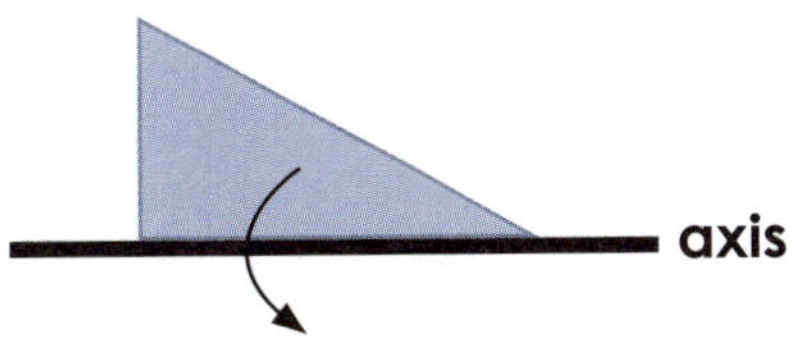

 ISBN 978-93-5103-033-1

Lesson 4 Nets

Forming solid figures

Let's Learn

Unfold a cubic box and lay it flat. We will get a **net** of the cube.

Maths Lab

Picture It

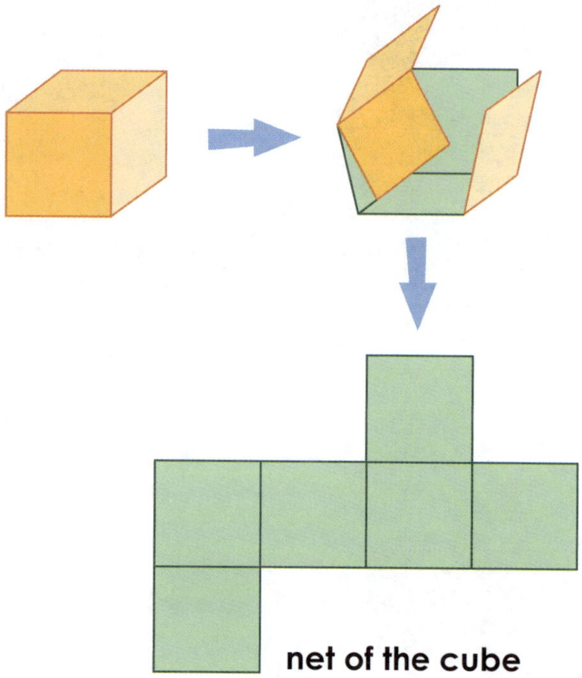

net of the cube

A cube has 6 square faces.
A net of the cube will also have 6 squares.

A net is a figure that can be folded to make a solid.

These are two more nets of a cube.

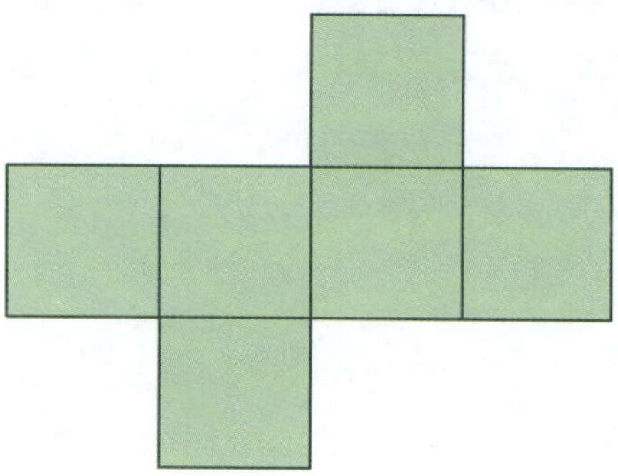

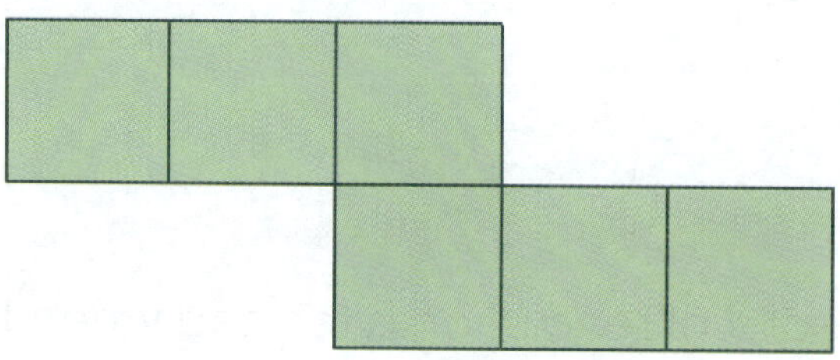

 ISBN 978-93-5103-033-1

Let's Do

1. Trace and cut out each net of a cube on a piece of paper.
   Fold each net into a cube.

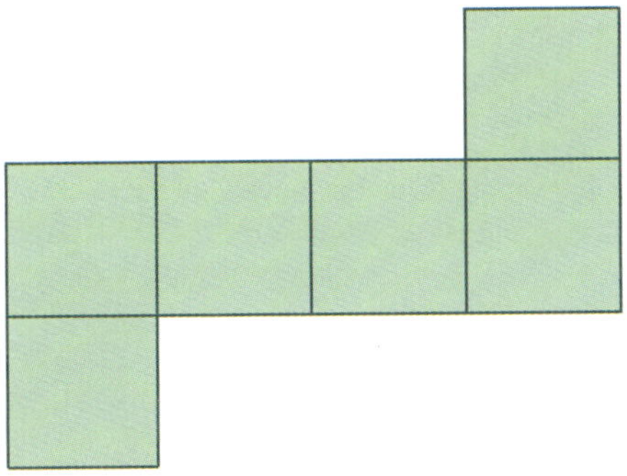

Net 1

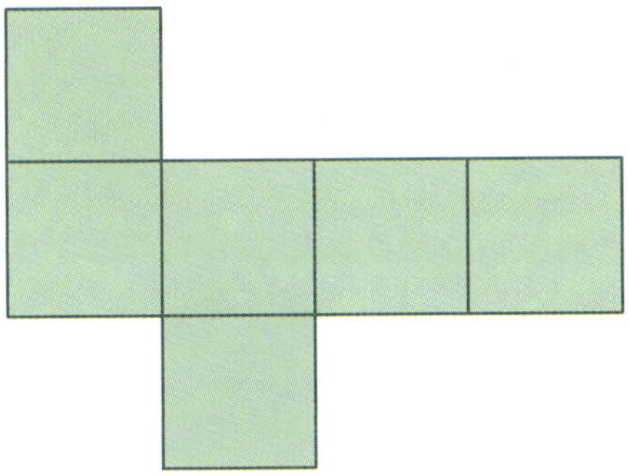

Net 2

Identifying nets of a cuboid, a prism and a pyramid

Let's Learn

Maths Lab

Picture It

a)

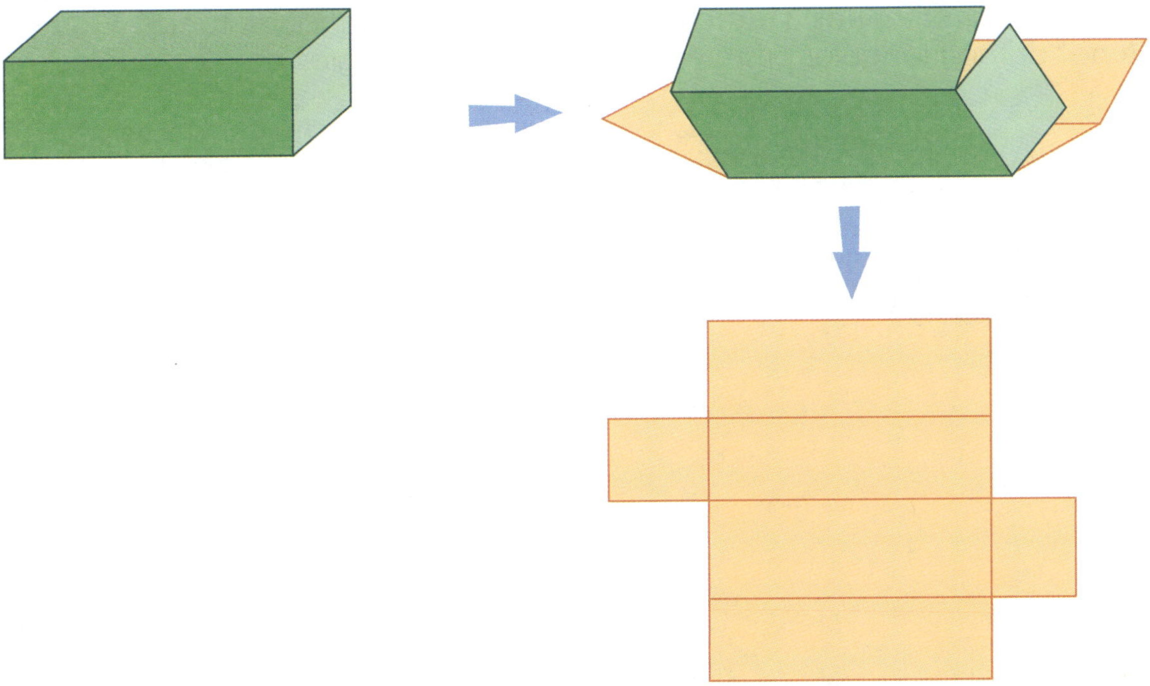

net of the cuboid

A cuboid has 6 rectangular faces.
A net of the cuboid will also have 6 rectangles.

 ISBN 978-93-5103-033-1

b)

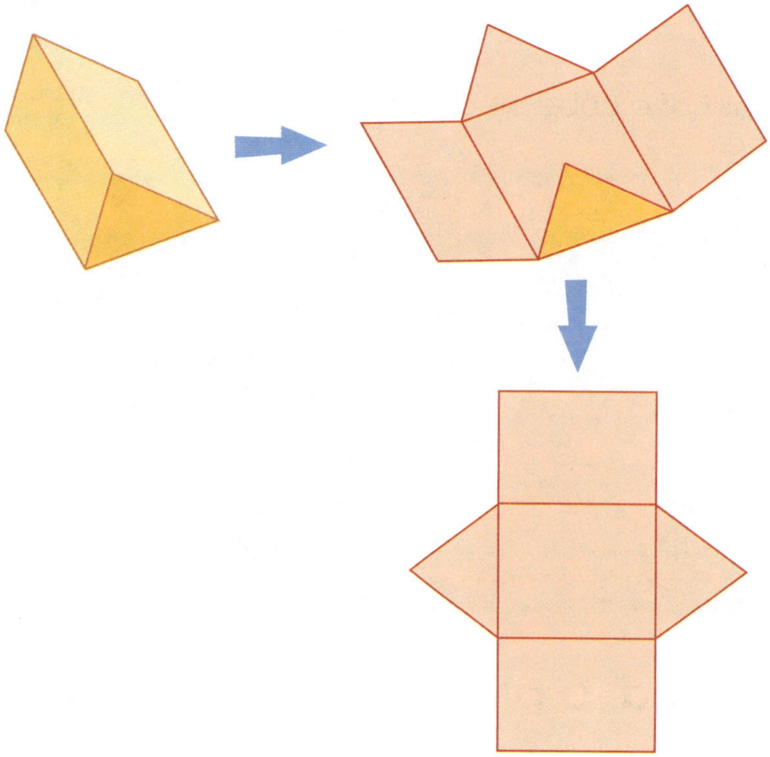

net of the prism

A triangular prism has 3 rectangular faces and 2 triangular faces.
A net of the triangular prism will also have 3 rectangles and 2 triangles.

c)

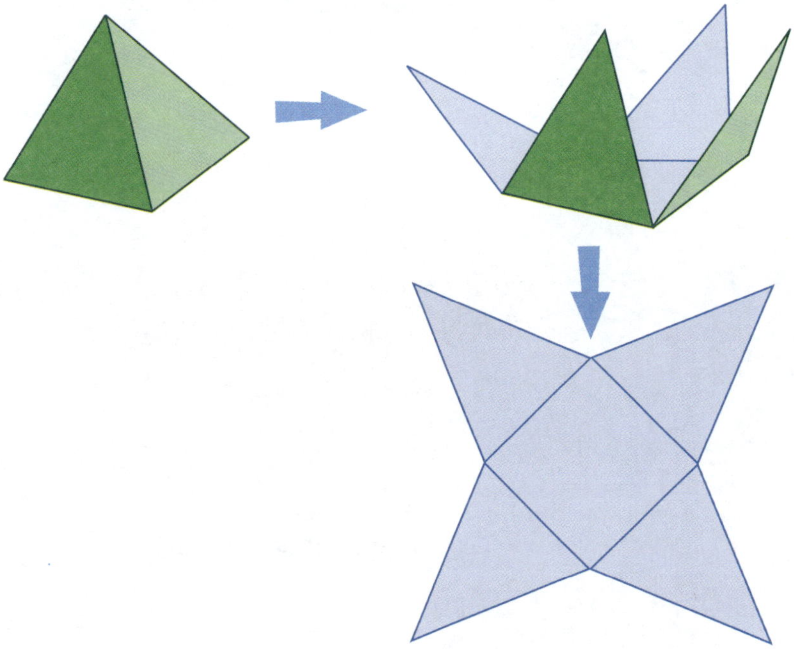

net of the pyramid

A square pyramid has 4 triangular faces and 1 square face.
A net of the square pyramid will also have 4 triangles and 1 square.

 ISBN 978-93-5103-033-1

Let's Do

1. Trace and cut out each figure on a piece of paper. Fold each figure to find out which of them are nets of solids.

A

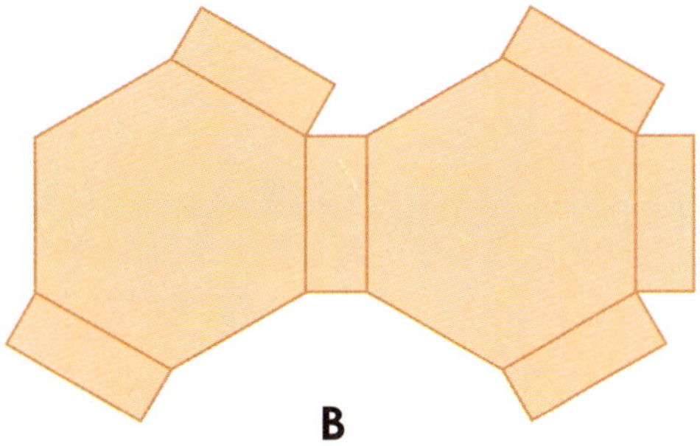

B

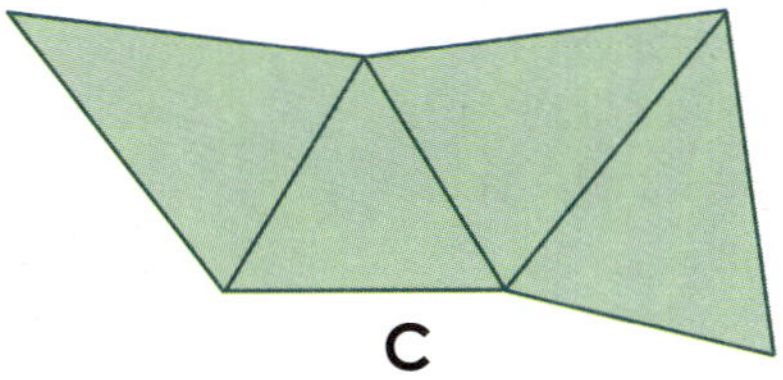

C

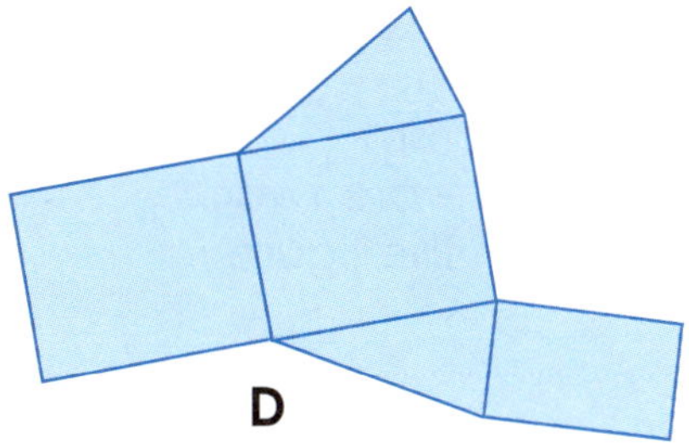

D

2. Circle the correct net of each solid.

Solid	Net	
a) 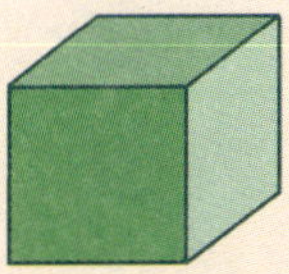		
b) 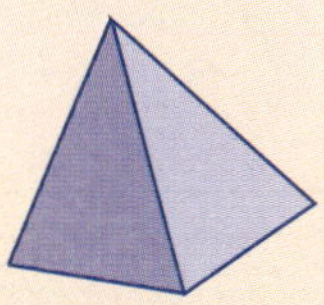	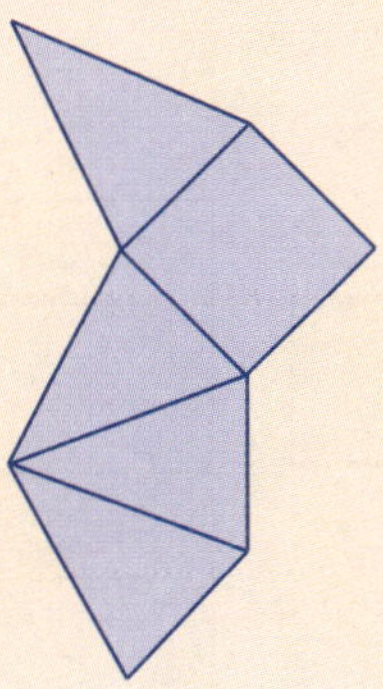	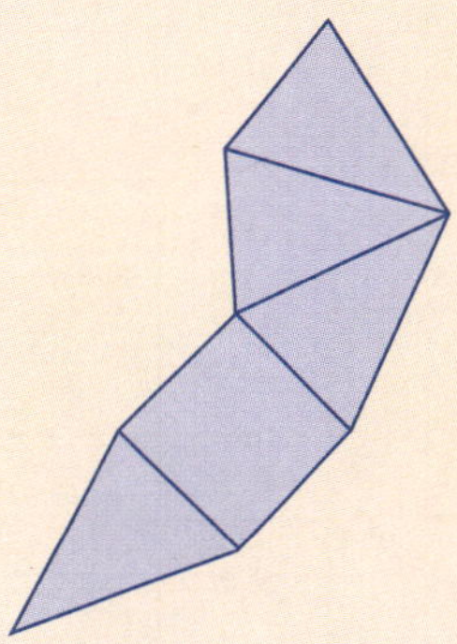

P/B Chapter 12: Exercise 8, pages 215–217

 ISBN 978-93-5103-033-1

Think About It

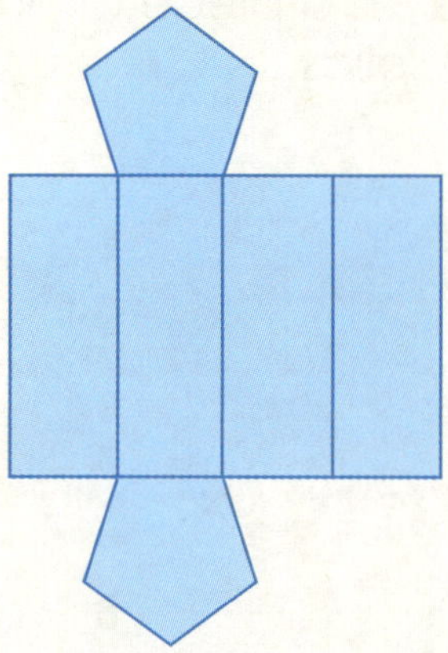

This is a net of a pentagonal prism because there are two pentagons in the figure.

Ria

No, this is not a net of a pentagonal prism. The figure should have 5 rectangles instead of 4 rectangles.

Sam

Who is correct? Explain why.

Practice 4

1. Identify the figure(s) that is a net of the cuboid.

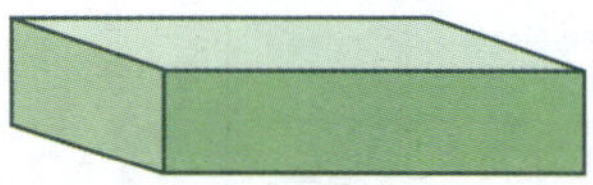

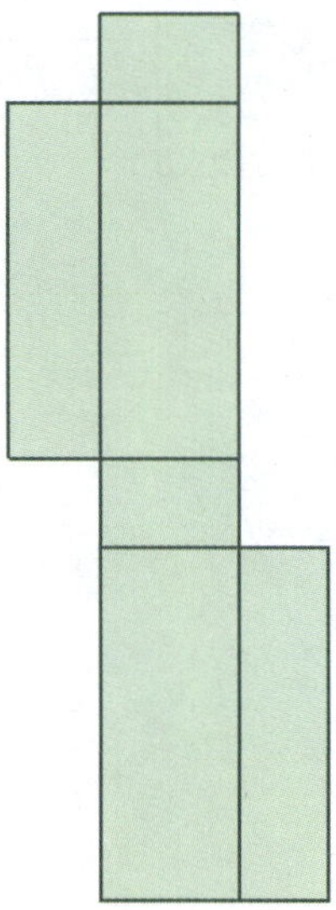

A

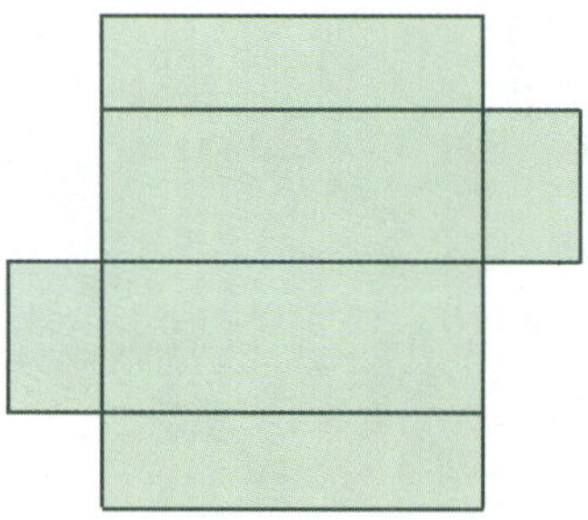

B

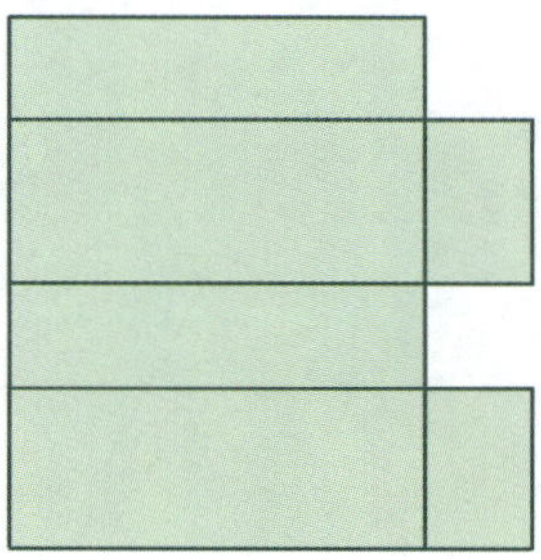

C

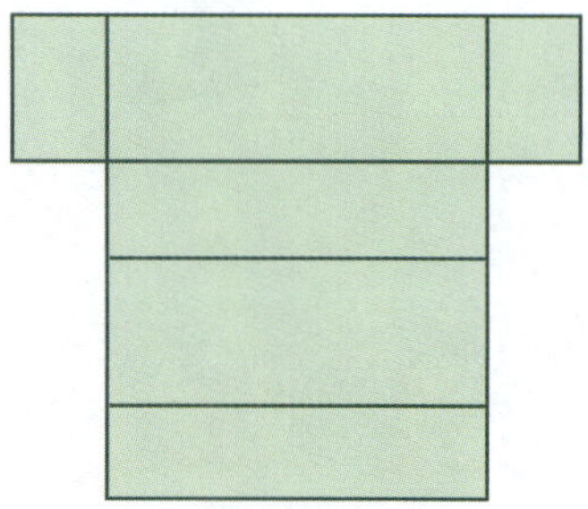

D

 ISBN 978-93-5103-033-1

2. Look at the nets below.

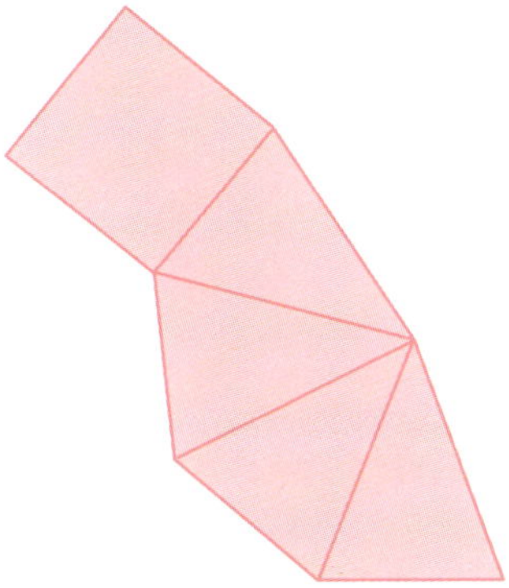

A

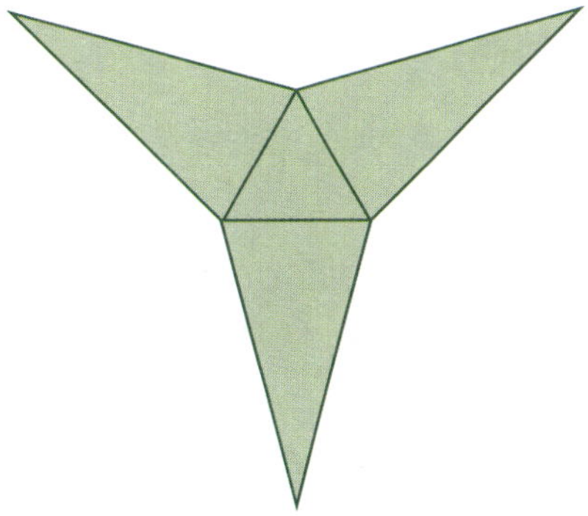

B

C

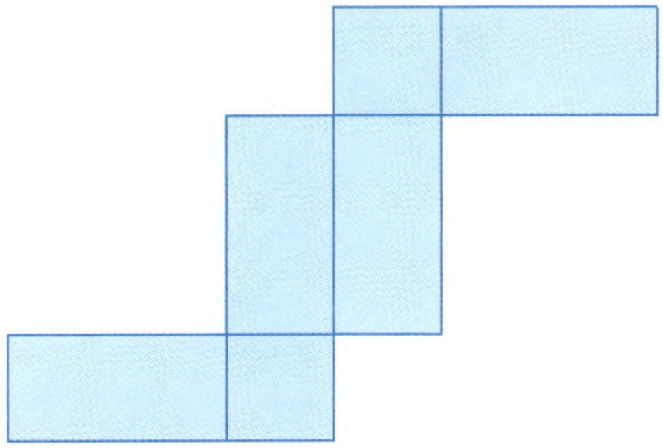

D

E

a) Which figure is a net of a triangular pyramid?

b) Which figure is a net of a cube?

c) Which figure is a net of a hexagonal prism?

d) Which figure is a net of a cuboid?

e) Which figure is a net of a square pyramid?

 ISBN 978-93-5103-033-1

Lesson 5 Problem Solving

Mind stretcher

Let's Learn

A cube has different pictures on its faces.
The figure below shows a net of the cube.

Sylvia folds the net to form the cube.
The front view of the cube is shown below.

Then she turns the cube to the right once. What picture will she see from the top of the cube?

1 **Understand** the problem.

What are the pictures on each face of the cube?
How does Sylvia turn the cube?
Which picture is seen on the front?

2 **Plan** what to do.

I can **act it out** to solve the problem. First, I fold the net to form the cube. Then, I turn the cube to the right once.

 ISBN 978-93-5103-033-1

3 Work out the **Answer**.

Fold the net to form the cube. Then, turn the cube to the right once.

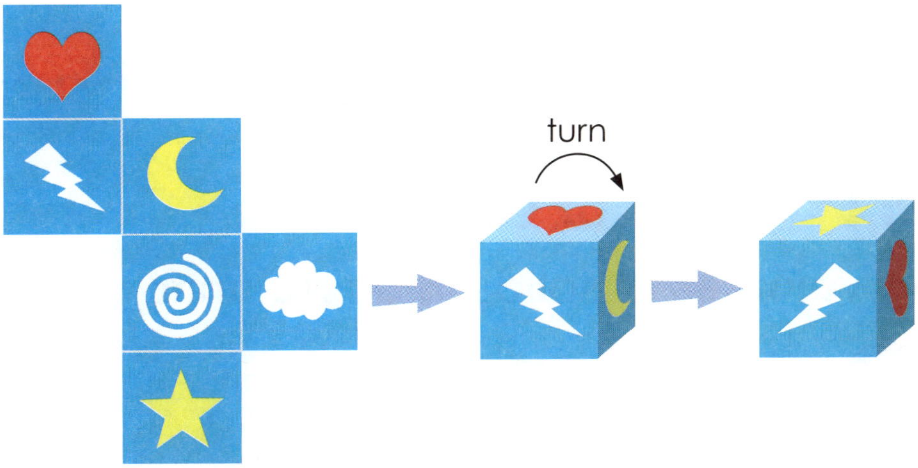

Sylvia will see  from the top of the cube.

4 **Check**
Did you answer the question?
Is your answer correct?

The picture on the left is .

When the cube is turned to the right once,  will be seen from the top.

My answer is correct.

☑ 1. Understand
☑ 2. Plan
☑ 3. Answer
☑ 4. Check

 ISBN 978-93-5103-033-1

13 Volume

Lesson 1 Units of Volume

Finding volumes of solids in cubic units

Let's Learn

a)

These solids are each made up of 8 unit cubes.
They have the same **volume**.

The volume of a solid is the amount of space it takes up.

The volume of a unit cube  is 1 **cubic unit**.

The volume of each solid is 8 cubic units.

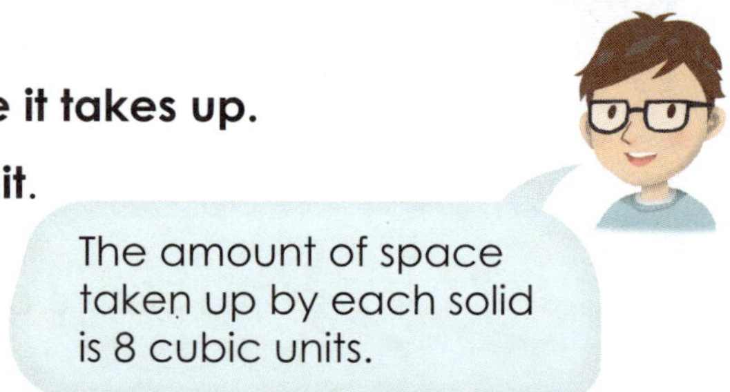

b) Use 6 unit cubes to build a solid like this:

Its volume is 6 cubic units.

Use 6 cubes to build another solid like this:

Its volume is ____ cubic units.

Do these solids have the same volume?

Use 6 cubes to build another solid.
Does the volume change?

 ISBN 978-93-5103-033-1

Let's Do

1. Count the unit cubes and fill in the blanks.

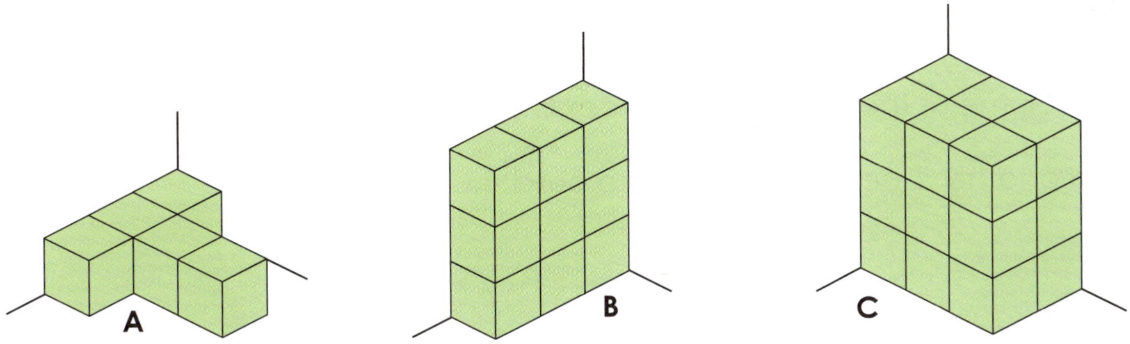

a) Solid A is made up of ______ unit cubes.
   Its volume is ______ cubic units.

b) The volume of Solid B is ______ cubic units.

c) The volume of Solid C is ______ cubic units.

d) Solid ______ has the greatest volume.

P/B Chapter 13: Exercise 1, page 218

Finding volumes of solids in cubic centimetres

Let's Learn

a) This is a 1-centimetre cube.
Each edge of the cube is 1 centimetre long.

Picture It

The volume of the cube is 1 **cubic centimetre**.

The cubic centimetre is a unit of volume.
We write cubic centimetre as **cm^3**.

 ISBN 978-93-5103-033-1

b) Use two 1-centimetre cubes to build this solid:

The volume of the solid is 2 cubic centimetres or 2 cm^3.

Add another 1-centimetre cube to build this solid:

The volume of the solid is ___ cubic centimetres.

How many 1-centimetre cubes are needed to build this solid?

The volume of the solid is ___ cubic centimetres.

c) The solid is made up of 1-centimetre cubes.
What is its volume?

There are 4 layers of .

Each layer is made up of 10 cubes.

$4 \times 10 = 40$

The volume of the solid is 40 cubic centimetres.

 ISBN 978-93-5103-033-1

Let's Do

1. The solids are made up of 1-centimetre cubes.
   Count the cubes and fill in the blanks.

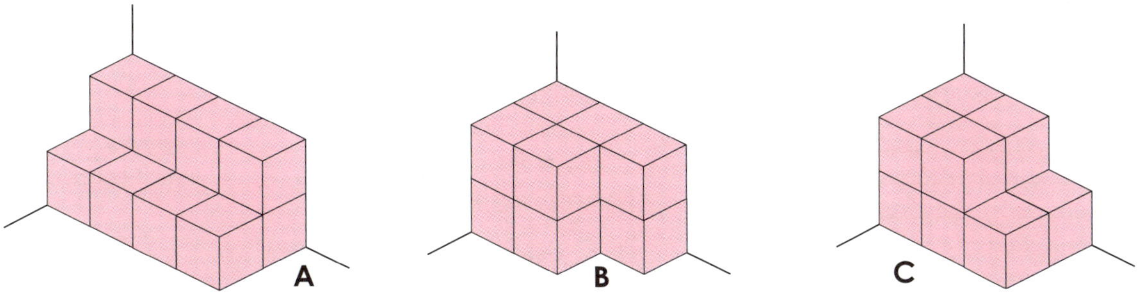

a) The volume of Solid A is ______ cubic centimetres.

b) The volume of Solid B is ______ cubic centimetres.

c) The volume of Solid C is ______ cubic centimetres.

d) Solid ______ and Solid ______ have the same volume.

e) Solid ______ has the greatest volume. P/B Chapter 13: Exercise 2, pages 219–220

Practice 1

1. The solids are made up of unit cubes. Find the volume of each solid.

a) 

b) 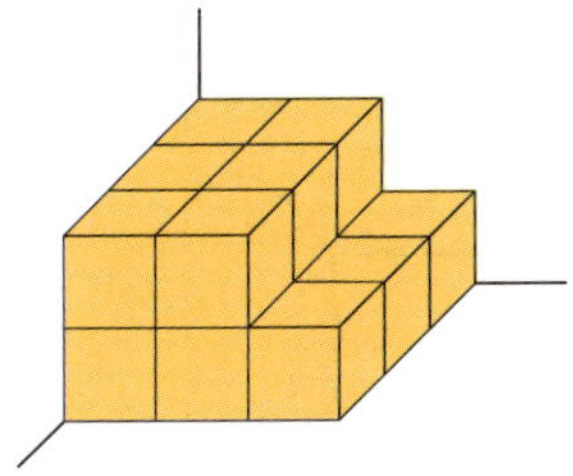

2. The solids are made up of 1-centimetre cubes.

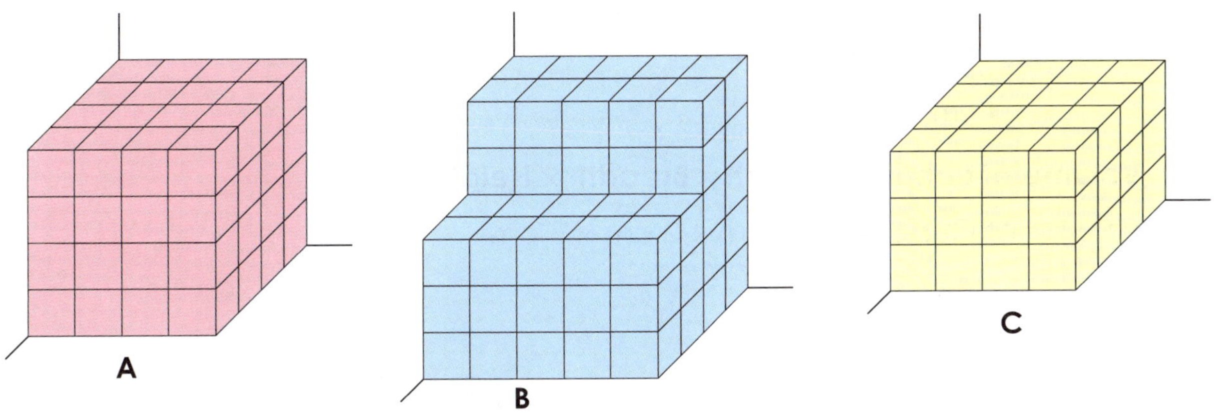

a) What is the volume of Solid A?
b) What is the volume of Solid B?
c) What is the volume of Solid C?
d) Which solid has the greatest volume?

 ISBN 978-93-5103-033-1

Lesson 2 Volume of a Cuboid and of Liquid

Finding volumes of cuboids in cubic centimetres

Let's Learn

a) Cuboid A is made up of 1-centimetre cubes.

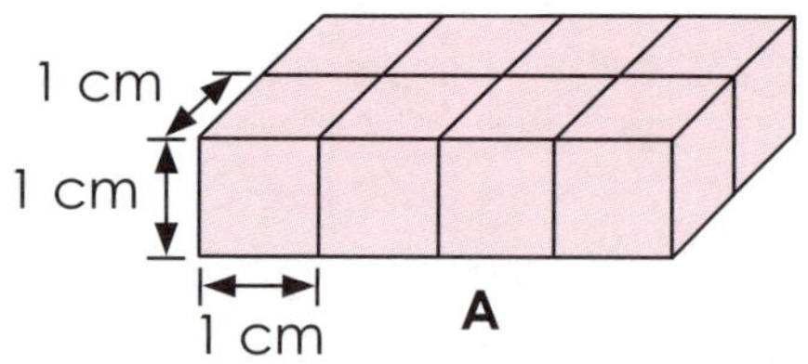

$2 \times 4 = 8$
There are 8 cubes.

The volume of Cuboid A is 8 cubic centimetres.

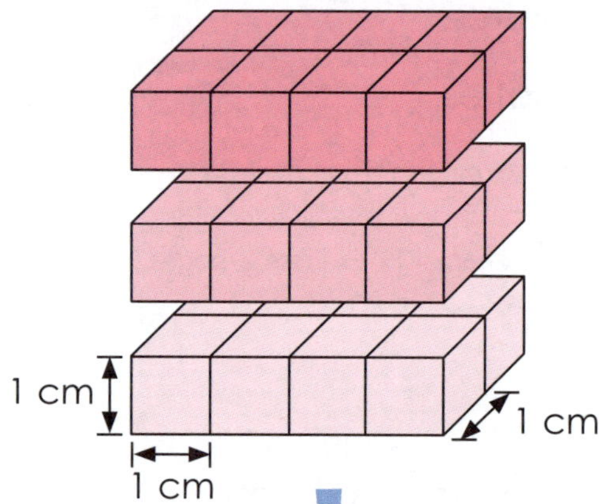

Add two layers of cubes to Cuboid A to build Cuboid B.

There are 3 layers of cubes.

$3 \times 8 = 24$
There are 24 cubes altogether.

The volume of Cuboid B is 24 cubic centimetres.

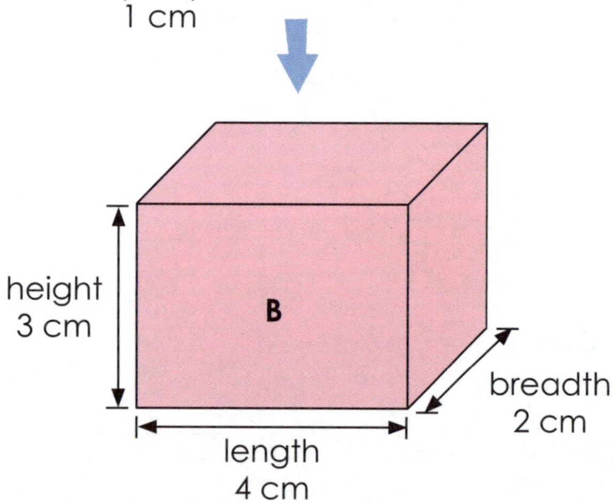

The length of Cuboid B is 4 centimetres.
Its breadth is 2 centimetres.
Its height is 3 centimetres.

Volume of cuboid = Length × Breadth × Height

Volume of Cuboid B $= 4\text{ cm} \times 2\text{ cm} \times 3\text{ cm}$
$= 24\text{ cm}^3$

 ISBN 978-93-5103-033-1

b) A cuboid measures 8 centimetres by 2 centimetres by 5 centimetres. Find its volume.

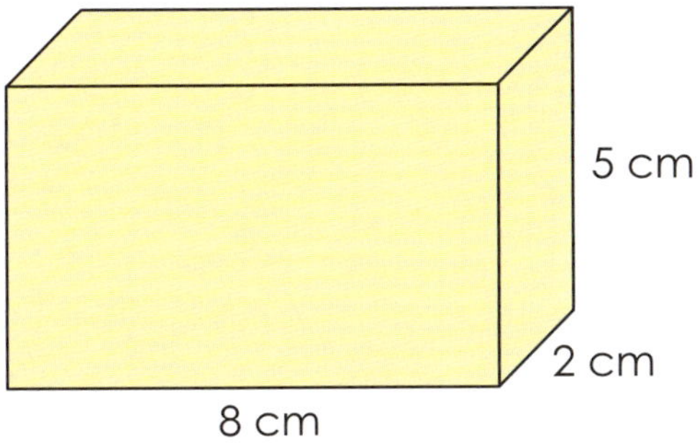

How many 1-centimetre cubes are needed to build this cuboid?

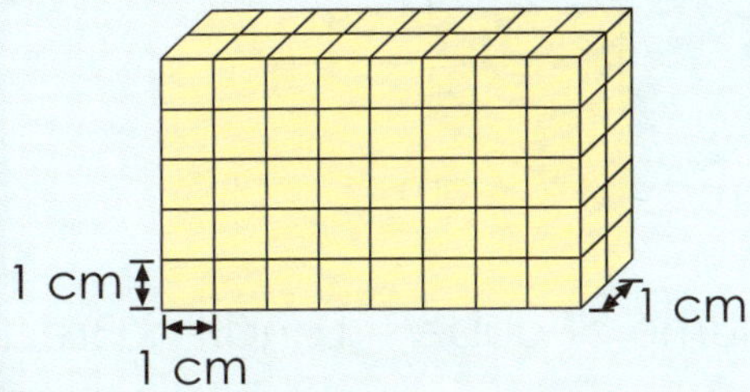

Volume of cuboid = Length × Breadth × Height

= ____ cm × ____ cm × ____ cm

= ____ cm^3

The volume of the cuboid is ____ cubic centimetres.

Let's Do

1. These cuboids are made up of 1-centimetre cubes. Count the cubes and fill in the blanks.

a)

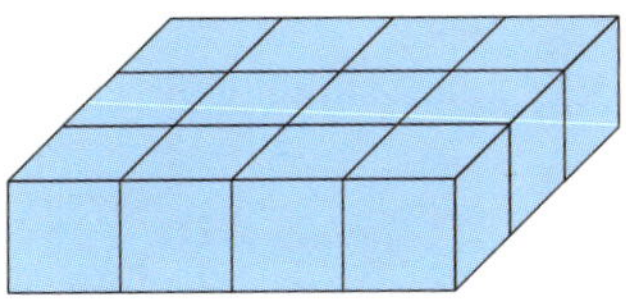

Length = ________ cm

Breadth = ________ cm

Height = ________ cm

Volume = ________ cm^3

b)

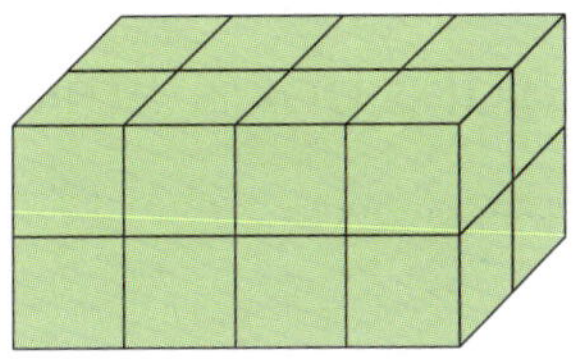

Length = ________ cm

Breadth = ________ cm

Height = ________ cm

Volume = ________ cm^3

2. a) Find the volume of a cuboid which measures 5 centimetres by 3 centimetres by 4 centimetres.

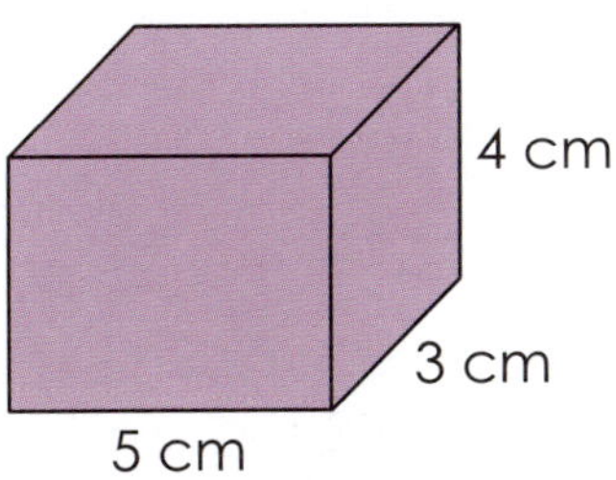

How many 1-centimetre cubes are needed to build this cuboid?

Volume of cuboid = Length × Breadth × Height

= ________ cm × ________ cm × ________ cm

= ________ cm^3

 ISBN 978-93-5103-033-1

b) Find the volume of a cube of edge 4 centimetres.

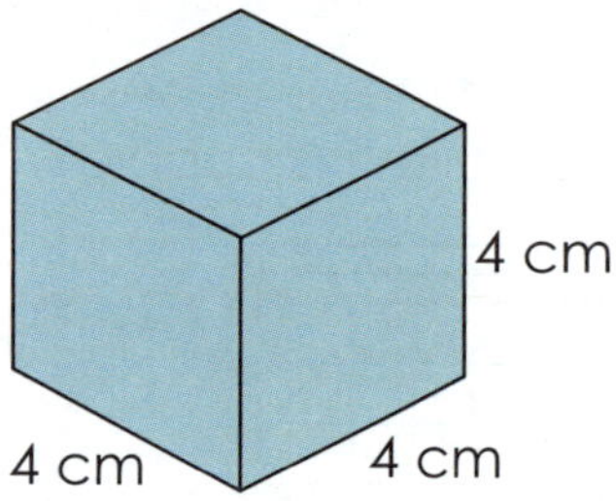

Volume of cube = Length $\times$ Breadth $\times$ Height

= ______ cm $\times$ ______ cm $\times$ ______ cm

= ______ cm^3

c) Which solid has a greater volume, the cuboid or the cube?

Chapter 13: Exercise 3, pages 221–222

Finding volumes of cuboids in cubic metres

Let's Learn

a) Each edge of this box is 1 metre long.

1-metre box

1-centimetre cube

We use cubic metres for bigger volumes.

The volume of the box is 1 **cubic metre**.

The cubic metre is also a unit of volume.
We write cubic metre as $\mathbf{m^3}$.

How many 1-centimetre cubes do you need to fill the box completely?

1 m = 100 cm

 ISBN 978-93-5103-033-1

b) A cuboid measures 2 metres by 1 metre by 1 metre. Find its volume.

Picture It

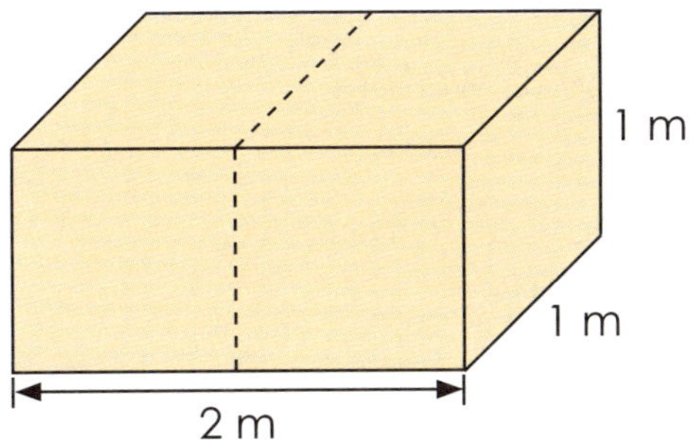

Volume of cuboid = Length × Breadth × Height
= 2 m × 1 m × 1 m
= ___ m^3

The volume of the cuboid is ___ cubic metres.

Let's Do

1. Fill in the blanks with **cm^3** or **m^3**.
   a) The volume of my eraser is about 5 ______.
   b) A big storage box has a volume of about 1 ______.

2. Find the volume of a cube of edge 3 metres.

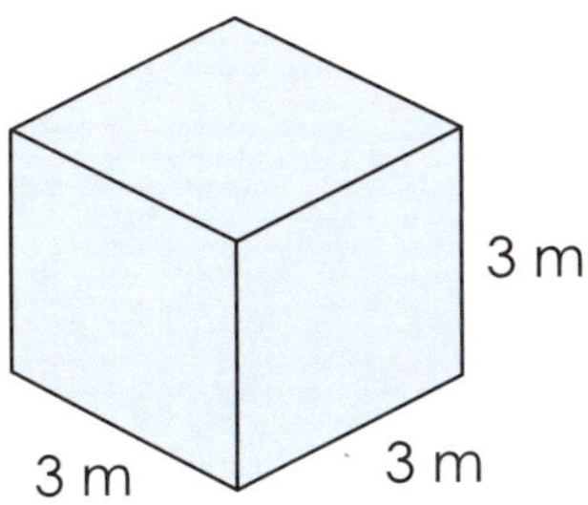

Volume = ______ m × ______ m × ______ m
= ______ m^3

3. Find the volume of a cuboid which measures 6 metres by 3 metres by 5 metres.

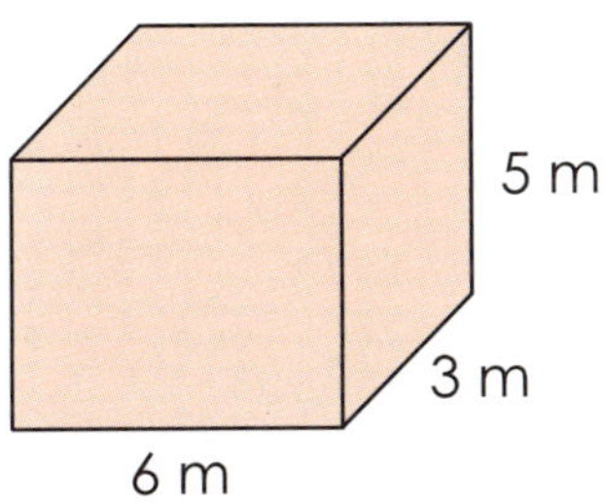

Volume = ______ m × ______ m × ______ m
= ______ m^3

PB Chapter 13: Exercise 4, page 223

 ISBN 978-93-5103-033-1

Converting units of volume

Let's Learn

a) Fill a 10-centimetre cubic container completely with water.

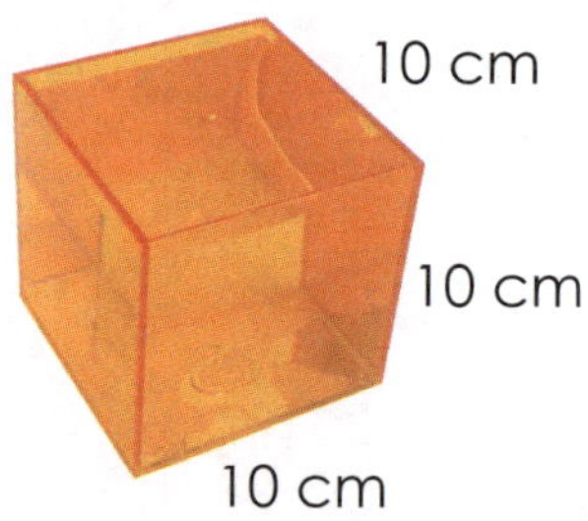

Volume of water in the container
$= 10 \text{ cm} \times 10 \text{ cm} \times 10 \text{ cm}$
$= 1000 \text{ cm}^3$

Pour all the water into a measuring jug.

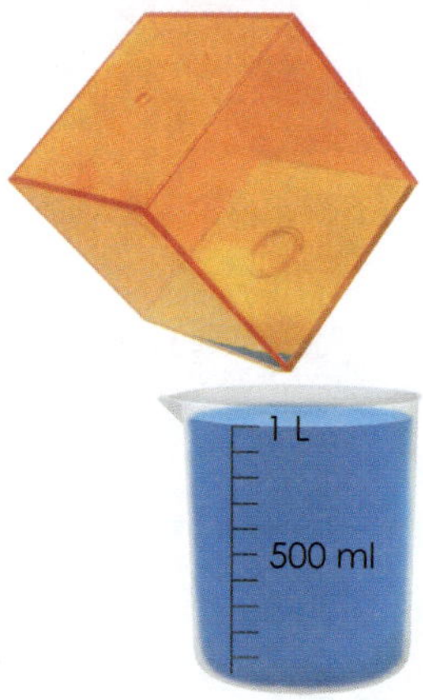

The water measures 1 litre.

$1000 \text{ cm}^3 = 1 \text{ L}$
$1000 \text{ cm}^3 = 1000 \text{ ml}$
$1 \text{ cm}^3 = 1 \text{ ml}$

b) What is 2 litres 750 millilitres in cubic centimetres?

2 L 750 ml
- $2 \text{ L} = 2000 \text{ ml} = 2000 \text{ cm}^3$
- $750 \text{ ml} = 750 \text{ cm}^3$

$2 \text{ L } 750 \text{ ml} = 2000 \text{ cm}^3 + 750 \text{ cm}^3$
$= 2750 \text{ cm}^3$

c) What is 1505 cubic centimetres in litres and millilitres?

1505 cm^3
- $1000 \text{ cm}^3 = 1 \text{ L}$
- $505 \text{ cm}^3 = 505 \text{ ml}$

$1505 \text{ cm}^3 = 1 \text{ L} + 505 \text{ ml}$
= ____ L ____ ml

ISBN 978-93-5103-033-1

Let's Do

1. Write in cubic centimetres.

a) 400 ml = _____ cm^3

b) 1 L 200 ml = _____ ml
= _____ cm^3

2. Write in litres and millilitres.

a) 2450 cm^3 = _____ ml
= _____ L _____ ml

b) 3050 cm^3 = _____ ml
= _____ L _____ ml

Finding volumes of liquids

Let's Learn

Picture It A rectangular fish tank measures 30 centimetres by 20 centimetres by 20 centimetres.

a) Find its capacity in cubic centimetres.

b) If the tank is filled with water to a depth of 8 centimetres, find the volume of the water in litres and millilitres.

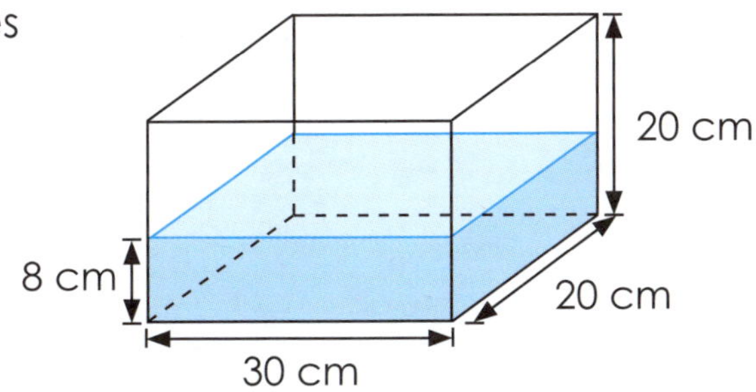

a) Capacity of the tank = 30 cm × 20 cm × 20 cm
= 12,000 cm^3

b) Volume of water = 30 cm × 20 cm × 8 cm
= 4800 cm^3
= 4 L 800 ml

Let's Do

1. A rectangular tank is 15 centimetres long, 12 centimetres wide and 9 centimetres high. If it is filled with water to a depth of 7 centimetres, find the volume of the water in litres and millilitres.

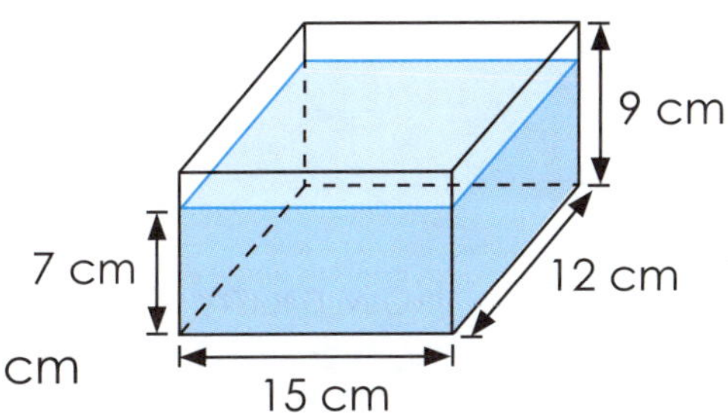

Volume of water = _______ cm × _______ cm × _______ cm
= _______ cm^3
= _______ L _______ ml

PB Chapter 13: Exercise 5, pages 224–226

 ISBN 978-93-5103-033-1

Practice 2

1. Find the volume of each cuboid.

a)

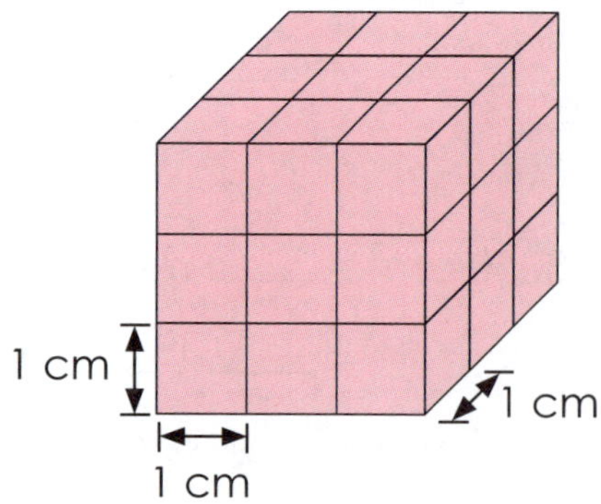

b)

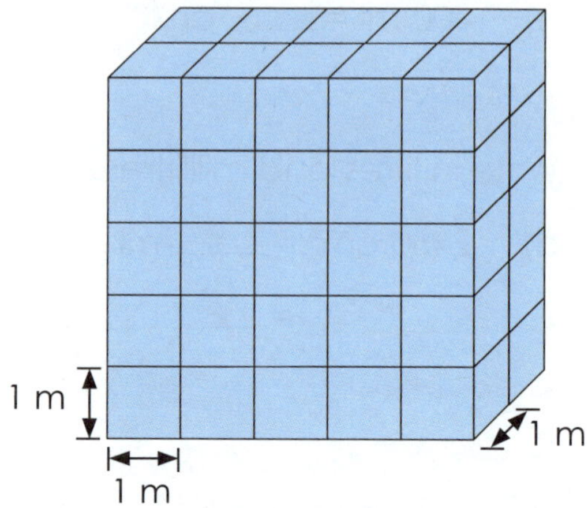

2. Find the volume of each cuboid.

a)

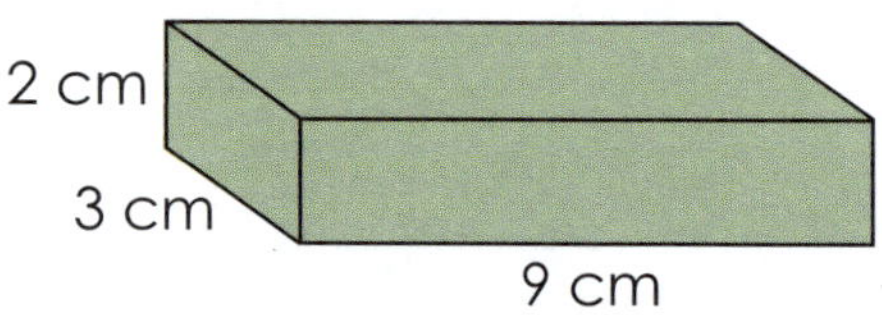

b)

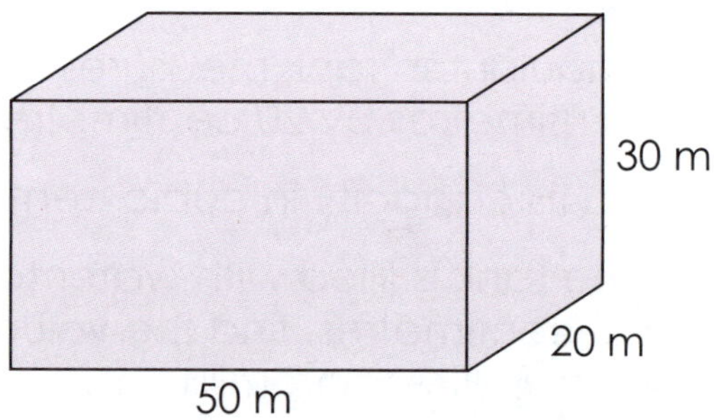

3. A cuboid measures 30 centimetres by 25 centimetres by 15 centimetres. Find its volume.

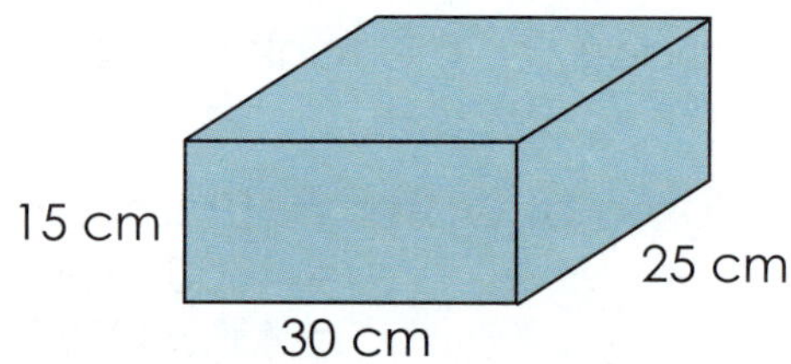

4. Find the volume of a cube of edge 5 centimetres.

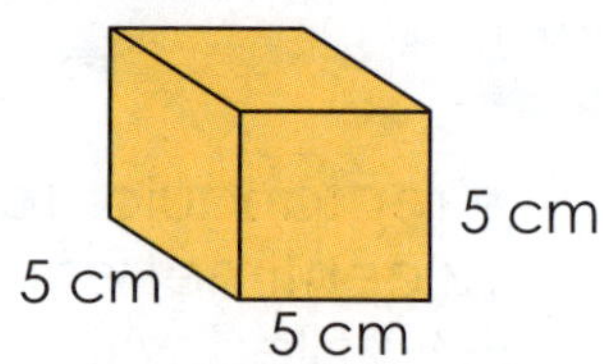

5. How many 1-centimetre cubes are needed to build the cuboid on the right?

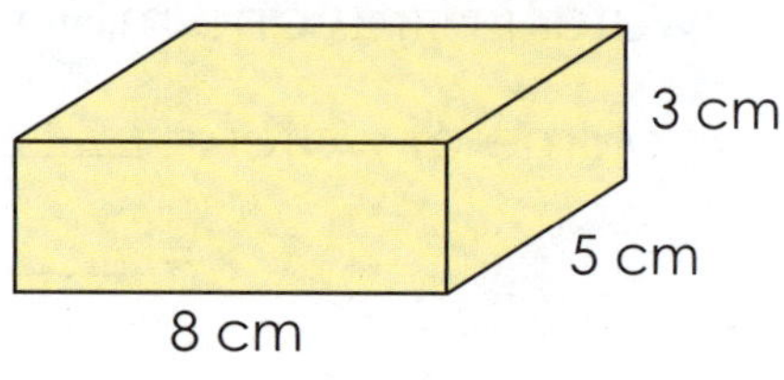

 ISBN 978-93-5103-033-1

6. Fill in the blanks with **cm³** or **m³**.

   a) The volume of a home refrigerator is about 1 ______.

   b) The volume of my textbook is about 650 ______.

7. Find the capacity of the rectangular box in cubic metres.

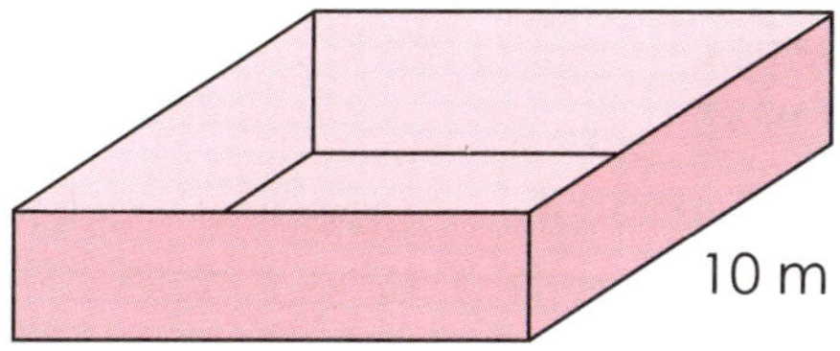

8. Write in cubic centimetres.

   a) 250 ml   b) 2 L   c) 2 L 60 ml

9. Write in litres and millilitres.

   a) 1050 cm^3 b) 1800 cm^3 c) 3500 cm^3

10. A rectangular container measures 15 centimetres by 10 centimetres by 3 centimetres. How many millilitres of water can it hold?

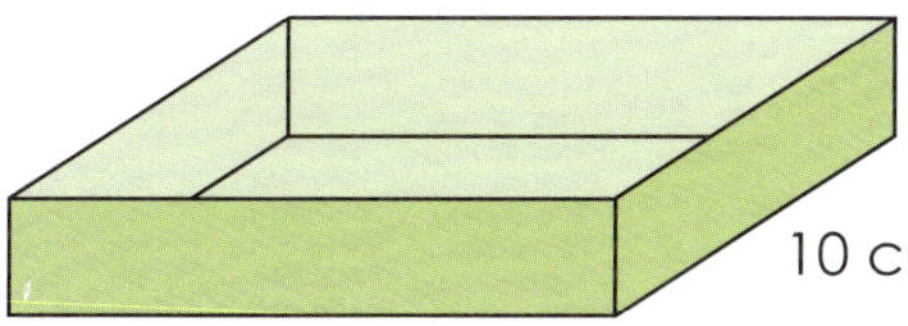

11. What is the volume of water in each rectangular container? Express your answer in litres and millilitres.

   a)

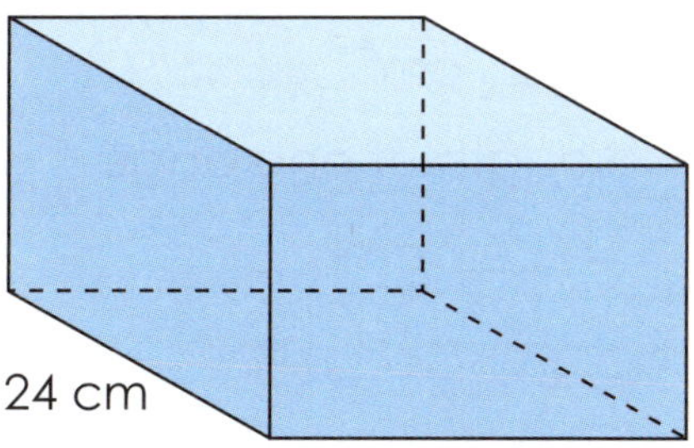

   b)

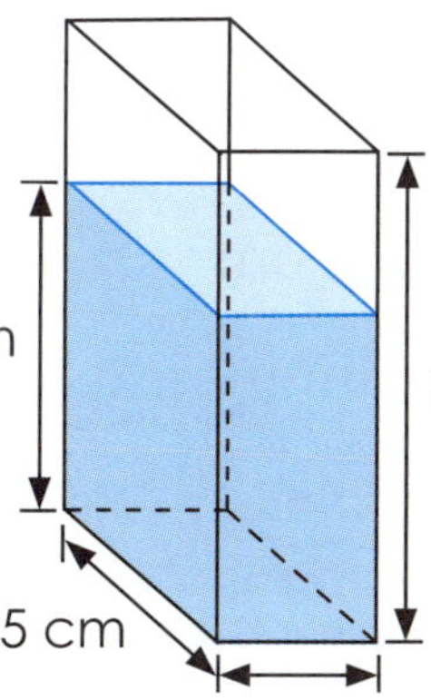

 ISBN 978-93-5103-033-1

Lesson 3 Cubes and Cuboids

Finding the length of one edge of a cube given its volume

Let's Learn

The volume of a cube is 27 cubic centimetres.
Find the length of one edge of the cube.

Picture It

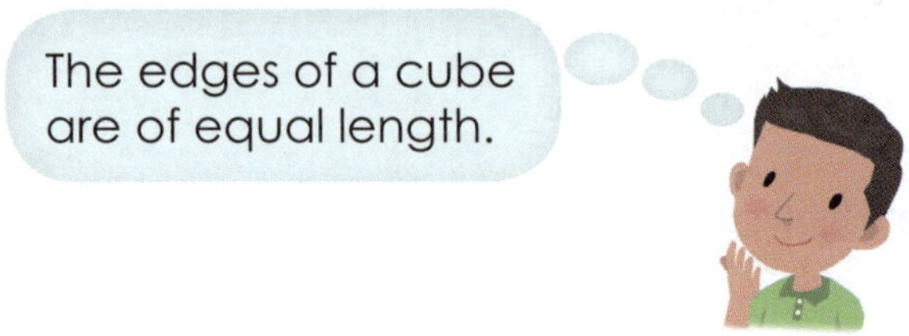

Volume of cube = Edge × Edge × Edge
$27\ cm^3 = 3\ cm \times 3\ cm \times 3\ cm$

The length of one edge of the cube is 3 centimetres.

Let's Do

1. Find the length of one edge of each cube.

a) Volume of cube= $64\ cm^3$

_____ cm × _____ cm × _____ cm

= $64\ cm^3$

Length of one edge

= _____ cm

b) Volume of cube= $125\ cm^3$

_____ cm × _____ cm × _____ cm

= $125\ cm^3$

Length of one edge

= _____ cm

  ISBN 978-93-5103-033-1

Finding the length of one edge of a cuboid given its volume and two other edges

Let's Learn

Picture It The volume of a cuboid is 24 cubic centimetres. The length of the cuboid is 3 centimetres and its breadth is 2 centimetres. Find its height.

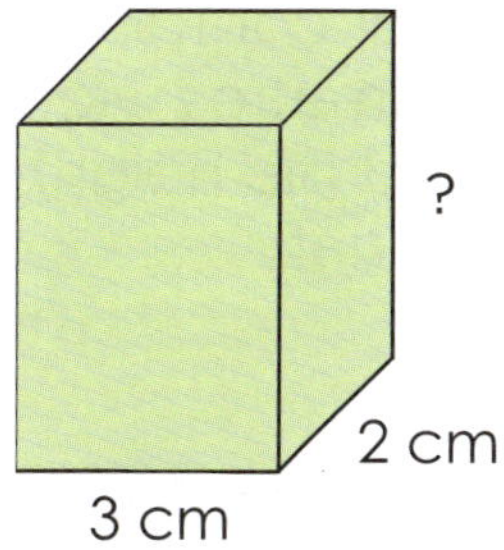

Method 1

Length $\times$ Breadth $\times$ Height = Volume of cuboid

$$3 \text{ cm} \times 2 \text{ cm} \times \text{Height} = 24 \text{ cm}^3$$
$$6 \text{ cm}^2 \times \text{Height} = 24 \text{ cm}^3$$
$$\text{Height} = (24 \div 6) \text{ cm}$$
$$= 4 \text{ cm}$$

The height of the cuboid is ▢ centimetres.

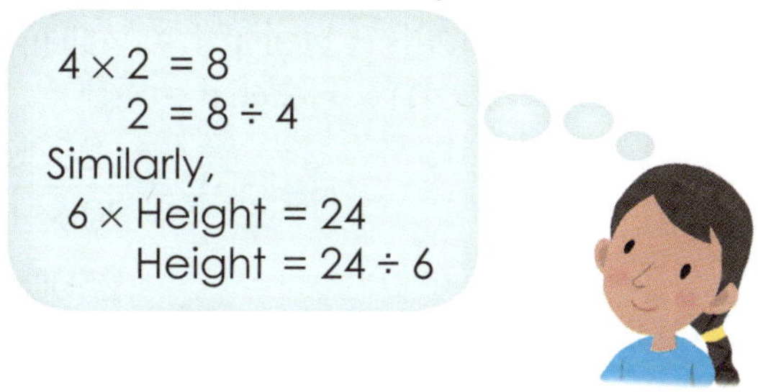

Method 2

$$3 \text{ cm} \times 2 \text{ cm} \times \text{Height} = 24 \text{ cm}^3$$
$$\text{Height} = \frac{24}{3 \times 2} \text{ cm}$$
$$= \frac{24}{6} \text{ cm}$$
$$= 4 \text{ cm}$$

The height of the cuboid is ▢ centimetres.

Let's Do

1. Find the length of CD.

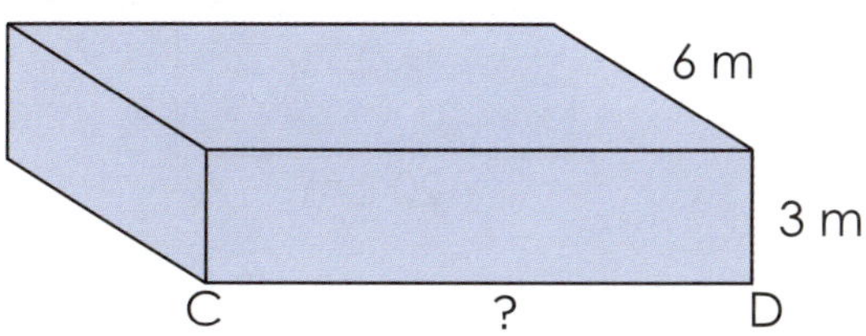

CD × ______ m × ______ m = 216 m^3

$$CD = \frac{\square}{\square} \text{ m}$$

= ______ m

Chapter 13: Exercise 6, pages 227–228

 ISBN 978-93-5103-033-1

Finding the height of water level given the length, width and volume

Let's Learn

Picture It A rectangular container, 20 centimetres long and 10 centimetres wide, contains 2.5 litres of water. Find the height of the water level in the container.

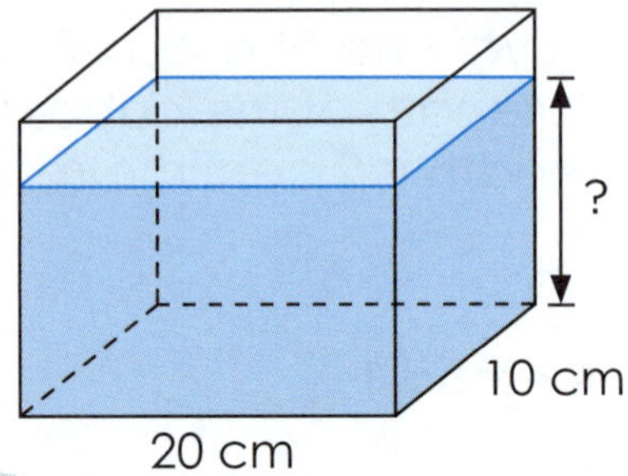

Volume of water = 2.5 L

$= 2.5 \times 1000 \text{ cm}^3$

$= 2500 \text{ cm}^3$

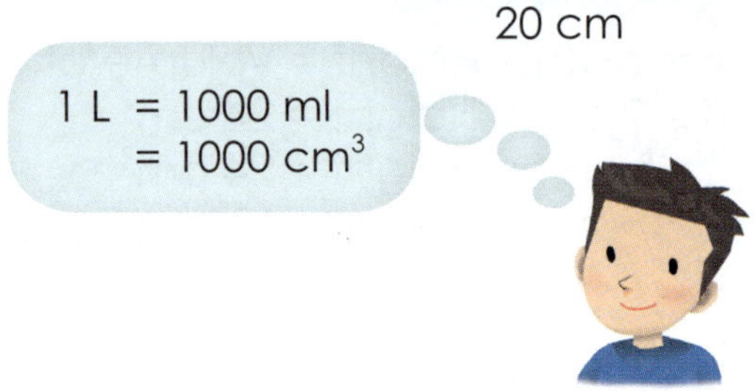

Length × Breadth × Height = Volume

20 cm × 10 cm × Height = 2500 cm^3

$$\text{Height} = \frac{2500}{20 \times 10} \text{ cm}$$

$$= \frac{\cancel{2500}^{25}}{\cancel{200}_{2}} \text{ cm}$$

$$= 12.5 \text{ cm}$$

The height of the water level in the container is 12.5 centimetres.

Let's Do

1. A rectangular tank, 20 centimetres long and 18 centimetres wide, contains 3.6 litres of water. Find the height of the water level in the tank.

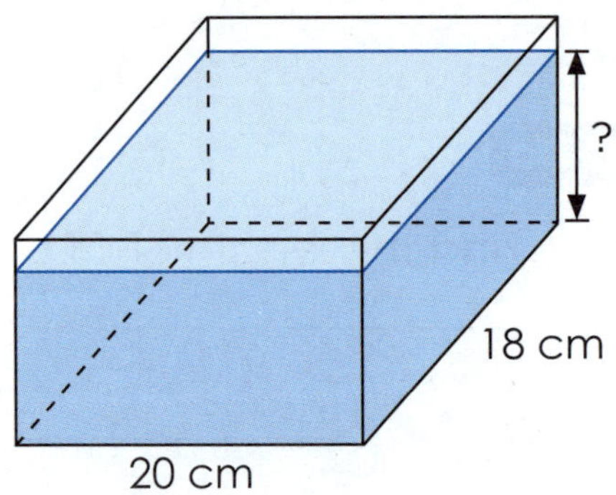

Volume of water = 3.6 L

= ______ cm^3

$$\text{Height} = \frac{\square}{\square \times \square} \text{ cm}$$

= ______ cm

The height of the water level in the tank is ______ centimetres.

PB Chapter 13: Exercise 7, pages 229–230

  ISBN 978-93-5103-033-1

Finding the length of one edge of a cuboid given the area of one face and volume

Let's Learn

The volume of the cuboid is 288 cubic metres.
Find the length of AB.

Picture It

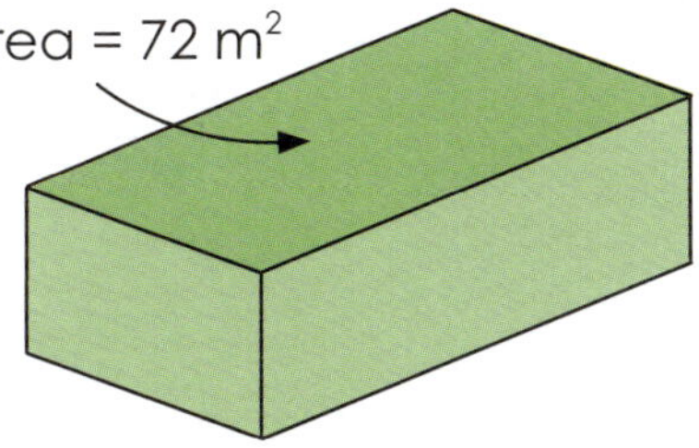

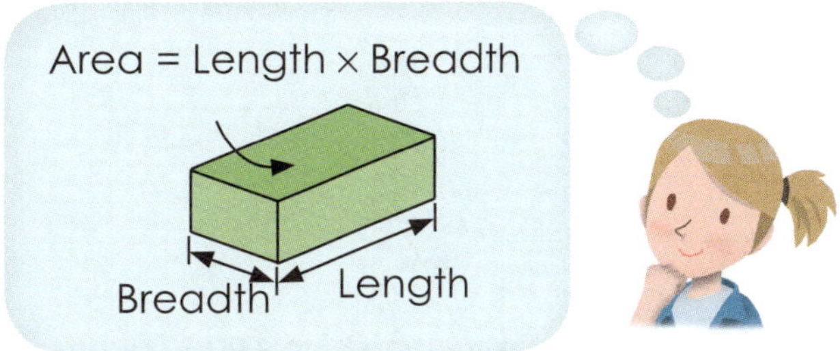

$\text{Length} \times \text{Breadth} = 72\ \text{m}^2$

$$\begin{aligned} \text{Length} \times \text{Breadth} \times \text{Height} &= \text{Volume} \\ 72\ \text{m}^2 \times AB &= 288\ \text{m}^3 \\ AB &= (288 \div 72)\ \text{m} \\ &= 4\ \text{m} \end{aligned}$$

The length of AB is 4 metres.

Let's Do

1. Find the unknown edge of each cuboid.

a)

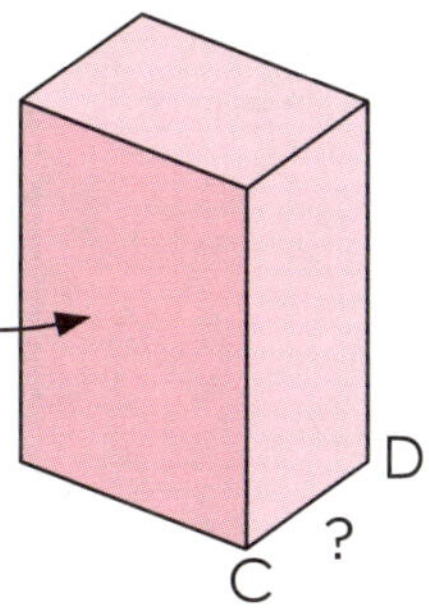

$\text{Volume} = 264\ \text{cm}^3$

$66\ \text{cm}^2 \times CD = 264\ \text{cm}^3$

CD = (______ ÷ ______) cm

= ______ cm

b)

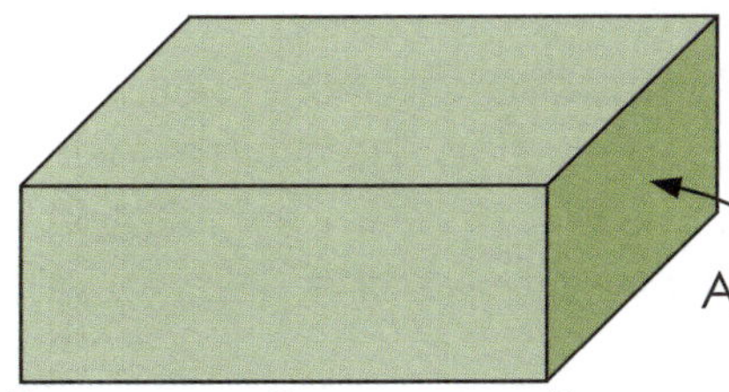

$\text{Volume} = 768\ \text{m}^3$

$48\ \text{m}^2 \times EF = 768\ \text{m}^3$

EF = (______ ÷ ______) m

= ______ m

 ISBN 978-93-5103-033-1

Finding the height of water level given the area and volume

Let's Learn

There are 2080 cubic centimetres of water in a rectangular container.
The area of the base of the container is 260 square centimetres.
Find the height of the water level in the container.

Picture It

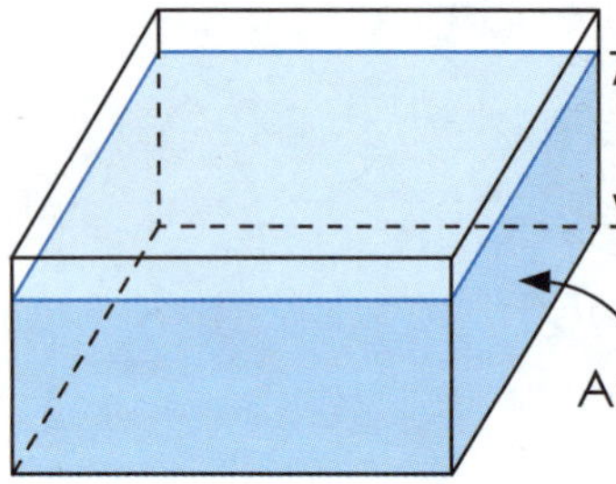

$$\text{Length} \times \text{Breadth} \times \text{Height} = \text{Volume}$$
$$260 \text{ cm}^2 \times \text{Height} = 2080 \text{ cm}^3$$
$$\text{Height} = (2080 \div 260) \text{ cm}$$
$$= 8 \text{ cm}$$

The height of the water level is 8 centimetres.

Let's Do

1. There are 1.2 litres of water in a rectangular container. The area of the base of the container is 96 square centimetres. Find the height of the water level in the container.

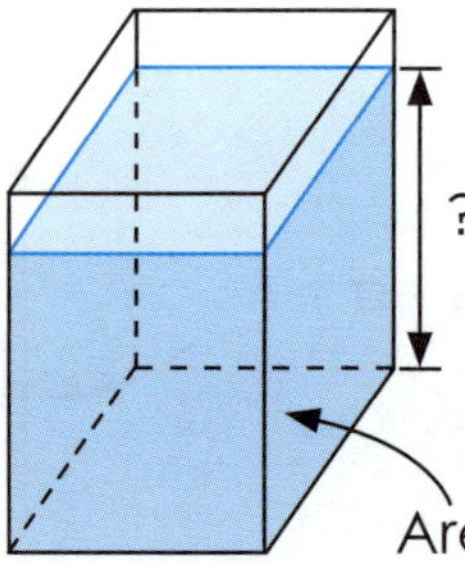

Volume of water = 1.2 L

= ______ cm^3

Length × Breadth × Height = Volume

______ cm^2 × Height = ______ cm^3

Height = (______ ÷ ______) cm

= ______ cm

The height of the water level is ______ centimetres.

P/B Chapter 13: Exercise 8, pages 231–232

 ISBN 978-93-5103-033-1

Practice 3

1. The volume of a cube is 343 cubic centimetres. Find the length of each edge of the cube.

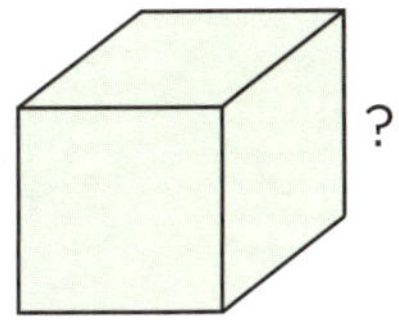

2. Find the unknown edge of each cuboid.

a)

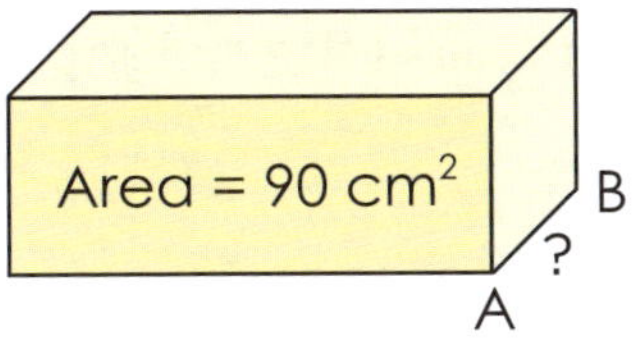

Volume = 360 cm^3

b)

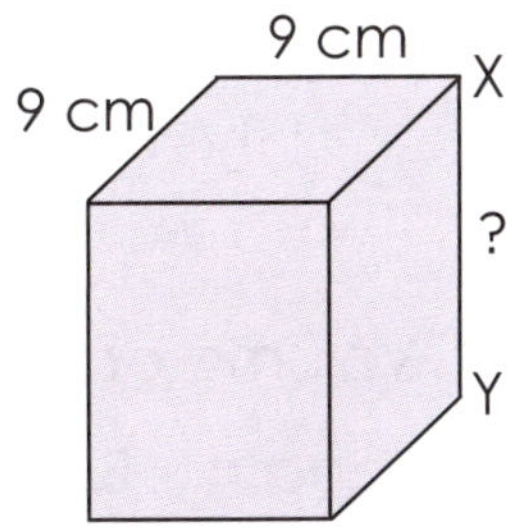

Volume = 972 cm^3

Solve the word problems. Show your work clearly.

3. A rectangular container, 40 centimetres long and 25 centimetres wide, is filled with 12 litres of water. Find the height of the water level in the container.

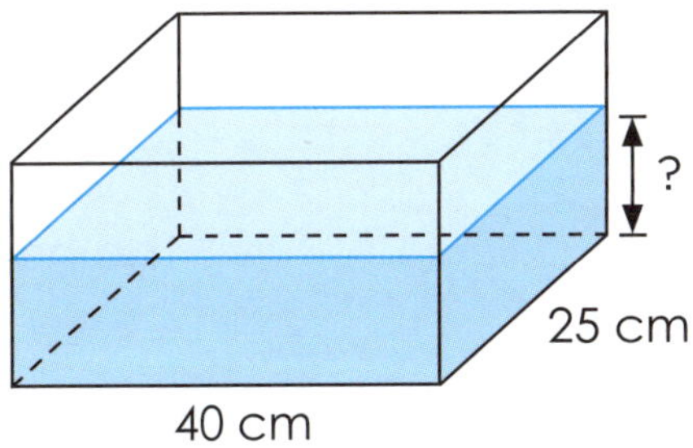

4. There are 4.5 litres of water in a rectangular container. The area of the base of the container is 225 square centimetres. Find the height of the water level in the container.

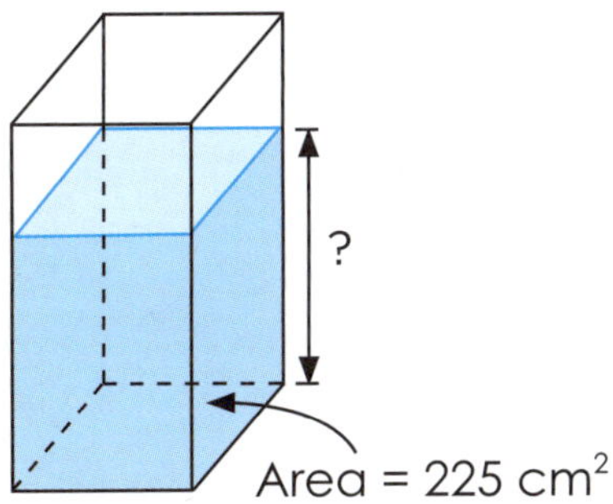

Lesson 4 Problem Solving

Word problems

Let's Learn

A rectangular container was filled to its brim with water. If 360 cubic centimetres of water were poured out from the container, what would be the height of the new water level?

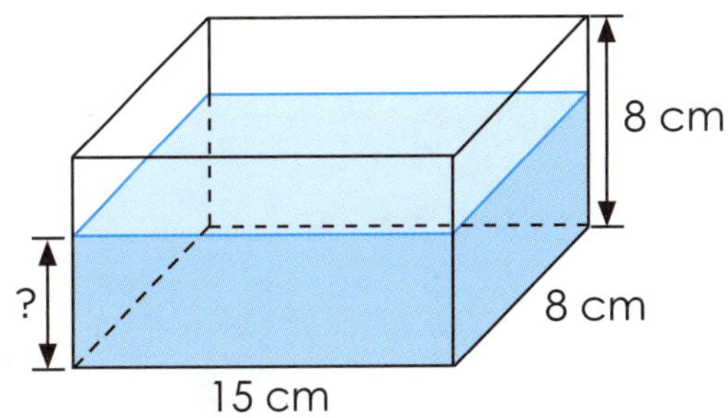

 ISBN 978-93-5103-033-1

1 Understand the problem.

What was the volume of water in the container at first?
How much water was poured out?
What happened to the water level in the container after some water was poured out?
What do I have to find?

2 Plan what to do.

First, I find the drop in the water level in the container after the water was poured out. Then, I find the height of the new water level.

3 Work out the **Answer**.

Volume of water poured out = 360 cm^3

Length × Breadth × Height = Volume
15 cm × 8 cm × Height = 360 cm^3

$$\text{Drop in height of water level} = \frac{360}{15 \times 8} \text{ cm} = 3 \text{ cm}$$

$$\text{Height of new water level} = 8 - 3 = 5 \text{ cm}$$

The height of the new water level is 5 centimetres.

4 Check
Did you answer the question?
Is your answer correct?

I can check the answer by solving the problem in another way.

Volume of water in the container at first
= 15 cm × 8 cm × 8 cm
= 960 cm^3

Volume of water left in the container = 960 – 360
= 600 cm^3

Length × Breadth × Height = Volume
15 cm × 8 cm × Height = 600 cm^3

$$\text{Height of new water level} = \frac{600}{15 \times 8} \text{ cm} = 5 \text{ cm}$$

My answer is correct.

☑ 1. Understand
☑ 2. Plan
☑ 3. Answer
☑ 4. Check

 ISBN 978-93-5103-033-1

Let's Do

1. A rectangular container, 20 centimetres long and 16 centimetres wide, is filled with water to a depth of 8 centimetres. Another 320 millilitres of water are then poured into the tank. What is the height of the new water level?

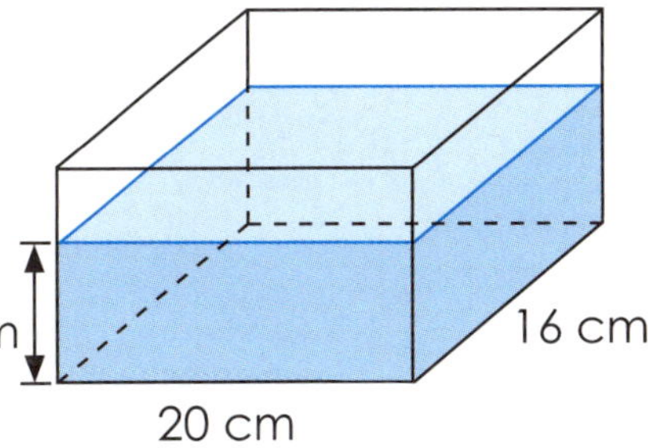

First, find the total volume of water after 320 millilitres of water are added. Then, find the height of the new water level.

- ☐ **1. Understand**
- ☐ **2. Plan**
- ☐ **3. Answer**
- ☐ **4. Check**

Let's Learn

Rohan wants to pack his 2-centimetre toy cubes into a storage box. How many cubes can he fit into the box?

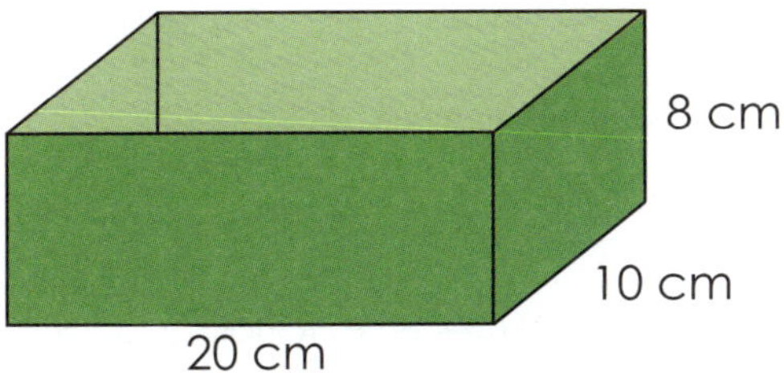

2-centimetre cube

1 Understand the problem.

What are the measurements of the box?
What are the measurements of a cube?
How many cubes do I need to build the box?

2 Plan what to do.

I have to find the volume of the box and the volume of a cube.

 ISBN 978-93-5103-033-1

3 Work out the **Answer**.

$$\begin{aligned}\text{Volume of box} &= \text{Length} \times \text{Breadth} \times \text{Height}\\ &= 20\text{ cm} \times 10\text{ cm} \times 8\text{ cm}\\ &= 1600\text{ cm}^3\end{aligned}$$

The volume of the box is 1600 cubic centimetres.

$$\begin{aligned}\text{Volume of cube} &= 2\text{ cm} \times 2\text{ cm} \times 2\text{ cm}\\ &= 8\text{ cm}^3\end{aligned}$$

The volume of the cube is 8 cubic centimetres.

$1600 \div 8 = 200$

He can fit 200 cubes into the box.

4 **Check**
Did you answer the question?
Is your answer correct?

Volume of 200 cubes
$= 200 \times 8\text{ cm}^3$
$= 1600\text{ cm}^3$
My answer is correct.

☑ **1. Understand**
☑ **2. Plan**
☑ **3. Answer**
☑ **4. Check**

Let's Do

1. How many 3-centimetre cubes are needed to build the solid below?

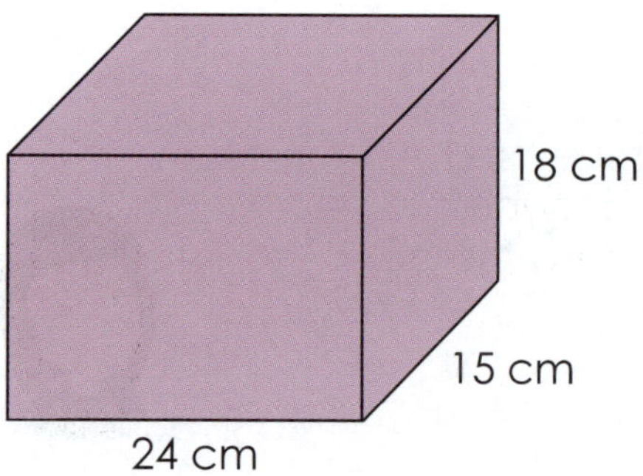

3-centimetre cube

☐ **1. Understand**
☐ **2. Plan**
☐ **3. Answer**
☐ **4. Check**

What is the volume of each cube?
What is the volume of the solid?

PB Chapter 13: Exercise 9, pages 233–235

  ISBN 978-93-5103-033-1

Practice 4

Solve the word problems. Show your work clearly.

1. Container A was filled to its brim with water. Container B was empty. If all the water in Container A was poured into Container B, what would be the height of the water level in Container B?

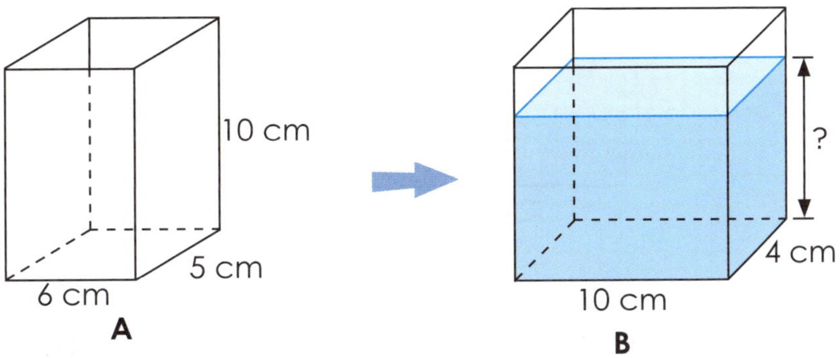

2. A rectangular container measuring 60 centimetres by 20 centimetres by 30 centimetres is filled with 28 litres of water. How many more litres of water are needed to fill the container to the brim?

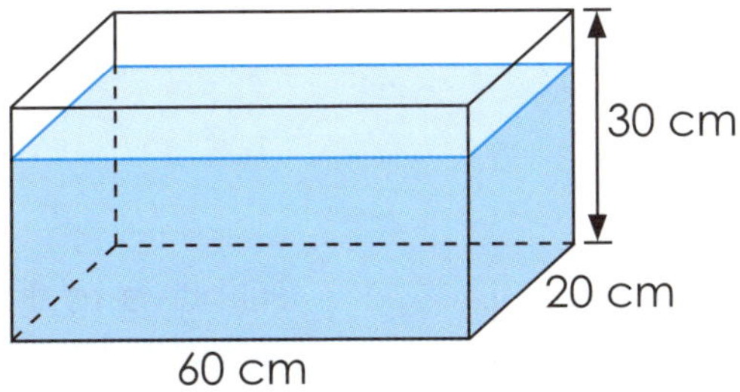

3. How many 5-centimetre cubes are needed to build the cuboid?

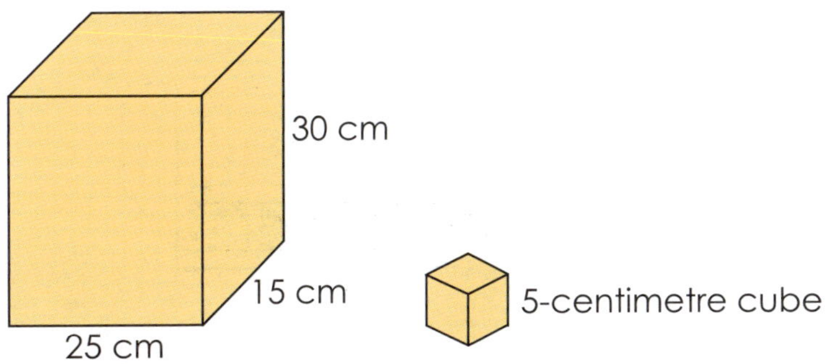

4. A cubical tank of edge 14 centimetres is half-filled with water. The water is poured into an empty rectangular tank measuring 10 centimetres by 8 centimetres by 8 centimetres until it is full. How much water is left in the cubical tank?

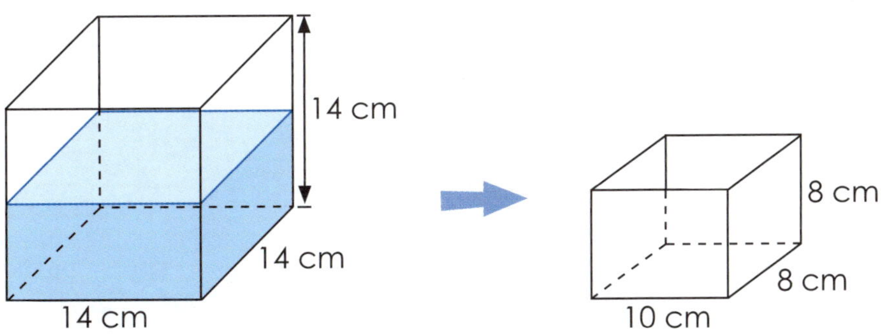

 ISBN 978-93-5103-033-1

Mind stretcher

Let's Learn

What is the maximum number of 3-centimetre cubes that can be put into the rectangular box?

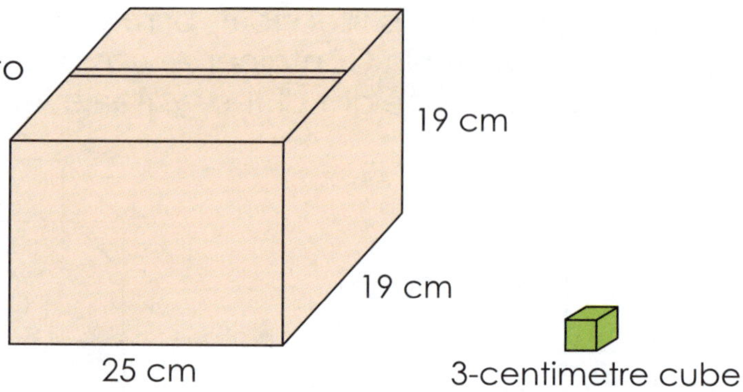

1 **Understand** the problem.

What are the measurements of a cube?
What are the measurements of the box?
Can I fill the box completely with the cubes?

2 **Plan** what to do.

I have to find the number of cubes that can fit along the length, breadth and height of the box.

3 Work out the **Answer**.

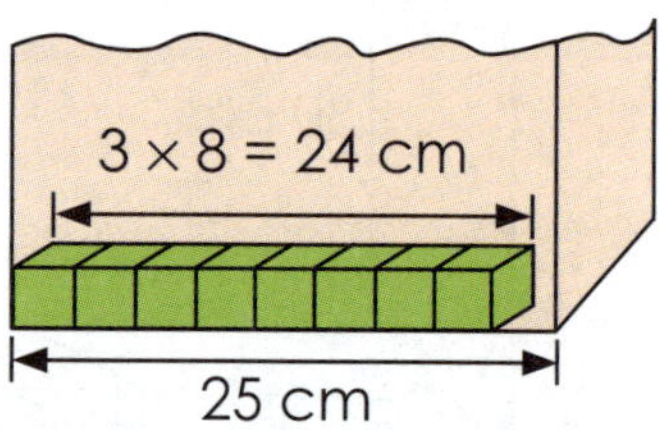

$25 \div 3 = 8$ R1
8 cubes can fit along the length of the box.

$19 \div 3 = 6$ R1
6 cubes can fit along the breadth and also the height of the box.

$8 \times 6 \times 6 = 288$
The maximum number of 3-centimetre cubes that can be put into the rectangular box is 288.

 ISBN 978-93-5103-033-1

4 Check

Did you answer the question?
Is your answer reasonable?

$$\text{Volume of box} = 25\text{ cm} \times 19\text{ cm} \times 19\text{ cm}$$
$$\approx 30\text{ cm} \times 20\text{ cm} \times 20\text{ cm}$$
$$= 12{,}000\text{ cm}^3$$

$$\text{Volume of a cube} = 3\text{ cm} \times 3\text{ cm} \times 3\text{ cm}$$
$$= 27\text{ cm}^3$$

$$\text{Total volume of 288 cubes} = 288 \times 27\text{ cm}^3$$
$$\approx 300 \times 30\text{ cm}^3$$
$$= 9000\text{ cm}^3$$

$12{,}000 > 9000$
My answer is reasonable.

- ✓ **1. Understand**
- ✓ **2. Plan**
- ✓ **3. Answer**
- ✓ **4. Check**

Think About It

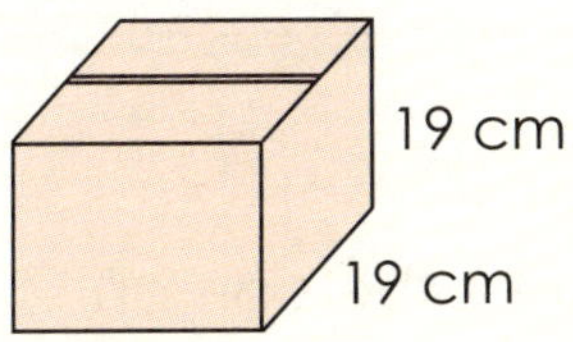

3-cm cube

For this problem, I cannot find the number of cubes that can be put into the box using:
Volume of box ÷ Volume of cube

Sam

Is Sam correct? Explain why.

ISBN 978-93-5103-033-1

Glossary

A

- **angles at a point**
  The sum of the angle measures at a point is 360°.

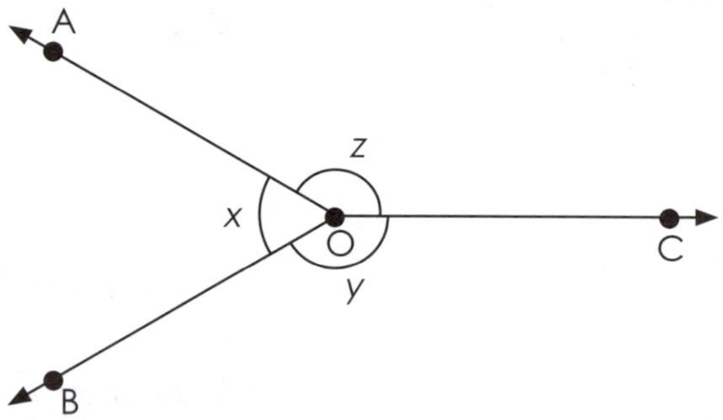

$\angle x$, $\angle y$ and $\angle z$ are **angles at a point**.
$m\angle x + m\angle y + m\angle z = 360°$

- **angles on a line**
  The sum of the angle measures on a line is 180°.
  AOB is a line.

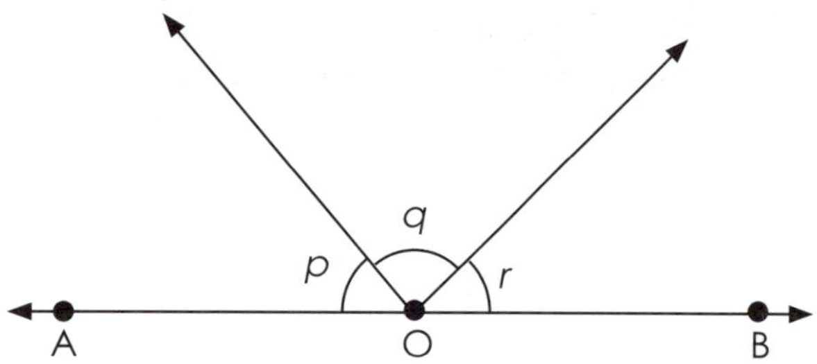

$\angle p$, $\angle q$ and $\angle r$ are **angles on a line**.
$m\angle p + m\angle q + m\angle r = 180°$

- **arc**
  An **arc** is the curved part of a circle.

  D and E are two points on this circle. The curved part from point D to point E is an arc.

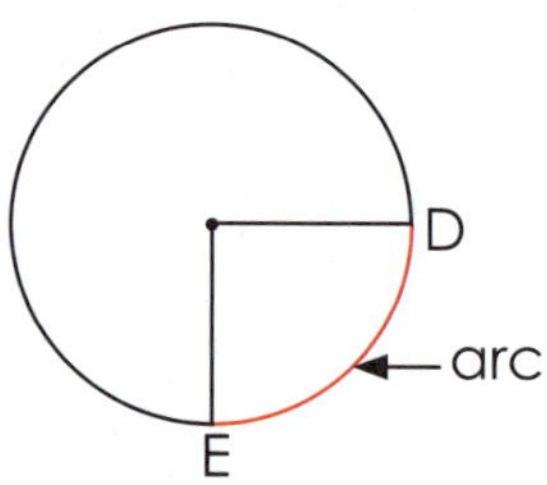

- **average**

$$\text{Average} = \frac{\text{Sum of data}}{\text{Number of data}}$$

The average of 7, 3, 10 and 4 is

$$\frac{7 + 3 + 10 + 4}{4} = \frac{24}{4} = 6.$$

- **axis of revolution**
  The line around which a shape revolves to form a solid of revolution is known as an **axis of revolution**.

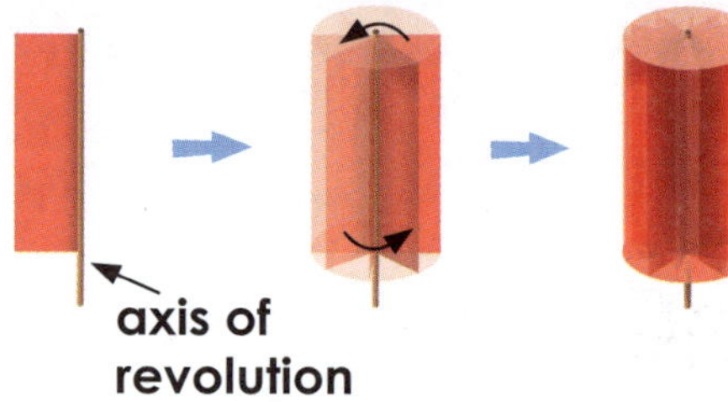

B

- **base (triangle)**
  The **base** of a triangle is the side on which it rests. Any side of a triangle can be its base.

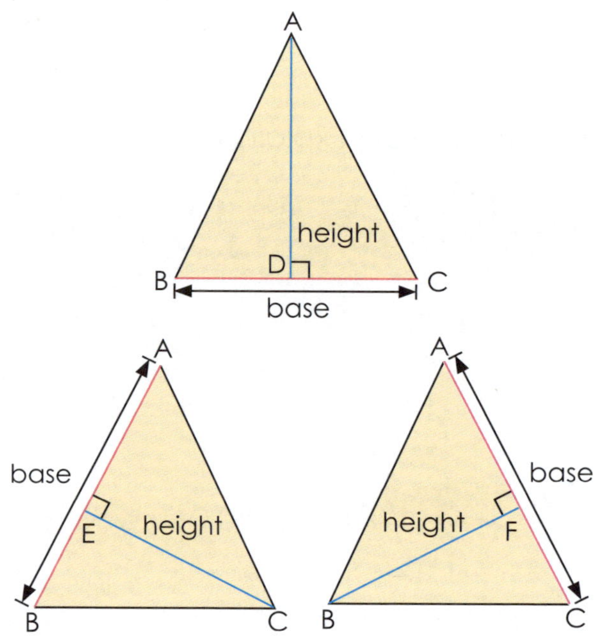

 ISBN 978-93-5103-033-1

- **base (solid)**
  The **base** of a solid is the face on which it rests.

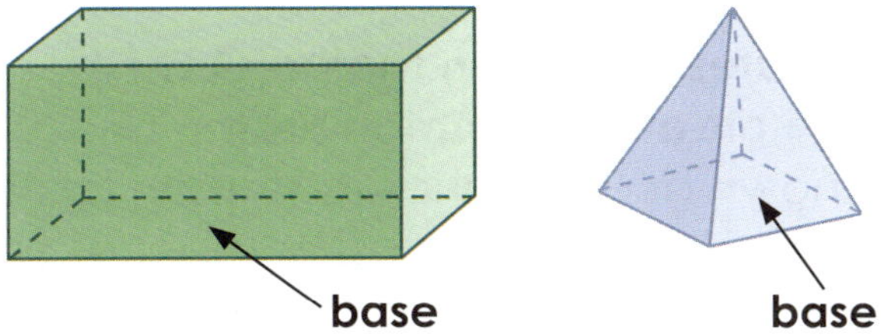

C

- **chord**
  A **chord** is a line segment which has both its end points on a circle. AB is a chord of this circle.

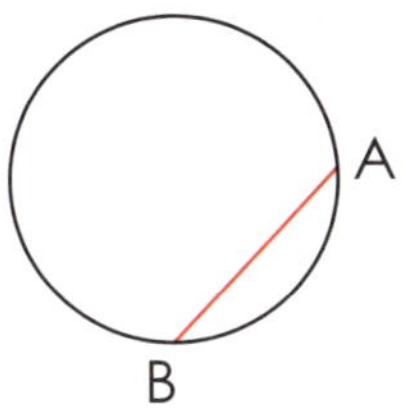

- **circumference**
  Circumference is the perimeter of a circle or the length around a circle.

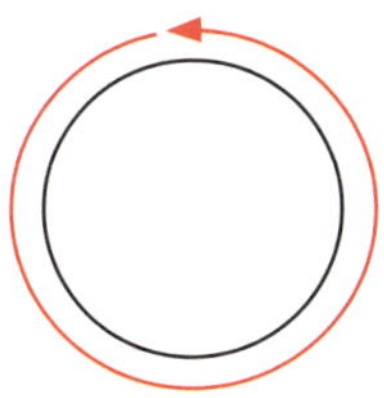

- **common factor**
  A **common factor** is a factor of two or more numbers.
  The factors of 30 are 1, 2, 3, 5, 6, 10, 15 and 30.
  The factors of 42 are 1, 2, 3, 6, 7, 14, 21 and 42.
  The common factors of 30 and 42 are 1, 2, 3 and 6.

- **common multiple**
  A **common multiple** is a multiple of two or more numbers.
  The multiples of 4 are 4, 8, 12, 16, 20, 24, 28, 32, 36, …
  The multiples of 6 are 6, 12, 18, 24, 30, 36, …
  The first three common multiples of 4 and 6 are 12, 24 and 36.

- **cone**
  A **cone** is a solid that has one circular flat face (its base), a curved surface and a vertex.

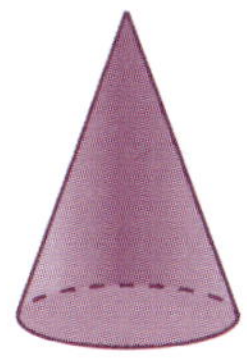

cone

- **crore**
  1 **crore** = 100 lakh = 1,00,00,000

- **cross section**
  A **cross section** of a solid is the shape made when the solid is cut parallel to its base.

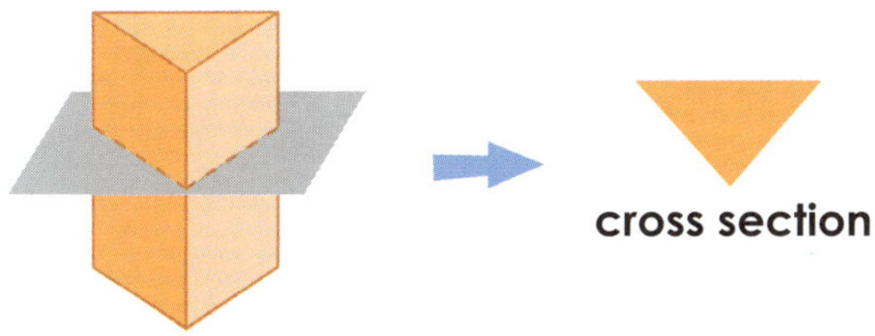

- **cubic centimetre (cm^3)**
  The **cubic centimetre** is a unit of volume.
  We write cubic centimetre as **cm^3**.

- **cubic metre (m^3)**
  The **cubic metre** is a unit of volume.
  We write cubic metre as **m^3**.

- **cubic unit**
  The volume of a unit cube is 1 **cubic unit**.

- **cylinder**
  A **cylinder** is a solid that has two identical circular flat faces that are parallel to each other and a curved surface.

cylinder

 ISBN 978-93-5103-033-1

D

- **diameter**
  A **diameter** of a circle is a line segment that passes through the centre of the circle and joins two points on the circle.
  The diameter of a circle is two times the length of its radius.

  PQ is a diameter of the circle.

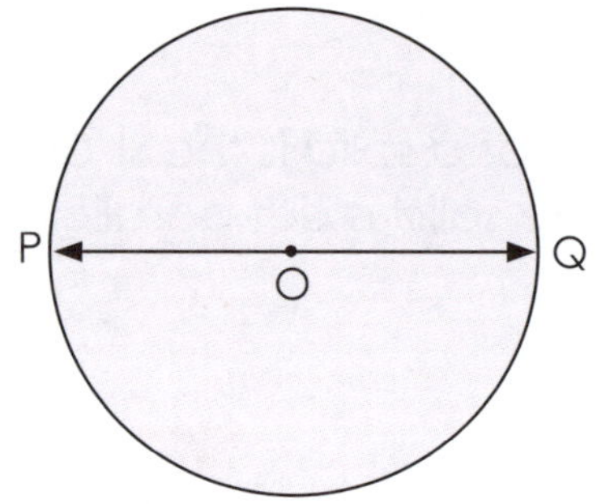

- **discount**
  Discount is the amount of money you save when buying things.
  Discount = Usual price – Selling price

E

- **equilateral triangle**
  A triangle with three equal sides is called an **equilateral triangle**.

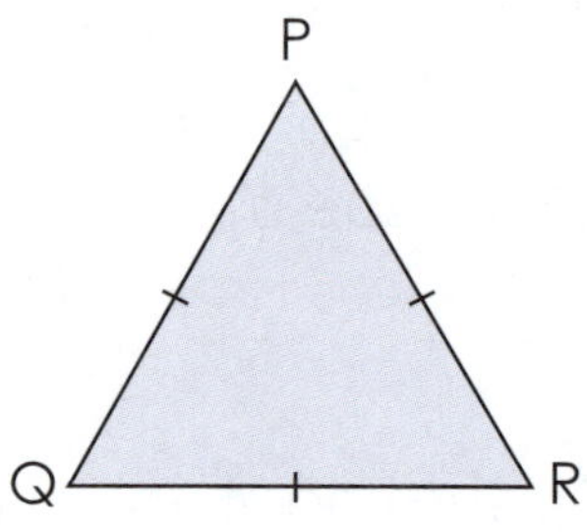

G

- **greatest common factor (G.C.F.)**
  The **greatest common factor**, also known as the highest common factor (H.C.F.), is the greatest number of all the common factors of two or more numbers.
  The common factors of 30 and 42 are 1, 2, 3 and 6.
  The greatest common factor of 30 and 42 is 6.

H

- **height (triangle)**
  The **height** of a triangle is the perpendicular distance from the base to the opposite vertex.

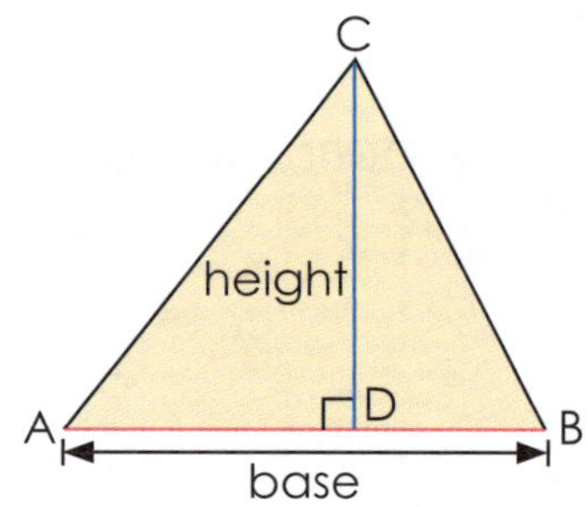

- **hexagon**
  A **hexagon** is a shape with 6 sides.

I

- **interest**
  Interest is the amount of money the bank pays you for depositing money with them.

- **isosceles triangle**
  A triangle with only two equal sides is called an **isosceles triangle**.

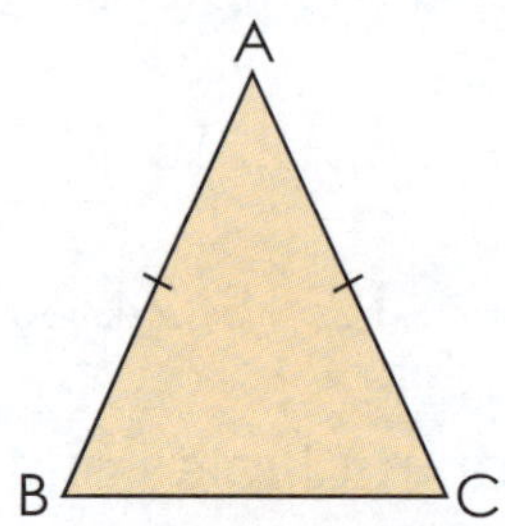

 ISBN 978-93-5103-033-1

L

- **lakh**
  1 **lakh** = 100 thousand = 1,00,000

- **least common multiple (L.C.M.)**
  The **least common multiple** is the smallest number of all the common multiples of two or more numbers.
  The first three common multiples of 4 and 6 are 12, 24 and 36.
  The least common multiple of 4 and 6 is 12.

- **like fractions**
  Like fractions are fractions that have the same denominator.
  $\frac{3}{8}$ and $\frac{7}{8}$ are like fractions because they have the same denominator, 8.

N

- **net**
  A **net** is a flat figure that can be folded to form a solid.

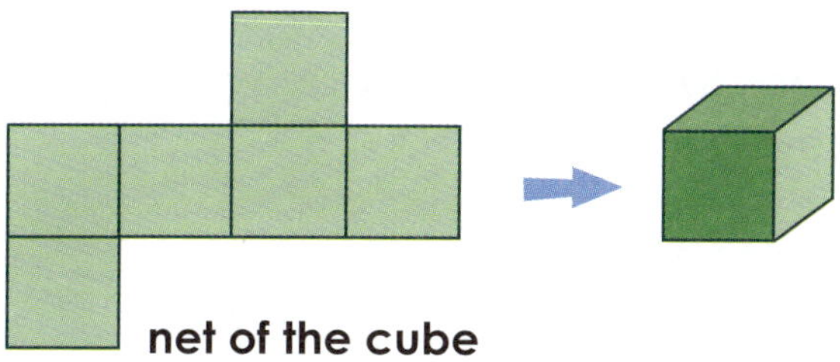

net of the cube

P

- **parentheses**
  Parentheses are a pair of round brackets used to enclose words or figures.

- **pentagon**
  A **pentagon** is a shape with five sides.

- **per cent**
  Per cent means 'out of 100'.
  54% means 54 out of 100.

- **pie chart**
  A **pie chart** is a circle graph divided into sectors, with each sector showing the relative size of a quantity of the whole.

  The pie chart below shows the quantities of four types of fruits sold at a supermarket in a day.

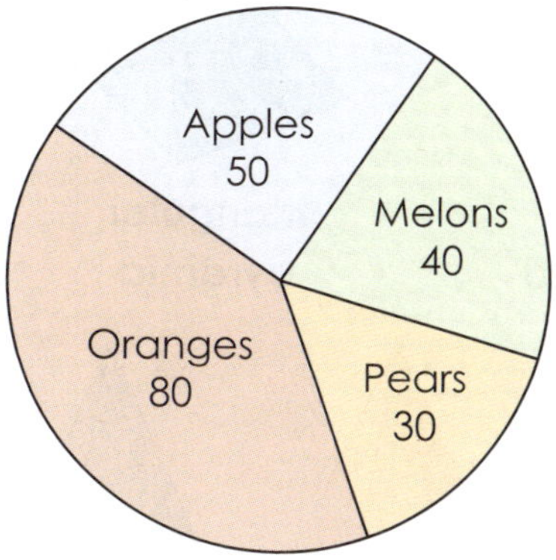

- **prism**
  A **prism** is a solid with two parallel identical faces of any shape that are joined by rectangular faces.

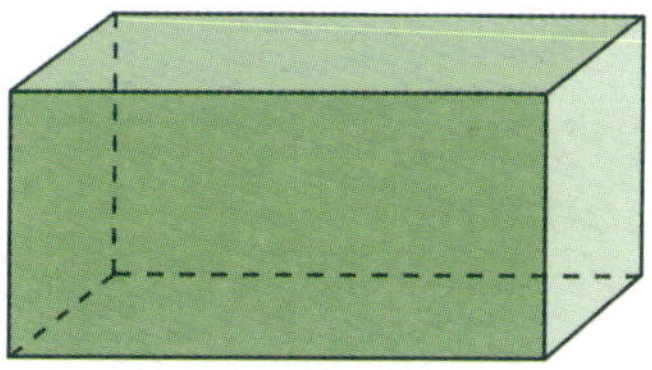

rectangular prism

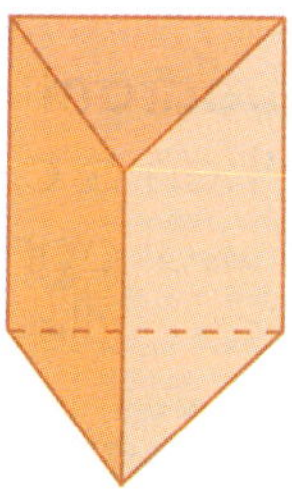

triangular prism

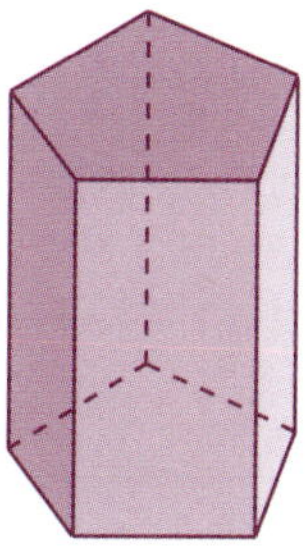

pentagonal prism

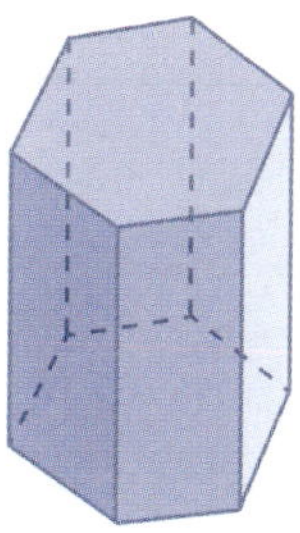

hexagonal prism

 ISBN 978-93-5103-033-1

- **pyramid**
  A **pyramid** is a solid that has a base and three or more triangular faces that meet at a common vertex.

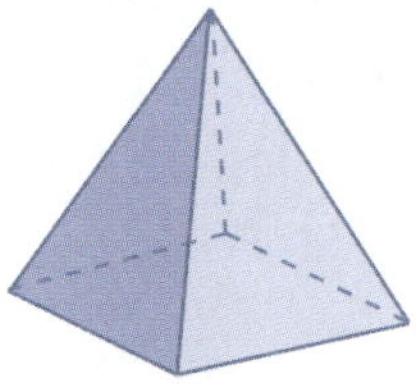

square pyramid

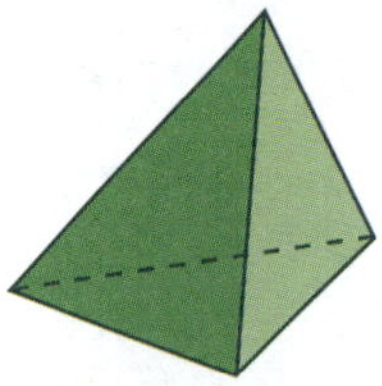

triangular pyramid

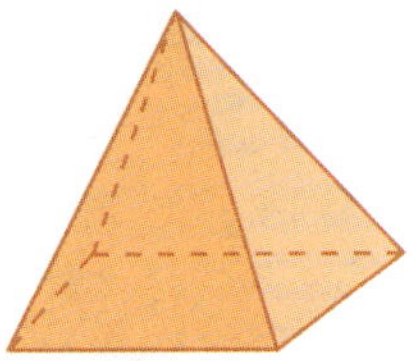

rectangular pyramid

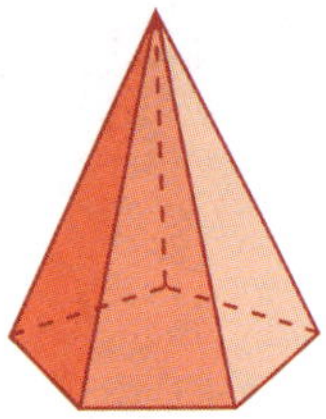

pentagonal pyramid

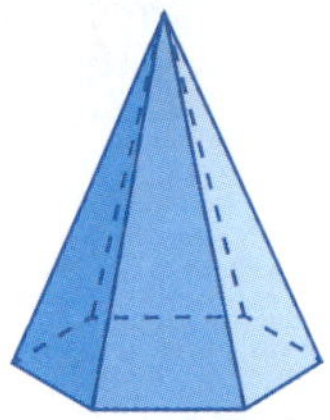

hexagonal pyramid

Q

- **quadrant**
  When a circle is divided into four equal parts, a quarter of the circle is also called a **quadrant**.

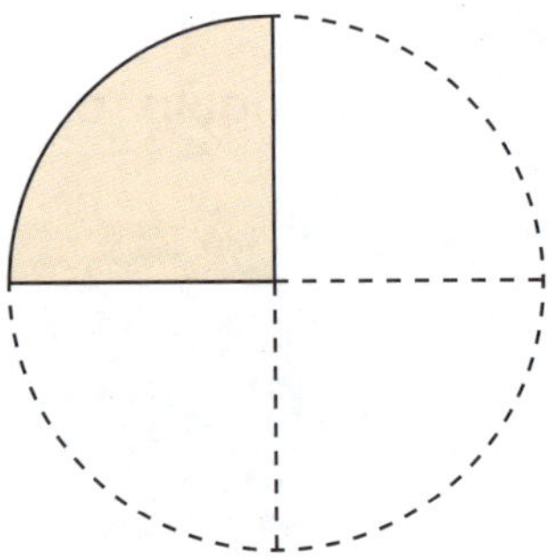

R

- **radius (radii)**
  A **radius** of a circle is a line segment from the centre of the circle to any point on the circle.

  The radius of a circle is half the length of its diameter.

  ON is the radius of the circle. OP is also a radius of the circle.
  ON and OP are **radii** of the circle.

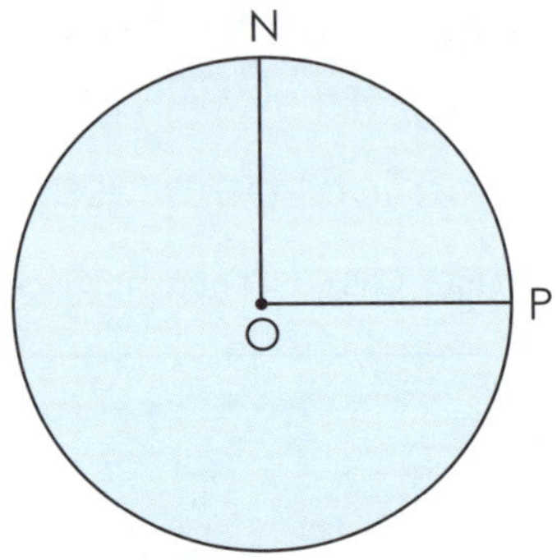

S

- **sales tax**
  Sales tax is a tax we pay when we buy things.

- **scalene triangle**
  A triangle with all three sides of different lengths is called a **scalene triangle.**

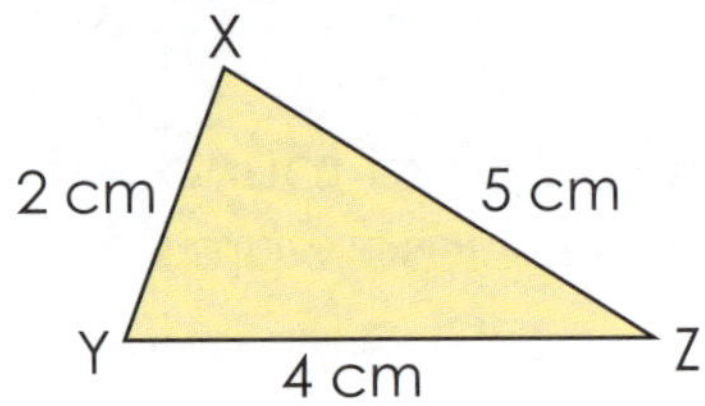

- **sector**
  A **sector** is the region between two radii and an arc.

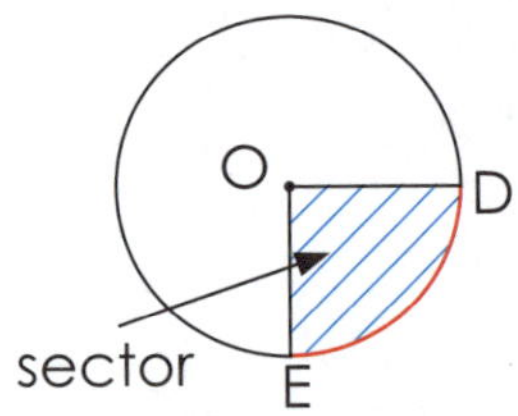

 ISBN 978-93-5103-033-1

- **segment**
  A **segment** is the region between a chord and an arc.

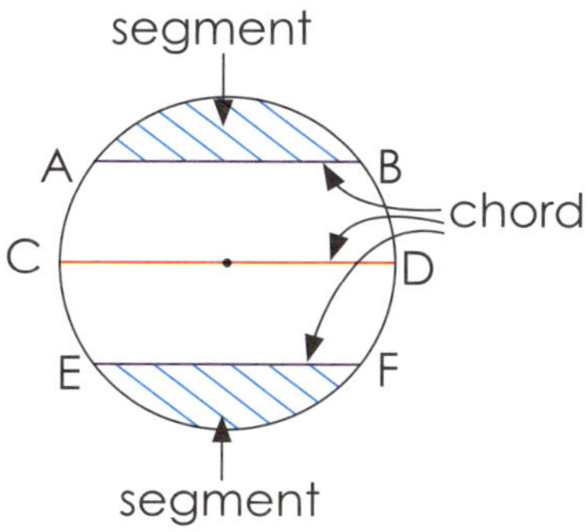

- **semicircle**
  When a circle is divided into two equal parts, a half of the circle is called a **semicircle**.

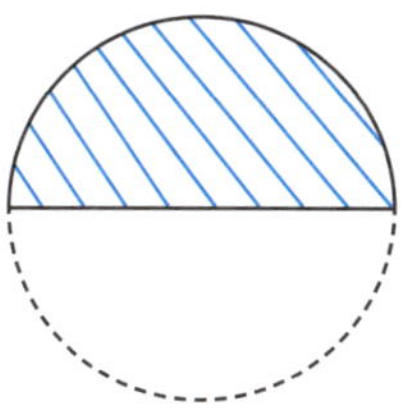

- **solid of revolution**
  A solid figure formed by the revolution of a shape around the axis of revolution is known as a **solid of revolution**.

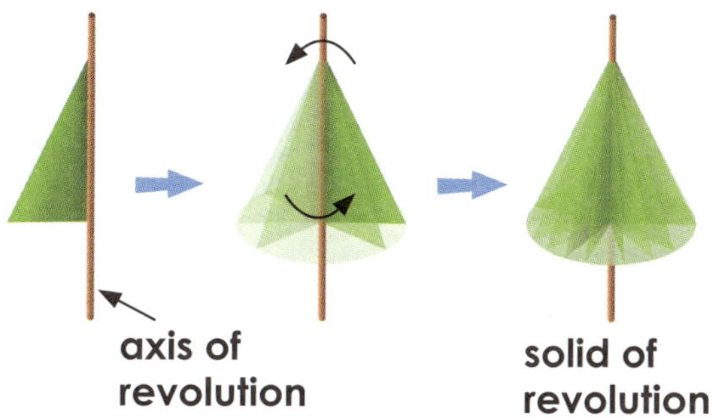

T

- **tessellation**
  A **tessellation** is an arrangement of shapes fitted together, in a repeated pattern, without gaps or overlaps.

U

- **uniform cross section**
  A solid has a **uniform cross section** when the cross sections of the solid are identical in shape and size.

  Prisms and cylinders have uniform cross sections.

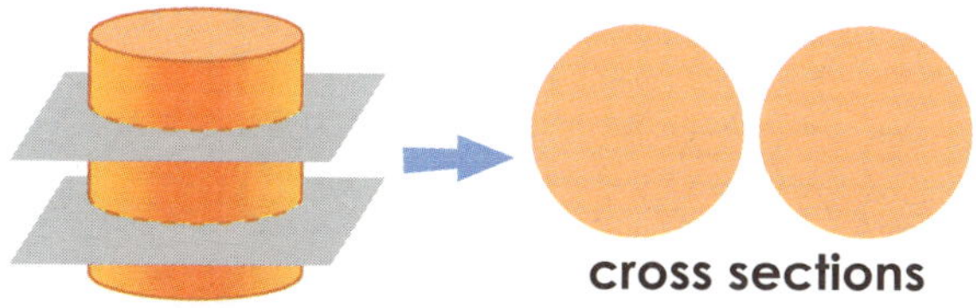

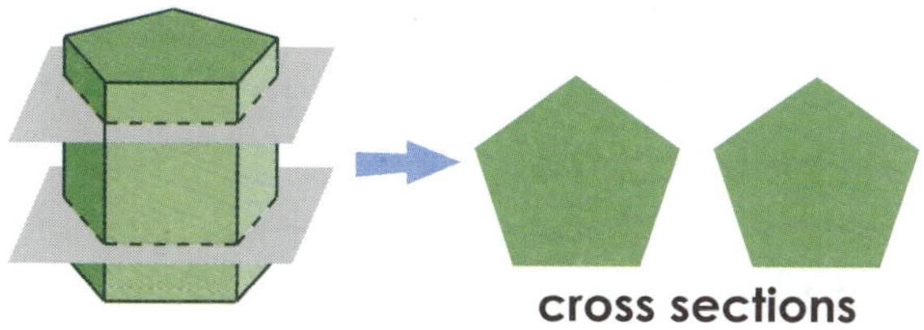

Pyramids and cones do not have **uniform cross sections**.

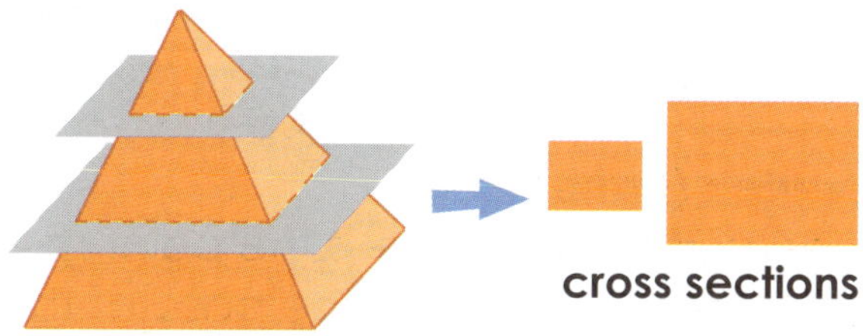

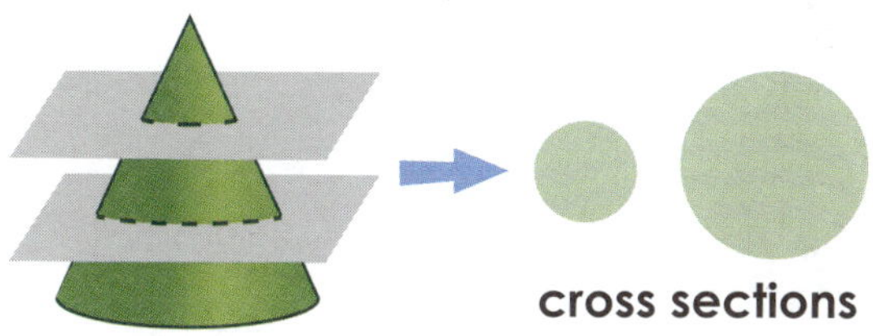

- **unit cube**
  A **unit cube** is a cube whose edges are 1 unit long.

 is a **unit cube**.

 ISBN 978-93-5103-033-1

- **unit shape**
  In a tessellation, the shape that is repeated to form the pattern is called the **unit shape**.

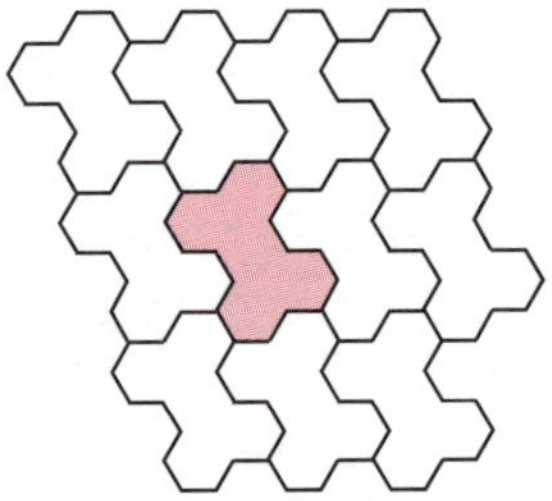

  The shaded shape is the **unit shape** of this tessellation.

- **unlike fractions**
  Unlike fractions are fractions that do not have the same denominator.
  $\frac{2}{3}$ and $\frac{2}{5}$ are **unlike fractions** because they have different denominators, 3 and 5.

V

- **vertex (cone)**
  The **vertex of a cone** is the point that is furthest away from the base of the cone.

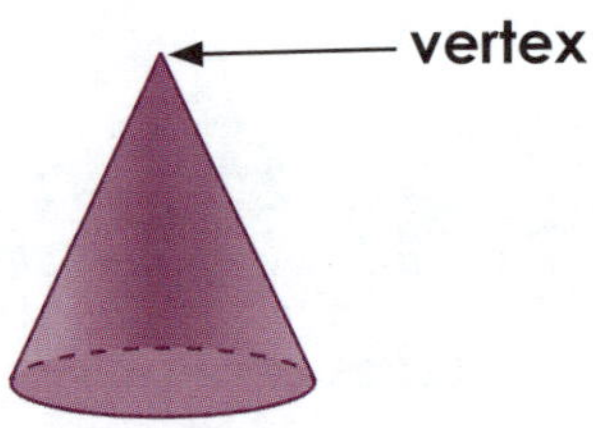

- **vertex (triangle)**
  The **vertex of a triangle** is the point where any two sides meet.

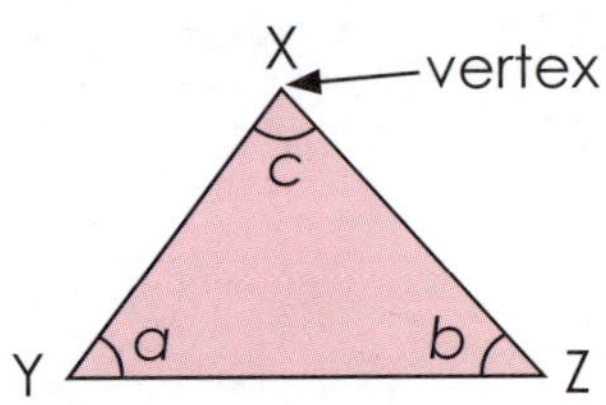

- **vertically opposite angles**
  Vertically opposite angles are the angles opposite each other when two lines cross. Vertically opposite angles have equal measures.

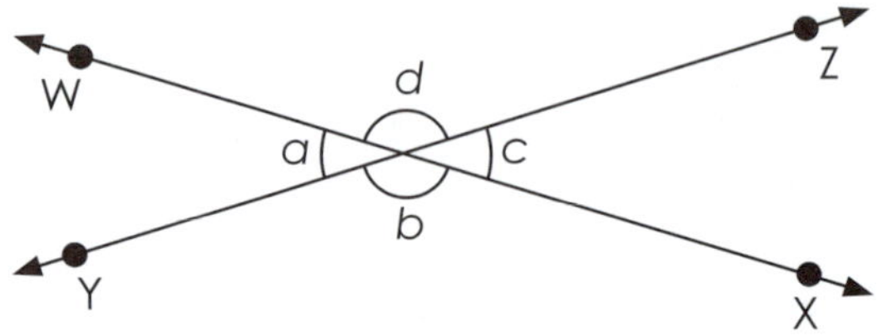

  $\angle a$ and $\angle c$ are a pair of vertically opposite angles.
  $m\angle a = m\angle c$

  $\angle b$ and $\angle d$ are also a pair of vertically opposite angles.
  $m\angle b = m\angle d$

- **volume (solid)**
  The **volume** of a solid is the amount of space it takes up.

 ISBN 978-93-5103-033-1

Answers

Chapter 1

Page 8, Let's Do

1. **a)** 4,01,062; **b)** 9,70,505
2. **a)** four lakh thirty-five thousand six hundred seventy-two;
b) three lakh eleven thousand twelve

Page 9, Let's Do

1. **a)** 3, 3,00,000; **b)** ten thousands, 40,000; **c)** 70,000

Page 10, Let's Do

1. **a)** 2,31,375; **b)** 2,13,538; **c)** 2,31,375, 2,31,358, 2,13,538

Page 11, Let's Do

1. **a)** 70,03,000; **b)** 90,23,000; **c)** 24,05,049
2. **a)** forty-one lakh twenty-six thousand;
b) thirty-six lakh ninety thousand five hundred eighty

Page 12, Let's Do

1. **a)** 5, 5,00,000; **b)** ten lakhs, 40,00,000; **c)** 20,00,000

Page 13, Let's Do

1. **a)** 4,30,20,300; **b)** 8,19,12,201
2. **a)** nine crore sixteen lakh eighty thousand three hundred;
b) two crore two lakh seventy-five thousand eight hundred thirty-four
3. **a)** 1, 10,00,000; **b)** ten lakhs, 30,00,000

Page 14, Let's Do

1. **a)** seven hundred thousand, 700,000; **b)** ₹ 2,00,00,000;
c) 2,14,70,300, twenty-one million four hundred seventy thousand three hundred

Page 15, Practice 1

1. **a)** 1,15,600; **b)** 8,80,005; **c)** 3,52,41,070
2. **a)** two lakh seven thousand three hundred six;
b) five lakh sixty thousand three; **c)** thirty-four lakh fifty thousand;
d) one crore sixty-five lakh eight thousand seventy
3. **a)** 80; **b)** 8000; **c)** 80,00,000 4. **a)** 2,00,000; **b)** 30,000;
c) 8,00,00,000 5. **a)** 4,61,668; **b)** 56,23,000 6. **a)** 73,500, 74,500;
b) 1,03,002, 1,13,002; **c)** 7,74,20,000, 5,74,20,000
7. 5,62,370, 5,32,760, 5,32,670, 5,32,607
8. 74,25,700, 7,23,57,000, 7,25,37,000, 7,32,57,000
9. **a)** 8000, 8000; **b)** 2,00,000, 200,000; **c)** 50,00,000, 5,000,000

Page 16, Let's Do

1. **a)** 20,81,971; **b)** 33,90,996; **c)** 59,67,469
2. 2,09,11,956

Page 17, Let's Do

1. **a)** 9,02,911; **b)** 21,92,229; **c)** 18,21,921
2. 59,03,492

Page 18, Let's Do

1.
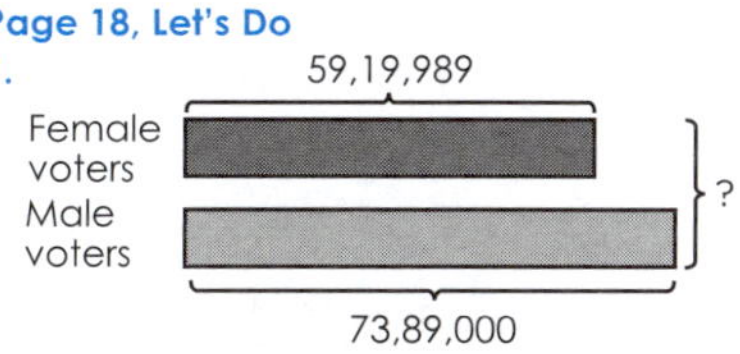

59,19,989 + 73,89,000 = 1,33,08,989
The total number of voters was 1,33,08,989.

2.
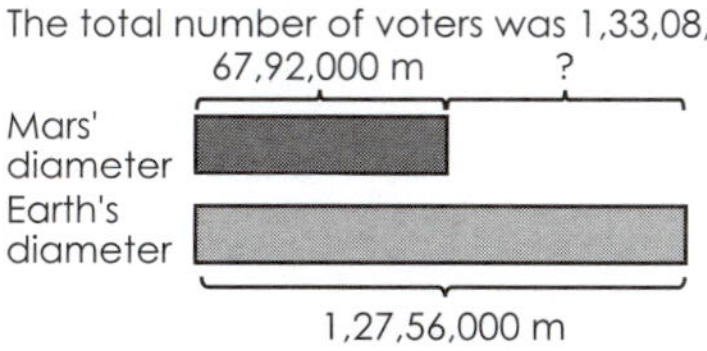

1,27,56,000 – 67,92,000 = 59,64,000
The difference between their diameters is 59,64,000 metres.

3.
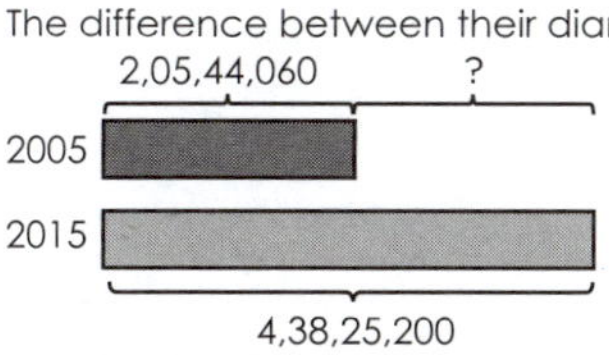

4,38,25,200 – 2,05,44,060 = 2,32,81,140
The population of Country A increased by 2,32,81,140 in ten years.

Page 19, Practice 2

1. **a)** 6,96,790; **b)** 13,49,048; **c)** 1,32,05,763; **d)** 1,92,69,247
2. **a)** 4,40,235; **b)** 62,10,001; **c)** 10,09,564; **d)** 5,03,07,904
3.
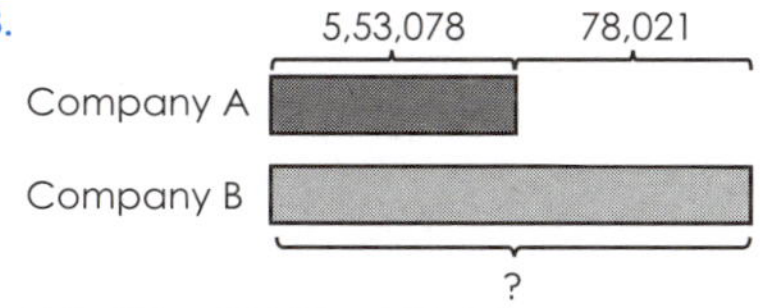

5,53,078 + 78,021 = 6,31,099
Company B collected 6,31,099 clothes.

4.
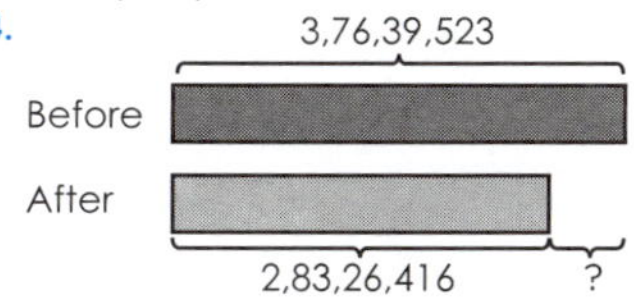

3,76,39,523 – 2,83,26,416 = 93,13,107
The property developer must buy 93,13,107 more bricks.

5.
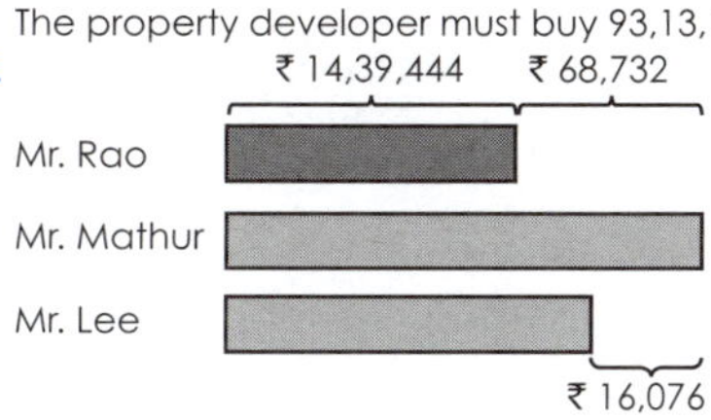

₹ 14,39,444 + ₹ 68,732 = ₹ 15,08,176
Mr. Mathur saved ₹ 15,08,176.
₹ 15,08,176 – ₹ 16,076 = ₹ 14,92,100
Mr. Lee saved ₹ 14,92,100.

Pages 20–21, Let's Do

1. **a)** 23,000; **b)** 55,000; **c)** 40,000

Page 22, Let's Do

1. **a)** 2,34,60,000; **b)** 2,35,00,000; **c)** 2,30,00,000; **d)** 2,00,00,000

Page 22, Let's Do

1. Estimates vary. **a)** 7,90,000; **b)** 3,00,00,000

Page 23, Let's Do

1. Estimates vary. **a)** 25,00,000; **b)** 90,000

Page 24, Practice 3

1. **a)** 7000; **b)** 11,000; **c)** 1,25,000
2. 10,00,000 kilometres
3. ₹ 11,00,000
4. ₹ 2,00,00,000
5. Estimates vary. **a)** 77,000; **b)** 75,000; **c)** 4,00,000; **d)** 4,72,000
6. Estimates vary.
City A: 18,00,000;
City B: 17,60,000;
City C: 17,10,000
The total number of people living in the three cities is approximately 52,70,000.
7. Estimates vary. **a)** 1,60,000; **b)** 5,40,000; **c)** 90,000; **d)** 60,000

Page 26, Let's Do

1. **a)** $2 \times 2 \times 3 \times 5$; **b)** $2 \times 3 \times 5 \times 7$

Page 27, Let's Do

1. is

Page 28, Let's Do

1. **a)** 1; 2; 5; 10; **b)** 10 2. 12

Page 29, Let's Do

1. is not

Page 30, Let's Do

1. **a)** 3; 6; 9; 12; 15; 18; 21; 24; 27; 30;
b) 5; 10; 15; 20; 25; 30; 35; 40; 45; 50;
c) 15; 30; **d)** 15
2. 324

Page 33, Let's Do

1. 108 and 2079 2. 2152 and 4140 3. 162 and 1458 4. 175
5. 2584 and 4280 6. 6579

Page 33, Practice 4

1. **a)** 1 and 3; **b)** 1, 2 and 4; **c)** 1, 3, 5 and 15; **d)** 1, 2, 4 and 8
2. **a)** Yes, because 60 is exactly divisible by 4.
b) Yes, because 84 is exactly divisible by 4.
c) Yes, because 60 and 84 are both divisible by 4.
3. **a)** 3; **b)** 4; **c)** 15; **d)** 8

ISBN 978-93-5103-033-1

4. Yes 5. **a)** 330; **b)** 288; **c)** 168; **d)** 540 6. **a)** 2, 4, 6, 8, 10, 12, 14, 16, 18, 20; **b)** 7, 14, 21, 28, 35, 42, 49, 56, 63, 70; **c)** 14
7. 513 – Yes; No; No; No; No; Yes
319 – No; No; No; No; No; No
3642 – Yes; No; Yes; No; No; No
4050 – Yes; No; Yes; No; No; Yes
6566 – No; No; No; Yes; No; No
1920 – Yes; Yes; Yes; No; Yes; No

Chapter 2

Page 35, Let's Do
1. **a)** 3280; **b)** 53,600; **c)** 6,30,000

Page 35, Let's Do
1. **a)** 1440; **b)** 14,400; **c)** 1,44,000

Page 36, Let's Do
1. Answers vary. Examples: **a)** 15,000; **b)** 32,000; **c)** 4,80,000

Page 37, Practice 1
1. **a)** 2380; **b)** 70,000; **c)** 37,000; **d)** 4000; **e)** 28,000; **f)** 5,20,000
2. 392; **a)** 3920; **b)** 39,200; **c)** 3,92,000 3. 2700; **a)** 27,000; **b)** 2,70,000; **c)** 27,00,000 4. Answers vary. Examples: **a)** 28,000; **b)** 30,000; **c)** 35,000; **d)** 42,000; **e)** 40,000; **f)** 3,60,000

Page 38, Let's Do
1. **a)** 52; **b)** 74; **c)** 40

Page 39, Let's Do
1. **a)** 7; **b)** 80; **c)** 40

Page 40, Let's Do
1. Answers vary. Examples: **a)** 80; **b)** 70; **c)** 90

Page 40, Practice 2
1. **a)** 47; **b)** 47; **c)** 47; **d)** 72; **e)** 72; **f)** 72 2. 9; **a)** 9000; **b)** 900; **c)** 90
3. 150; **a)** 1500; **b)** 150; **c)** 15 4. Answers vary. Examples: **a)** 80; **b)** 80; **c)** 80; **d)** 700; **e)** 400; **f)** 800

Page 41, Let's Do
1. **a)** 32; **b)** 44

Page 42, Let's Do
1. **a)** 45; **b)** 81

Page 44, Let's Do
1. **a)** 27; **b)** 0

Page 45, Let's Do
1. **a)** 276; **b)** 5; **c)** 14

Page 46, Practice 3
1. **a)** 356; **b)** 356; **c)** 298; **d)** 298 2. **a)** 16; **b)** 64; **c)** 64; **d)** 16 3. **a)** 56; **b)** 300; **c)** 3; **d)** 15; **e)** 37; **f)** 68; **g)** 37; **h)** 10; **i)** 21; **j)** 70; **k)** 50; **l)** 4

Page 47, Let's Do
1. **a)** 1,62,127; **b)** 4,40,510

Page 48, Let's Do
1. **a)** 1,73,240; **b)** 30,07,641

Page 49, Let's Do
1. 6,79,768

Page 49, Practice 4
1. **a)** 3,41,880; **b)** 3,42,020; **c)** 6,92,576; **d)** 2,75,968; **e)** 63,08,208; **f)** 19,57,236 2. 1077 × ₹ 13 = ₹ 14,001; It costs ₹ 14,001.
3. 150 × 526 = 78,900; 78,900 balloons needed
4. 128 × 2314 = 2,96,192; 2,96,192 almonds

Page 50, Let's Do
1. **a)** 2 R10; **b)** 4 R9; **c)** 8 R65

Page 51, Let's Do
1. **a)** 3 R12; **b)** 2 R15; **c)** 6 R5

Page 53, Let's Do
1. **a)** 4; **b)** 2 R28; **c)** 3 R20

Page 54, Let's Do
1. **a)** 9; **b)** 6; **c)** 8 R60

Page 56, Let's Do
1. **a)** 30 R22; **b)** 14 R45; **c)** 40 R12

Page 59, Let's Do
1. **a)** 70 R35; **b)** 33 R10; **c)** 106 R36

Page 60, Let's Do
1. **a)** 1329 R12; **b)** 10,563 R24

Page 61, Let's Do
1. 68 2. 129

Page 62, Practice 5
1. **a)** 2 R8; **b)** 1 R28; **c)** 2 R7; **d)** 9 R20; **e)** 4 R55; **f)** 4 R7
2. **a)** 37 R2; **b)** 28; **c)** 31 R11; **d)** 530 R5; **e)** 60 R11; **f)** 95 R17; **g)** 1901 R20; **h)** 3868 R1; **i)** 2378 R34; **j)** 9851 R34; **k)** 5828 R6; **l)** 17908 R46
3. ₹ 6048 ÷ 16 = ₹ 378
Each envelope held ₹ 378.
4. 2145 ÷ 64 = 33 R33
The maximum number of pens Mr. Gupta can buy is 33.
5. 10,650 ÷ 38 = 280 R10
Each school received 280 balloons. There was 10 balloons left.

Page 63, Let's Do
1. Number of bales of fabric = 11,904 ÷ 96
= 124
Amount of money she received = 124 × ₹ 56
= ₹ 6944
Mita received ₹ 6944.

Page 64, Let's Do
1. Cost of the cell phone = 15 × ₹ 830 + ₹ 310
= ₹ 12,760
Amount to pay for 1 instalment = ₹ 12,760 ÷ 44
= ₹ 290
Arun has to pay ₹ 290.

Pages 64–65, Practice 6
1. 1,55,640 ÷ 24 = 6485
There were 6485 packs of 24 erasers.
6485 × ₹ 70 = ₹ 4,53,950
The company made ₹ 4,53,950 after the sale of all the erasers.
2. 368 × 144 = 52,992
He bought 52,992 buttons altogether.
3. Number of students in each school = 7840 ÷ 14
= 560
Number of boys in each school = 560 – 240
= 320
14 × 320 = 4480
There were 4480 boys altogether.
4. Number of yellow chairs = 42 × 16
= 672
Number of red chairs = 1104 – 672
= 432
432 ÷ 18 = 24
There are 24 rows of red chairs.

Chapter 3

Page 67, Let's Do
1. **a)** 3; **b)** $2\frac{3}{5}$

Page 68, Let's Do
1. **a)** $2\frac{1}{3}$; **b)** $1\frac{3}{4}$

Page 69, Let's Do
1. **a)** 5.3; **b)** 5.1

Page 70, Let's Do
1. 1.3

Page 70, Practice 1
1. **a)** 7; **b)** $2\frac{2}{3}$; **c)** $8\frac{1}{3}$; **d)** 8 2. **a)** $3\frac{3}{4}$; **b)** $5\frac{1}{4}$; **c)** $3\frac{1}{2}$; **d)** $11\frac{1}{7}$
3. **a)** 1.7; **b)** 1.2; **c)** 6.3; **d)** 5.6
4. 26 ÷ 8 = 3.25
$= 3\frac{1}{4}$
Each piece was $3\frac{1}{4}$ metres long.
5. $3 \div 9 = \frac{1}{3}$
She used $\frac{1}{3}$ metre of cloth for each pillow cover.
6. $10 \div 4 = 2\frac{1}{2}$
There were $2\frac{1}{2}$ cakes in each share.
7. $2 \div 5 = \frac{2}{5}$
There was $\frac{2}{5}$ litre of milk in each jug.

 ISBN 978-93-5103-033-1

8.

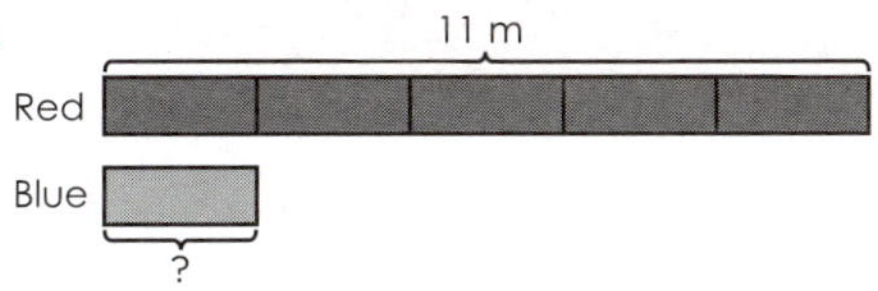

5 units → 11 m

1 unit → 11 ÷ 5

$= 2\frac{1}{5}$ m

The blue ribbon is $2\frac{1}{5}$ metres long.

Page 72, Let's Do

1. a) $1\frac{1}{15}$; b) $1\frac{8}{15}$

Page 74, Let's Do

1. a) $\frac{17}{24}$; b) $\frac{5}{12}$

Page 75, Let's Do

1. $\frac{19}{36}$

Page 75, Practice 2

1. a) $1\frac{5}{12}$; b) $\frac{3}{4}$; c) $\frac{13}{24}$; d) $\frac{7}{15}$; e) $1\frac{17}{24}$; f) $1\frac{1}{15}$

2. a) $\frac{1}{4}$; b) $\frac{7}{12}$; c) $\frac{2}{15}$; d) $\frac{19}{24}$; e) $\frac{19}{30}$; f) $\frac{7}{15}$

3. $\frac{2}{5} + \frac{1}{4} = \frac{8}{20} + \frac{5}{20}$

$= \frac{13}{20}$

She spent $\frac{13}{20}$ of her money altogether.

4. $1\frac{1}{3} - \frac{3}{4} = \frac{4}{3} - \frac{3}{4}$

$= \frac{16}{12} - \frac{9}{12}$

$= \frac{7}{12}$

He took $\frac{7}{12}$ hour longer to return home.

Pages 77–78, Let's Do

1. a) $5\frac{5}{12}$; b) $5\frac{1}{15}$

Page 79, Let's Do

1. a) $1\frac{5}{8}$; b) $2\frac{13}{15}$

Page 80, Let's Do

1. $4\frac{1}{12}$

Page 81, Practice 3

1. a) $4\frac{2}{9}$; b) $8\frac{1}{3}$; c) $6\frac{1}{3}$; d) $3\frac{23}{24}$; e) $4\frac{7}{18}$; f) $4\frac{1}{12}$

2. a) $2\frac{1}{2}$; b) $2\frac{1}{2}$; c) $2\frac{1}{2}$; d) $3\frac{7}{12}$; e) $1\frac{1}{15}$; f) $2\frac{2}{15}$

3. $1\frac{1}{2} + 1\frac{1}{12} = 2\frac{1}{2} + \frac{1}{12}$

$= 2\frac{6}{12} + \frac{1}{12}$

$= 2\frac{7}{12}$

She spent $2\frac{7}{12}$ hours cooking altogether.

4. $2\frac{1}{2} - 1\frac{2}{5} = 1\frac{1}{2} - \frac{2}{5}$

$= 1\frac{5}{10} - \frac{4}{10}$

$= 1\frac{1}{10}$

Nisha jogged $1\frac{1}{10}$ kilometres further than her brother.

5. $2\frac{3}{4} - 1\frac{1}{3} = 1\frac{3}{4} - \frac{1}{3}$

$= 1\frac{9}{12} - \frac{4}{12}$

$= 1\frac{5}{12}$

The length of the other ribbon is $1\frac{5}{12}$ metres.

6. $3\frac{1}{6} - 1\frac{2}{3} = 2\frac{1}{6} - \frac{2}{3}$

$= 1\frac{7}{6} - \frac{4}{6}$

$= 1\frac{3}{6}$

$= 1\frac{1}{2}$

She bought $1\frac{1}{2}$ kilograms more potatoes than carrots.

Page 83, Let's Do

1. $\frac{3}{10}$ 2. $\frac{5}{18}$

Page 84, Let's Do

1. a) $\frac{1}{4}$; b) 10

Page 86, Let's Do

1. a) $10\frac{2}{5}$; b) $7\frac{1}{3}$

Page 87, Let's Do

1. a) $\frac{22}{27}$; b) 8

Page 87, Let's Do

1. $3\frac{3}{4}$

Page 88, Practice 4

1. a) $\frac{1}{4}$; b) $\frac{2}{9}$; c) $\frac{1}{6}$; d) $\frac{5}{8}$; e) $\frac{1}{2}$; f) $\frac{3}{8}$ 2. a) 12; b) $2\frac{2}{3}$; c) 4; d) 5; e) 4; f) 5 3. a) $\frac{3}{5}$; b) $2\frac{1}{8}$; c) $2\frac{2}{3}$; d) 4; e) 5; f) 4

4. $\frac{2}{3} \times 2\frac{3}{4} = \frac{2}{3} \times \frac{11}{4}$

$= \frac{11}{6}$

$= 1\frac{5}{6}$

He uses $1\frac{5}{6}$ kilograms of flour.

5. $2\frac{1}{2}\text{ m} \times 3\frac{3}{4}\text{ m} = \frac{5}{2}\text{ m} \times \frac{15}{4}\text{ m}$

$= \frac{75}{8}\text{ m}^2$

$= 9\frac{3}{8}\text{ m}^2$

The area of the land is $9\frac{3}{8}$ square kilometres.

Page 90, Let's Do

1. $\frac{2}{9}$ 2. $\frac{1}{8}$

Page 91, Let's Do

1. $\frac{1}{20}$

Page 91, Practice 5

1. a) $\frac{4}{15}$; b) $\frac{5}{28}$; c) $\frac{1}{5}$; d) $\frac{3}{7}$; e) $\frac{1}{12}$; f) $\frac{3}{20}$

2. $\frac{7}{8} \div 4 = \frac{7}{8} \times \frac{1}{4}$

$= \frac{7}{32}$

Each club received $\frac{7}{32}$ of the money.

3. $\frac{2}{5} \div 3 = \frac{2}{5} \times \frac{1}{3}$

$= \frac{2}{15}$

There was $\frac{2}{15}$ litre of fruit juice in each cup.

4. $\frac{3}{4} \div 4 = \frac{3}{4} \times \frac{1}{4}$

$= \frac{3}{16}$

The length of each side is $\frac{3}{16}$ metre.

5. $\frac{3}{4} \div 6 = \frac{3}{4} \times \frac{1}{6}$

$= \frac{3}{24}$

$= \frac{1}{8}$

Each child received $\frac{1}{8}$ kilogram of walnuts.

 ISBN 978-93-5103-033-1

Page 94, Let's Do

1. **a)** 20; **b)** 8; **c)** $6\frac{2}{3}$

Page 95, Let's Do

1. $4\frac{4}{5}$

Pages 95–96, Practice 6

1. **a)** 10; **b)** 21; **c)** 16; **d)** 24; **e)** 45; **f)** 56; **g)** 72; **h)** 66; **i)** 120
2. **a)** 6; **b)** 6; **c)** $7\frac{1}{2}$; **d)** $13\frac{1}{2}$; **e)** $7\frac{1}{5}$; **f)** $10\frac{2}{7}$
3. $5 \div \frac{1}{5} = 5 \times \frac{5}{1}$

   $= \frac{25}{1}$

   $= 25$

   5 bottles of detergent will last 25 weeks.
4. $10 \div \frac{1}{4} = 10 \times \frac{4}{1}$

   $= \frac{40}{1}$

   $= 40$

   He needs 40 tins of milk powder.
5. $6 \div \frac{3}{4} = 6 \times \frac{4}{3}$

   $= \frac{24}{3}$

   $= 8$

   8 pots of soup can be made with 6 litres of water.
6. $3 \div \frac{2}{9} = 3 \times \frac{9}{2}$

   $= \frac{27}{2}$

   $= 13\frac{1}{2}$

   Lily will be able to fill 13 mugs completely.
7. $3 \div \frac{4}{7} = 3 \times \frac{7}{4}$

   $= \frac{21}{4}$

   $= 5\frac{1}{4}$

   The greatest number of pieces that can be cut is 5.

Page 97, Let's Do

1. **a)** 6; **b)** $2\frac{2}{3}$

Page 98, Let's Do

1. 4

Page 99, Practice 7

1. **a)** 2; **b)** 8; **c)** 2; **d)** $\frac{3}{5}$; **e)** $1\frac{1}{35}$; **f)** $1\frac{5}{9}$
2. $\frac{3}{4} \div \frac{1}{12} = \frac{3}{4} \times \frac{12}{1}$

   $= 9$

   Shelly has 9 blue pieces.
3. $\frac{7}{12}\text{ m}^2 \div \frac{3}{8}\text{ m} = \left(\frac{7}{12} \times \frac{8}{3}\right)\text{ m}$

   $= \frac{14}{9}\text{ m}$

   $= 1\frac{5}{9}\text{ m}$

   The length of the paper is $1\frac{5}{9}$ metres.
4. $\frac{7}{8} \div \frac{1}{4} = \frac{7}{8} \times \frac{4}{1}$

   $= \frac{7}{2}$

   $= 3\frac{1}{2}$

   3 bows can be made from $\frac{7}{8}$ metre of ribbon.
5. $\frac{11}{12} \div \frac{2}{5} = \frac{11}{12} \times \frac{5}{2}$

   $= \frac{55}{24}$

   $= 2\frac{7}{24}$

   3 containers are needed to hold $\frac{11}{12}$ litre of orange juice.

Page 102, Let's Do

1. Method varies. Example: $\frac{5}{8} \times 96 = 60$

   There are 60 girls.

   $96 - 60 = 36$

   There are 36 boys.
2. 5 units → 300

   1 unit → 300 ÷ 5

   = 60

   8 units → 8 × 60

   = 480

   There were 480 rolls.

Page 103, Let's Do

1. 8 units → 192

   1 unit → 192 ÷ 8

   = 24

   3 units → 3 × 24

   = 72

   72 marbles were neither blue nor green.

Pages 104–105, Let's Do

1. 4 units of the total → 300

   1 unit of the total → 300 ÷ 4

   = 75

   3 units of remainder → 75

   1 unit of remainder → 75 ÷ 3

   = 25

   2 units of remainder → 2 × 25

   = 50

   Mrs. Singh had 50 samosas left.
2. 1 unit of the remainder → 300

   2 units → 2 × 300

   = 600

   3 units → 600

   1 unit → 600 ÷ 3

   = 200

   5 units → 5 × 200

   = 1000

   Mr. Manny had ₹ 1000 at first.

Pages 105–106, Practice 8

1. 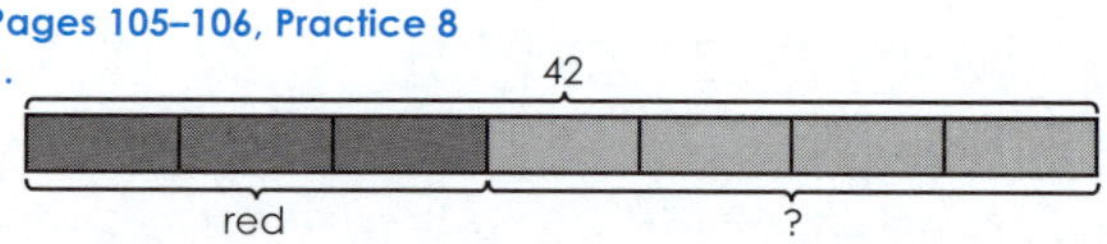

   Method varies. Example: $\frac{4}{7} \times 42 = \frac{168}{7}$

   $= 24$

   There are 24 green apples.
2. 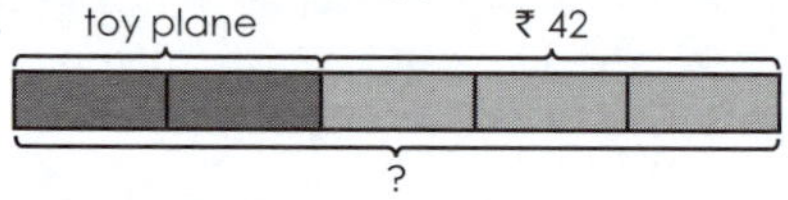

   3 units → ₹ 42

   1 unit → ₹ 42 ÷ 3

   = ₹ 14

   5 units → 5 × ₹ 14

   = ₹ 70

   She had ₹ 70 at first.

 ISBN 978-93-5103-033-1

3.

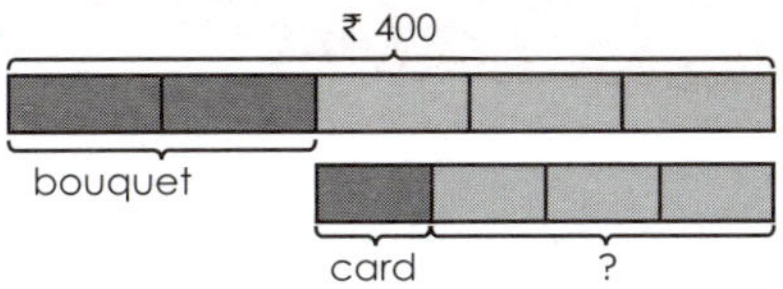

4 units → $\frac{3}{5}$ × ₹ 400
= ₹ 240
1 unit → ₹ 240 ÷ 4
= ₹ 60
3 units → 3 × ₹ 60
= ₹ 180
He had ₹ 180 left.

4.

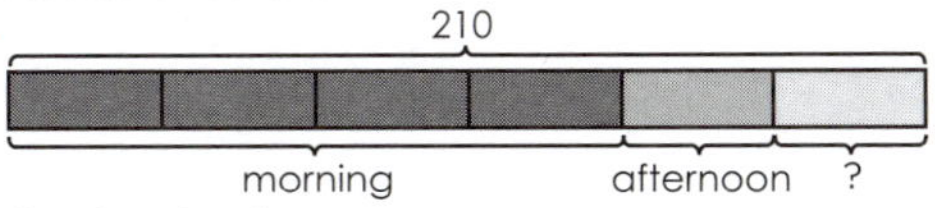

$\frac{2}{3} + \frac{1}{6} = \frac{4}{6} + \frac{1}{6}$
$= \frac{5}{6}$

$\frac{5}{6}$ of the sandwiches were sold.
6 units → 210
1 unit → 210 ÷ 6
= 35
35 sandwiches were not sold.

5.

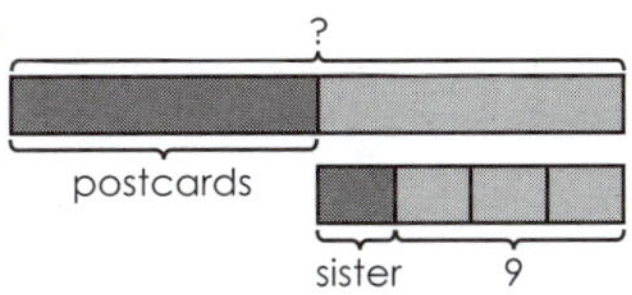

3 units → 9
1 unit → 9 ÷ 3
= 3
4 units → 4 × 3
= 12
2 × 12 = 24
He bought 24 stamps.

6.

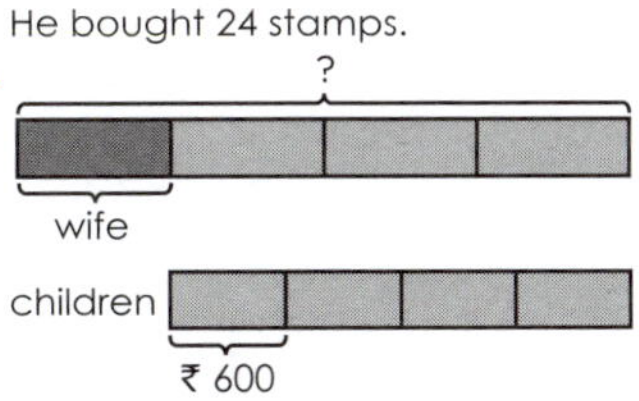

4 × ₹ 600 = ₹ 2400
He gave his children ₹ 2400.
3 units → ₹ 2400
1 unit → ₹ 2400 ÷ 3
= ₹ 800
4 units → 4 × ₹ 800
= ₹ 3200
He had ₹ 3200 at first.

7.

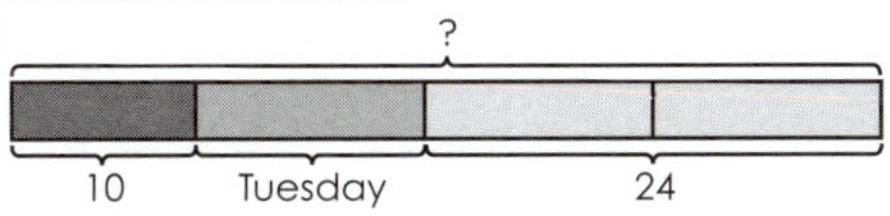

2 units → 24
1 unit → 24 ÷ 2
= 12
3 units → 3 × 12
= 36
10 + 36 = 46
There were 46 pages in the book.

Chapter 4

Page 109, Let's Do

1. 60°, 65°, 55°, 60°, 65°, 55°, 180°, Yes, because the sum of the angle measures is 180°.

Page 110, Let's Do

1. 75°, 141°, 144°, 75°, 141°, 144°, 360°, Yes, because the sum of the angle measures is 360°.

Page 111, Let's Do

1. 114°, 66°, 114°, 66°, ∠*a* and ∠*c*; ∠*b* and ∠*d*

Page 112, Practice 1

1. **a)** 180°; **b)** 360° 2. **a)** 180°; **b)** 360° 3. ∠COF and ∠EOD; ∠COE and ∠FOD

Pages 113–114, Let's Do

1. 90° 2. 35° 3. 68°

Page 115, Let's Do

1. 134°, 46°, 134°

Pages 115–117, Practice 2

1. **a)** 118°; **b)** 52°; **c)** 56°; **d)** 105°; **e)** 29°; **f)** 124° 2. 155° 3. 40°, 40° 4. 44°

Chapter 5

Page 120, Let's Do

1. **a)** 3.15; **b)** 3.14; **c)** 3.15 2. 7.00

Page 121, Let's Do

1. **a)** 0.09; **b)** 1.21; **c)** 6.92

Page 122, Let's Do

1. **a)** 5.78; **b)** 4.71; **c)** 8.38

Page 122, Practice 1

1. **a)** 0.12; **b)** 7.51; **c)** 40.08; **d)** 81.14; **e)** 0.73; **f)** 3.12; **g)** 59.01; **h)** 18.61 2. **a)** 6.27 km; **b)** 4.08 kg; **c)** 0.19 L; **d)** 20.25 L 3. **a)** 0.07; **b)** 0.26; **c)** 0.46; **d)** 8.96; **e)** 6.92; **f)** 6.98 4. **a)** 1.33; **b)** 2.57; **c)** 2.56; **d)** 5.67

Page 124, Let's Do

1. **a)** 6, 0.6, 0.06; **b)** 9, 0.9, 0.09

Page 125, Let's Do

1. **a)** 1.2; **b)** 0.68; **c)** 3.45

Page 125, Let's Do

1. **a)** 45; **b)** 3.2; **c)** 476.7

Page 126, Let's Do

1. **a)** 0.3; **b)** 320; **c)** 132.5

Page 127, Let's Do

1. **a)** 90; **b)** 3620; **c)** 13,400

Page 128, Let's Do

1. **a)** 72; **b)** 616; **c)** 150; **d)** 20,480

Page 129, Practice 2

1. **a)** 2; **b)** 0.2; **c)** 0.02; **d)** 8; **e)** 0.8; **f)** 0.08 2. **a)** 75; **b)** 57; **c)** 20.5; **d)** 32.1; **e)** 14.39; **f)** 50.76 3. **a)** 0.08; **b)** 6.4; **c)** 343.2; **d)** 0.06; **e)** 259.2; **f)** 194.88 4. **a)** 2; **b)** 40; **c)** 150.8; **d)** 50; **e)** 7250; **f)** 32,400 5. **a)** 2.8; **b)** 18; **c)** 725; **d)** 1316; **e)** 1338; **f)** 1038 6. **a)** 20,400; **b)** 1500; **c)** 31,150; **d)** 15,750; **e)** 16,450; **f)** 12,064

Page 131, Let's Do

1. **a)** 0.8, 0.08, 0.008; **b)** 0.6, 0.06, 0.006

Page 132, Let's Do

1. **a)** 0.023; **b)** 0.045; **c)** 1.2

Page 132, Let's Do

1. **a)** 0.2; **b)** 0.08; **c)** 0.043

Page 133, Let's Do

1. **a)** 0.08; **b)** 0.9; **c)** 0.015

Page 135, Let's Do

1. **a)** 0.004; **b)** 0.2; **c)** 0.324

Pages 135–136, Let's Do

1. **a)** 0.004; **b)** 0.016; **c)** 0.002; **d)** 0.102

Page 136, Practice 3

1. **a)** 0.2; **b)** 0.02; **c)** 0.002; **d)** 0.5; **e)** 0.05; **f)** 0.005 2. **a)** 0.012; **b)** 0.036; **c)** 0.47; **d)** 0.53; **e)** 3.9; **f)** 10.3 3. **a)** 0.3; **b)** 0.2; **c)** 0.7; **d)** 0.125; **e)** 0.016; **f)** 0.121 4. **a)** 0.07; **b)** 0.007; **c)** 0.342; **d)** 0.009; **e)** 0.043; **f)** 0.506 5. **a)** 0.002; **b)** 0.004; **c)** 0.018; **d)** 0.03; **e)** 2.16; **f)** 2.065 6. **a)** 0.03; **b)** 0.012; **c)** 0.015; **d)** 0.033; **e)** 0.103; **f)** 0.013

Page 137, Let's Do

1. **a)** 300; **b)** 615; **c)** 4200; **d)** 185

Page 138, Let's Do

1. **a)** 400; **b)** 6

Page 139, Let's Do

1. **a)** 0.35; **b)** 0.625; **c)** 4.07; **d)** 6.05

Page 139, Let's Do

1. **a)** 4.35; **b)** 5.09

Page 140, Practice 4

1. **a)** 285; **b)** 2750; **c)** 85; **d)** 706; **e)** 154; **f)** 3825 2. **a)** 20, 80; **b)** 16, 500; **c)** 2, 80; **d)** 40, 6; **e)** 56, 75; **f)** 64, 104 3. **a)** 0.67; **b)** 0.105; **c)** 0.069; **d)** 2.87; **e)** 3.5; **f)** 4.06 4. **a)** 9.6; **b)** 4.705; **c)** 20.4; **d)** 54.06; **e)** 120.04; **f)** 63.08

Page 141, Let's Do

1. Answers vary. Examples: **a)** 90,000; **b)** 9000; **c)** 900

Pages 142–143, Let's Do

1. Answers vary. Examples: **a)** 32; **b)** 2000

Page 144, Let's Do

1. 8

 ISBN 978-93-5103-033-1

Page 144, Practice 5

1. Answers vary. Examples: **a)** 200; **b)** 600; **c)** 2000; **d)** 160; **e)** 450; **f)** 900
2. **a)** 115.92; **b)** 37.41; **c)** 113.04; **d)** 10.92; **e)** 12,458.4; **f)** 1274.65
3. 18 × 1.75 kg = 31.5 kg
   She bought 31.5 kilograms of flour.
4. 31 × ₹ 2.75 = ₹ 85.25
   He spends ₹ 85.25.
5. 12 × 18.3 cm = 219.6 cm
   The length of the table is 219.6 centimetres.

Page 145, Let's Do

1. **a)** 0.15; **b)** 0.032

Page 147, Let's Do

1. Answers vary. Examples: **a)** 1600; **b)** 16; **c)** 1.6

Page 148, Let's Do

1. 29.25

Page 148, Practice 6

1. Answers vary. Examples: **a)** 2; **b)** 20; **c)** 36; **d)** 8; **e)** 30; **f)** 9
2. **a)** 6.96; **b)** 22.44; **c)** 68.53; **d)** 227.712; **e)** 24.817; **f)** 135.558
3. 4.6 × ₹ 34.50 = ₹ 158.70
   She paid ₹ 158.70 for the sugar.
4. 7.5 × ₹ 6.20 = ₹ 46.50
   He paid ₹ 46.50 for the electric wire.
5. 25.74 km × 6.8 km = 175.032 km^2
   ≈ 175 km^2
   The area of the plot of land is 175 square kilometres.

Page 150, Let's Do

1. **a)** 200; **b)** 20; **c)** 2

Page 151, Let's Do

1. **a)** 0.7; **b)** 2

Page 152, Let's Do

1. **a)** 1.25; **b)** 0.23

Page 153, Let's Do

1. 24.68

Pages 153–154, Practice 7

1. Answers vary. Examples: **a)** 2; **b)** 2; **c)** 2; **d)** 4; **e)** 3; **f)** 4
2. **a)** 0.6; **b)** 3.7; **c)** 2.9 3. **a)** 0.08; **b)** 1.13; **c)** 0.24
4. ₹ 161.25 ÷ 75 = ₹ 2.15
   The cost of each visiting card was ₹ 2.15.
5. 158.4 L ÷ 45 = 3.52 L
   The capacity of the water tank is 3.52 litres.
6. 9.15 L ÷ 37 ≈ 0.25 L
   There is 0.25 litre of ketchup in each bottle.
7. 56.18 cm ÷ 24 = 2.34 cm
   Each book is 2.34 centimetres thick.

Page 155, Let's Do

1. 0.325 L × 12 = 3.9 L
   Sue used 3.9 litres of water to make 12 cups of tea.
   7.5 – 0.415 – 3.9 = 3.185 L
   She had 3.185 litres of water left.

Page 155, Practice 8

1.

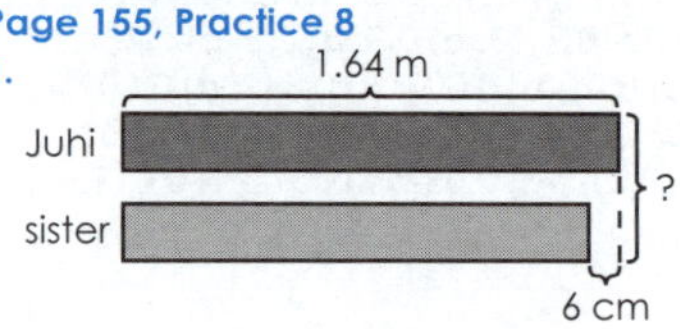

   Juhi's sister's height = 1.64 – 0.06
   = 1.58 m
   1.64 + 1.58 = 3.22 m
   Their total height is 3.22 metres.
2. Cost of 17 packets of needles = 17 × ₹ 2.45
   = ₹ 41.65
   ₹ 41.65 + ₹ 3.85 = ₹ 45.50
   Mrs. Lal spent ₹ 45.50 altogether.
3.

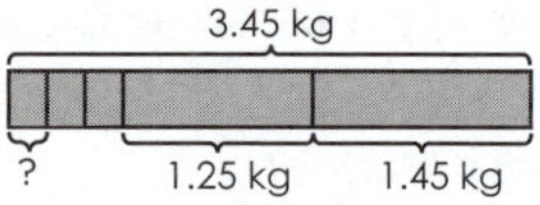

   Flour used for 3 loaves of bread = 3.45 – 1.25 – 1.45
   = 0.75 kg
   0.75 kg ÷ 3 = 0.25 kg
   ≈ 250 g
   She used 250 grams of flour for each loaf of bread.
4. Weight of one marble = 31.75 g ÷ 25
   = 1.27 g
   Weight of one tennis ball = 45.5 × 1.27 g
   = 57.785 g
   1.27 + 57.785 = 59.055 g
   The total weight of one marble and one tennis ball is 59.055 grams.

Chapter 6

Page 158, Let's Do

1. **a)** 67; **b)** 50; **c)** 100 2. **a)** 33; **b)** 20; **c)** 5

Page 159, Let's Do

1. **a)** 45; **b)** 30

Page 160, Let's Do

1. **a)** 53; **b)** 85; **c)** 2; **d)** 70

Page 160, Let's Do

1. **a)** 0.28; **b)** 0.88; **c)** 0.3; **d)** 0.05

Page 161, Let's Do

1. **a)** $\frac{1}{10}$; **b)** $\frac{3}{4}$; **c)** $\frac{1}{20}$; **d)** $\frac{2}{25}$

Page 162, Practice 1

1. **a)** 25%; **b)** 40% 2. **a)** 46%; **b)** 80%; **c)** 8% 3. **a)** 70%; **b)** 25%; **c)** 9%; **d)** 50% 4. **a)** 63%; **b)** 5%; **c)** 20%; **d)** 40% 5. **a)** 0.15; **b)** 0.41; **c)** 0.09; **d)** 0.8 6. **a)** $\frac{23}{50}$; **b)** $\frac{2}{5}$; **c)** $\frac{7}{25}$; **d)** $\frac{3}{50}$
7. 15 out of 100 = $\frac{15}{100}$
   = 15%
   15% of the oranges are rotten.
8. Number of red cups = 100 – 37
   = 63
   63 out of 100 = $\frac{63}{100}$
   = 63%
   63% of the cups are red.
9. 60% = $\frac{60}{100}$
   = $\frac{3}{5}$
   The football team won $\frac{3}{5}$ of the matches.

Page 164, Let's Do

1. **a)** 45; **b)** 80; **c)** 56

Page 165, Let's Do

1. 40 2. 65

Page 167, Let's Do

1. **a)** 4; **b)** 20; **c)** 32

Page 168, Let's Do

1. **a)** 28; **b)** 72

Page 169, Let's Do

1. Number of questions answered incorrectly = 20 – 18
   = 2
   2 out of 20 = $\frac{2}{20}$
   = $\frac{10}{100}$
   = 10%
   He answered 10% of the questions incorrectly.

Page 169, Practice 2

1. **a)** 30%; **b)** 60%; **c)** 25%; **d)** 55%; **e)** 36%; **f)** 15%; **g)** 20%; **h)** 20%
2. **a)** 80%; **b)** 75%; **c)** 72%
3. 100% – 70% = 30%
   30% of the tank is not filled.
4. $\frac{4}{5} = \frac{80}{100}$
   = 80%
   80% of the books are fiction books.
5. **a)** $\frac{14}{50} = \frac{28}{100}$ = 28%
   28% of the vehicles are motorcycles.
   b) Number of vehicles that are not motorcycles = 50 – 14
   = 36
   $\frac{36}{50} = \frac{72}{100}$
   = 72%
   72% of the vehicles are not motorcycles.

 ISBN 978-93-5103-033-1

6. Number of adults = 1500 – 450
= 1050

$1050/1500 = \frac{70}{100}$
$= 70\%$

70% of the participants were adults.

7. Length of wire used to make the jewellery = 5 – 2
= 3 m

$\frac{3}{5} = \frac{60}{100}$
$= 60\%$

He used 60% of the wire to make the jewellery.

Page 171, Let's Do

1. 108 2. **a)** 15; **b)** 16; **c)** 10

Page 172, Let's Do

1.
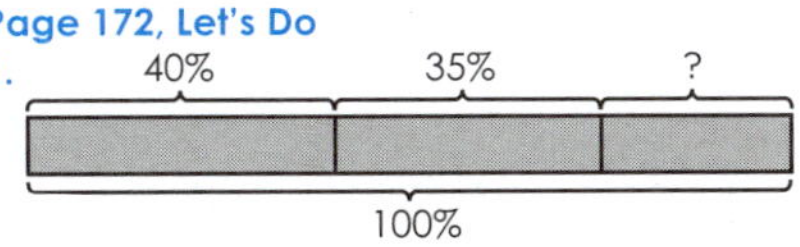

100% – 40% – 35% = 25%

$25\% \times 600 = \frac{25}{100} \times 600$
$= 150$

150 children visited the museum.

Page 173, Let's Do

1. Method varies. Example:
100% – 98% = 2%
2% of the students did not pass the test.
2% × 150 = 3
3 students did not pass the test.

Page 175, Let's Do

1. Sales tax = 3% × ₹ 9500
= ₹ 285
₹ 9500 + ₹ 285 = ₹ 9785
The cost of the bicycle with the tax is ₹ 9785.

2. Discount = 20% × ₹ 94
= ₹ 18.80
₹ 94 – ₹ 18.80 = ₹ 75.20
The selling price of the pair of earrings was ₹ 75.20

Page 176, Let's Do

1. **a)** Decrease = 10% × 500
= 50
500 – 50 = 450
There are 450 boys this year.

b) Increase = 8% × 450
= 36
450 + 36 = 486
There are 486 girls this year.

Page 177, Practice 3

1. **a)** 6; **b)** ₹ 121.50; **c)** 33; **d)** 123.2; **e)** 111 kg; **f)** 322.4 m

2. $45\% \times 1200 = \frac{45}{100} \times 1200$
$= 540$
There are 540 children.

3. $7\% \times 60\ m^2 = \frac{7}{100} \times 60\ m^2$
$= 4.2\ m^2$
The area of the pond is 4.2 square metres.

4. $90\% \times 50 = \frac{90}{100} \times 50$
$= 45$
She spelt 45 words correctly.

5. $30\% \times ₹\ 1350 = \frac{30}{100} \times ₹\ 1350$
= ₹ 405
She saves ₹ 405 each week.

6. 100% – 55% = 45%
$45\% \times 20 = \frac{45}{100} \times 20$
$= 9$
There are 9 male staff members.

7. Increase = 5% × 720
$= \frac{5}{100} \times 720$
$= 36$
720 + 36 = 756
There are 756 members this year.

8. Sales tax = 10% × ₹ 50
$= \frac{10}{100} \times ₹\ 50$
= ₹ 5
₹ 50 + ₹ 5 = ₹ 55
She paid ₹ 55 for the comic.

9. Discount = 30% × ₹ 190
$= \frac{30}{100} \times ₹\ 190$
= ₹ 57
₹ 190 – ₹ 57 = ₹ 133
The sale price was ₹ 133.

10. 100% – 40% = 60%
$60\% \times 15 = \frac{60}{100} \times 15$
$= 9$
9 arrows did not hit the target.

11.
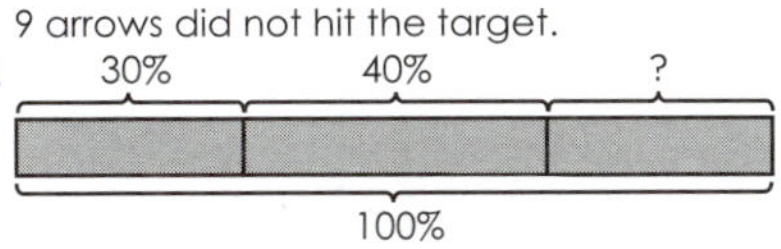

100% – 30% – 40% = 30%
$30\% \times 280 = \frac{30}{100} \times 280$
$= 84$
There are 84 adults.

12.
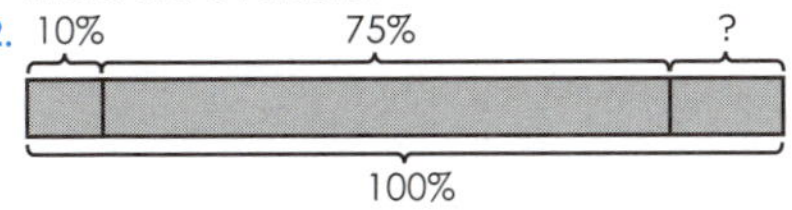

100% – 10% – 75% = 15%
$15\% \times 200 = \frac{15}{100} \times 200$
$= 30$
30 parking spaces are for motorcycles.

Chapter 7

Pages 180–181, Let's Do

1. 5 2. 38

Page 182, Let's Do

1. 77.5

Page 182, Let's Do

1. 143

Page 183, Let's Do

1. 37.20

Page 184, Let's Do

1. 7, 35

Page 185, Let's Do

1. 2, 230

Page 185, Practice 1

1. **a)** 145; **b)** 26.3; **c)** 2.39 m

2. 5460 km ÷ 3 = 1820 km
The average distance he travelled each month was 1820 kilometres.

3. 6 × 18 kg = 108 kg
The total weight of the 6 crates of pears is 108 kilograms.

4. 4 × ₹ 23.75 = ₹ 95
The total amount of money spent on the games stalls was ₹ 95.

5. 4 × 2 m 30 cm = 8 m 120 cm
= 9 m 20 cm
The total length of the planks is 9 metres 20 centimetres.

6. 10 L 275 ml ÷ 3 = 9 L 1275 ml ÷ 3
= 3 L 425 ml
He used 3 litres 425 millilitres of petrol each day.

Page 187, Let's Do

1. Total cost of 3 gel pens = 3 × ₹ 4.50
= ₹ 13.50
Cost of 2 gel pens = 2 × ₹ 3.90
= ₹ 7.80
₹ 13.50 – ₹ 7.80 = ₹ 5.70
The cost of the third gel pen is ₹ 5.70.

Page 188, Let's Do

1. Number of eggs laid in the first 4 weeks = 4 × 387
= 1548
Total number of eggs laid in 5 weeks = 1548 + 157
= 1705
1705 ÷ 5 = 341
The average number of eggs laid each week was 341.

 ISBN 978-93-5103-033-1

Page 189, Let's Do

1. 9 units = 144
   1 unit = 144 ÷ 9
   = 16
   8 units = 16 × 8
   = 128
   The greater number is 128.

Page 189, Practice 2

1. Total weight of the four packages = 4 × 33 kg
   = 132 kg
   132 kg – 18 kg – 27 kg – 37 kg = 50 kg
   The weight of the fourth package is 50 kilograms.
2. 3 × 70 = 210
   210 – 76 – 65 = 69
   Kenny has to get a minimum score of 69 points to win a prize.
3. Total weight of 3 packets of peanuts = 3 × 2.2 kg
   = 6.6 kg
   Total weight of 2 packets of peanuts = 2 × 1.8 kg
   = 3.6 kg
   6.6 kg – 3.6 kg = 3 kg
   The weight of the third packet is 3 kilograms.
4. Total number of people in the first 3 days = 3 × 108
   = 324
   Total number of people in 4 days = 324 + 124
   = 448
   448 ÷ 4 = 112
   The average number of people who came each day was 112.
5. 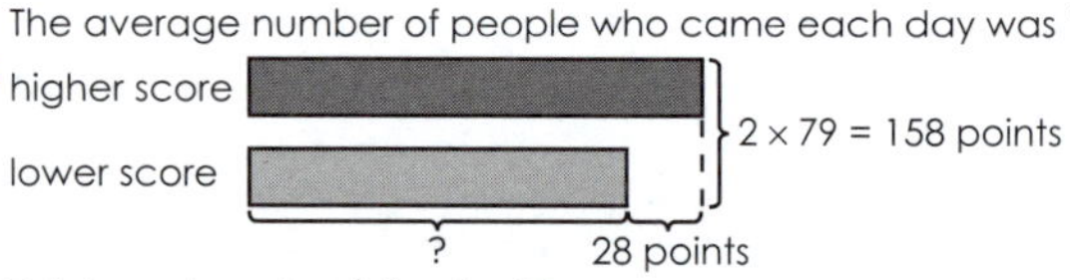

   Total number of points = 2 × 79
   = 158
   (158 – 28) ÷ 2 = 65
   The lower score is 65 marks.

Chapter 8

Page 191, Let's Do

1. **a)** vertex; **b)** side; **c)** z

Page 192, Let's Do

1. **a)** XY; **b)** ZY; **c)** YW

Page 193, Let's Do

1. **a)** XU; **b)** YT; **c)** ZV

Page 194, Practice 1

1. **a)** LM and LN; **b)** L; M; N
2. BD; CF; AE

Page 195, Let's Do

1. C
2. B and D
3. E; equilateral
4. scalene

Page 196, Practice 2

1. equilateral; scalene; isosceles
2. **a)** 65°; **b)** 60°

Pages 198–199, Let's Do

1. **a)** 24; **b)** 40; **c)** 60

Page 200–201, Let's Do

1. **a)** 42; **b)** 30

Page 201, Let's Do

1. **a)** 36;

b) Shaded area = Area of rectangle – Area of triangle
   Area of rectangle = 14 cm × 20 cm
   = 280 cm^2
   Area of triangle = $\frac{1}{2}$ × 14 cm × 8 cm
   = 56 cm^2
   Shaded area = 280 – 56
   = 224 cm^2

Page 202, Let's Do

1. 27

Pages 203–204, Practice 3

1. **a)** 20 cm^2; **b)** 54 cm^2; **c)** 31.5 m^2; **d)** 240 m^2
2. **a)** 24 cm^2; **b)** 25 cm^2; **c)** 10 cm^2; **d)** 240 cm^2
3. **a)** 63 cm^2; **b)** 5104 m^2
4. **a)** 88 cm^2; **b)** 750 cm^2; **c)** 260 cm^2

Chapter 9

Page 205, Let's Do

1. Accept a circle with a radius of 3 centimetres.
2. Accept a circle with a radius of 4 centimetres.

Pages 207, Let's Do

1. **a)** PQ and RS; **b)** OP, OQ, OR and OS;
c) TU and VW; **d)** Accept any arc marked and labelled on the circle;
e) Accept any segment shaded and labelled on the circle.

Pages 208–209, Let's Do

1. **a)** 12; **b)** 43 2. **a)** 3; 6; **b)** 4.2; 8.4; **c)** 6.5; 13

Page 210, Practice 1

1. Accept a circle with a radius of 6 centimetres.
2. Accept a circle with a diameter of 7 centimetres.
3. **a)** CD and EF; **b)** OC, OD, OE and OF; **c)** Answers vary.
Example: AB; **d)** Accept any arc marked and labelled on the circle;
e) Accept any sector and segment shaded and labelled on the circle.
4. **a)** 8 cm; **b)** 9 cm
5. **a)** A – 16 m; B – 10 m; C – 18 cm; D – 22 cm; **b)** B; **c)** C

Chapter 10

Page 213, Let's Do

1. **a)** $\frac{1}{4}$; **b)** 12,000; **c)** 1200

Page 215, Let's Do

1. **a)** $\frac{1}{2}$; **b)** 25%; **c)** $\frac{1}{8}$; **d)** 600

Page 217, Let's Do

1. **a)** shopping; **b)** 35%; **c)** 30%; **d)** ₹ 2000

Page 219, Practice 1

1. **a)** 40; **b)** 25%; **c)** 8; **d)** 80 2. **a)** Games; **b)** 18%; **c)** $\frac{1}{5}$; **d)** 150

Chapter 11

Page 223, Let's Do

1. Accept any one shaded unit for **a)** – **d)**.

Page 224, Let's Do

1. **a)** Yes; **b)** No

Page 225, Practice 1

1. Accept any one shaded unit for **a)** – **d)**.
2. **b)** and **c)**

Chapter 12

Page 234, Let's Do

1. 5, 6, 9, 9

Pages 236–237, Let's Do

1. Figure A 2. Figure C

Page 238, Let's Do

1. 2 2. 2

Pages 239–240, Practice 1

1. 10, 9, 8, 13 2. Top view, Front view, Side view 3. 3 4. 3

Pages 242–243, Let's Do

1. Solid B 2. **a)** hexagon, hexagonal; **b)** 8, 12, 18

Page 246, Let's Do

2. **a)** 5; **b)** 5

Page 248, Let's Do

1. **b)** different

Pages 249, Practice 2

1. **a)** rectangular pyramid; **b)** pentagonal prism; **c)** triangular prism;
d) pentagonal pyramid 2. **a)** 6, 7; **b)** 12, 12; **c)** 8, 7;
d) rectangular prism; **e)** hexagonal pyramid

Page 251, Let's Do

2. **a)** cone; **b)** cylinder

Page 253, Let's Do

1. cone

 ISBN 978-93-5103-033-1

Page 253, Practice 3
1. **a)** cone; **b)** cylinder
2. cylinder, rectangular or square pyramid, triangular pyramid
3. **a)** cylinder; **b)** cone

Pages 258–259, Practice 4
1. A, D 2. **a)** B; **b)** C; **c)** E; **d)** D; **e)** A

Chapter 13

Page 263, Let's Do
1. **a)** 5, 5; **b)** 9; **c)** 18; **d)** C

Page 265, Let's Do
1. **a)** 12; **b)** 10; **c)** 10; **d)** B, C; **e)** A

Page 265, Practice 1
1. **a)** 9 cubic units; **b)** 15 cubic units 2. **a)** 64 cm^3; **b)** 80 cm^3; **c)** 48 cm^3; **d)** Solid B

Pages 267–268, Let's Do
1. **a)** 4, 3, 1, 12; **b)** 4, 2, 2, 16 2. **a)** 60 cm^3; **b)** 64 cm^3; **c)** The cube has a greater volume

Page 269, Let's Do
1. **a)** cm^3; **b)** m^3 2. 27 m^3 3. 90

Page 271, Let's Do
1. **a)** 400; **b)** 1200 2. **a)** 2, 450; **b)** 3, 50

Page 271, Let's Do
1. 1, 260

Pages 272–273, Practice 2
1. **a)** 27 cm^3; **b)** 50 m^3 2. **a)** 54 cm^3; **b)** 30,000 m^3 3. 11,250 cm^3 4. 125 cm^3 5. 120 1-centimetre cubes 6. **a)** m^3; **b)** cm^3 7. 360 m^3 8. **a)** 250 cm^3; **b)** 2000 cm^3; **c)** 2060 cm^3 9. **a)** 1 L 50 ml; **b)** 1 L 800 ml; **c)** 3 L 500 ml 10. 450 ml 11. **a)** 14 L 400 ml; **b)** 3 L

Page 274, Let's Do
1. **a)** 4; **b)** 5

Page 275, Let's Do
1. 12

Page 276, Let's Do
1. 10

Page 277, Let's Do
1. **a)** 4; **b)** 16

Page 278, Let's Do
1. 12.5

Page 279, Practice 3
1. 7 cm 2. **a)** 4 cm; **b)** 12 cm 3. 12 cm 4. 20 cm

Page 281, Let's Do
1. Volume of water in the container at first = 20 cm × 16 cm × 8 cm = 2560 cm^3

   New volume of water in the container = 2560 + 320 = 2880 cm^3

   Height of new water level = $\frac{2880}{(20 \times 16)}$ cm = 9 cm

   The height of the new water level is 9 centimetres.

Page 282, Let's Do
1. Volume of solid = 24 cm × 15 cm × 18 cm = 6480 cm^3

   Volume of cube = 3 cm × 3 cm × 3 cm = 27 cm^3

   Number of cubes needed to build the solid = 6480 ÷ 27 = 240

   240 3-centimetre cubes are needed.

Page 283, Practice 4
1. Volume of water in Container A = 6 cm × 5 cm × 10 cm = 300 cm^3

   10 cm × 4 cm × Height = 300 cm^3

   Height = $\frac{300}{(10 \times 4)}$ cm = 7.5 cm

   The height of the water level in Container B would be 7.5 centimetres.
2. Capacity of the container = 60 cm × 20 cm × 30 cm = 36,000 cm^3 = 36 L

   36 – 28 = 8 L

   8 more litres of water are needed.
3. Volume of solid = 25 cm × 15 cm × 30 cm = 11,250 cm^3

   Volume of cube = 5 cm × 5 cm × 5 cm = 125 cm^3

   11,250 ÷ 125 = 90

   90 5-centimetre cubes are needed.
4. Volume of water in the cubical tank = $\frac{1}{2}$ × 14 cm × 14 cm × 14 cm = 1372 cm^3

   Volume of water poured into the rectangular tank = 10 cm × 8 cm × 8 cm = 640 cm^3

   1372 – 640 = 732 cm^3

   732 cubic centimetres of water is left in the cubical tank.

 ISBN 978-93-5103-033-1

Problem Solving Process

Solve problems using these 4 steps:

1 **Understand** the problem.
Can you describe the problem in your own words?
What information is given?
What do you need to find?
Is there information that is missing or not needed?

2 **Plan** what to do.
What can you do to help you solve the problem?
Here are some things you can do:
- Draw a picture
- Make a list
- Make a supposition
- Guess and check
- Look for a pattern
- Act it out
- Work backwards

3 Work out the **Answer**.
Solve the problem using your plan in Step 2.
If you cannot solve the problem, make another plan.
Show your work clearly.
Write the answer statement.

4 **Check**
Read the question again. Did you answer the question?
Does your answer make sense?
Is your answer correct?
You may use the following to help you check your answer:
- fact families
- replace the unknown in the problem with your answer

If your answer is not correct, go back to Step 1.

 ISBN 978-93-5103-033-1

The content of this Scholastic ALPHA™ Mathematics Coursebook 5 Edition is adapted from Primary Mathematics Project 4A, 4B, 5A, 5B, 6A, 6B (3rd Edition) originally developed by the Ministry of Education, Singapore. This edition contains new content developed by Scholastic Education International (Singapore) Private Limited which is not attributable to the Ministry of Education, Singapore. We would like to acknowledge the Project Team from the Ministry of Education, Singapore, who developed the original Singapore Edition:

Project Director: Dr Kho Tek Hong
Team Members: Hector Chee Kum Hoong, Liang Hin Hoon, Lim Eng Tann, Rosalind Lim Hui Cheng, Ng Hwee Wan, Ng Siew Lee, Chip Wai Lung

Original edition published under the title of Primary Mathematics Project 4A, 4B, 5A, 5B, 6A, 6B (3rd Edition)

Published by Marshall Cavendish Education Pte Ltd

This edition

Published by Scholastic Education International (Singapore) Private Limited